The Future of Catholicism in America

THE FUTURE OF RELIGION IN AMERICA

THE FUTURE OF RELIGION IN AMERICA
Series Editors Mark Silk and Andrew H. Walsh

The Future of Religion in America is a series of edited volumes on the current state and prospects of the principal religious groupings in the United States. Informed by survey research, the series explores the effect of the significant realignment of the American religious landscape that consolidated in the 1990s, driven by the increasing acceptance of the idea that religious identity is and should be a matter of personal individual choice and not inheritance.

The Future of Evangelicalism in America, edited by Candy Gunther Brown and Mark Silk

The Future of Mainline Protestantism in America, edited by James Hudnut-Beumler and Mark Silk

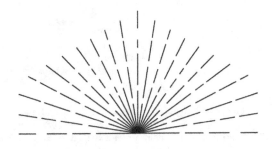

THE FUTURE
OF CATHOLICISM
IN AMERICA

EDITED BY

Patricia O'Connell Killen and Mark Silk

Columbia University Press
New York

Columbia University Press
Publishers Since 1893
New York   Chichester, West Sussex
cup.columbia.edu
Copyright © 2019 Columbia University Press
All rights reserved

Library of Congress Cataloging-in-Publication Data
Names: Killen, Patricia O'Connell, editor.
Title: The future of Catholicism in America / edited by Patricia O'Connell
Killen and Mark Silk.
Description: New York : Columbia University Press, 2019. | Series: The future
of religion in America | Includes bibliographical references and index.
Identifiers: LCCN 2018039213 (print) | LCCN 2018053784 (e-book) |
ISBN 9780231549431 (e-book) | ISBN 9780231191487 (cloth : alk. paper) |
ISBN 9780231191494 (pbk. : alk. paper)
Subjects: LCSH: Catholic Church—United States—History—21st century.
Classification: LCC BX1406.3 (e-book) | LCC BX1406.3 .F88 2019 (print) |
DDC 282/.7309051—dc23
LC record available at https://lccn.loc.gov/2018039213

Columbia University Press books are printed on permanent
and durable acid-free paper.
Printed in the United States of America

Cover design: Lisa Hamm
Cover image: Cathedral of Christ the Light © *The Catholic Voice*

Contents

Series Editors' Introduction

THE FUTURE OF RELIGION IN AMERICA

Mark Silk and Andrew H. Walsh

What is the future of religion in America? Not too good, to judge by recent survey data. Between 1990 and 2015, the proportion of adults who said they had no religion—the so-called Nones—increased from the middle single-digits to over 20 percent, a startling rise and one that was disproportionately found among the rising "Millennial" generation. If the Millennials remain as they are, and the generation after them follows their lead, one-third of Americans will be Nones before long. To be sure, there are no guarantees that this will happen; it has long been the case that Americans tend to disconnect from organized religion in their twenties, then reaffiliate when they marry and have children. It is also important to recognize that those who say they have no religion are not saying that they have no religious beliefs or engage in no religious behavior. Most Nones in fact claim to believe in God, and many engage in a variety of religious practices, including prayer and worship attendance. Meanwhile, nearly four in five Americans continue to identify with a religious body or tradition—Christian for the most part but also Jewish, Muslim, Hindu, Buddhist, Sikh, Baha'i, Wiccan, New Age, and more. How have these various traditions changed? Which have grown and which declined? What sorts of beliefs and practices have Americans gravitated toward and which have they moved away from? How have religious impulses and movements affected public policy and the culture at large? If we are to project the future of religion in America, we need to know where it is today and the trajectory it took to get there.

Unfortunately, that knowledge is not easy to come by. For nearly half a century, the historians who are supposed to tell the story of religion in

America have shied away from bringing it past the 1960s. One reason for this has been their desire to distance themselves from a scholarly heritage they believe to have been excessively devoted to Protestant identities, perspectives, and agendas. Placing Protestantism at the center of the story has seemed like an act of illegitimate cultural hegemony in a society as religiously diverse as the United States has become over the past half-century. "Textbook narratives that attempt to tell the 'whole story' of U.S. religious history have focused disproportionately on male, northeastern, Anglo-Saxon, mainline Protestants and their beliefs, institutions, and power," Thomas A. Tweed wrote in 1997, in a characteristic dismissal. Indeed, any attempt to construct a "master narrative" of the whole story has been deemed an inherently misleading form of historical discourse.

In recent decades, much of the best historical writing about religion in America has steered clear of summary accounts altogether, offering instead tightly focused ethnographies, studies based on gender and race analysis, meditations on consumer culture, and monographs on immigrants and outsiders and their distinctive perspectives on the larger society. Multiplicity has been its watchword. But as valuable as the multiplicity approach has been in shining a light on hitherto overlooked parts of the American religious landscape, it can be just as misleading as triumphalist Protestantism. To take one prominent example, in 2001 Diana Eck's *A New Religious America: How a "Christian Country" Has Become the World's Most Religiously Diverse Nation* called for an end to conceptualizing the United States as in some sense Christian. Because of the 1965 immigration law, members of world religions were now here in strength, Eck (correctly) claimed. What she avoided discussing, however, was the relative weight of the world religions in society as a whole. As it turns out, although twenty-first-century America counts millions of Muslims, Hindus, Buddhists, Jains, Sikhs, Taoists, and adherents of other world religions in its population, they total less than 5 percent of the population. Moreover, Eck omitted to note that the large majority of post-1965 immigrants have been Christian—for the most part Roman Catholics. Overall, close to three-quarters of Americans still identify as Christians of one sort or another.

While there is no doubt that the story of religion in America must account for the growth of religious diversity, since the 1970s substantial changes have taken place that have nothing to do with it. There is, we believe, no substitute for comprehensive narratives that describe and assess how religious identity has changed and what the developments in the major religious institutions and traditions have been—and where they are headed. That is what the Future of Religion in America series seeks to provide. For the series, teams of experts have been asked to place the tradition they study in the contemporary American context, understood in quantitative as well as qualitative terms.

The appropriate place to begin remapping the religious landscape is with demographic data on changing religious identity. Advances in survey research now provide scholars with ample information about both the total national population and its constituent parts (by religious tradition, gender, age, region, race and ethnicity, education, and so on). As a resource for the series, the Lilly Endowment funded the 2008 American Religious Identification Survey, the third in a series of comparable, very large random surveys of religious identity in the United States. With data points in 1990, 2001, and 2008, the ARIS series provided robust and reliable data on American religious change over time down to the state level that is capable of capturing the demography of the twenty largest American religious groups. Based on interviews with 54,000 subjects, the 2008 Trinity ARIS has equipped our project to assess in detail the dramatic changes that have occurred over the past several decades in American religious life and to suggest major trends that organized religion faces in the coming decades. It has also allowed us to equip specialists in particular traditions to consider the broader connections and national contexts in which their subjects "do religion."

The ARIS series suggests that a major reconfiguration of American religious life has taken place over the past quarter-century. Although signs of this reconfiguration were evident as early as the 1960s, not until the 1990s did they consolidate into a new pattern—one characterized by three salient phenomena. First, the large-scale and continuing immigration inaugurated by the 1965 immigration law not only introduced significant populations of adherents of world religions hitherto little represented in the United States but also, and more significantly, changed the face of American Christianity. Perhaps the most striking impact has been on the ethnic and geographical rearrangement of American Catholicism. There have been steep declines in Catholic affiliation in the Northeast and rapid growth in the South and West, thanks in large part to an increase in the population of Latinos, who currently constitute roughly one-third of the

American Catholic population. California now has a higher proportion of Catholics than New England, which, since the middle of the nineteenth century, had been by far the most Catholic region of the country.

A second major phenomenon is the realignment of non-Catholic Christians. As recently as 1960, half of all Americans identified with mainline Protestant denominations—Congregationalist, Disciples of Christ, Episcopalian, Lutheran, Methodist, and Northern Baptist. Since then, and especially since 1980, such identification has undergone a steep decline, and by 2015 was approaching 10 percent of the population. The weakening of the mainline is further revealed by the shrinkage of those simply identifying as "Protestant" from 17.2 million in 1990 to 5.2 million in 2008, reflecting the movement of loosely tied mainline Protestants away from any institutional religious identification. By contrast, over the same period those who identify as just "Christian" or "non-denominational Christian" more than doubled their share of the population, from 5 to 10.7 percent. Based on current demographic trends, these people, who tend to be associated with megachurches and other nondenominational Evangelical bodies, will soon equal the number of mainliners. In most parts of the country, adherents of Evangelicalism now outnumber mainliners by at least two to one, making it the normative form of non-Catholic American Christianity. Simply put, American Protestantism is no long the "two-party system" that historian Martin Marty identified a generation ago.

The third phenomenon is the rise of the Nones. Their prevalence varies from region to geographic region, with the Pacific Northwest and New England at the high end and the South and Midwest at the low. Americans of Asian, Jewish, and Irish background are particularly likely to identify as Nones. Likewise, Nones are disproportionately male and younger than those who claim a religious identity. But there is no region, no racial or ethnic group, no age or gender cohort that has not experienced a substantial increase in the proportion of those who say they have no religion. It is a truly national phenomenon, and one that is at the same time more significant and less significant than it appears. It is less significant because it implies that religious belief and behavior in America have declined to the same extent as religious identification, and that is simply not the case. But that very fact makes it more significant, because it indicates that the rise of the Nones has at least as much to do with a change in the way Americans understand religious identity as it does with a disengagement from religion. In a word, there has been a shift from understanding one's religious identity as inherited or "ascribed" toward seeing it as something that individuals choose for themselves. This shift has huge implications for all religious groups in the country, as well as for American civil society as a whole. In order to make sense of it, some historical context is necessary.

During the colonial period, the state church model dominated American religious life. There were growing pressures to accommodate religious dissent, especially in the Middle Atlantic region, a hotbed of sectarian diversity. But there wasn't much of a free market for religion in the colonial period because religious identity was closely connected to particular ethnic or immigrant identities: the Presbyterianism of the Scots-Irish; the Lutheranism, Calvinism, and Anabaptism of various groups of Pennsylvania Germans; the Judaism of the Sephardic communities in Eastern seaboard cities; the Roman Catholicism of Maryland's English founding families. The emergence of revivalism in the late eighteenth century and the movement to terminate state establishments after the Revolution cut across this tradition of inherited religious identity. Different as they were, Evangelical Protestants and Enlightenment deists—the coalition that elected Thomas Jefferson president—could together embrace disestablishment, toleration, and the primacy of individual religious conscience and choice. This introduced amazing diversity and religious change in the early nineteenth century, in what came to be known as the Second Great Awakening. Within a few decades, however, ascribed religious identity was back in the ascendancy. By the 1830s, Baptists, Methodists, Presbyterians, Congregationalists, Disciples, and Episcopalians were establishing cultural networks—including denominational schools and colleges, mission organizations, and voluntary societies—within which committed families intermarried and built multigenerational religious identities.

The onset of massive migration from Europe in the 1840s strengthened the salience of ascribed religious identity, creating new, inward-looking communities as well as a deep and contentious division between the largely Roman Catholic immigrants and the Protestant "natives." Moderate and liberal Protestant denominations moved away from revivalism and sought self-perpetuation by "growing their own" members in families, Sunday schools, and other denominational institutions. Religion as a dimension of relatively stable group identities persisted into the middle of the twentieth century; indeed, after World War II, sociologists saw it as a key foundation of the American way. Will Herberg famously argued that the American people were divided into permanent pools of Protestants, Catholics, and Jews, with little intermarriage. Yet by the end of the 1960s, it was clear that the century-long dominance of ascribed religious identity was under challenge. Interfaith marriage had become more common as barriers of prejudice and discrimination fell; secularization made religion seem optional to many people; and internal migration shook up established communities and living patterns.

In addition, conversion-oriented Evangelical Protestantism was dramatically reviving, with an appeal based on individuals making personal decisions to follow Jesus. At the same time, a new generation of spiritual seekers was exploring religious frontiers beyond Judaism and Christianity. As at the end of the eighteenth century, Evangelicals and post-Judeo-Christians together pushed Americans to reconceptualize religion as a matter of individual choice. By the 1990s, survey research indicated that religious bodies that staked their claims on ascribed identity—mainline Protestants and Roman Catholics above all, but also such ethno-religious groupings as Lutherans, Jews, and Eastern Orthodox—were suffering far greater loss of membership than communities committed to the view that religion is something you choose for yourself (Evangelicals, religious liberals, and the "spiritual but not religious" folk we call Metaphysicals). Within the religious communities that have depended on ascription, that news has been slow to penetrate.

The bottom line for the future of religion in America is that all religious groups are under pressure to adapt to a society where religious identity is increasingly seen as a matter of personal choice. Ascription won't disappear, but there is little doubt that it will play a significantly smaller role in the formation of Americans' religious identity. This is important information, not least because it affects various religious groups in profoundly different ways. It poses a particular challenge for those groups that have depended upon ascribed identity to guarantee their numbers, challenging them to develop not only new means of keeping and attracting members but also new ways of conceptualizing and communicating who and what they are. Preeminent among such groups are the Jews, whose conception of religious identity has always been linked to parentage; only converts are known as "Jews by choice." If to a lesser degree, Catholics and Mormons have historically been able to depend on ascriptive identity to keep their flocks in the fold. But in a world of choice, American Catholicism has increasingly had to depend on new Latino immigrants to keep its numbers up, while the LDS Church, focused more and more on converts from beyond the Mountain West, has had to change its ways to accommodate "Mormons by choice."

In the wide perspective, what choice has done is to substantially weaken the middle ground between the extremes of religious commitment and indifference. With the option of "None" before them as an available category of identity, many Americans no longer feel the need to keep up the moderate degree of commitment that once assured that pews would be occupied on Sunday mornings. American society has become religiously bifurcated—a bifurcation signaled by political partisanship. Since the 1970s, the Republican Party has increasingly become the party of the more religious; the Democratic Party, the party of the less religious. In order to take account of this growing divide between the religious and the secular, the narrative of religion in America must thus go beyond both the Protestant hegemony story and the multiplicity story. The new understanding of religious identity as chosen, in a society where "None" is increasingly accepted as a legitimate choice, stands at the center of the narrative this series will construct.

The Future of Catholicism in America

Introduction

THE FUTURE OF ROMAN CATHOLICISM IN THE UNITED STATES: BEYOND THE SUBCULTURE

Patricia O'Connell Killen

> Catholic historians take it for granted that they will deal with diversity, eclecticism, even chaos in the history of the church.
>
> —Jon Butler

Three years after the Second Vatican Council concluded in 1965, the Harvard-trained Catholic sociologist Thomas F. O'Dea assessed its project of *aggiornamento*—becoming up-to-date. This fundamental conciliar purpose was, he wrote, Christianity's "probably final opportunity . . . to confront modernity within the context of a unified religious community" possessing "great creative energies" and maintaining "genuine and currently operative ties with the past."[1]

O'Dea's bold claim exemplifies two elements crucial to understanding Catholicism's present and future in the United States. The first is his confidence. Like his Catholic compatriots, O'Dea was sure of his church, a robust faith community that by any measure had arrived, a success on the American religious scene. That confidence colored their excitement about the prospect of renewal. The second is his concern. A respected scholar of religion in the modern era, O'Dea understood that change in any religious organization—let alone one as large, complex, and tied to the authority of tradition and a hierarchical structure as Roman Catholicism—was a high-stakes venture, the outcome of which could not be predetermined. But, in the face of global modernization, it was a project that, in his view, had to be undertaken.

A half-century later, O'Dea's confidence in the church's unity, its stability rooted in robust and "genuinely operative ties to the past," and its "creative" resources may seem implausible, even quaint. After a half-century of contestation over the meaning and implementation of Vatican II, a decades-long scandal over sexual abuse, and stark differences between the hierarchy and laity on a range of issues, a quite different American Catholic Church exists today from the one that embarked on the project of *aggiornamento*.

The mid-twentieth-century Roman Catholic Church was a highly cohesive community forged as an ethnic/class/religious subculture.[2] Today it is thoroughly assimilated into its American context; clergy and laity alike exemplify the sensibilities of this voluntary, individualistic, market- and media-saturated milieu. Then, most American Catholics shared an understanding of the church as a supernatural institution, protected from the vagaries of history, and existing to mediate and dispense the means of salvation. Today, Catholics, as Joseph Chinnici notes in chapter 5, make their journey of faith through "the politics of history." The scandals over fiscal malfeasance as well as clergy sexual abuse have eroded trust among large numbers of current and former Catholics, undercutting the credibility and authority of the hierarchy. Far fewer Catholics now view the church as essential to salvation.

Then, family, ethnicity, and neighborhood provided social reinforcement for being a practicing Catholic. Today, Catholicism, like every other religious option in the United States, is a matter of choice. Regular participation in the practices of parish life has declined steeply since the Second Vatican Council concluded. Growing numbers, especially of those under age thirty, no longer consider such participation important to being Catholic.[3] Many of all ages have opted out of the church, and disaffiliation is accelerating, especially among the young—starkly among young women. Former Catholics now make up more than 10 percent of the adult population.[4]

Then, Catholic life largely revolved around the territorial parish to which all Catholics within its boundaries belonged. Today, Catholics freely migrate to parishes that most reflect their sensibilities and views. Even the majority of those still participating in parishes are at odds with formal church teaching on a range of topics, including divorce, homosexuality, contraception, abortion, and women's roles in the church.[5] Then, the presence and labor of ranks of vowed religious and ordained clerics in parishes, schools, health care, and social services symbolized and enacted institutional Catholicism. Those ranks have shriveled. The number of women religious (sisters and nuns) plummeted more than 70 percent between 1965 and 2016, and religious brothers 66 percent during the same period; equally severe declines among the ordained, always a smaller population than sisters, are, for the moment, buffered by reliance on priests from other countries and supplemented with permanent deacons.[6] Today, laypeople, both volunteers and professionals, are a permanent feature of Catholic liturgical, parish, and broader church structural roles, but too often as second-class ecclesial actors, and not always in easy relationship with the ordained personnel who hold power.[7] Then, there was no question that students in Catholic institutions of higher education would study theology and philosophy in the neoscholastic tradition of Thomas Aquinas. Today, the Catholic identity of these institutions is, in the minds of some bishops, priests, and laity, suspect. Then, the ritual, if not always the conviction, of deference to ecclesial authority prevailed. Today, ordained and lay Catholics engage publicly across all media platforms in conflict over, dissent from, and critique of church teaching and discipline, and employ the power of interest groups to bend leaders, people, and the public to their points of view—a mode of interaction with designated church authority and teaching virtually unimaginable in 1960.

In sum, American Catholicism today is pluriform, composed of a wide and diverse range of communities—liturgical, theological, and ethnic. Except for the most recent immigrants, its members are fully assimilated into American society, participants in the individualistic, democratic American milieu. They continue to interact with the symbols, teachings, and practices of their faith. They continue to participate in rituals that mark the cycle of life, to experience community with fellow parishioners, and to interpret the meaning of their living, loving, suffering, and dying within the rich narratives and rituals of the Catholic tradition. But they are far less bound to the uniform moral, intellectual, and disciplinary authority of the church hierarchy than were their forbears. They follow their own paths.

How did this pluriform American Catholicism come about? What are its prospects—up to and including its capacity to be an influential public presence? These are the questions this volume explores. To answer them, the contributors consider demographic data, immigration, liturgy and spirituality, institutional leadership, intra-ecclesial developments and conflicts, and the church's public engagement over the past half-century. These topics, integrally connected to the church's self-understanding, emerged as crunch points where the Second Vatican Council's project of ecclesial renewal met the reality of massive social and cultural change.

At the moment the Council was convened, American Catholics were moving rapidly out of a religious-ethnic-class subculture into wider American life.[8] Today's Catholicism is *post*-subcultural. But at the time of the Council, the church in the United States had hardly begun to consider a post-subcultural existence. As a result, the development of practices for being and doing Catholicism beyond the enclave became inseparable from the project of renewal. Over the past half-century, the Second Vatican Council has been promoted, resisted, blamed, and claimed as authorization for ideas, practices, and change more aptly attributed to being religious in a post-subcultural mode. Second, Catholics entered fully into the American milieu at a moment when it was undergoing rapid change, economically, politically, socially, culturally, and religiously. Catholics and their church participated in, propelled forward, and protested sweeping changes in American society and culture. The civil rights movement, the feminist movement, oral contraceptives, the war in Vietnam and concomitant anti-war activism, the organizing of Latino farm laborers, the budding of the environmental movement—all of these and more were both the context against which and subjects engaged during the process of renewal. Third, the Catholic Church was a hierarchical religious institution, wedded to historical teaching, practice, and structures as primary sources of religious authority that undertook the project of updating itself and engaging the modern world. The personality, power, and influence of the reigning pope, the most powerful institutional figure in the Catholic Church, would mark profoundly the tone, pace, and direction of the project of renewal at any given point, and so the shape of engagement with the modern world. So, too, would the views of the American bishops—themselves participants in the move from a subcultural to a post-subcultural existence—who wielded almost unlimited power within their dioceses. Yet neither pope nor local ordinary could direct and control fully the creative religious ferment unleashed by the project of *aggiornamento*.

THE SECOND VATICAN COUNCIL AND THE U.S. CATHOLIC CHURCH, 1959–1978

Pope John XXIII announced that he would convene an ecumenical council to address the church's relationship with the modern world on January 25, 1959, three months into his papacy. His announcement surprised Catholics, including some cardinals present for it, and quickly began to elicit excitement, anticipation, and resistance.[9]

When John made his announcement, the Catholic Church in the United States was robust and by all measures thriving.[10] Driven by waves of immigration, the ambition to succeed, and a need to fend off the hostility of Protestant neighbors, the Catholic community had, over a century and a half, created a subculture for itself woven of religion, ethnicity, and social class. Powerful bishops and wealthy lay leaders had succeeded in garnering both power and grudging respect from the frequently antagonistic Protestant majority. By 1959, the Catholic bishops had contained—though not eliminated—ethnic conflict within the Catholic community and had inculcated a sense of national Catholic identity. A worldview drawn from the works of the great medieval theologian Thomas Aquinas provided a highly functional, unifying intellectual vision for all Catholics, one that stressed common membership in a global, supernatural organization.[11] Experience serving in the military during World War I and World War II strengthened a sense of national Catholic identity. Yet, even as Catholics played out a return to normalcy in postwar suburban parishes by building schools and holding public displays of Catholic devotion and strength, the boundaries around their subculture were becoming more porous. Expanding educational opportunities provided by the GI Bill, along with a growing national economy, changed the fortunes of Catholics.

Successive waves of immigrants had built and sustained the Catholic Church in the United States. More than a million Irish and millions of others—Germans, Poles, French Canadians, Slavs, Mexicans, and more—arrived during the nineteenth and early twentieth centuries. Most turned to the church for assistance in adapting to their new setting. Protestants were the brokers of power in the United States, and most were uneasy with the scale of immigration and the growing presence of Catholic foreigners. The church, seeking to meet the needs of its people and to establish itself on par with Protestant religious communities, responded by building parishes that offered pastoral care, social services, and education whenever possible. The cycle of sacraments that mark the life span and a rich array of liturgical devotions proved an anchor for many Catholic laity, especially when priests, sisters, and other parishioners shared their countries of origin. Staffed by an abundance of priests and women religious from World War I through 1965, parishes created the world within which most American Catholics lived. Many urban Catholics of the mid-twentieth century made little distinction between living in their parish and living in their city. The physical plant and programs of large parishes in the nation's major cities and in the burgeoning postwar suburbs testified to what an unfriendly Protestant writer of the time famously called "Catholic Power."[12]

The growing numbers of Catholics who advanced educationally and economically during the first half of the twentieth century created separate Catholic professional organizations such as the Catholic Medical Association, the Catholic Sociological Association, and the Catholic Education Association. These organizations reinforced a sense of distinctive Catholic identity and of a Catholic world, while bridging educated Catholics into wider professional spheres where they defended Catholicism by demonstrating high standards of professionalism in a Catholic key. The dual task of these organizations and their members was to promote distinctive Catholic perspectives and to counter the anti-Catholic sentiment that was a pervasive dimension of American Catholics' experience in the United States into the 1960s.[13]

The activities and opportunities within the church, an ethnic and familial intimacy with it, and a larger environment often uncongenial to Catholics helped to cement affiliation and reinforce a lived experience of Catholicism as a distinctive, supernaturally infused, religious world. This world provided a stable base for Catholics negotiating the confusion attendant to immigration and the massive economic and social disruptions of the Great Depression and World War II and its aftermath. The church was unchanging even when everything else around them was in flux. It was this American Catholic Church—a subculture making good—that received the news of the impending ecumenical council.

The Second Vatican Council opened in October 1962, after three years of preparation, and a year and a half into John F. Kennedy's first term as president of the United States. Catholics and non-Catholics alike viewed television coverage of the more than 2,400 bishops, cardinals, *periti* (experts), representatives from other Christian rites in communion with Rome, lay observers, and visitors from other religious bodies assembled for the opening session. Over the Council's four sessions (October 11–December 8, 1962; September 29–December 4, 1963; September 14–November 21, 1964; September 14–December 8, 1965), the assembled hierarchs debated, revised, and promulgated documents on liturgy, ecclesiology, Scripture and divine revelation, religious life, religious freedom, ecumenism, relationship with non-Christian groups, and the intra-ecclesial relationship of bishops to each other and to the pope. By the time the Council ended, the Roman Catholic Church had been irrevocably changed.[14]

News of events in Rome contributed to Catholics' growing awareness that their church actually did change over time. More influential, though, was the implementation of Council documents and directives, perhaps most significantly *Sacrosanctum Concilium*, the Constitution on the Sacred Liturgy, approved in December 1963. The implementation of new liturgical texts and practices forcefully implanted the reality of change.[15] The shift from Latin to the vernacular (language of the people) and alterations in prayers and actions at the celebration of Mass made ordinary Catholics participants in this change. In many dioceses, the liturgical reforms were accompanied by the removal of statues of saints, the elimination of devotional practices, and the remodeling of churches. Priests now faced people at Mass. New hymns and music, guitars in church, an emphasis on the assembled community as the "People of God" and "a pilgrim people"— all of which emphasized God's intimate presence in the community as it moved through time, not solely in the consecrated bread and wine—drove home the fact of change in the church. Both the people's sense of themselves as Catholics and their relationship to church leaders became foci of attention and reflection as never before in the history of Catholicism in the United States.

The reforms of Vatican II were alternately intoxicating and alarming. Brought up to understand themselves as members of a supernatural society and the church as a timeless mediator of grace, many American Catholics struggled to understand and embrace the changes they were experiencing.[16] Others welcomed them with relief, banking on *aggiornamento* to resolve the strain they felt from living in two worlds.

To be sure, the changes ushered in by the Second Vatican Council did not surprise everybody. A liturgical movement, aimed at retrieving the practices of liturgy from the early church and revising the liturgy of the 1950s, had been growing since the first years of the twentieth century in the United States, earlier in Europe.[17] The theologians and liturgists associated with this movement were important *periti* at the Council, and they advised bishops on implementing the changes in the liturgy in their home dioceses. Liturgical change was directed toward making the Eucharistic celebration more central in the lives of Catholics. It also attempted to bring the connection between the Eucharist and social justice into focus.[18]

Many ordinary Catholics eagerly embraced Vatican II's emphasis on the laity and on the church as the entire "People of God." This theme gave their religious experience an independent validity previously unacknowledged by the hierarchy. The ministry of the laity mattered by virtue of their baptism and was not simply an extension of the apostolate of the bishop. Interest in spirituality grew. Members of religious communities and the laity brought fresh questions to traditional spiritual writings. Attention turned to retrieving older prayer forms, from centering prayer based on the fourteenth-century classic on contemplation, *The Cloud of Unknowing*, to the more action-oriented *Spiritual Exercises* by sixteenth-century Catholic Reformation hero Ignatius Loyola, the founder of the Society of Jesus (Jesuits).[19] New spiritual movements and organizations emerged, such as the Charismatic movement and the World Community for Christian Meditation. Members of the laity, female as well as male, undertook the advanced study of theology, some with a hope to assume pastoral and educational roles in parishes. Still others were drawn into activism in pursuit of justice.

Pope John XXIII died in early June 1963, six months after the end of the Council's first session and five months before the assassination of John F. Kennedy. Within three weeks the papal enclave elected his successor, Giovanni Cardinal Montini, who took the name Paul VI. Quickly announcing that Vatican II would continue, the new pope presided over the deliberations, decisions, and documents of the Council's final three sessions. Through the remainder of his reign, he worked to guide the interpretation and implementation of Council documents, emphasizing dialogue with other faith communities and with those of no faith. He traveled to India and to the United States, where both his address to the United Nations General Assembly and his Mass in Yankee Stadium in October 1965 were televised. In his travels, speeches, and encyclicals, Paul VI enacted the openness to the world for which John had invoked the Council. Paul expected the churches of the United States and Europe, the wealthiest of all Catholic communities, to take seriously the gospel admonition of good news to the poor. His writings on evangelization continued the Council's commitment to engage culture seriously as a factor relevant to faith. Liberation theology emerged as one expression of renewal.[20]

Vatican II's teachings empowered all American Catholics to claim their own voices. Some of those voices dissented from church teaching and practices—including those of the Council itself. Some members of the clergy and laity alike expressed concern over what they considered excesses of liturgical experimentation. Many were uncomfortable with the Council's documents being more pastoral than doctrinal and dogmatic, which led to a questioning of their authority. In 1968, traditionalists established Catholics United for the Faith (CUF) to strengthen the faith and protect what the group considered essential church teaching. Some traditionalists attached themselves to groups like the Society of St. Pius X, an organization founded by the French archbishop Marcel Lefebvre in 1970 that claimed Vatican II taught heretical positions.[21]

The most notable example of post–Vatican II dissent from church teaching was the response of American Catholics to *Humanae Vitae*, Pope Paul VI's 1968 encyclical reiterating a prohibition "on any form of artificial contraception for Catholics."[22] Theologians, some pastors, and many laity criticized the document, theologians claiming that because the teaching was not infallible they were free to do so. Much of the criticism was public, which set up a confrontation with bishops; in Washington, D.C., the moral theologian Fr. Charles Curran was forced to resign his position on the faculty of Catholic University.[23] Both the enthusiasm to extend the reforms of Vatican II and resistance to its teaching and instructions indicated the degree to which the Council had altered how

U.S. Catholics related to their church, and the extent to which they were adopting democratic strategies into their hitherto heavily top-down religious world.

For American Catholics, the Second Vatican Council and its heady aftermath were intertwined with rapid change occurring across multiple dimensions of society and culture in the 1960s and 1970s. Between Pope John's January 1959 announcement that he would convene an ecumenical council and its conclusion in December of 1965, the pace of social change and resistance to change accelerated. Civil rights activists staged six months of sit-ins at lunch counters in Greensboro, North Carolina, from February through July 1960. The Federal Drug Administration approved the first oral contraceptive that same year, and John F. Kennedy became the first Catholic elected president of the nation. In 1962, the year the Council convened, Cesar Chavez founded the National Farm Workers Association. Rachel Carson's *Silent Spring* was published two weeks before the Council opened. In 1963, President Kennedy signed the Equal Pay Act. Almost exactly a month before the Council's third session began, Martin Luther King, Jr. led the March on Washington and delivered his "I Have a Dream" speech. Two weeks before the second session began, the bombings at the Sixteenth Street Baptist Church in Birmingham, Alabama, killed four young girls. President Kennedy was assassinated on November 22, 1963, twelve days before the session concluded. The following year, President Johnson announced his Great Society agenda and signed the Civil Rights Act, which outlawed discrimination based on race, color, religion, sex, or national origin and prohibited unequal application of voter registration requirements. Congress passed the Gulf of Tonkin Resolution. Before the Council's final session in the fall of 1965, civil rights activists, including priests and sisters, marched from Selma to Montgomery; the Voting Rights Act was signed; riots, looting, and burning gripped the Watts area of Los Angeles; and the Supreme Court rendered its decision establishing the right of married couples to use contraceptives. As the bishops deliberated, the number of U.S. troops in Vietnam reached 200,000.

During the reign of Paul VI (1963–1978), social and cultural change continued apace. On April 4, 1967, Martin Luther King, Jr. delivered his Vietnam War speech, asserting the disproportionate burden on persons of color and the poor to fight wars. That year, in Detroit and 158 other cities, riots erupted, born of despair over racism and poverty. Exactly a year after his Vietnam speech, King was assassinated in Memphis. Two months later, on June 6, 1968, Robert F. Kennedy was assassinated. Television coverage of the 1968 Democratic Convention showcased student demonstrations and police brutality. That same year, the Indian Civil Rights Act responded to activism on the part of indigenous peoples and Dennis Banks established the American Indian Movement (AIM). In 1969, the Stonewall riots in New York became the public symbol for the rights of sexual minorities. In 1970, New York State legalized abortion on demand and a case began its journey through the judicial system that in 1973 would reach the Supreme Court as *Roe v. Wade*, ultimately establishing women's right to abortion. The Equal Rights Amendment passed in 1972 but would fail to be ratified by a sufficient number of states, in part because of the opposition of conservative Catholic activist Phyllis Schlafly. The acceleration of change—the civil rights movements (African American, Hispanic, Asian, indigenous), women's and gay rights movements, the sexual revolution, the Vietnam War and the protests against it, the movement to widen access to legal abortion, and more—provided the backdrop and sometimes the focus for the growing conflict and contest over the meaning and implementation of the Council. The conflict was theological, liturgical, and organizational. Through all of it, American Catholics absorbed and contributed to a growing suspicion and distrust of government and other institutions that defined the last third of the twentieth century.[24]

As the project of *aggiornamento* proceeded in the rapidly changing context of the United States and Catholics experienced multiple changes within the church in the 1960s and 1970s, questions about boundaries of Catholic identity and belonging became increasingly problematic. In a subculture, religious identity is ascribed as a dimension of one's inherited identity. It is part of a nexus of identities—ethnic, economic, racial, regional. Beyond a subcultural context, and increasingly in twenty-first-century America, religious identity becomes a matter of individual choice, self-determined according to one's personal spiritual quest or comfort level or association. By the late 1980s, the majority of adults in the United States believed that the appropriate way to determine one's religious beliefs and belonging was "on one's own."[25] The expansion of religious publishing, activism leading to religious interest groups independent of parish or diocese, and the emergence of web-based communications propelled individual religious searching. Philip Hammond described this process as a "third disestablishment."[26] Personal autonomy triumphed over constraint, and the individual became the center of religious experience, truth, and authenticity. Catholic teaching, practice, and organization are experienced, lived, and understood differently in a society where religious affiliation and participation are a matter of individual choice and intention.

In such a society, establishing boundaries of belief and belonging becomes more challenging and, for many, fraught. These boundaries make a religious community identifiable to itself and to others. They assure a degree of internal theological and organizational coherence that contributes to a strong sense of identity and affiliation on the part of those within the community. They bolster confidence in the trustworthiness of the community's teachings. The post–Vatican II challenge to American Catholicism was to preserve authentic Catholic identity and practice in a post-subcultural world. What was becoming of the nexus of stories, relationships, practices, and institutional structures that had kept the community together?

"THE REFORM OF THE REFORM," 1978–2013

In the wake of Paul VI's death in 1978, the papacy passed (after the very short tenure of John Paul I) to Karol Wojtyla, the cardinal archbishop of Krakow, Poland, who as John Paul II ruled until his death in 2005. His twenty-seven-year reign, the second longest in the history of the papacy, was in critical ways dedicated to scaling back Vatican II's opening up and democratizing of the church—a process that came to be known as the "reform of the reform." Under John Paul, ascendency passed to ecclesiastical leaders who believed that the reforms of the Second Vatican Council had gone too far, or had been coopted by radicals, or had been distorted by the influence of local cultures. Among John Paul's initiatives were weakening national bishops' conferences, centralizing authority in Rome, selecting as bishops men for whom loyalty to the institution was the preeminent value, elevating the status of the ordained, radically restructuring the International Commission on English in the Liturgy (ICEL), suppressing liberation theology, sanctioning inquiries and in some cases disciplining Catholic theologians teaching in seminaries and universities, gaining greater control over women religious, and containing doctrinal discussion within clearer bounds through the promulgation of a new catechism. A powerfully charismatic presence, John Paul II made good use of travel and emerging communication technologies to communicate an alluring global papacy. That allure continued, even in the face of growing revelations about clergy sexual abuse and fiscal malfeasance that dominated the last decade of his papacy.[27]

By the end of his reign, John Paul II had appointed virtually all the active bishops in the United States. In place of promoting a shared vision of Catholicism as a world community of the faithful, most focused on reestablishing control within their dioceses and supporting conservative social causes in the political arena. A Catholic-Evangelical alliance emerged in the public sphere. Equally if not more consequential for the institutional church, however, was the clergy sexual abuse scandal that became public in the late 1980s. Since then diocese by diocese, reports in waves have washed over the American Church. In 2002 the *Boston Globe's* reporting made clear how, for decades, bishops and their subordinates had shielded abusers from the law, transferring them from parish to parish and enabling them to victimize again. The cost in prestige, in credibility, in loss of parishioners, and in financial settlements has been incalculable. As the crisis grew, some bishops attributed it to the growing presence of homosexuals in the clergy since Vatican II, thereby deflecting attention from their responsibility for the situation. Many had a difficult time accepting the findings of the 2004 report on clergy sexual abuse from the John Jay College of Criminal Justice at the City University of New York, which emphasized that the crisis was, in large part, the result of a system of ecclesial leadership that placed loyalty and conformity above all other values. The "Charter for the Protection of Children and Young People," adopted by the U.S. Conference of Catholic Bishops at their 2002 meeting in Dallas, established important standards for protecting children from abuse, but the Vatican's weakening of the power of national bishops' conferences meant that the USCCB had no power to enforce them across dioceses. A few bishops openly refused to put the standards into effect; more gave them lip service but continued the longstanding practice of cover-up.[28]

John Paul II died on April 2, 2005. Within three weeks the papal conclave elected Cardinal Joseph Ratzinger to succeed him. As head of the Congregation on the Doctrine of the Faith, Ratzinger had taken the lead in pursuing the reform of the reform, so there was every reason to expect more of the same when he took charge as Benedict XVI. A more retiring and cerebral presence than his predecessor, Benedict focused attention on the rise of secularism in the West and the growth of Islam in Europe. His preoccupation with secularism spurred "the new evangelization," a project of the American hierarchy represented in such organization as "Catholics Come Home" and in the writings of conservative intellectuals like Princeton University's Robert George, George Weigel of the Ethics and Public Policy Institute in Washington, and Auxiliary Bishop of Los Angeles Robert E. Barron, who at the time was at Mundelein Seminary in Chicago.

Benedict desired a purer, more uniform, less pluralistic church, smaller if it need be—a model embraced by many U.S. bishops pushing for clearer boundaries to communion and greater respect for hierarchical authority. They took actions to move the church in this direction, focusing on liturgy, the central ritual of Catholic identity. The new General Instruction on the Roman Missal (GIRM), begun under John Paul II, was promulgated. It replaced the more open, colloquial liturgical English put in place after Vatican II with Latinate translations emphasizing the majesty and power of God, spiritual reality, and the centrality of the priest in liturgy. Another highly visible project was bringing nuns into line, which some bishops in the United States embraced enthusiastically. Criticizing women religious publicly, the Vatican launched an examination of the Leadership Conference of Women Religious and a review of women's religious communities in the United States. Emboldened by these actions, in some U.S. dioceses, bishops systematically removed women from significant roles in liturgy and in diocesan offices. At the same time, pressure to push gay priests back into the closet intensified. When coupled with the clear message that U.S. bishops would brook no quarter with dissent—a message communicated through disciplinary measures directed at theologians in Catholic universities, such as Roger Haight and

Elisabeth Johnson—these actions, in the view of the majority of American Catholics, amounted to a repudiation of much of what Vatican II had stood for. Some Catholic clerics and laity received these moves with relief, others with sorrow.[29]

During Benedict's papacy, the clergy sexual abuse scandal enveloped the church as a whole, reaching countries around the world and into the Vatican itself. As Benedict wrote his learned tomes and treatises, his house seemed increasingly out of order—beset by revelations of ongoing corruption in the Vatican bank and a Roman curia that seemed out of control. Citing age and ill health, and perhaps feeling incapable of resolving the institutional challenges, on February 28, 2013, Benedict XVI became the first pope in centuries to resign his office voluntarily.

POPE FRANCIS: RESTORING THE SPIRIT OF VATICAN II, 2013–

On March 12, 2013, the papal conclave replaced Benedict with Jorge Mario Bergoglio, cardinal archbishop of Buenos Aires and the first Jesuit and Latin American to hold the position. Bergoglio took the name Francis after the beloved founder of the Franciscan Order. Immediately, the tone, style, and content of messages from the Vatican changed markedly. Here was a pope who carried his own bags, canceled his own newspaper subscriptions, cold-called people on his own phone, and chose to live in the Vatican guesthouse rather than the elegant papal apartments. Early statements indicated a turning away from consuming preoccupation with abortion and contraception, from harshness toward sexual minorities, and from an insistence on enforcing barriers to communion for divorced and remarried Catholics. Instead, Francis emphasized a church that was pastoral, unafraid to make mistakes, and above all, concerned for the poor and downtrodden. Again and again, he warned against the dangers of clericalism. Within three years he had reformed the Vatican bank, begun remaking the Curia, created a synod on the family, resolved the investigation of women religious, established a means of disciplining bishops who mishandled abuse cases, and issued an encyclical calling for the international community to take drastic steps to combat climate change. Not all of Francis's initiatives were successful, and his own understanding developed and evolved, notably around sexual abuse and women's issues.

Some of his decisions on both have displeased many across the ideological spectrum. Still, the effect of his actions was galvanizing, inside and outside the church. But as of this writing, it remained far from clear what the staying power of the Franciscan project would be. Francis was seventy-seven when elected, and he himself remarked that he did not expect his papacy to be a long one.

In the U.S. Catholic Church, Pope Francis evoked celebration and concern. His early choice of Cardinal Sean O'Malley, archbishop of Boston, to be one of his close advisers signaled that the Vatican was no longer interested in cultivating hardline bishops. This impression was strengthened by his removal of Cardinal Raymond Burke, a staunch hard-liner and formerly archbishop of St. Louis, as head of the Vatican's supreme court, as well as by the appointment of three notable progressives to important sees—Bishop Blaise Cupich of Spokane to Chicago, Auxiliary Bishop Robert McElroy of San Francisco to San Diego, and Archbishop Joseph Tobin of Indianapolis to Newark. Further indication of his plans came when he elevated Cupich and Tobin, but not Archbishop Charles Chaput of Philadelphia or Archbishop William Lori of Baltimore, to the cardinalate.

But if progressives saw Francis as a badly needed corrective to three decades of retrenchment from Vatican II, conservatives felt just the opposite. Within months of Francis's election, Chaput noted their unhappiness with his approach and vision for the church.[30] During the past four years of Francis's reign, the willingness of high-ranking clerics—bishops and cardinals—to criticize him publicly is unprecedented in the history of modern Catholicism.[31] To date, Francis has not altered any formal teaching of the church. Yet, by stressing the need for pastoral presence in the world, Francis has presented a serious challenge to those who had embraced John Paul's and Benedict's reform of the reform.

ANTICIPATING THE FUTURE OF CATHOLICISM: A PLURIFORM AMERICAN CHURCH

The majority of American Catholics alive today have never known a time in the church when there was not ongoing contestation over boundaries of institutional affiliation, liturgy, intra-ecclesial power and authority, and a raft of public policy, gender, and sexuality issues. These Catholics grew to adulthood hearing about the Second Vatican Council's project of *aggiornamento* as a yet unrealized aspiration and/or as the cause of all the church's current ills. Not without its own irony, the contest over the implementation of the Second Vatican Council's directives has, for decades, been a school for Catholics to learn to operate in the nation's voluntary religious milieu. The majority of Catholics today are fully post-subcultural, their sensibilities shaped profoundly by a culture of individualism, wary of institutional power and encouraging of personal spiritual journeys. While many choose to remain connected to their local parish or a Catholic community of some other kind, growing numbers find the church irrelevant to their lives.[32]

The contributors to this volume have taken the measure of American Catholicism at a pivotal moment of internal institutional and larger contextual challenge for the church. In this moment, three significant trends are operative. First, the U.S. Catholic Church is marked by a pattern of disconnection—among members of the hierarchy; the hierarchy, other church leaders, and the laity; Catholics of different class, ethnic, and generational backgrounds; and Catholics with different ideological commitments. This pattern of disconnection feeds multiple responses to the abuse crisis, discussions of homosexuality and same-sex relationships, immigration, climate change and environmental protection, the role of women in the church, and the readiness of Catholic politicians to vote contrary to episcopal pronouncements on legislation. It nurtures anxiety about the health of the church. It intersects with competing understandings of authority and influence; tensions between "tradition" and "spirit-inspired" faith; evolving conceptualizations of individual and communal identity; and questions about the relationship between church doctrine and devotional practice.

These disconnections exceed the normal operation of a hierarchical organization made more visible in today's digital world. To be sure, internal tensions have always been part of the life of the church, even when it presented a unified public face, maintaining for its people and the larger society the image of a monolithic, supernatural community of hierarchically defined consensus. But that exaggerated view of consensus, employed to unify a multiethnic religious organization, did align significantly with the on-the-ground experience of large numbers of American Catholics. Few American Catholics now have that experience. The extent and intensity of disconnection disclose unprecedented and irreversible shifts in the U.S. Catholic community, both in how Catholic identity is conceived and practiced and in how the coherence of the institutional church is understood and enacted.

Second, a sustained movement on the part of many bishops to reclaim the isolation of the subcultural enclave in order to bolster clarity of Catholic identity and boundaries of belonging has been underway since the papacy of John Paul II. The U.S. Catholic bishops have employed it in their opposition to same-sex marriage and the Affordable Care Act. It has been and remains attractive to those seeking to increase clarity and order in the U.S. church. While always a point of contention, alternatively welcomed and excoriated by various Catholic groups, this project now is misaligned with the vision and directives of Pope Francis, increasing internal ecclesial tensions. Ironically, this strategy of claiming to be separate from the larger society locates American Catholicism centrally in the milieu of America's voluntary religious culture, where groups as diverse as the Shakers, Latter Day Saints (Mormons), and contemporary Fundamentalists and Evangelicals have employed it to claim moral authority and strengthen boundaries of identity and belonging.[33]

It is unclear whether and how this project of reestablishing something of a Catholic subculture can and will be redirected to bring U.S. bishops, clergy, and laity who support the project more into line with Francis's vision for the church. As Katarina Schuth notes in chapter 4, the men increasingly occupying the ranks of the clergy define themselves as John Paul II priests and embrace the notions of purification and clarification of boundaries of identity and belonging. Whether they will adjust attitudes and behavior remains to be seen. As William Portier has argued, while they may hold minority views within the Catholic population more broadly, as younger lay adults who share the views of newer clergy occupy institutional positions in parishes, universities, and dioceses, they exercise and will continue to exercise outsized influence.[34] The extent to which Francis's teaching—including his repeated exhortation to bishops and priests to be pastoral and "smell like their sheep"—his appointments, and his influence will modulate these efforts is a major question. In this period of the Francis papacy, then, the American Catholic Church exemplifies a contest between visions, played out in an elaborate dance of the exercise of institutional power.

Third, forms of public Catholicism are now more fragmented and far less cohesive than even three decades ago. In the 1980s, the U.S. Catholic Bishops' pastoral letters on peace (1983) and the economy (1986) bore influence beyond the U.S. church and into wider society. Today, the influence of the bishops, even with their own people, has declined markedly.[35] Whether Francis's articulation of a vision for the office of bishop as pastor among the people or his reaffirmation of the authority of local episcopal conferences will contribute to stemming this decline is unclear. Also yet to be determined is the extent to which Francis's insistence on the Catholic Church as a church of the poor will elicit a shift in emphasis or direction among the U.S. Catholic bishops.

Over the past decades, as Steven Avella and Richard Wood point out in chapters 3 and 7, U.S. bishops increasingly have been unable to reach consensus among themselves on social issues beyond those related to gender and sexuality. Though they have promulgated documents on immigration and the death penalty, for example, those documents have not garnered the attention of the ones on gender and sexuality. How Francis's appeal to Catholics to care for the poor and his emphasis on the church's economic teaching will be accepted by the bishops and will be heard and internalized by lay Catholics remains to be seen.

All three of these realities—disconnection, preoccupation with boundaries, and fragmentation of public presence—have evolved in the effort of the Catholic Church to implement the directives of the Second Vatican Council and at the same time develop ecclesial practices and orientations at once continuous with the inherited hierarchical structure and suitable to the nation's voluntary, individualistic, pluralistic context. What has emerged is a pluriform American Catholicism, a church unlikely ever again to achieve the unity and coherence of earlier times.

While fragmentation, disconnection, and separation are powerful dynamics in contemporary U.S. Catholicism, they are not the entire story. Altered, innovative, even new expressions of Catholicism are emerging. Face-to-face, print, and web-based resources for spiritual guidance are more numerous and accessible than ever before. Faith-based, intentional communities of young adults, mostly college graduates, committed to service are popular. Families organize into small communities for mutual support and spiritual growth. Ethnically rich forms of prayer, devotion, and practice have been embraced anew in seeking to strengthen spiritual life and in welcoming new immigrants, as Timothy Matovina points out in chapter 2. In some places, parish-based initiatives in community organizing thrive. Women's religious communities have confronted new challenges, some transforming their motherhouses and grounds, now far too large for their communities' needs, into environmental centers for promoting simple living and community agriculture.[36] These all constitute emerging modes of Catholic presence and practice. What these developments point to, at least for now, is the ongoing power of Catholic thought, liturgy, and practice to shape and inspire the imaginations of Catholics. Disagreement and disconnection do not, it seems, tarnish the luster of powerful symbols, rituals, stories, and practices carried in the Catholic tradition, as Chinnici and Andrew Walsh detail in chapters 5 and 6, respectively. They continue to resonate, to attract, and to inculcate a sense of shared identity and shared responsibility, not only for the local parish but for the larger human community and natural environment as well.

Despite decades of trauma, disillusionment with church leaders, dissent from church teaching, defections, and pitched conflict over "true" *aggiornamento*, the Roman Catholic Church remains the single largest religious body in the United States, with nearly 70 million people, accounting for roughly a quarter of the U.S. population.[37] If that proportion has held steady for more than four decades, it is because of immigrants, primarily Hispanics; in the meantime, an unprecedented and accelerating loss of membership among Catholics of Western European descent is underway. The Catholic Church is now losing members at a faster rate than other religious bodies.[38] Yet, given its size, the Catholic Church in the United States will be a significant presence for the foreseeable future.[39] What its influence will be is a key question.

There is good evidence that large numbers of Americans will continue to identify as Roman Catholic despite disagreement with formal magisterial teaching and dissatisfaction with some dimensions of church life. Even in the face of the clergy abuse crisis, as William Dinges and Katarina Schuth show in chapters 1 and 4, most Catholics continue to report high levels of satisfaction with their local parish and their pastor. Large numbers of Catholics continue to do as they have long done—mark the transitions of life through sacramental practices within the bounds of a local parish. But as Dinges (chapter 1), Chinnici (chapter 5), and Walsh (chapter 6) describe, these same people see less difference between themselves and other Christians, so the salience of institutional affiliation is declining. Catholics act with increasing independence, defining their relationship to the church on their own terms and in ways that many in the hierarchy find increasingly troublesome but are largely helpless to resist, hamstrung as they are by a shortage of priests, which itself strains essential elements in the church's self-understanding and practice.

In delineating the emergence of today's pluriform American Catholicism, the contributors to this volume explore a set of key questions:

- Who are U.S. Catholics today, and what do they believe and practice?
- How is the U.S. Catholic Church coming to terms with its growing ethnic diversity?
- How successful is the U.S. Catholic Church in maintaining continuity of tradition and practice, especially around ecclesial office and sacrament?
- Can the U.S. Catholic Church develop a durable sense of shared unity in a situation of growing theological diversity among Catholic people and a sharp decline in the number of ordained clergy and vowed religious?
- How do Catholics encounter God in prayer and worship, and what difference does that make for their relationship to formal church leaders, to their neighbors outside the church, and in their civic lives?
- Will the conflicts over the trajectory of the Second Vatican Council's teaching and reform reach some resolution, and what influence are they having on the life of prayer and the forming of Catholics' beliefs, attitudes, and dispositions?
- What public role is Catholicism playing in the wider society today, and what changes in how it plays that role can be anticipated?

The public presence of Catholicism in twenty-first-century America is complex. At this moment, its visible force seems to depend on the ability of the hierarchy to reestablish its credibility and inspire or compel assent to official teaching and action on the part of Catholics. Its ability to do so is questionable. Yet public presence exists and is growing through another venue—the laity's encounter with Catholic theological and social teaching, coupled with liturgical practice, in ways that shape their imaginations and sensibilities and so inspire their political, economic, and social actions. The force of religious ideas and religious sensibilities on the lives of individuals in a voluntary and individualistic society, which also exists on a global stage that is becoming increasingly postmodern in its social, economic, and political dimensions, is fluid and elusive. As the essays in this volume show, a pluriform American Catholicism now exists. It will continue to evolve rapidly into the foreseeable future. Its shape will significantly determine Catholicism's fortunes, including its modes and the extent of its public influence.

NOTES

Jon Butler, "Historiographical Heresy: Catholicism as a Model for American Religious History," in *Belief in History: Innovative Approaches to European and American Religion*, ed. Thomas Kselman (Notre Dame, IN: University of Notre Dame Press, 1991), 291.

1. Thomas F. O'Dea, *The Catholic Crisis* (Boston: Beacon Press, 1968), 11–12.
2. Helpful introductory histories of American Catholicism that cover this period include Patrick W. Carey, *Catholics in America: A History* (Lanham, MD: Roman and Littlefield, 2008); Jay P. Dolan, *The American Catholic Experience: A History from Colonial Times to the Present* (Garden City, NY: Doubleday, 1985); James Terence Fisher, *Communion of Immigrants: A History of Catholics in America* (New York: Oxford University Press, 2002); and James M. O'Toole, *The Faithful: A History of Catholics in America* (New York: Belknap Press, 2010).
3. Between 1965 and 1972, one-third of adults under the age of thirty identified as Catholics; by 2008 only 26 percent did so, 22–23 percent when immigrants are excluded. See Barry A. Kosmin and Juhem Navarro-Rivera, "The Transformation of Generation X: Shifts in Religious and Political Self-Identification, 1990–2008: A Report Based on the American Religious Identification Survey 2008," https://commons.trincoll.edu/aris/files/2012/05/ARISGENX2012.pdf; see also chapter 1 in this volume.
4. Patricia Wittberg, "A Lost Generation?: Fewer Young Women Are Practicing Their Faith: How the Church Can Woo Them Back," *America: The Jesuit Review*, February, 20, 2012, https://www.americamagazine.org/issue/5129/article/lost-generation; see also Pew Research Center on Religion and Public Life, "Faith in Flux," April 27, 2009, revised February 11, 2012, http://pewforum.org/2009/04/27/faith-in-flux; and "America's Changing Religious Landscape," http://pewforum.org/2015/05/12/americas-changing-religious-landscape.
5. See chapter 1 in this volume.

6. Center for Applied Research in the Apostolate (CARA), Georgetown University, "Frequently Requested Church Statistics," https://cara.georgetown.edu/frequently-requested-church-statistics/; see also chapter 4 in this volume.

7. See chapter 4 in this volume. CARA reported a 16 percent drop in enrollment in lay ministry programs from 2015/16 to 2016/17, down from 23,681 to 19,969; Peter Feuerherd, "Participation in Lay Ministry Training Programs Down 16 Percent," *National Catholic Reporter*, October 12, 2017, https://www.ncronline.org/news/parish/participation-lay-ministry-training-programs-down-16-percent.

8. William L. Portier, "Here Come the Evangelical Catholics," *Communio* 31 (Spring 2004): 35–66; Robert Orsi, *Thank You, Saint Jude: Women's Devotion to the Patron Saint of Hopeless Causes* (New Haven, CT: Yale University Press, 1996).

9. Chester Gillis, *Roman Catholicism in America* (New York: Columbia University Press, 1999), 86; John W. O'Malley, *What Happened at Vatican II* (Cambridge, MA: Harvard University Press, 2010); and Massimo Faggioli, *Vatican II: The Battle for Meaning* (Mahwah, NJ: Paulist Press, 2012).

10. Carey, *Catholics in America*, 115; Mark S. Massa, *The American Catholic Revolution: How the Sixties Changed the Church Forever* (New York: Oxford University Press, 2010).

11. Carey, *Catholics in America*, 80–84.

12. Paul Blanshard, *American Freedom and Catholic Power* (Boston: Beacon Press, 1949).

13. Two examples of such societies are the American Catholic Sociological Society, which became the Association for the Sociology of Religion, and the Catholic Medical Association. See "American Catholic Sociological Society," in William H. Swatos, Jr., *Encyclopedia of Religion and Society*, http://hirr.hartsem.edu/ency/acss.htm; and "Catholic Medical Association," *New Catholic Encyclopedia*, 2nd ed., vol. 3, 285–286.

14. On the calling of the Second Vatican Council, see Guiseppe Alberigo and Joseph A. Komonchak, *The History of Vatican II* (Maryknoll, NY: Orbis, 1995). See also Faggioli, *Vatican II*; Massa, *The American Catholic Revolution*; and O'Malley, *What Happened at Vatican II*.

15. Gillis, *Roman Catholicism in America*, 90; Massa, *The American Catholic Revolution*, 9, 15–16.

16. Carey, *Catholics in America*, 81–82.

17. Carey, *Catholics in America*, 83–85; Keith F. Pecklers, *The Unread Vision: The Liturgical Movement in the United States of America, 1926–1955* (Collegeville, MN: Liturgical Press, 1998).

18. Gillis, *Roman Catholicism in America*, 72–74.

19. James Martin, *The Jesuit Guide to (Almost) Everything: A Spirituality for Real Life* (New York: HarperCollins, 2010) was a widely successful popular introduction to Jesuit spirituality. See also Louis K. Dupre, Don E. Saliers, John Meyendorff, *Christian Spirituality: Post-Reformation and Modern* (New York: Crossroad, 1989);

Carmen Acevedo Butcher, trans., *The Cloud of Unknowing: A New Translation* (Boulder, CO: Shambhala, 2009); and Richard Woods, *Mysticism and Prophecy* (Maryknoll, NY: Orbis, 1998).

20. "Vatican Council II," *New Catholic Encyclopedia*, 2nd ed., vol. 14, 407–418; "Paul VI, Pope," *New Catholic Encyclopedia*, 2nd ed., vol. 11, 26–33.

21. "Lefebvre, Marcel," *New Catholic Encyclopedia*, 2nd ed., vol. 8, 456–459.

22. Gillis, *Roman Catholicism in America*, 106.

23. Gillis, *Roman Catholicism in America*, 106–109; Massa, *The American Catholic Revolution*, 49–74.

24. Jim Callahan, *America in the 1960s* (Decades of American History) (New York: Facts on File, 2005); Charles Patterson, *The Civil Rights Movement* (New York: Facts on File, 1995); James T. Patterson, *Grand Expectations: The United States, 1945–1974* (New York: Oxford University Press, 1996).

25. Wade Clark Roof and William McKinney, *American Mainline Religion: Its Changing Shape and Future* (New Brunswick, NJ: Rutgers University Press, 1987), 40–71.

26. Philip E. Hammond, *Religion and Personal Autonomy: The Third Disestablishment in America* (Columbia: University of South Carolina Press, 1992).

27. "John-Paul II, Pope," *New Catholic Encyclopedia*, 2nd ed., vol. 7, 1002–1015.

28. John Jay College conducted two research projects for the U.S. Conference of Catholic Bishops. "The Nature and Scope of Sexual Abuse of Minors by Catholic Priests and Deacons in the United States 1950–2002," published in 2004, and "The Causes and Context of Sexual Abuse of Minors by Catholic Priests in the United States, 1950–2010: A Report Presented to the United States Conference of Catholic Bishops by the John Jay College Research Team," published in 2011. Both are available at http://usccb.org. The bishops adopted "The Charter for the Protection of Children and Young People" at their meeting in Dallas in June 2002. It also is available at http://usccb.org . As of this writing, the sexual abuse crisis had intensified once again with the removal/resignation of the former Archbishop of Washington, D.C., Cardinal Theodore McCarrick; the release of the report of the two-year grand jury investigation of clergy sexual abuse in six dioceses in the State of Pennsylvania; and the publication of the letter by Archbishop Carol Maria Viganò, Apostolic Nuncio to the United States from 2011 through 2016, asserting cover-up of McCarrick's misdeeds at top levels in the Vatican and calling on Pope Francis to resign. See Michael R. Sisak, "Cardinal Theodore McCarrick, former archbishop, removed from ministry after sex abuse reports," *Chicago Tribune*, June 20, 2018, http://www.chicagotribune.com/news/nationworld /ct-cardinal-theodore-mccarrick-sex-abuse-20180620-story.html; Laurie Goodstein and Sharon Otterman, "Catholic Priests Abused 1,000 Children in Pennsylvania, Report Says," *New York Times*, August 14, 2018, https://www .nytimes.com/2018/08/14/us/catholic-church-sex-abuse-pennsylvania.html;

and Joshua J. McElwee, "Former Ambassador Viganò Accuses Vatican of Covering Up McCarrick Scandal for Years," *National Catholic Reporter*, August 26, 2018, https://www.ncronline.org/news/accountability/former-ambassador -vigano-accuses-vatican-covering-mccarrick-scandal-years.

29. Joshua J. McElwee, "Visitation Report Takes Mostly Positive Tone Towards U.S. Sisters," Global Sisters Report, a project of the National Catholic Reporter, December 16, 2014, http://globalsistersreport.org/visitation -report-takes-mostly-positive-tone-towards-us-sisters-16701; Laurie Good-stein, "Vatican Ends Battle with U.S. Catholic Nuns' Group," *New York Times*, April 16, 2015, https://www.nytimes.com/2015/04/17/us/catholic-church -ends-takeover-of-leadership-conference-of-women-religious.html. On critique of Sr. Elisabeth A. Johnson, see Paul Vitello, "After Bishops Attack Book, Gauging Bounds of Debate," *New York Times*, April 11, 2011, https://www .nytimes.com/2011/04/12/nyregion/12fordham.html; on Roger Haight, see David Gibson, "The Vatican Levies further Penalties on Roger Haight, S.J.," *Commonweal*, June 2, 2009, https://www.commonwealmagazine.org/vatican -levies-further-penalties-roger-haight-sj.

30. John Allen interview with Charles Chaput, *National Catholic Reporter*, July 23, 2013, https://ncr.org.

31. "After Critical Letter to Pope, Theologian Resigns as Consultant to U.S. Bishops," November 1, 2017, http://cruxnow.com. See also the statement by the president of the USCCB, Cardinal Daniel N. DiNardo of Galveston-Houston, "U.S. Conference of Catholic Bishops President on Dialogue Within the Church," November 1, 2017, http://usccb.org; Edward Pentin, "Cardinal Burke Outlines Formal Correction of Pope Francis' Teaching," *National Catholic Register*, August 17, 2017, https://ncregister.com; Casey Egan, "American Cardinal Burke Criticizes Pope Francis in Irish Speech, November 17, 2014, https://irishcentral.com.

32. Christian Smith, Kyle Longest, Jonathan Hill, and Kari Christoffersen, *Young Catholic America: Young Adult Catholics In, Out of, and Gone from the Church* (New York: Oxford University Press, 2014); chapter 1 in this volume; Art Raney, Daniel Cox, and Robert P. Jones, "Searching for Spirituality in the U.S.: A New Look at the Spiritual but not Religious," Public Religion Research Institute, November 6, 2017, https://prri.org.

33. See R. Laurence Moore, *Religious Outsiders and the Making of Americans* (New York: Oxford University Press, 1987).

34. Portier, "Here Come the Evangelical Catholics."

35. See chapter 1 in this volume. The rapid movement from being a subcultural church through denomination to our current context of unraveling religious and other institutions and the growth of more fluid and temporary movements cannot help but challenge inherited Catholic understandings of hierarchical authority.

36. Bernard J. Lee and William D'Antonio, *The Catholic Experience of Small Christian Communities* (Mahwah, NJ: Paulist Press, 2000); Sarah McFarland Taylor, *Green Sisters: A Spiritual Ecology* (Cambridge, MA: Harvard University Press, 2009); Richard L. Wood, *Faith in Action* (Chicago: University of Chicago Press, 2002).

37. Chapter 1 in this volume; "The Global Catholic Population," Pew Research Center, February 13, 2013, http://www.pewforum.org/2013/02/13/the-global -catholic-population/.

38. Pew Religious Landscape Study, 2014, http://www.pewforum.org.

39. "Searching for Spirituality in the U.S.," https://prri.org; chapter 1 in this volume.

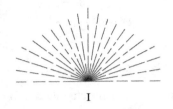

I

Catholicism Today

ADRIFT AND/OR ADJUSTING

William D. Dinges

An American Catholic Rip Van Winkle who slept through the mid-twentieth century and awoke in the early part of the twenty-first century would be decidedly stunned by the Catholic landscape. How things have changed!

If a singular concept has framed the discourse on Catholics in the United States over the last half-century, it is "change," and by "change" I mean tectonic shifts in Catholic theological formulations, institutional life, cultural norms, demographic realities, and religious self-understanding. The "unchanging" church and "perfect and juridical society" proclaimed by early scholastic manuals has transformed dramatically in the face of long-term social, cultural, and historical shifts, and in the wake of a half-century-long contesting over the meaning and implementation of the Second Vatican Council. The transition has not been easy.

For older and predominantly Euro-American Catholics, the church's post–Vatican II transformation has meant reconfiguring a religious identity against the gestalt of a previously stable set of religiocultural norms, symbols, and values.[1] For significant numbers of younger Catholics today, this process has often been characterized by discontinuity and fragmentation. Differing generational experiences have also been attended by alterations in Catholic class dynamics and in the church's regional, ethnic, and racial demographics, and more recently, by a disastrous sexual abuse and hierarchical malfeasance crisis. In stark contrast to the early euphoria surrounding the Council, much of the post–Vatican II narrative has been one of sobering institutional declension. Little wonder that Peter Steinfels, a perceptive observer of contemporary Catholicism, used the words "Adrift" and "Crisis" in the title of his 2003 book on the state of the church in America.[2]

AMERICAN CATHOLIC DEMOGRAPHICS

Social science research measuring change among American Catholics over the past half-century has proliferated, although interpretation of some of the data, like that of *aggiornamento* in general, remains contested. Nor has church leadership shown uniform enthusiasm for social science analysis of Catholic life and culture. Nevertheless, research initiatives on American Catholics today have moved far beyond pre–Vatican II parish census taking and narrow concerns over declining birth rates and "mixed marriages."

In what follows, I address three interrelated issues: I first summarize some of the contemporary demographic data on American Catholics. I then draw together key social science findings relating to Catholic institutional affiliation, sacramental participation, and identity construction. Last, I discuss interpretive themes operative in this literature and conclude by speculating on some of the implications of current research findings for the future of Catholicism in the American context.

As noted, numerous social and behavioral science studies of postconciliar Catholic life and culture have been done over the past half-century, including the research of well-known scholars such as Andrew M. Greeley, James D. Davidson, Dean Hoge, Christian Smith, Michele Dillon, and others. Relevant data on American Catholics can also be found in large-scale research projects funded by Lilly Endowment and the Pew Charitable Trusts.[3] In addition, CARA, the Center for Applied Research in the Apostolate in Washington, D.C., has produced numerous studies on Catholic life, including its most recent *Catholic Parishes of the 21st Century* (2017).

One of the most comprehensive analyses of post–Vatican II Catholicism is a quarter-century longitudinal work led by the sociologist William D'Antonio and various collaborators. The D'Antonio research began on the eve of John Paul II's second visit to the United States in 1987 and was completed with the results of a 2011 survey. Five volumes of this wide-ranging project have been published (1989, 1996, 2001, 2007, 2013).[4]

There are currently around seventy million Catholics in the United States.[5] In national surveys of U.S. residents, about one-quarter self-identify as Catholics. This figure has held relatively steady since the Second World War and continues to make Catholics one of the largest religious groups in the country.

The overall demographic picture is that of a church that is still predominantly white and non-Hispanic, though just barely. About four in ten Catholics are Hispanic/Latino, and another 10 percent are non-Hispanic black, Asian, or Native American.[6] Catholicism has a slight female majority (54 percent women /46 percent men) and is a population that is mostly married (70 percent).[7]

An estimated eighteen to twenty million Catholics are inactive, disaffiliated, or only sporadically involved in church life.[8] Lapsed Catholics constitute the second largest "religious" group in the United States—behind practicing Catholics and ahead of Southern Baptists. Kosmin and Keysar's *American Religious Identification Survey* (ARIS 2008) put the number of Catholics who "switched out" (to other religious groups, or to no religion as of 2001) at a net loss (factoring in 4.3 million newcomers who "switched in") of about five million adults, or around 9 percent of the Catholic population.[9] However, the more recent Pew Religious Landscape Surveys (2008, 2015) suggest an even greater extent of Catholic losses.

According to Pew, the number of Catholics who have actually "switched out" is higher than all other previous estimates and higher than the net losses of any other religious body in the United States today. Nearly 13 percent of all Americans are former Catholics.[10] Among Latino/a Catholics, an estimated 1.3 million have left the church for Pentecostal and Evangelical Protestant denominations.[11] Pew researchers speculate that Catholic losses overall would be even greater were it not for the offsetting impact of immigration (see below). However, the Pew "switched out" figures have been contested by CARA researchers, who estimate that those raised Catholic but who no longer identify as such are closer to 8 percent.[12]

Growth Rate

The current growth rate of Catholics in the United States has been estimated at around 10 to 12 percent, due in large part to a second great wave of immigration from the Philippines and Vietnam and to large numbers of Latino/a immigrants with larger family sizes.[13] About 42 percent of immigrants to the United States each year say they are Catholic.[14] In high-immigrant areas of the country, such as Los Angeles, Dallas, Las Vegas, and Miami, the Catholic population has increased rapidly. The primary shift in the regional distribution of Catholics has been from the Northeast to the

West and South. While dioceses in the former region are closing parishes and schools, many in the latter are scrambling to open new facilities.[15]

In spite of the immigrant growth factor, Catholics in the United States appear to be declining both in absolute numbers and as a percentage of the U.S. population, following the broader decline of the U.S. Christian population as a whole. The Pew 2015 survey estimates the number of U.S. adult Catholics now at about 51 million, roughly three million fewer than in 2007.[16]

While immigration and the previously noted "switched out" factor impact the Catholic growth rate in the United States, this figure should be situated within the larger global framework. The global Catholic population has grown by nearly 30 percent since 1985, with the most dynamic growth of global Christianity overall in Africa and East Asia—105 percent in the former, 58 percent in the latter. By contrast, the growth rate in Latin America was 31 percent and in Europe, zero.[17] In spite of the long-term shift toward lower global fertility, most of the Christians of the future—including the bulk of Roman Catholics—will be in Latin America, Africa, and Asia, not in Europe or North America.

Class

One of the major long-term changes tracked by scholars is the transformation of the Catholic class structure, especially among Euro-American Catholic populations (e.g., Irish and German) that dominated much of American church life through the later nineteenth and first half of the twentieth centuries. The descendants of these immigrants are now at or above national averages of educational attainment, occupational status, and family income. Overall, 70 percent of Vatican II and young adult Catholics today are college graduates, and 27 percent have attended graduate or professional schools.[18] Although wealth among American Catholics is not distributed uniformly, some 60 percent now have incomes above $50,000 per year.[19]

The advances in affluence and social mobility among Euro-American Catholics are products of assimilation, waning anti-Catholic bias, and the educational benefits of the GI Bill for earlier generations. Although assimilation dynamics remain at play among "new immigrant" Catholics—even if in different ways—the church in America today is hardly an underclass one. This long-term transformation of the Catholic class structure has impacted the Catholic presence in the power structures of American society. Internally, the shift has produced a better-educated and more democratically inclined laity, many of whom are more Americanized in outlook and behavior and less accepting of traditional religious authority. However, the fact that Catholic class dynamics remain stratified along ethnic lines, especially relating to non-Hispanic/Hispanic differences, poses important questions about a two-church, ethno-class Catholic presence in the American context.

Ethnicity

American Catholics remain an ethnically diverse lot, even as ethnicity as a prime carrier of Euro-American Catholic identity continues its long-term demise. The 1990 ARIS data indicated that around 20 percent of American Catholics were minority-group members, notably Hispanic or Latino/a, African American, Asian, and other.[20] By 2007, however, this figure had jumped to around one-third of the Catholic population, owing to accelerating rates of legal and illegal immigration.[21]

Latino/a Catholics are the largest group overall, with Mexican Americans, Puerto Ricans, and Cubans representing the largest segments of this population. While the actual count remains unknown, most projections put the current number of Latino/a Catholics in the United States at nearly 40 percent of the Catholic population.[22] Given their higher representation in the 18–29 age cohort and larger family sizes, Latino/a Catholics will account for an even greater share of the church in America in the future. Aside from their demographic significance, Latino/a Catholics tend to be slightly more "orthodox" on various church teachings, while also bringing a spiritual sensibility rooted in Spanish popular Catholicism that accentuates their importance as one of the most conspicuous contributors to the "changing face" of American Catholicism.[23] The question remains open, however, as to whether the tight affiliation of the Latino/a population with the church may loosen as their ethnic identity and religious identity become unbound—as was the case for other immigrant groups.

African American Catholics have increased to around 5 percent of the Catholic population, due largely to the high proportion of recent African and Caribbean immigrants who are Catholic, and to an alleged "evangelizing dividend" associated with non-Catholic inner-city black residents attending parochial schools.[24]

About 2 percent of the Catholic population is Asian. The most significant numbers here are Vietnamese and Filipino/a.[25]

Gender

A renewed struggle for gender equality across a broad array of social spectra has persisted over the past half-century. Subsequent waves of feminism have challenged lingering gender inequities, traditional work and family roles have been altered, and greater numbers of women have moved into positions of equality in various institutional spheres. Religious traditions, particularly mainstream ones, have moved to expand ministerial opportunities for women—including ordination.

Although research has shown that Catholics want women to have more influence in the church,[26] efforts in this regard have met with only limited success outside of the conventional roles that women have traditionally played in Catholic institutional life. The Vatican prohibition notwithstanding, six out of ten American Catholics support the ordination of women as priests,[27] a position many consider theologically acceptable and a legitimate response to pressing pastoral needs.

Of perhaps more far-reaching significance than ordination is the fact that women's long-standing loyalty and commitment to the church can no longer be taken for granted. As D'Antonio and colleagues found, Catholic women, especially non-Hispanic ones, "show a steep trajectory of decline over the past 25 years" on key indicators of that commitment: weekly Mass attendance, attitudes about the importance of church in their lives, and whether they might ever leave the church. Women's commitment levels to the church are now on par with men's, which have historically been lower. Given the important role played by women in the religious socialization of the young, this decline in commitment will likely have serious long-term institutional consequences.[28]

Age or Generational Cohort

As we will see later, age cohort is one of the strongest predictors of attitudes, practices, and beliefs among American Catholics. Studies by

Andrew Greeley (*Young Catholics in the United States and Canada*, 1980) and Patrick McNamara (*Conscience First, Tradition Second: A Study of Young American Catholics*, 1992) were among the first to draw attention to the significance of age-related factors for post–Vatican II Catholic identity and church involvement. Subsequent research by James Davidson (1997), Dean Hoge et al. (2001), and D'Antonio et al. (1989, 1996, 2001, 2007, 2013) further highlighted the importance of age-related demographics.[29]

The pre–Vatican II generation is now just a tenth of all adult Catholics, while the two generations with no experience of that era of church life (Gen X and Millennials) account for more than half of all adult Catholics.[30] Racial and ethnic diversity also affects these figures, as Gen X and Millennial Catholics, who make up more than half of all Catholics, are in almost equal proportions non-Hispanic white, Hispanic, and other race or ethnicity.[31]

The purported demographic dividend relative to the graying Catholic population is another noteworthy generational factor today. U.S. Census data reported in 2007 that the thirty-five million Americans who were sixty-five or older at that time would more than double to seventy-one million by 2030, a trend driven by better health care and longer life expectancy. Given that sixty-five-and-older individuals are more likely to be religious practitioners and church connected, this demographic factor presents a potential "Grayby boom" for churches as a whole, and Catholicism in particular.[32]

Geographic Profile

As noted, the past quarter-century has seen dramatic shifts in Catholic populations, beyond the movement of white Catholics out of once ethnically homogenous neighborhoods into suburbia. For the most part, Catholics maintain a relatively even national spread. The most significant drop over the past quarter-century has been in the number of Catholics in the Northeast (New England and Mid-Atlantic)—from 37 percent to 28 percent—with the real growth areas in the South and West.[33] The internal migration of northern Catholic retirees along with the mounting Hispanic presence has accelerated this shift. However, relative to religious population trends in general, Catholics still remain underrepresented in the South.

CATHOLIC RELIGIOUS IDENTITY

Social science research on American Catholics since the Second Vatican Council paints a complex picture of stability, vitality, transformation, and decline—all of which pose the proverbial "half-empty, half-full" hermeneutic conundrum.

On the positive side, studies show more lay involvement in parish life and ministry, more individual appropriation of the faith, strong commitment to elements of the church's social teachings and peace and justice initiatives, the rise of small faith communities and religious movements, and the presence of some very robust parish communities.[34] At the national level, the church remains the largest nonpublic provider of education and health care and one of the biggest providers of social services. Polling also shows high levels of support for Pope Francis (70 percent) among American Catholics, although lower levels for the church itself (55 percent).[35]

On the challenging side, and although mitigated by non-Hispanic/Hispanic differences, research points to institutional instability, internal fragmentation, ongoing contesting (e.g., "liturgical wars") and polarization, declining financial and organizational resources, declining vocations to the ordained and nonordained religious life, declining sacramental participation, weakening connectedness to local Catholic institutions (parish and school), and lower levels of adherence to formal church teachings and discipline. These last trends are especially prevalent among Catholic Millennials, many of whom remain nominally Catholic but have little knowledge of the tradition, less social embeddedness in it, fewer church-related commitments, and scant regard for church authority.[36]

The causes of Catholicism's institutional malaise stem from a complex array of internal and external factors. The former include neuralgic contesting over the meaning and implementation of Vatican II (most recently the "reform of the reform" debates), inadequate catechesis and religious socialization, liturgical deficiencies, and the demoralizing impact of the sexual abuse and hierarchical malfeasance crises. The latter include cultural trends toward an increasingly secular and post-denominational society, America's superheated culture of individualism, and the accelerating rise of (ex)religious "Nones" who, even where they embrace a spiritual identity, do so in ways that have little or nothing to do with organized religion.[37] Declines in the importance of creed and doctrine to religious identity,[38] the spread of "choice" in identity formation, and overall declines in traditional forms of religious authority, along with a preference for direct encounters with the sacred, are additional trends impacting contemporary Catholicism.

As we will see, the critical issue here is not that of maintaining a Catholic identity per se, or whether individual Catholics hold to core beliefs regarding the death, resurrection, and salvific role of Jesus Christ. It centers, rather, on the imperative of Catholic institutional affiliation or church belonging and involvement as prerequisites for doing so. While large numbers of Catholics continue to self-identify as Catholic and retain in varying ways core Catholic beliefs, their commitment to the church as an institution *essential* to their identity as Catholics, as a *necessary* instrument of salvation, and as an *objective* source of truth and sacraments has become increasingly tenuous. Where individuals maintain a Catholic identity, many do so on their own terms and with decreasing deference to, or connection with, institutional lines of authority. For some—in a revealing shift in identity construction—the appellation "Christian" has more often than not supplanted "Catholic" as a first-term indicator of religious identity.

ADHERENCE TO FORMAL CHURCH TEACHING

Post–Vatican II research has consistently pointed to significant gaps between official church teachings and the beliefs and behaviors of many America Catholics. Putnam and Campbell in their acclaimed *American Grace* (2010) noted the "striking" nature of the low percentage of Catholics who endorse orthodox Catholic doctrine.[39] How gaps of this nature compare historically with pre–Vatican II Catholic populations is open to question, although the general assumption has been that Catholics in the earlier era were more doctrinally compliant.

Since the Second Vatican Council, gaps between church teachings and lay belief and practice have been especially pronounced in the area of human sexuality, but hardly confined to it. The widespread rejection of Pope Paul VI's prohibition of artificial birth control (*Humanae Vitae*, 1968) first highlighted the scope of this gap. Subsequent research has tracked declines in doctrinal fidelity along an even broader range of church teachings. In addition, Catholic views on specific social and political issues (capital punishment, immigration, military policy, end of life) have become more congruent with general public ones—although Catholics tend to be slightly more liberal than Protestants on sex- and marriage-related matters.[40] In the area of social justice and concern for the poor, studies show that compliance with official church teaching has strengthened and is central to the Catholic identity of significant numbers of American Catholics today.[41]

In addition to gaps between official teachings and actual belief and practice, research also shows that a declining percentage of Catholics believe that the hierarchy's teaching authority is an important part of their faith. D'Antonio et al. (2013) found that only about 30 percent believed that "Vatican authority" was personally "very important" to them, while nearly a quarter (23 percent) claimed it was "not important at all.[42] As education and income increase, this importance further declines.[43] Although the majority of Catholics continue to attribute importance to hierarchical authority and official church teachings, this attachment hardly translates into uniform compliance. Even where adherence is present, questions have arisen about what individual Catholics actually believe surrounding these issues.[44]

PARISH INVOLVEMENT

For a communally rich tradition like Roman Catholicism, the importance of parish affiliation can hardly be overstated. The vast majority of American Catholics experience themselves as "church" in parish settings. Parishes form and sustain Catholic identity. They nurture a Catholic sensibility, signify institutional connectedness, and provide a primary venue for ritualized solidarity. Parishes have been the normal means for strengthening the inner structure of the church, for administering the sacraments, and for channeling Catholic influence into American public life. Not surprisingly, as Davidson and others have shown, parish involvement has a significant impact on institutional connectedness: parish-affiliated Catholics hold stronger traditional beliefs and practices, go to Mass and communion more frequently, pray more frequently, and are more likely to agree that Catholicism is the one true church.[45]

In 2001, there were slightly more than 19,000 Catholic parishes in the United States. As of around 2016, that number declined to 17,233, owing to closings and consolidations due primarily to demographic shifts.[46] Some parishes are increasingly large, complex, and ethnically diverse. More are now "shared" in this regard, while a "mismatch" continues to exist between Catholic population densities and parish locations, especially as the church in America becomes an increasingly "southern" one.

What is the state of contemporary parish life with respect to Catholic institutional commitment?

For Euro-American Catholics in particular, the reality of a tight-knit urban parish with a staff of priests and women religious has generally come to an end. As noted, mobility and new immigration patterns have transformed the social and ethnic profiles of many of these once-dominant urban parishes. The majority of parishes today have some degree of multiple ethnic populations. Where contemporary national parishes exist—either *de facto* or officially—they are now more commonly Hispanic, Polish, or Vietnamese.[47]

On the positive side, research points to vibrant parishes that work well, have a strong sense of vision, nurture and engage the local Catholic population, run successful RCIA programs, provide diverse and edifying liturgies, and have multiple ministerial opportunities.[48] These conditions are especially prevalent in some of the newer immigrant parishes, in some larger southern and western Catholic parish variants on the megachurch phenomenon, and in parishes with strong collaborative and social-justice ministries.[49]

The Notre Dame Study of Catholic Parish Life (CPL) in the early 1980s was one of the first major analyses of its kind following Vatican II.[50] Researchers found an overall level of satisfaction with parish life, in spite of lingering problems with uninspiring liturgies and contesting over clerical authority. Parish Catholics were particularly happy when a conscious effort was made to meet the expectations of a "postconciliar style" in terms of role diversification and liturgical styles. The CPL study also found that the accessibility of the pastor and his ability to be emphathic and supportive were important parish attachment factors.[51] Subsequent studies have also shown that, overall, American Catholics are satisfied with their parishes. Most find their pastor approachable, appreciate the welcoming atmosphere and friendliness at church, and have many of their spiritual needs met within the parish setting.[52] The vast majority agree that parish priests do a good job; only a minority feels their parish today is "too big and impersonal."[53] Research also shows that parishes remain highly relevant as a central focus of Catholic community experience.[54]

Virtually all post–Vatican II studies show that laity are playing an increasing role in parish life. Following a theological legitimation that fosters a type of ecclesial democratization on the basis of baptism, and as the number of priests and vowed religious decline, opportunities for lay participation and leadership in parish settings have increased.[55] In 2014, there were 3,488 parishes without a resident pastor.[56] Lay Catholics— overwhelmingly laywomen—currently fill a wide variety of parish administrative and ministerial roles. According to CARA's *Catholic Parishes* study, some 40,000 lay ministers now work at the local or diocesan level.[57] Research has also shown that parishes that provide multiple opportunities for lay involvement and ministry have higher levels of commitment and vitality.[58] Individuals involved in activities and service-oriented groups experience stronger parish attachment. Having social and spiritual needs met, frequent conversations with the pastor, high-quality homilies, and music at liturgical services are also relevant attachment dynamics.

While the overall portrait of contemporary Catholic parish life shows positive elements, various concerns are also evident. To begin with, about one-third of American Catholics are not registered in any parish.[59] Among Latino/a Catholics, less than half are registered.[60] Many who arrive in the United States come with little or no tradition of parish registration. Overall, parish-involved Catholics remain predominantly older and female, a pattern following broader trends in church participation in general. Reasons for parish disconnectedness vary from specific needs not being met (e.g., of divorced and separated Catholics or young adults) to banal and uninviting liturgies, the lack of effective adult-education programming, little leadership vision or energy, clerical resistance to lay ministry, or simply the failure of individuals to reconnect following a move. Other challenges include tepid interest in parish initiatives (outreach to youth, volunteering, small faith communities), conflicts over management and professionalism in parish administration, and difficulties in "shared" parishes over priorities and the use of resources. Financial support and, in some instances, severe financial situations are additional parish-related challenges.[61]

Parish attachment is also influenced by mobility factors and, in the case of younger adults, by lifestyle transience and low levels of commitment in all social domains. While only 17 percent of pre–Vatican II Catholics are without parishes, 47 percent of post–Vatican II Catholics lack such attachment.[62] Even when connected, young adults are less likely to have significant numbers of close friends who belong to the same parish, an associational factor known to enhance commitment.[63]

Parish membership is not parish involvement. Studies show that significant numbers of Catholics, including registered parish members, are inactive in parish life or leadership roles outside of parochial school involvement or the servicing of their own sacramental needs. The CPL study found that less than half of all parish-affiliated Catholics (48 percent) took part in *any* type of parish activity outside of Mass.[64] Other research confirms that American Catholics participate far less in parish activity than members of many Protestant denominations.[65] The 2009 ARIS survey indicated that only slightly more than half of American Catholics (54 percent) considered "active participation in the parish community" as important or very important.[66] This lack of parish attachment and involvement is also evident financially. Catholic churches are eight times as large as Protestant ones, but produce annual revenues that are only twice as large.[67]

Other trends also affect Catholic parish life today even while their long-term outcomes remain uncertain. For example, independent of factors of time or convenience, more Catholics now shop for a parish to their liking. This tendency was already evident in the CPL study, which found that about 15 percent had crossed boundaries in the selection of a parish.[68] The 2017 CARA *Catholic Parishes* study indicates that 35 percent of parishioners—especially younger ones and those who identify their race and ethnicity as something other than non-Hispanic white—are attending Mass at a parish of their own choosing rather than their territorial parish.[69] While parish shopping promotes attachment to the church, along with more positive evaluations of parish life, it also produces homogenization, illustrates a more individualized and "seeker" approach to meeting spiritual needs, and expresses a Catholic variant of the denominational dynamic of voluntarism in American religious life.

As noted, some Catholic parishes today are being reconstituted in significant ways via wide-scale migration patterns. These include movements of Latino/a migrants/immigrants along with a regional flow of northern Catholic retirees into southern states. In the former case, tensions over identity and intercultural practices within shared parishes have proved challenging.[70] In the latter, older retirees sometimes bring with them differing community and liturgical experiences, along with differing ecclesial expectations surrounding church authority and the role of laity in parish life. The long-term impact of this internal retiree migration on parish life remains largely unexamined.[71]

The proliferation of small faith communities and the growth of various "apostolic movements" or "new movements" (such as RENEW, Cursillo, Focolare, the Neo-Catechumenal Way, and TEC [Teens Encounter Christ]) also affects Catholic parish life today. A study by Bernard Lee and William D'Antonio in 2000, one of the first of its kind, claimed about 37,000 small faith communities.[72]

Positively, small faith communities and new movements facilitate church connectedness and involvement in parish ministry. In ways paralleling Protestant megachurch practice, they provide parishioners with specialized or more intimate participatory niches within a larger church setting. However, while the vast majority of small faith communities have operated successfully within parishes, some have proven problematic, especially those characterized by "covenanted" relationships—notably in the case of some Catholic Charismatic Renewal groups that have been overshadowed by issues of elitism, sectarianism, and issues of authority.

While small faith communities and apostolic movements can be viewed as forms of parish innovation, they also suggest a judgment on local parish life. Many of these smaller associations provide participants with a deeper sense of spirituality, belonging, sharing, and community than is experienced in the local parish. In so doing, they suggest new models of Catholic solidarity. They also represent a restructuring of the church itself, not merely a social mechanism for maintaining attachment to it. Small faith communities and apostolic movements foster a more explicit sense of being Catholic, along with an implicitly more critical view of church structures. They also give expression to another element of U.S. Catholic acculturation, notably toward broader social patterns of small group involvement.[73]

Catholic Schools

The state of Catholic elementary and secondary schools is another indicator of lessening institutional attachment among Catholics in the North American context.

Catholic schools have played an important historic role in maintaining Catholic identity and morale, in instilling the discipline and skills needed for entry into the American mainstream, and in engendering a trans-ethnic Catholic identity.[74] In the peak years of the 1950s, close to half of all Catholic children attended Catholic schools, but enrollment has been steadily declining over the post–Vatican II era as parochial schools close and consolidate and as the mainstay of their traditional teaching staffs—sisters, brothers, and priests—declines. Approximately 40 percent of Catholic elementary and secondary schools have closed since 1965 in the face of a 50 percent decline in enrollment.[75] According to Froehle and Gautier, about one in five Catholic K–8 students and about one in seven Catholic high school students attend Catholic schools.[76] Fewer Catholics at all levels (elementary, high school, college) are getting an education today in church-affiliated institutions, while a greater percentage of those enrolled is non-Catholic, especially in Mid-Atlantic and urban inner-city settings. Where parochial schools were once run primarily for urban immigrants and their children, some are now increasingly prep-like schools with higher tuitions for those escaping public education or in suburban parishes.

The decline in Catholic schools is a complex issue related to demographic shifts, assimilation trends, economic downturns, the availability of public vouchers or tax credits, tuition costs, and fewer religious teachers. Here, I highlight the role of these schools in connecting individuals and families to an institutional expression of the church. That fewer Catholics are now being socialized formally by church-sponsored educational institutions is both cause and effect of weakening institutional attachment. The waning influence of Catholic schools on Catholic identity and commitment has also been compounded by widely perceived deficiencies surrounding other venues of Catholic religious education.[77]

Sacramental and Devotional Life

Virtually all studies of postconciliar Catholicism point to declines in traditional forms of piety and devotionalism, especially surrounding Mary and the saints. Where active, these forms are often associated with ethnicity (Latinos/as) or with the conditions of diaspora Catholicism—meaning they are more prevalent where Catholics are in a minority. Roman Catholic traditionalists, a small and highly sectarian subculture, also promote traditional devotions as part of an overall campaign against Vatican II reforms.[78] A resurgence in traditional devotions—notably in Eucharistic forms—can also be found among younger "(neo)orthodox" or "evangelical" Catholics,[79] although a case can be made that the interest here has as much to do with the quest for tangible identity markers in a flattened ecumenical environment as it does with resurgent religious conservatism.

While older forms of piety and devotionalism have declined, new forms have arisen. One of the most studied of these has been the Catholic Charismatic Renewal, a "spirit-filled" manifestation of religious enthusiasm that emerged in the 1960s in many American mainline denominations. Although now considerably less visible than during its high-water mark through the 1980s and early 1990s, Catholic Charismatic Renewal remains a vibrant form of spirituality in many Latino parishes.[80] By 2007, more than half of Latino/a Catholics identified themselves as "charismatic."[81]

Beyond stylistic or cultural changes in traditional patterns of Catholic piety and devotionalism, however, participation in Catholic sacramental life has not kept pace with Catholic growth since the 1960s. Only slightly more than half of American Catholics (55 percent) now consider themselves "practicing" ones.[82] While the number of infant baptisms has remained relatively constant over the past half-century, significant declines have occurred in the number of Catholics going to confession and receiving Holy Orders. In addition, somewhere between 20 and 30 percent of young adult Catholics today have never been confirmed, a sacrament intended to signify and seal commitment to the church.[83] Significant numbers of Catholics are also marrying non-Catholics, or marrying other Catholics outside the church's sacramental context.[84]

One of the most noteworthy signs of waning sacramental attachment is the decline in regular Sunday Mass attendance. Since the 1980s, attendance has fluctuated between 25 and 42 percent. According to a 2003 Gallup Poll, a higher percentage of Protestants (overall) than Catholics now attend church on a weekly basis.[85] In 2015, the Pew Research Center estimated the number of regular Catholic Sunday Mass attendees at around 39 percent.[86] D'Antonio et al. (2013) reported 31 percent;[87] an earlier CARA report (2008) gave a figure of 23 percent.[88] Data variations notwithstanding, the overall trend has clearly been downward, and dramatically so, from the peak years on the eve of the Second Vatican Council.

Even more telling, however, is the fact that significant numbers of American Catholics no longer consider regular Mass participation as essential to being a "true," "good," or "core" Catholic.[89] The most recent D'Antonio study (2013) indicated that nearly 50 percent of highly committed Catholics maintain that one can be a "good Catholic" without going to church each week.[90] Aside from its spiritual implications in light of the Vatican II Liturgical Constitution's affirmation of the liturgy as the "summit toward which the activity of the church is directed . . . [and the] fountain from which all her power flows" [*Sacrosanctum Concilium*, I.10]), this diminishing sense of the centrality of the liturgy to Catholic life and identity is highly significant.

Sunday Mass attendance is a behavioral norm linked directly with the church's disciplinary authority. Although few Catholics today find the pre–Vatican II "go-to-Mass-or-go-to-hell" mantra compelling, the "serious obligation" to attend Sunday Mass has been repeatedly affirmed by the church's magisterium.[91] The fact that many Catholics do not go today, or go only sporadically, highlights both loose institutional attachment and diminishing church authority.

Sunday Mass attendance is also significant because studies show that higher rates correlate positively with other church-related norms. These include higher levels of overall sacramental practice and doctrinal fidelity, encouraging a child to pursue a religious vocation, enrollment in Catholic schools, approval of church leadership, attitudes towards marriage, and Catholic political attitudes.[92]

In addition, regular Mass participation facilitates what Andrew Greeley famously dubbed the "Catholic imagination," a concept that draws on insights of Weber and Durkheim, and on the theologian David Tracey's "analogical imagination."[93] Given the manner in which ritualized prayer and devotional life nurture such an imagination—wherein images are evoked, accentuated, objectified, formalized, and shared—the durability of the "Catholic imagination" remains unclear when Catholics attend Mass less frequently or not at all or when the liturgy's importance to Catholic identity is marginalized.

SUMMARY: LOOSE BONDS

Although Catholic identity endures today, it does so with diminished fidelity to significant elements of official church teachings, with lessened institutional attachment and loyalty, and with declining patterns of sacramental and devotional practice. In this respect there is little reason to contest claims like that of D'Antonio et al. (2007) that "Commitment to the Church is in gradual decline"—and especially so among younger Catholics, who are more aligned to faith than to church.[94] What this and other studies show is that while many Catholics remain in the church today, they negotiate the content and meaning of their faith and give more authority to their own judgment and conscience than to church authorities.[95] For significant numbers, submission to episcopal authority is only weakly operative as a constituent element of what it means to be Catholic. Instead, religious sensibilities are negotiated and governed by patterns of personal choice and preference, not those of inheritance or authority. Spirituality and "faith" trump institutional commitment. Fewer are involved in church life, and fewer appear to have the same needs for the church as a historical tradition or bonded community or as an exclusive spiritual and sacramental source that characterized the attachment of earlier generations of American Catholics. Catholic institutional connectedness, especially for non-Latino Catholics, is in many ways now more akin to the cultural phenomenon that Robert Wuthow dubbed "loose connections."[96] While religious and spiritual sensibilities remain strong and at least nominally Catholic, the need or desire to belong to a religious institution appears more transient and tentative. This is not a surprising development.

For a broad segment of the American population—including American Catholics—religious affiliation over the past half-century has become increasingly fluid. Numerous studies have shown that religious mobility and switching are more pervasive as mainstream denominational loyalties weaken and/or become more diffused and difficult to catalog and index.[97] Like many other Americans, many Catholics—especially better-educated and more affluent ones—have been influenced by cultural codes of individualism and by a free-market religious economy marked by differentiation and commodification, where moral authority is seen as an individual prerogative and where religious identity is a lifestyle choice among an ever-expanding array of spiritual possibilities. Within this milieu of religious pluralism, diversity, and voluntarism, what Catholicism offers is but one possible source of spiritual edification, even while the religious life-world of the individual remains loosely attached to symbolic markers from within the tradition, along with elements of its moral and communal dimensions.

CATHOLIC IDENTITY CONSTRUCTION

While much of the commentary on the transformation of Catholicism following Vatican II has emphasized polarization and conflict in the form of ecclesial culture wars between liberal and conservative factions, since the 1990s attention has increasingly shifted to the issue of Catholic identity.[98] What does it mean to be Catholic? According to whom, and by what criteria? These questions animate virtually all discussions of Catholic ecclesiology, culture, and institutional life today.[99] Two aspects of this identity issue—namely, boundaries and salience—have received considerable attention in the literature reviewed here.

Boundary Diffusion

The decline in institutional commitment among American Catholics has been attended by the diffusion of Catholic boundaries in a cultural climate of ecumenism, inculturation, and waning anti-Catholicism. The boundaries highlighted here are not those between Catholics and secularists, or Catholics and non-Christians, but internal boundaries relating to who is, and who is not, considered "in" as a Catholic, along with the perceived boundaries between Catholics and non-Catholics within the broad Christian tradition. Boundary diffusion among Catholics matters because this is a known factor that has been explicitly linked with institutional decline among other mainline traditions.[100]

The subjective boundaries perceived by many American Catholics have changed significantly over the past half-century. Few today consider the traditional way of identifying a "lapsed" Catholic—whether the individual attended Mass or made his/her Easter Duty—as putting a person outside the church. In addition, significant numbers believe that one can be a "good Catholic" ("in") without obeying church teachings on various matters of faith and doctrine. There is widespread reluctance on the part of many Catholics to draw any lines at all regarding "in" and "out" categories, although rejection of church teachings on abortion, homosexuality, the Resurrection, and the Eucharist remain significant markers of perceived "out" status.[101] However, even in this last regard, the D'Antonio et al. (2013) *American Catholics in Transition* research indicated that four in ten believe you can be a "good Catholic" without believing that in the Mass, the bread and wine actually become the body and blood of Jesus.[102]

During this same period, again owing to both internal and external factors, boundaries between American Catholics and Protestants, especially mainline Protestants, have become more diffused. This is true not only in regard to the broader convergence of ecumenical-inspired religious practice and spirituality discussed in chapter 5, but also in terms of the traditional Catholic affirmation that the Roman Catholic Church is a divine structure unique in its fidelity to Christ's will, imbued with his teaching authority through Peter (Mat. 16:18). Almost half of the respondents in the Hoge et al. *Young Adult Catholics* study (2001) saw few substantive differences between Catholics and mainline Protestants. Nor did the majority believe that Catholicism was more faithful to the will of Christ than other expressions (mostly mainline) of Christian self-understanding. In their central beliefs, the two traditions are increasingly perceived as the same, especially by younger Catholics.[103] Other research has also shown that, among post–Vatican II Catholics, a little over half (57 percent) agree that Catholicism contains a greater share of truth than other religions do, while only half (50 percent) remain convinced that the Catholic Church is "the one true church."[104] Studies like the Baylor Research Project (2008) also point to a remarkable degree of convergence between Catholics and mainline Protestants on a wide variety of measures of religious and spiritual belief.[105]

As Catholics acquire a more fluid sense of the boundaries of their faith, as they perceive themselves as less distinct ("just Christian"[106]) from other expressions of Christian self-understanding, as they become more accustomed to an emphasis on what mainstream Christian traditions have "in common," and as they become more accepting of the spiritual parity of other Christian denominations—and, by extension, of other religions— Catholic boundaries have become less exclusive, less differentiated, and more diffuse. For some, Catholic identity has also become less distinct and compelling.

Salience

Salience is a measure of the pertinence and intensity of a belief, not its content. Salience accentuates the importance of a set of convictions or identity(ies) to an individual within a general configuration of identity values. Salience can also be affected by external factors. For example, where Catholicism is a minority status, Catholic identity tends to be stronger.

Research on the salience of Catholic identity shows mixed results. On the one hand, it is high among core Catholics (typically estimated at about 10 percent of the Catholic population), among those in religious life and in the various movements mentioned earlier, and among those working to effect change in the church. Large majorities of Catholics at large report "being a Catholic is a very important part of who I am" (75 percent) and "I cannot imagine being anything but Catholic" (68 percent). An equally high proportion (75 percent) want the younger generation of the family to grow up as Catholics.[107]

On the other hand, research suggests that salience has slowly declined in general over Catholic generations. Studies by D'Antonio and colleagues have consistently shown gradual declines in the importance of the Church to individual Catholics.[108] In 2013, the Pew Research Center reported that its analysis of data from the General Social Survey (GSS) showed that those who called themselves "strong" Catholics were down more than 15 percentage points since the mid-1980s—a four-decade low.[109] The Smith et al. *Young Catholic America* study (2014) also pointed to waning salience as a factor in the role of religious decline among Catholic youth.

What does this decline in the salience of Catholic identity mean?

It does not mean that most Catholics no longer identify with their faith, that they do not enjoy being Catholic, or that they intend to leave the church. Large majorities continue to report that they "like being Catholic," that they "would not change to another religion," or would "never leave the Church."[110] A 2008 CARA poll found that 77 percent of American Catholics agree at least somewhat with the statement "I'm glad to be a Catholic."[111] Catholic identity endures even as it is diffuse, contested, and transformed.

Pride and endurance, however, are not always commensurate with *importance*. For greater numbers of American Catholics, especially post–Vatican II ones, Catholic identity is simply less compelling. Put another way, Catholic identity is no longer at the top of the identity hierarchy for significant numbers of laity.[112]

This salience dynamic is important because of its obvious impact on commitment to the life of the church. Studies show—and common sense dictates—that those who attach more importance to being Catholic are more likely to be committed to the church and its ministries, more active in it, and more likely to comply with its teachings. A salient Catholic identity also has significant behavioral consequences for lifestyle choices that affect the intergenerational transmission of the faith. These choices include the religious education of children, institutional support, parish belonging, and perhaps most significantly, marital choice—given the importance of parental roles in the religious socialization of children.

DECLINE OR SOMETHING ELSE?

With the growth of social science research on American Catholics in the post–Vatican II era, interpretations of the data have been diverse and, in some cases, contentious. In general terms, the church's institutional decline has been viewed as an inevitable consequence of deep changes in the locus of religious authority in the modern/postmodern context. Accordingly, Catholicism has been decisively impacted by the shift in the legitimation of authority from traditional sources to more rational/ bureaucratic and charismatic ones, or to sources that prioritize seeker-oriented experience and agency. Catholicism's authority structure, like that of monarchies, is based on a belief in the sanctity of traditions and those who hold authority accordingly. However, authority claims of this nature are problematic in a postmodern context. Where power and decision making are not shared in some fashion, and where compliance behavior cannot be forced, traditional models of authority are delegitimated and, more often, simply disregarded.[113] As noted earlier, a declining percentage of American Catholics believe that the teaching authority of the hierarchy is an important part of their faith. When asked to rank what they see as most essential to their identity, factors such as "helping the poor" and "the sacraments, such as the Eucharist," remain at the top of the list, while "the teaching authority claimed by the Vatican" remains near the bottom.[114]

Other social science–inspired interpretations—often by Catholics on the right of the ecclesial spectrum—read the postconciliar data in a more ideologically critical way. Here, shifts (declines) in belief and behavior are often viewed as the ill-begotten fruits of Vatican II, coupled with the corrosive effects of the cultural upheavals of the 1960s. The emergence of "Catholic lite" and pick-and-choose Catholicism has been caricatured in this literature as a "culture of dissent" registering the negative impact of moral liberalism, campus radicalism, the critique of authority, and the flowering of expressive individualism—all of which allegedly combined with progressive theological shifts and "dissenting theologians" to destabilize Catholicism's traditional teaching authority and lead to the current malaise.[115] More recently, the debilitating impact of these trends has been further compounded by the serious failures of church leadership surrounding the sexual abuse crisis.[116]

Criticism similar to these, although less driven by Catholic in-house ideological contesting, can also be found in the work of scholars who analyze contemporary religious trends from a rational-choice (or market-economy) perspective. These individuals assert that various institutional and normative changes within the church since Vatican II have weakened distinctive cultural and social patterns that once facilitated "strictness" central to Catholicism's organizational vitality. This weakening, in turn, produced a loss of religious capital and a diminished capacity to sustain high levels of church commitment. The adverse effects of such waning strictness, along with the unbalancing of the cost/benefit ratios of belonging to the church since Vatican II, have been especially conspicuous in the decline in contemporary vowed religious life.[117]

But not all social science interpretations of post–Vatican II change embrace a hermeneutics of decline. Among mainstream studies—many of which have been done by more progressive-minded Catholic researchers—assessments of the belief/behavior gap, loose institutional affiliation, and declining sacramentalism have been given a more positive tack. Here the argument is advanced that Catholics today, especially younger ones, are not any less "Catholic" than older generations; they are simply "different" in how they express their faith. This interpretative frame, which has been a prominent leitmotif in the research of sociologists like Greeley, Davidson, D'Antonio, Hoge, Dillon, and others, includes two key concepts—core and periphery—relevant to assumptions about religious identity.

Core and Periphery

A core-and-periphery approach to Catholic identity rests on the commonsense assumption that some components in a belief system are more important than others. While Catholicism contains a multitude of beliefs, practices, and disciplines, these elements hardly carry equal weight, either theologically or as identity markers. They rank in a hierarchy of value and significance. Belief in mandatory celibacy as a precondition of ordination, or the discipline of Eucharistic fasting, for example, are hardly of the same gravitas as belief in the divinity of Christ, or His Resurrection.

Implicit in the core-and-periphery approach is the assumption that much of the conflict among Catholics today, along with what appears to be institutional tepidness and declension, centers not on what is essential to the faith, but on what is secondary or peripheral. While aspects of the latter are a source of conflict and polarization, or have simply weakened or disappeared, core "pan–Vatican II" beliefs (Trinity, Divinity of Christ, Resurrection, Mary as the Mother of God, the Real Presence) remain strong. Catholics today differentiate between the essentials and nonessentials of their faith; they hold to the former while minimizing or disregarding the latter. Davidson and colleagues (1997) were among the first to elaborate on this core-and-periphery argument. Their study of Indiana Catholics (along with a national sampling) highlighted distinct patterns of belief and practice among three generational cohorts—pre–Vatican II, Vatican II, and post–Vatican II Catholics. These three groups came of age during different historical periods. The overall transformation across generations was toward expressing their faith in more individualist terms. Davidson concluded that while the religious and spiritual interests of post–Vatican II Catholics were as strong as anyone else's, their interests were *different*—less oriented toward institutional and obligatory concerns. Accordingly, the greatest unity among Catholics centered on pan–Vatican II beliefs, along with consensus about the church's social teachings. Catholics quarreled little over these matters. They were, in fact, the core or "single most important basis of Catholic unity," the alleged glue that held Catholics together. Where conflict existed, it centered on "recent ideas, pre–Vatican II practices, and sexual and reproductive ethics."[118]

The D'Antonio (1989, 1996, 2001, 2007, 2013) and Hoge (2001) studies also probed core and peripheral orientations among lay Catholics. Here, too, pan–Vatican II beliefs proved more central to most than did adherence to specific rules and moral teachings of the church. Respondents considered God's presence in the sacraments and concern for the poor ("donating time or money to help the poor") much more relevant to being a "good Catholic" than teachings like the belief that only men could be priests or private confession to a priest.[119]

From the perspective of the core/periphery argument, things are not as bad as they appear; pre– and post–Vatican II differences should not be read as *ipso facto* signs of declension.

BOUNDED DIVERSITY

A related interpretive frame informing research on contemporary Catholics also concludes that the selective appropriation of the faith is not a diminishing of Catholic identity, but a theologically legitimate act of constructing that identity. Michele Dillon, notably in *Catholic Identity: Balancing Reason, Faith, and Power* (1999), has forcefully advanced this argument for an authentic community of "bounded diversity" in the church. Dillon's research on three activist and dissenting groups (Dignity, Women's Ordination Conference, and Catholics for a Free Choice) echoes a proposition long pressed by Andrew Greeley—namely, that American Catholics remain in the church because they do so primarily on their own terms.[120]

The operative assumption in Dillon's study was that the plurality of symbols and traditions within Catholicism are appropriated and reinterpreted in multiple ways. Accordingly, the church hierarchy is not the sole or primary producer of Catholicism. Church symbols and commitments are passed on more through social networks (parents, spouses, peers, friends) than through official church programs. In addition, Vatican II validated the idea that doctrinal and institutional changes were necessary. Theologians and "pro-change Catholics" who contest the boundaries of Catholic identity delineated by the Vatican are in fact legitimately reconstructing from within what it means for individuals and the church to be Catholic.

Dillon drew legitimation for her "bounded diversity" argument by accentuating the tradition's theological emphasis on the dignity of the human person, respect for the primacy of informed conscience, the compatibility of faith and reason, and the necessity of a living, embodied, and enculturated Catholic identity.[121]

Virtually all of the post–Vatican II social science assessments of institutional instability and the transformation of Catholic identity over the past half-century root the conflict and changes in multiple causes inside and outside of the Council itself. It is worth noting, however, that much of this assessment—especially in light of assumptions about social science's "value-free" nature—is laden implicitly, if not explicitly, with sociologies of knowledge expressing backstage theological presuppositions. Many social science interpretations of change among American Catholics in the wake of the Council are themselves *de facto* arguments for or against Vatican II *aggiornamento*, or for or against a more inclusive, participatory, and pluralistic church. While these interpretations operate outside the theological domain, they often do not operate outside theological assumptions.

More progressive assessments of the situation in the church today preference individualism and individual experience, along with the postmodern assumption that identity—religious or otherwise—is largely a "reflexive" or self-constructive process.[122] These assessments also implicitly preference the "new voluntarism" at the heart of a denominational sensibility that understands "church" as a strictly voluntary association created by, and at the service of, individual believers, rather than a heritage or (as *Lumen Gentium* stated) a divinely ordered and spiritually sustained reality into which the individual is incorporated by sacraments of initiation. The core-and-periphery interpretive frame also harbors dichotomies that reflect implicit theological perspectives. This is evident, for example, in the delineation of factors deemed axial or core (e.g., "sacraments") to Catholic identity, and those dubbed elements of the "institutional church" (e.g., "teaching authority claimed by the church")—with the latter often construed as marginal or peripheral, or simply the consequence of obligation or guilt.[123] Assumptions are also at work in dismissing dissent on moral claims on the grounds that these issues are not theologically informed and, therefore, can be changed or dismissed—as though moral maxims relating to the sanctity of human life are unrelated to core creedal and theological presupposition about the nature and dignity of the human person.

Likewise, more negative social science–informed interpretations of the post–Vatican II transformations of Catholic life and identity found in the research of conservative scholars also work with implicit theological and ecclesial assumptions—ones that suggest deficiencies in understanding the intricacies of the development of doctrine in the church, that are more congenial to pre–Vatican II models of Catholic identity, or that express heightened forms of Catholic sectarianism and counterculture opposition to secularism—along with the impetus to protect the church's hierarchical power structure.[124]

The point is that while post–Vatican II social science research on American Catholics presents a rich array of data, little of its analysis has escaped in-house ideological struggles to control the narrative of the Council and to shape the meaning and interpretation of its outcome. This situation has been compounded by ambiguities in the Council documents and by the mixed and sometimes unintended consequences surrounding their implementation. The situation also reflects the proverbial "half full" or "half empty" interpretive potential inherent in much of the data, along with the religious commitments and sensibilities of the researchers themselves. The hermeneutic captivity of the latter means that their interpretive themes embody multiple—and oft times hidden—theological assumptions about the nature of church, the content of orthodoxy, the role of tradition and revelation, and the nature of religious authority. As such, these themes and their advocacy express another dimension of the problematic relationship between facts and values in social science research, along with the rhetoric of contestation and inclusion that has dominated so much of Catholic life since the mid-1960s.

THE AMERICAN CULTURE FUTURE: THREE PRIORITIES

The capacity of the Catholic Church to maintain the fidelity of its membership and to promote an effective public witness in American culture depends upon multiple factors. Internally, and in light of data trends reviewed here, three issues strike this author as particularly urgent: organizational coherence, lay/clerical relations, and the intergenerational transmission of the faith.

Organizational Coherence

The unity of creed and cult generally embraced by the hierarchy is considerably less conspicuous among Catholic laity today. Especially in regard to Euro-American Catholics, the decline in ethnicity, the rise in socioeconomic status, and the achievement of high levels of education—coupled with Vatican II theological shifts toward greater responsibility assumed by the laity for their own spiritual maturation and roles in the church—have meant that Catholic religious self-understanding has moved toward a more subjective, individualist, and freedom-of-choice approach. Catholic communal and institutional attachments have declined, while thinking and acting more autonomously—from "tradition" to "conscience," from inherited communalism (expressed symbolically as the Body of Christ) to lifestyle choice—have become more pervasive. In short, Catholics are making up their own minds on issues of faith and morals and following broader American cultural patterns of religious change, especially tendencies to differentiate "faith" from "religion," to prefer choice over inheritance, and for spiritual meaning to unfold increasingly outside of institutional religion, although not entirely independent of it.[125]

Catholics today also remain more or less internally conflicted on matters of authority, gender, sexual orientation, and liturgy, among other issues. Nor should Catholic class divisions be minimized, especially when reinforced along ethnic and racial lines. The polarization and ideological tension between liberal/conservative/traditionalist Catholics that earmarked the initial furor over Vatican II reforms has hardly disappeared, despite Common Ground initiatives led by the late Cardinal Joseph Bernardin and the "culture of encounter" tone of Pope Francis. Conflicting groups, institutions, and organizations continue to lay claim to diverse visions of Catholic identity and fidelity to the Tradition. In so doing, they express many of the classic church/sect dynamics that paralleled the Protestant engagement with modernity and the ensuing split between mainline and Evangelical Protestantism.[126] Contemporary Catholic ideological sorting must also be situated within the hyperpolarization on virtually all American socioeconomic, cultural, and political fronts today.

These centrifugal trends of individualism, lifestyle orientation, internal fragmentation, and cultural polarization mean that Catholicism's institutional coherence is more problematic and unstable. As noted, these trends both express and produce pressures toward a more individualized and denominational-like Catholic identity, on the one hand, and toward a more sect-like high-tension posture, on the other. Their impact has been compounded by what the historian Scott Appleby calls the "social thinning" of Catholicism,[127] and by the fact that many of the structural and societal conditions (ethnicity, anti-Catholicism) that gave rise to earlier patterns of the culture system of Catholicism are no longer operative or have altered dramatically over the past half-century.

Few post–Vatican II research scholars have failed to recognize the important influence of the American context on Catholic identity and organizational dynamics, and perhaps none has done so as poignantly as priest, sociologist, and popular novelist Andrew Greeley.

Nearly four decades ago, Greeley observed that Catholics in the United States were becoming more "Protestantized" or, as he put it at the time, "Americanized." His point was not that Catholics were becoming Protestant in a doctrinal sense or abandoning their union with Rome, but that their organizational style was becoming more Protestant-like and impacting a wide array of Catholic structures and relationships—including pressures for more popular participation in decision making and leadership selection, a more democratic approach to church governance, a more social service concept of ministry, and significantly more room for individual decision making. Greeley also predicted

a much more relaxed attitude toward authority, the collapse of the caste barriers between clergy and laity . . . much greater freedom for discussion and criticism, and more openness toward non-Catholic religion—all these seem to be an inevitable part of the future of the Roman Catholic church in this country as it realizes that such styles of ecclesiastical organization are inevitable when one is dealing with a thoroughly Americanized population.[128]

It remains an academic question whether the changes Greeley described are a "Protestantizing" or "Americanizing" process, or simply a return to a situation akin to an eighteenth- and early nineteenth-century mode of American Catholicism characterized by an attachment to the faith that was strong but largely devoid of hierarchical control, ecclesiastical structures and participation, and clerical influence.

As the twenty-first century unfolds, individual American Catholics will continue to witness publicly to their faith. Catholic grassroots interest groups will do likewise, even when this witness is through, although not necessarily in the name of, their church. Demographic and immigration patterns will also influence Catholicism's public presence, as will the split between observant and less observant Catholics. The point I emphasize here is that the capacity of Catholics *collectively* to engage American culture will depend, in part, on some modicum of organizational coherence and effective church leadership. Put another way, the cultural power exercised by the church—its moral appeal and its capacity to create meaning, mobilize resources, and inform American civic and political discourse—necessitates not only institutional credibility but also institutional coherence and stability, especially in an increasingly pluralistic and secular society that is far less supportive of religion in general and rampant with the lures of hedonistic consumerism. A Catholicism that lacks organizational coherence, that remains fragmented and institutionally unstable, or in which the plurality of strands or bonded diversity proves too diverse, will have limited public impact in such an environment—as will a winnowed-down Catholicism that inclines too sharply toward high-tension sectarianism.

In light of the above, it is no small irony that the values of greater freedom, toleration, freedom of conscience, and democracy at the heart of the American experiment, and that achieved varying degrees of legitimation within the church in the context of Vatican II *aggiornamento*, also represent values that have made the institution's organizational coherence—and therefore its capacity to exercise public influence—more problematic. While the revitalization of parish life is one antidote to the church's organizational malaise, this revitalization is itself part of the task of addressing the broader atrophy of Catholic communal participation and the need for a socially embedded Catholicism in the face of the nation's fragmenting cultural pressures.

Lay/Clerical Relations

A second and related area that will impact the future of the church in America is the cooperation between laity and clergy. The church's organizational coherence and the vitality of Catholic parish life previously discussed are affected in no small way by the atmosphere of this relationship.

Like many aspects of contemporary Catholic life, lay and clerical relations have altered significantly over the past half-century. Vatican II's validation of the spiritual parity of the laity ("universal call to holiness") has been especially important. The clerical model of spiritual virtuosity that dominated so much of Catholicism's religious symbolism has lost hegemonic influence. More lay Catholics now embrace not only the legitimacy of their own spiritual vocation *qua* laity, but their ministerial responsibilities within the Catholic community. It is clear that significant numbers of committed laity, especially those influenced by the effervescence of Vatican II, along with some segments of the young adult Catholic population, *want* to be involved in a more democratic church and in meaningful decision-making roles,[129] notably in regard to spending priorities and parish life.[130] This desire for greater involvement in ministry roles and as facilitators, leaders, and coordinators in the local church is seen as a central aspect of their "baptismal call."

Lay aspirations for more meaningful influence in the church, however, face serious challenges. These challenges include structural conditions (Catholicism's hierarchical and nondemocratic nature) and the fact that, in spite of their expanding roles today, the laity have no *legally* decisive voice in any of the church's key decision-making bodies.[131] Tensions over the common priesthood of the baptized and the ministerial or hierarchical priesthood of the ordained are also relevant, as are recent trends toward more conservative priests and seminarians who are enamored of a cultic sense of the priesthood and are more prone to traditional attitudes toward liturgy and authority and more resistant to greater lay influence, especially on the part of women. Tension here is particularly evident where lay activism is perceived as a threat to clerical status, security, and self-validation.[132]

Social, theological, and interpersonal dynamics governing lay/clerical interactions invite further research. Here I emphasize the implications of the current situation for the future of the church in America, especially where the refusal of collaborative ministry contributes to lay perceptions that parish priests are out of touch, look upon the laity as more followers than leaders, and underestimate lay commitment to change in the church.[133]

The lingering promotion of clericalism and refusal of collaborative ministry will exercise an adverse effect on the institutional attachment of some Catholics, promote an ecclesial divorce-in-place response among others, and foster further disaffiliation. These factors will also fuel a continuing denomination-like dynamic as individual Catholics sort themselves out (where possible) in accordance with parish and pastoral environments more congenial to their own ministry and participatory aspirations.

The importation of foreign-born priests in response to the priest shortage is an additional factor that will affect lay/clerical relations. As of 2014, some 6,500 international priests were serving in American parishes.[134]

The ability of foreign-born priests to minister effectively to American Catholics remains an open question.[135] Problems with "fathers without borders" typically arise when priests have little in common culturally with those whom they serve—even when, as individuals, they are valued and appreciated. Language and communication can be problematic, as are issues of justice when priests are imported from countries that, in some cases, have even greater priest shortages than the United States. The importation of foreign-born priests also presents a solution to the priest shortage at variance with American Catholic acceptance of women and noncelibate men as ministers.

Intergenerational Transmission of Faith

A third issue looming large in the future of Catholicism in America is the status of young adult Catholics. Few observers of the church today have failed to recognize the serious challenges surrounding the intergenerational transmission of the faith. These are hardly new nor unique to Catholicism. Their causes are multiple and rooted in a complex array of changes, including the fact that social relationships, identities, and institutions are increasingly disconnected from the localized interactions that once defined everyday life and that facilitated transmission of the faith in an everyday way. In addition, because age cohorts in the church are more differentiated today—as they are in society at large—effective religious socialization is more challenging.[136] Given the current higher levels of disconnectedness among Catholic Millennials, the long-term decline in commitment to the church is likely to continue, if not accelerate, with increasing generational replacement.

As we have seen, research shows that generation is one of the strongest predictors of beliefs and practices among American Catholics. Arguments about fidelity to core beliefs notwithstanding, identity and commitment levels are weakest among younger Catholic cohorts, and especially Millennials. Fewer report that "being a Catholic is a very important part of who you are" or that they "would never leave the Church."[137] Young Catholics are less likely than older ones to have celebrated their first reconciliation, first communion, or the sacrament of confirmation.[138] Among virtually all Catholic ethnic groups, weekend Mass attendance is lower for Millennials than for Vatican II and post–Vatican II generations.[139] Catholic teenagers also lag significantly behind their Protestant peers when measured by general standards of religious belief, practice, experience, and commitment. Their most common pathway of change is religious decline[140]— a trajectory that has been attributed to multiple factors, including ineffective catechesis, decline in the number of priests and men and women religious, weak religious socialization, and parental failures in transmitting the faith.[141]

It has traditionally been assumed that institutional disconnectedness is a normal aspect of young adult ("life cycle") development: Once married and raising families, Catholics return to the church. This trajectory is now less feasible. Young adult Catholics are spending longer periods of time away from the church. They marry later, have fewer children, and are more likely to be in interfaith marriages. In addition, an increasing number of their marriages, even when to fellow Catholics, are non-church-sanctioned ones.[142] These trends raise serious cautions about expectations that younger Catholics will return to church involvement once they embrace marriage.

In addition, the destabilization of Catholic family life—following broader cultural patterns surrounding marriage and divorce—also affects Catholicism's weakening social ecology. Outside of its celibate ranks, Catholicism has traditionally been based on the two-parent, heterosexual, nuclear family. However, as more Catholics are raised in single-parent, blended, or otherwise nontraditional families, and as Catholic divorce rates come to parallel national ones, exposure to traditional Catholic family socialization patterns will likely decline.

Research on American Catholics also substantiates the common-sense observation that active, practicing and committed Catholic parents are more likely to produce young adults who behave likewise.[143] In this regard, lower levels of religious commitment among Millennial Catholics reflects lower levels of commitment among their Gen X parents. Likewise, the growing rate of interfaith marriages will likely continue to weaken young adult attachment to the church. Married Catholics are more likely to be church-affiliated than married Americans in general.

Where marriages are same-faith ones, they tend to foster higher levels of adherence to church teachings, facilitate "domestic church" theology, and contribute positively to the religious formation of young Catholics.[144] In fact, Catholics are marrying non-Catholics at an increasing rate, even while ethnic factors mitigate the overall pattern. The 1980s CPL study found that among married Catholics over fifty, 14 percent were married to Protestants; among those in their twenties, the figure was 28 percent.[145] Davidson's 1997 research placed the Catholic interfaith marriage rate at 40 percent,[146] while the Hoge et al. 2001 study found that nearly 50 percent of marriages of Euro-American young adult Catholics were to someone of another Christian or faith tradition.[147] Kosmin and Keysar reported in 2006 that two million Catholic children had a parent who was not Catholic.[148]

Catholic out-marriages will have significant consequences for the future of the church. This is especially so in a more ecumenically inclined age in which Protestant spouses of Catholics are less likely than in the past to convert to Catholicism, and in a cultural context that prioritizes religious identity in terms of "choice" rather than an ascribed status.

Other factors will also continue to affect the church connectedness of young adult Catholics. Davidson, for example, pointed to the significant gap between the age of young adults and the average age of a Catholic priest today—now about sixty-eight. While the percentage of older priests is more than twice as large as the percentage of older laypeople, the percentage of younger laity is seven times larger than the percentage of younger priests.[149] Given human preferences to interact with those similar in age, young adult connectedness to the church stands to be disadvantaged by an aging priesthood.[150]

In addition to age differentials between younger Catholics and clergy, other demographic factors are at play. Young adult Catholics—or at least those already "more active than average" in the church[151]—want be involved in parish ministry and practices. One difficulty is that parish ministries are often monopolized by Baby Boomers, a large demographic who are living longer and healthier lives. While these individuals may represent a boon for the church, their numbers are problematic insofar as younger adults perceive themselves to be shut out of parish responsibilities for service and ministry.

The question of young adults in the church today (and tomorrow) will also be affected by the influence of the "new faithful" or "evangelical Catholics." Significant numbers of these individuals are converts, from broken homes, or refugees from liberalism and religious relativism. They are more conservative in theology, more traditional in piety, and more likely to enter consecrated life. They are also less enamored of Vatican II reforms and less concerned about disputes over the Council's legacy. Many have come to Catholicism out of a strong need for identity, connectedness, and certitude—although they are not "traditionalist" in the strict sense of that term. The enthusiasm and commitment of these "new faithful" will likely thrust some into leadership roles in which they may have a disproportionate influence in the church relative to their actual numbers.[152]

The need for a preferential option in the church for young adult Catholics is clear. Pastoral strategies will be successful when young adults are empowered and their talents utilized. Previous remarks about polarization among Catholics notwithstanding, most Millennials do not come to the church today with the baggage of that intra-church conflict that decisively shaped the religious sensibilities of many older (especially Baby Boomer) Catholics. Their relationship to the tradition is more akin to religious anomie—uncertainty and lack of knowledge of their own home—along with a desire to know more about it. They also embrace broader cultural patterns that preference social-justice initiatives and engagement in voluntary or civic activity at school, at work, or in their communities. These interests suggest an openness to church teachings that accentuate social justice and service, especially when presented in compelling and convincing ways.

There is also evidence that some young adults today, including young adult Catholics, are drawn to more experiential and physical expressions of faith. This attraction includes a recovery of ritual and a new enthusiasm for the experience of community.[153] Catholicism's rich liturgical tradition and inherently communal nature can be creatively exploited in this regard.

It goes without saying that young Catholics today have been profoundly affected by the technological and digital revolution in which they have come of age. Successful outreach and ministry must address this reality. Without such engagement, serious opportunities to evangelize successfully among this digitally savvy population will be lost.

CONCLUSION

In his classic narrative, *The Uprooted: The Epic Story of the Great Migrations That Made the American People* (1951), Oscar Handlin observed that the Catholic Church's claim to its members' allegiance "rested on a solid basis of authority. It was not an individual choice that was involved in the process of belonging, but conformity."[154]

Social science research on American Catholics over the past half-century definitively negates Handlin's assessment. Long-term changes in Catholic social dynamics, theological shifts associated with Vatican II, the ever-changing contours of the American religious landscape, and the commanding influences of a culture of individualism and consumption have increasingly led to a preference for choice over conformity and authority—or inheritance—as a key determinant in the social construction of religious identity, Catholic or otherwise.

Few scholars who have mapped postconciliar Catholicism would disagree that tensions between laity and ordained officials—and not just between liberals and conservatives—is likely to be a permanent fixture of American Catholicism for the foreseeable future, especially as many who remain in the church increasingly transform elements of it in their own image and likeness.[155] Tendencies to view this tension as insignificant—notably in a cultural environment in which "faith" is privileged over "institution"—or to assume that the hierarchy is peripheral in Catholic identity construction are additionally telling.[156]

Catholicism is a lived tradition with a formal and hierarchical authority structure, a deeply communal and sacramental nature, and one in which doctrine matters. It is also a tradition that calls for freedom of conscience, personal appropriation, and reinterpretation. The situation is inherently problematic, however, when religious identity is increasingly differentiated from, or only weakly linked to, a coherent nexus of believing, belonging, and praxis. Minus the deep social ecology of ethnic bonds, and recognizing that Catholicism is more than simply a cultural system, assertions about allegiance to the faith, but not to the institution or church, are necessarily challenging.

The contemporary contesting over Catholic identity will continue. Tensions will persist between those who look positively upon more emphasis on personal responsibility for faith, more shared authority, greater lay participation, more women in leadership roles, more deacons, more ecumenism, greater dialogue with and tolerance of other faiths, and more contemporary liturgical idioms, and those who view these developments as *de facto* compromises with secular impulses inimical to the tradition. Nor is social science research on American Catholics likely to be exempt from these tensions, given that much of the research reported here has itself been instrumental in both articulating and interpreting the process of change and, in some cases, fostering and (de) legitimating it, too.

NOTES

1. See, for example, Thomas H. Groome and Michael J. Daley, eds., *Reclaiming Catholicism: Treasures Old and New* (Maryknoll, NY: Orbis, 2010); Thomas J. Ferraro, ed., *Catholic Lives / Contemporary America* (Special Issue), *South Atlantic Quarterly* 93, no. 3 (Summer 1994).

2. Peter Steinfels, *A People Adrift: The Crisis of the Roman Catholic Church in America* (New York: Simon & Schuster, 2003).

3. Including the Pew Religious Landscape Surveys (2008, 2015).

4. William V. D'Antonio, James D. Davidson, Dean R. Hoge, and Ruth A. Wallace, *American Catholic Laity in a Changing Church* (Kansas City, MO: Sheed & Ward, 1989); William V. D'Antonio, James D. Davidson, Dean R. Hoge, and Ruth A. Wallace, *Laity: American and Catholic Transforming the Church* (Kansas City, MO: Sheed & Ward, 1996); William V. D'Antonio, James D. Davidson, Dean R. Hoge, and Katherine Meyer, *American Catholics: Gender, Generation, and Commitment* (Walnut Creek, CA: AltaMira Press, 2001); William V. D'Antonio, James D. Davidson, Dean R. Hoge, and Mary L. Gautier, *American Catholics Today: New Realities of Their Faith and Church* (Lanham, MD: Rowman & Littlefield, 2007); and William V. D'Antonio, Michele Dillon, and Mary L. Gautier, *American Catholics in Transition* (Lanham, MD: Rowman & Littlefield, 2013).

5. These numbers vary. Bryan T. Froehle and Mary L. Gautier, *Catholicism USA: A Portrait of the Catholic Church in the United States* (New York: Orbis, 2000), put Catholics at about 27 percent of the national population; Barry A. Kosmin and Ariela Keysar, *American Religious Identification Survey [ARIS 2008]: Summary Report*, March 2009, Trinity College, Hartford, CT, https://commons.trincoll.edu /aris/files/2011/08/ARIS_Report_2008.pdf, 3, reported Catholics as about 25 percent of the total adult population. The more recent Pew Research Center, "America's Changing Religious Landscape," May 12, 2015, http://www .pewforum.org/2015/05/12/americas-changing-religious-landscape/, put the Catholic population at around 51 million. D'Antonio et al., *American Catholics*

in Transition, 29, claim about 75 million while the current CARA Research Report (Summer 2017) places the number at 72.4 million. The undercounting of Hispanic Catholics may contribute, in part, to these discrepancies in the total Catholic count.

6. Charles E. Zech, Mary L. Gautier, Mark M. Gray, Jonathon L. Wiggins, and Thomas P. Gaunt, *Catholic Parishes in the 21st Century* (New York: Oxford University Press, 2017), 11. As Puerto Ricans, Cubans, Mexicans, and other groups from predominantly Spanish-speaking backgrounds come into greater contact in the United States and collaborate on mutual concerns, they more frequently employ umbrella designations such as "Hispanic," "Latino," "Latina," and more recently "Latinx" to accentuate commonalities of language and ethnic heritage, as well as perceived differences with other U.S. residents. "Hispanic" is more commonly used in official Catholic documents and among Catholic leaders, while "Latino" and "Latinx" are gaining ascendancy among scholars and activists. Regional differences influence choice of term; for example, "Latino" and "Latinx" are strongly preferred in California and elsewhere on the west coast. Since no one designation enjoys universal acceptance, the most common ones are employed interchangeably in this volume. Moreover, every attempt is made to respect the terminology particular individuals and groups use in referring to themselves.

7. D'Antonio et al., *American Catholics Today*, 8. CARA puts these figures at 66 percent non-Hispanic white; 53 percent female; 47 percent male; 53 percent married. See Mark M. Gray, Paul M. Perl, and Tricia C. Bruce, *Marriage in the Catholic Church: A Survey of U.S. Catholics*, CARA Project Report, October 2007, https://cara.georgetown.edu/MarriageReport.pdf, 15, 13, 18.

8. D'Antonio et al., *American Catholics in Transition*, 3; James D. Davidson et al., *The Search for Common Ground: What Unites and Divides Catholic Americans* (Huntington, IN: Our Sunday Visitor, 1997), 195.

9. Barry A. Kosmin and Ariela Keysar, *Religion in a Free Market and Non-Religious Americans: Who, What, Why, Where* (Ithaca, NY: Paramount Market, 2006), 58.

10. Pew Research Center, "America's Changing Religious Landscape," 35.

11. Fernanda Santos, "A Populist Threat Confronts the Catholic Church," *New York Times*, April 20, 2008, 30.

12. CARA claims a 72 percent Catholic retention rate. See "The Impact of Religious Switching and Secularization on the Estimated Size of the U.S. Adult Catholic Population," 2008, https://cara.georgetown.edu/caraservices/FRStats/Winter2008.pdf, 5.

13. Dean R. Hoge, "A Demographic Framework for Understanding Catholicism in America," *Seminary Journal* 12, no. 3 (2006): 61. The Pew Religious Landscape Survey (2008) puts the figure at 46 percent.

14. James D. Davidson, *Catholicism in Motion: The Church in American Society* (Liguori, MO: Liguori/Triumph, 2005), 18. See also Guillermina Jasso, Douglas S. Massey, Mark R. Rosenzweig and James P. Smith, "Exploring the Religious

Preferences of Recent Immigrants to the United States," in *Religion and Immigration*, ed. Yvonne Y. Haddad, Jane I. Smith, and John L. Esposito (Walnut Creek, CA: AltaMira Press, 2003), 217–253. The Pew Religious Landscape Survey (2008) placed the number of immigrants who report themselves Catholic at 46 percent.

15. Zech et al., *Catholic Parishes*, 9–11.
16. Pew Research Center, "America's Changing Religious Landscape," 9.
17. Philip Jenkins, *The Next Christendom: The Coming of Global Christianity* (Oxford: Oxford University Press, 2002). See also John L. Allen, Jr., *The Future Church: How Ten Trends Are Revolutionizing the Catholic Church* (New York: Doubleday, 2009), esp. 141–169.
18. Froehle and Gautier, *Catholicism USA*, 16.
19. D'Antonio et al., *American Catholics Today*, 8.
20. Barry A. Kosmin and Seymour P. Lachmann, *One Nation Under God: Religion in Contemporary American Society* (New York: Crown, 1993), 127.
21. Gray, Perl, and Bruce, *Marriage in the Catholic Church*, 15.
22. See, for example, Hosffman Ospino, *Hispanic Ministry in Catholic Parishes: A Summary Report of Finding from the National Study of Catholic Parishes with Hispanic Ministry*, Boston College, School of Theology and Ministry, 2014, https://www.bc.edu/content/dam/files/schools/stm/pdf/2014/Hispanic MinistryinCatholicParishes_2.pdf, 5.
23. See Timothy Matovina, *Latino Catholicism: Transformation in America's Largest Church* (Princeton, NJ: Princeton University Press, 2012); Hoffsman Ospino, ed., *Hispanic Ministry in the Twenty-First Century: Present and Future* (Miami, FL: Convivium Press, 2010).
24. Kosmin and Lachmann, *One Nation*, 127.
25. Kosmin and Lachmann, *One Nation*, 127.
26. For example, Robert D. Putnam and David E. Campbell, *American Grace: How Religion Divides and Unites Us* (New York: Simon & Schuster, 2010), 243–245.
27. D'Antonio et al., *American Catholics in Transition*, 104–105. Hispanics, however, are less receptive to "strongly agree[ing]" on the issue.
28. D'Antonio et al., *American Catholics in Transition*, esp. 89–105.
29. Although there is no firm agreement on the age breakdown of Catholic cohort populations, most researchers identify four groups: Pre–Vatican II Catholics are those born before 1940; Vatican II Catholics came of age during Vatican II and were born between 1941 and 1960. Post–Vatican II Catholics grew up in the aftermath of the Council (1961–1978); Gen Xers and Millennials (1978–1987) are both subpopulations within the post–Vatican II generations. See also "American Catholics Across Generations: Glimpsing the Future," *Seminary Journal* 12, no. 3 (2006): 69–70.
30. D'Antonio et al., *American Catholics Today*, 110.
31. Zech et al., *Catholic Parishes*, 13–15.

32. See John L. Allen, Jr., "More Catholics on the Way," *National Catholic Reporter*, February 2, 2007, 6. According to Allen, this aging trend is also true of the Hispanic population. The U.S. Census Bureau estimates that the Hispanic sixty-five-plus population will rise from 4 percent to 16 percent by 2050.

33. Zech at al., *Catholic Parishes*, 7–19.

34. See Zech et al., *Catholic Parishes*, passim.

35. Michael S. Rosenwald, Michelle Boorstein, and Scott Clement, "Poll: Americans Widely Admire Pope Francis, but His Church Less So," September 20, 2015, https://www.washingtonpost.com/local/poll-americans-widely-admire-pope-francis-but-his-church-less-so/2015/09/19/f7f46188-5d71-11e5-b38e-06883aacba64_story.html?utm_term=.91e5ce36df9e.

36. D' Antonio et al., *American Catholics in Transition*, 139–150; see also Christian Smith, Kyle Longest, Jonathan Hill, and Kari Christoffersen, *Young Catholic America: Emerging Adults in, Out of, and Gone from the Church* (New York: Oxford University Press, 2014).

37. On the general decline of religion, see Mark Chaves, *American Religion: Contemporary Trends* (Princeton, NJ: Princeton University Press, 2011). On the "None" phenomenon, see Phil Zuckerman, *Faith No More: Why People Reject Religion* (New York: Oxford University Press, 2012); Linda A. Mercadante, *Belief Without Borders: Inside the Minds of the Spiritual but Not Religious* (New York: Oxford University Press, 2014); and Elizabeth Drescher, *Choosing Our Religion: The Spiritual Lives of America's Nones* (New York: Oxford University Press, 2016). See also Wade Clark Roof, *Spiritual Marketplace: Baby Boomers and the Remaking of American Religion* (Princeton, NJ: Princeton University Press, 1999); Michael Hout and Claude S. Fischer, "Why More Americans Have No Religious Preference: Politics and Generations," *American Sociological Review* 67 (2002): 165–190.

38. See, for example, Leonard Sweet, *Post-Modern Pilgrims: First Century Passion for the Twenty-First Century World* (Nashville, TN: Broadman and Holman, 2000).

39. Putnam and Campbell, *American Grace*, 301.

40. See, for example, Pew Research Center, "Strong Public Support for Right to Die: More Americans Discussing—and Planning—End-of-Life Treatment," January 5, 2006, http://people-press.org/reports/display.php3?ReportID=266; Pew Research Center, "U.S. Catholics Open to Non-Traditional Families," September 2, 2015, http://www.pewforum.org/2015/09/02/u-s-catholics-open-to-non-traditional-families/.

41. Davidson, *Catholicism in Motion*, 165–167. CARA reports that 83 percent of Catholics say that helping those in need is "somewhat" or "very" important to their sense of what it means to be Catholic. *CARA Report* 14, no. 1 (Summer 2008): 11.

42. D'Antonio et al., *American Catholics in Transition*, 49.

43. Davidson, *Catholicism in Motion*, 86–89. The most recent ARIS study (2009) indicated that about a third of Catholics do not see the Church's magisterial

authority as particularly important to their identity as Catholics. Hoge et al. found that less than half (42 percent) of those surveyed considered that "Teaching that Christ established the authority of bishops by choosing Peter to head the Church" was "essential to faith"; Dean R. Hoge, William D. Dinges, Mary Johnson, S.N.D.d.N, and Juan L. Gonzales, Jr., *Young Adult Catholics: Religion in the Culture of Choice* (Notre Dame, IN: University of Notre Dame Press, 2001), 201.

44. See, for example, the discussion about what Catholics actually understand by the "Real Presence" in Davidson, *Catholicism in Motion*, 164–165. See also James D. Davidson, "Yes, Jesus Is Really There: Most Catholics Still Agree," *Commonweal*, October 12, 2001, 14–16. In 2008, CARA *Sacraments Today: Beliefs and Practices Among U.S. Catholics* reported that 43 percent of Catholics said their belief in the Real Presence was best reflected in the statement "Bread and wine are symbols of Jesus, but Jesus is not really present," 4.

45. Davidson et al., *The Search for Common Ground*, 177–197. See also William V. D'Antonio et al., *American Catholics: Gender, Generation, and Commitment*, esp. appendix B, 157–158.

46. CARA, "Frequently Requested Church Statistics," http://cara.georgetown.edu/frequently-requested-church-statistics/.

47. Froehle and Gautier, *Catholicism USA*, 54–57.

48. Some such parishes are identified in Paul Wilkes, *Excellent Catholic Parishes* (Mahwah, NJ: Paulist Press, 2001).

49. Anthony Stevens-Arroyo et al., *The National Survey of Leadership in Latino Parishes and Congregations* (Brooklyn, NY: Program for the Analysis of Religion Among Latinas/os, 2003).

50. The study was funded by Lilly Endowment and involved multiple researchers, directed by Msgr. John J. Egan, Michael Welch, David Leege, Jay Dolan, Msgr. Joseph Gremillion, Mark Searle, and Philip Murnion under the Institute for Pastoral and Social Ministry at the University of Notre Dame. For summary results, see Joseph Gremillion and Jim Castelli, *The Emerging Parish: The Notre Dame Study of Catholic Parish Life Since Vatican II* (San Francisco: Harper & Row, 1987).

51. Mark Searle, "The Notre Dame Study of Catholic Parish Life," *Worship* 60, no. 4 (July 1986): 323. For the significance of lay relationships with priests, see also Andrew M. Greeley, *The Catholic Myth: The Behavior and Beliefs of American Catholics* (New York: Scribner, 1990).

52. Davidson, *Catholicism in Motion*, 68; Hoge et al., *Young Adult Catholics*, 48–53.

53. The figures were 91 percent and 40 percent, respectively; D'Antonio et al., *American Catholics Today*, 109. These positive assessments can be attributed, in part, to the fact that increasing numbers of Catholics are self-selecting ("parish shopping") into their parish choice. CARA puts the number doing so at 35 percent; Zech et al., *Catholic Parishes*, 119.

54. See Jerome P. Baggett, *Sense of the Faithful: How American Catholics Live Their Faith* (New York: Oxford University Press, 2009), esp. 125–168.

55. D'Antonio et al., *American Catholics Today*, 108; Zech et al., *Catholic Parishes*. See also David DeLambo, *Lay Parish Ministry: A Study of Emerging Leadership* (New York: National Pastoral Life Center, 2005).

56. Zech et al., *Catholic Parishes*, 45.

57. Zech et al., *Catholic Parishes*, 36. For earlier data, see Mark M. Gray and Mary L. Gautier, *Understanding the Experience: A Profile of Lay Ecclesial Ministers Serving as Parish Life Coordinators* (Washington, DC: National Association for Lay Ministry, 2004); Delambo, *Lay Parish Ministry*.

58. James C. Cavendish, "Church-Based Community Activism: A Comparison of Black and White Catholic Congregations," *Journal for the Scientific Study of Religion* 39 (2000): 371–384.

59. Davidson et al., *The Search for Common Ground*, 180; D'Antonio et al., *American Catholics in Transition*, 109–110. Davidson et al. report that significant numbers of these unattached or "informally" affiliated individuals were African Americans, Latino/as, and young people, along with those who were economically and emotionally distressed or who had learned early that religion is not an important part of life, 194–195.

60. D'Antonio et al., *American Catholics in Transition*, 110.

61. Zech et al., *Catholic Parishes*.

62. Davidson, *The Search for Common Ground*, 185.

63. Hoge et al., *Young Adult Catholics*, 222.

64. Gremillion and Castelli, *The Emerging Parish*, 4.

65. Sidney Verba, Kay Lehman Scholzman, and Henry E. Brady, *Voice and Equality: Civic Voluntarism in American Politics* (Cambridge, MA: Harvard University Press, 1995); see also Nancy Ammerman, "Religious Narratives in the Public Square," in *Taking Faith Seriously*, ed. Mary Jo Bane, Brent Coffin, and Richard Higgins (Cambridge, MA: Harvard University Press, 2005), 146–174.

66. ARIS, 2009.

67. Dean R. Hoge, Charles Zech, Patrick McNamara, and Michael J. Donahue, *Money Matters: Personal Giving in American Churches* (Louisville, KY: Westminster John Knox, 1996), 31. CARA research also shows that parish Catholics continue to be notoriously poor givers relative to Protestants—contributing about half as much to their parishes, as a percentage of household income, as Protestants contribute to their congregations; Zech et al., *Catholic Parishes*, 77.

68. David C. Leege and Joseph Gremillion, "The U.S. Parish Twenty Years After Vatican II: An Introduction to the Study," *Notre Dame Study of Catholic Parish Life*, Report No. 1, December 1984, 6.

69. Zech et al, *Catholic Parishes*, 119.

70. See Brett C. Hoover, *The Shared Parish: Latinos, Anglos, and the Future of U.S. Catholicism* (New York: New York University Press, 2014).

71. For initial research on this issue, see Christopher J. Born, "Post-Retirement Religiosity Among Migrating Northern Catholic Baby Boomers" (Ph.D. diss., Catholic University of America, 2011).

72. Bernard J. Lee, *The Catholic Experience of Small Christian Communities* (Mahwah, NJ: Paulist Press, 2000).

73. Lee, *Small Christian Communities*, 145.

74. For a positive assessment of the impact of Catholic schools, see Andrew M. Greeley, William C. McCready, and Kathleen McCourt, *Catholic Schools in a Declining Church* (Kansas City, MO: Sheed & Ward, 1976).

75. Steinfels, *A People Adrift*, 213.

76. Froehle and Gautier, *Catholicism USA*, 72–73. D'Antonio et al., *American Catholics in Transition*, 41, report that between 1987 and 2011, the number of Catholic elementary schools and elementary school enrollment declined by more than 25 percent.

77. Hoge et al., *Young Adult Catholics*, 131–148.

78. William D. Dinges, "Roman Catholic Traditionalism," in *Fundamentalisms Observed*, ed. Martin E. Marty and R. Scott Appleby (Chicago: University of Chicago Press, 1991), 66–101.

79. See Colleen Carroll, *The New Faithful: Why Young Adults Are Embracing Christian Orthodoxy* (Chicago: Loyola Press, 2002).

80. On the movement in general, see Joseph H. Fichter, *The Catholic Cult of the Paraclete* (New York: Sheed & Ward, 1975); Richard J. Bord and Joseph E. Faulkner, *The Catholic Charismatics: The Anatomy of a Modern Religious Movement* (University Park: Pennsylvania State University Press, 1983).

81. Pew Research Center, "Changing Faiths: Latinos and the Transformation of American Religion," April 25, 2007, http://assets.pewresearch.org/wp-content/uploads/sites/11/2007/04/hispanics-religion-07-final-mar08.pdf, 32–38.

82. *CARA Report* 14, no. 1 (Summer 2008): 11.

83. Hoge et. al., *Young Adult Catholics*, 116.

84. Davidson, *Catholicism in Motion*, 159–161. Where divorce has occurred, fewer Catholic are now seeking annulments.

85. Reported in *Christian Century* 121, no. 13 (January 13, 2004): 13.

86. Pew Research Center, "U.S. Public Becoming Less Religious," November 3, 2015, http://assets.pewresearch.org/wp-content/uploads/sites/11/2015/11/201.11.03_RLS_II_full_report.pdf, 70.

87. D'Antonio et al., *American Catholics in Transitions*, 110.

88. *CARA Report* 14, no. 1 (Summer 2008): 10. See also CARA, *Sacraments Today: Belief & Practices Among U.S. Catholics* (Washington, DC: Georgetown University, April 2008), 20.

89. CPL found that nearly 50 percent responded "yes" to the question "In your judgment, should persons be considered 'true' Catholics if they rarely go to Mass?" Violations of sexual norms drew much higher "no" responses, with urging or undergoing an abortion as the most serious basis for placing oneself outside the Church; Gremillion and Castelli, *The Emerging Parish*, 50. CARA, *Sacraments Today*, 61, reports that more than two-thirds of American Catholics

agree with the statement "I can be a good Catholic without going to Mass every Sunday."

90. D'Antonio et al., *American Catholics in Transition*, 59.

91. More recently in John Paul II's 1998 Apostolic Letter, *Dies Domini* [On Keeping the Lord's Day Holy], https://w2.vatican.va/content/john-paul-ii/en/apost_letters/1998/documents/hf_jp-ii_apl_05071998_dies-domini.html.

92. Regarding the last, see, for example, Gregory Allen Smith, *Politics in the Parish: The Political Influence of Catholic Priests* (Washington, DC: Georgetown University Press, 2008), 187.

93. According to Greeley, the fundamental difference between Catholics and Protestants is not doctrinal or ethnic. Instead, Catholics imagine in an analogical way, Protestants in a dialectical fashion. Catholics allegedly stay attached to Catholicism because they like their images of God and are disinclined to give them up. See Andrew M. Greeley, *The Catholic Imagination* (Berkeley: University of California Press, 2000).

94. D'Antonio et al., *American Catholics Today*, 104, 155.

95. See also, for example, Baggett, *Sense of the Faithful*.

96. Robert Wuthnow, *Loose Connections: Joining Together in America's Fragmented Communities* (Cambridge, MA: Harvard University Press, 1998).

97. See Pew Research Center, "America's Changing Religious Landscape," 33–47. See also Richard Cimino and Don Latin, *Shopping for Faith: American Religion in the New Millennium* (San Francisco: Jossey-Bass, 2002); Wade C. Roof, *Spiritual Marketplace: Baby Boomers and the Remaking of American Religion* (Princeton, NJ: Princeton University Press, 1999).

98. For insightful commentary on the enduring polarization, see Mary Ellen Konieczny, Charles C. Camosy, and Tricia C. Bruce, *Polarization in the US Catholic Church: Naming the Wounds, Beginning to Heal* (Collegeville, MN: Liturgical Press, 2016).

99. For example, Robert A. Ludwig, *Reconstructing Catholicism for a New Generation* (New York: Crossroad, 1996); Francis J. Butler, *American Catholic Identity: Essay in an Age of Change* (Kansas City, MO: Sheed & Ward, 1994); Daniel Donovan, *Distinctively Catholic: An Exploration of Catholic Identity* (New York: Paulist Press, 1997); Robert P. Imbelli, ed., *Handing on the Faith: The Church's Mission and Challenge* (New York: Crossroad, 2006); Thomas P. Rausch, *Being Catholic in a Culture of Choice* (Collegeville, MN: Liturgical Press, 2006). For issues relating to defining "Catholic" among youth, see Smith et al., *Young Catholic America*.

100. See especially Dean R. Hoge, Benton Johnson, and Donald A. Luidens, *Vanishing Boundaries: The Religion of Mainline Protestant Baby Boomers* (Louisville, KY: Westminster/John Knox Press, 1994).

101. Hoge et al., *Young Adult Catholics*, 208–209; Searle, "The Notre Dame Study of Catholic Parish Life," 332.

102. D'Antonio et al., *American Catholics in Transition*, 50, 114. See also CARA, *Sacraments Today*, 54–57.

103. Hoge et al., *Young Adult Catholics*, 211.

104. D'Antonio et al., *American Catholics*, 44–45.

105. Rodney Stark, *What Americans Really Believe: New Findings from the Baylor Surveys of Religion* (Waco, TX: Baylor University Press, 2008.)

106. Smith et al., *Young Catholic America*, 128–132.

107. D'Antonio et al., *American Catholics in Transition*, 52.

108. William V. D'Antonio, James D. Davidson, Dean R. Hoge, Katherine Meyer, *American Catholics*, 22.

109. These figures were even starker when compared with American Protestants, whose strength of religious identification has been rising in recent years. See Pew Research Center, " 'Strong' Catholic Identity at a Four-Decade Low in U.S.,' " March 13, 2013, http://www.pewforum.org/2013/03/13/strong-catholic-identity-at-a-four-decade-low-in-us/.

110. In Hoge et al., *Young Adult Catholics*, 57, 75 percent of the respondents agreed that "I cannot imagine myself being anything other than Catholic"; D'Antonio et al., *American Catholics Today*, 20, reported that 70 percent said they "can't imagine themselves being anything but Catholic."

111. CARA *Sacraments Today: Belief and Practice among U.S. Catholics* (Washington, D.C.: Georgetown University, 2008), 8.

112. D'Antonio et al., *American Catholics Today*, 15–48.

113. These dynamics relate to secularization theories highlighting the significance of the differentiation of temporal and religious authority and the declining scope of the latter. See Mark Chaves, "Secularization as Declining Religious Authority," *Social Forces* 72, no. 3 (1994): 74.

114. D'Antonio et al., *American Catholics Today*, 92–94.

115. David Carlin, *The Decline and Fall of the Catholic Church in America* (Manchester, NH: Sophia Institute Press, 2003), 377. For similar negative assessments see Ken Jones, *Index of Leading Catholic Indicators: The Church Since Vatican II* (St. Louis, MO: Oriens, 2003); James Lothian, "*Novus Ordo Missae*: The Record After Thirty Years," *Homiletic and Pastoral Review* CI, no. 1 (October 2000): 27–32; Joseph Varacalli, "Conflict and Change in the Catholic Church," *Journal for the Scientific Study of Religion* 29, no. 3 (September 1990): 417–418.

116. George Weigel, *The Courage to Be Catholic: Crisis, Reform and the Future of the Catholic Church* (New York: Basic Books, 2002).

117. See, for example, Roger Finke and Rodney Stark, *The Churching of America, 1776–1990: Winners and Losers in Our Religious Economy* (New Brunswick, NJ: Rutgers University Press, 1992), esp. 255–275.

118. Davidson et al., *The Search for Common Ground*, 55.

119. Hoge et al., *Young Adult Catholics*, 203.

120. Andrew M. Greeley, *The Communal Catholic: A Personal Manifesto*, (NY: Seabury Press, 1976), 47.

121. Dillon, *Catholic Identity*. For a critique of Dillon's argument, see John A. Coleman, "Dissenting in Place," *America*, May 6, 2000, 18–20.

122. Anthony Giddens, *Modernity and Self-Identity: Self and Society in the Late Modern Age* (Stanford, CA: Stanford University Press, 1991).

123. Dean R. Hoge, "Core and Periphery in American Catholic Identity," *Journal of Contemporary Religion* 17, no. 3 (2002): 293–307.

124. See, for example, Carlin, *The Decline and Fall*, and Varacalli, "Conflict and Change."

125. See Linda Mercadante, *Belief Without Borders: Inside the Minds of the Spiritual but Not Religious* (New York: Oxford University Press, 2014); Elizabeth Drescher, *Choosing Our Religion: The Spiritual Lives of America's Nones* (New York: Oxford University Press, 2016).

126. For thoughtful discussion of polarization and the "broken" state of contemporary Catholicism, see Konieczny, Camosy, and Bruce, *Polarization*.

127. R. Scott Appleby, "Surviving the Shaking of the Foundations: United States Catholicism in the Twenty-First Century," in Katarina Schuth, *Seminaries, Theologates, and the Future of Church Ministry: An Analysis of Trends and Transitions* (Collegeville, MN: Liturgical Press, 1999), 9.

128. Andrew M. Greeley, *The Denominational Society: A Sociological Approach to Religion in America* (Glenview, IL: Scott, Foresman, 1972), 193–194.

129. Dean R. Hoge and Marti R. Jewell, "Young Adult Catholics and Their Future in Ministry," National Association of Lay Ministry, 2007, https://nalm.org /wp-content/uploads/2016/05/Young-Adult-Catholics-Interim-Report.pdf.

130. D'Antonio et al., *American Catholics Today*, 111.

131. This point is highlighted by theologian Paul Lakeland in "Maturity and the Lay Vocation," in *Catholic Identity and the Laity: College Theological Society Annual Volume 54*, ed. Tim Muldoon (Maryknoll, NY: Orbis, 2009), 241–260.

132. For discussion of the traditional bent among seminarians, including significant numbers who are insecure, rigid, overly scrupulous, and fearful and reactionary toward change, American culture, and critical thought, see Schuth, *Seminaries, Theologates*. Dean Hoge and Jacqueline Wenger identify tensions between laity and clergy in reference to two dominant models of the priesthood operative today. In the "cultic" model, the priest is an individual set apart from the laity who provides worship and sacraments, and there is greater emphasis on a putative higher clerical status and privilege. The "servant leader" model stresses the universal call to ministry, emphasizes collaboration with the laity, and is less clerically privileged and distinctive. Young priests today are considerably more inclined to the former model than are those who were seminarians in the 1960s and '70s, who put more emphasis on the servant leader model in light of Vatican II. See Dean R. Hoge and Jacqueline Wenger, *Evolving Visions of the Priesthood* (Collegeville, MN: Liturgical Press, 2003).

133. D'Antonio et al., *American Catholics Today*, 109, 146; Gremillion and Castelli, *The Emerging Parish*, 46.

134. Mary L. Gautier, Melissa A. Cidade, Paul M. Perl, and Mark Clark, *Bridging the Gap: The Opportunities and Challenges of International Priest Ministering in the United States* (Huntington, IN: Our Sunday Visitor, 2014), 53.

135. See "Serving U.S. Parishes, Fathers Without Boarders," *New York Times*, December 28, 2008.

136. William D. Dinges, "Faith, Hope and (Excessive) Individualism," in *Handing on the Faith: The Church's Mission and Challenge*, ed. Robert P. Imbelli (New York: Crossroad, 2006), 30–43.

137. Davidson, *Catholicism in Motion*, 136.

138. CARA, *Sacraments Today*, 3.

139. Zech et al., *Catholic Parishes*, 142.

140. Christian Smith and Melinda Lundquist Denton, *Soul Searching: The Religious and Spiritual Lives of American Teenagers* (New York: Oxford University Press, 2005), 193–217.

141. Smith and Denton, *Soul Searching*, 193–217.

142. Davidson, *Catholicism in Motion*, 161.

143. Smith et al., *Young Catholic America*, 186.

144. Hart M. Nelsen, "The Religious Identification of Children in Interfaith Marriages," *Review of Religious Research* 32 (1990): 122–134; see also CARA, *Sacraments Today*, 3.

145. Gremillion and Castelli, *The Emerging Parish*, 33.

146. Davidson, *The Search for Common Ground*, 192.

147. Hoge et al., *Young Adult Catholics*, 43. Alan McCutcheon's earlier 1988 study reported the Catholic out-marriage rate at 43 percent. See Alan L. McCutcheon, "Denominations and Religious Intermarriage: Trends Among White Americans in the Twentieth Century," *Review of Religious Research* 29, no. 3 (March 1988): 213–227.

148. Kosmin and Keysar, *Religion in a Free Market*, 102.

149. Davidson, *Catholicism in Motion*, 104.

150. Davidson, *Catholicism in Motion*, 105–106.

151. See, for example, Hoge and Jewell, "Young Adult Catholics."

152. For an excellent discussion of the possible impact of this more conservative group of young adults, see Rausch, *Being Catholic*, esp. 87–100, and Carroll, *The New Faithful*.

153. See Richard Flory and Donald E. Miller, *Finding Faith: The Spiritual Quest of the Post-Boomer Generation* (New Brunswick, NJ: Rutgers University Press, 2008), 119.

154. Oscar Handlin, *The Uprooted: The Epic Story of the Great Migrations That Made the American People* (Boston: Little, Brown, 1951), 119.

155. Baggett, *Sense of the Faithful*.

156. For an insightful historical analysis of this process in relation to the reconfiguration of spiritual authority in the Church, and one that augments current findings in social science research, see James P. McCartin, *Prayers of the Faithful: The Shifting Spiritual Life of American Catholics* (Cambridge, MA: Harvard University Press, 2010).

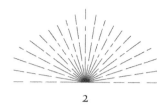

Becoming Latino

THE TRANSFORMATION OF U.S. CATHOLICISM

Timothy Matovina

Immigrant clergy can border on the hagiographic when they exalt the influence of Catholicism in their native land. One émigré priest lauded his compatriots' "simple yet strong piety and trust in God," the influence of a Catholic ethos in everyday life, and the "deep religious feeling [and] love for the Madonna" that "alone would be proof of the strength of their religion." His depiction elicited a two-month dispute in the pages of the national Catholic weekly *America*. The first respondent retorted that "piety does not consist in processions or carrying lighted candles, in prostrations before a statue of the Madonna, in processions in honor of the patron saints of villages." Others characterized immigrants as ignorant of their Catholic faith, infrequent in church attendance, and unwilling to offer financial or other support to parishes. For these reasons, critics deemed the émigrés "easy victim[s] to the Protestant proselytizer." Immigrant defenders questioned the legitimacy of such claims. They opined that immigrants' practice of their faith was remarkable when one considered that most of them were poor workers struggling for their very survival. Most had endured the ordeal of migrating from their homelands to blighted neighborhoods in U.S. cities, where they found relatively few priests prepared to serve them in their native tongue. Several respondents in the debate pointed out the enthusiastic immigrant response to pastoral outreach efforts. Some considered the real issue to be the hostility the immigrants so frequently met in the United States, even from members of their own church.[1]

The short statement with which the editors of *America* closed this controversy sided with the critics: "When all has been said and due discount has been made for the insufficiency of the data offered as the basis of a judgment, the conviction, we think, will cling to most readers' minds that there is an Italian problem, and that it clamors for solution." The year was 1914, three decades after debate about the "Italian problem" surfaced among U.S. Catholic bishops at their 1884 Plenary Council in Baltimore. Pope Leo XIII even weighed in on the situation in an 1888 letter urging the U.S. bishops to provide his immigrant compatriots "the saving care of ministers of God familiar with the Italian language."[2]

Accusations and rebuttals regarding the Italian immigrants of yesteryear are strikingly parallel to perceptions of today's Latino Catholics.[3] Indeed, the protracted debate about Italians reveals a central and long-standing feature of U.S. Catholicism: the varied attempts to incorporate new groups into a unified body of faith. Though for much of U.S. Catholic history Hispanics have constituted a relatively small and frequently overlooked group, since World War II their numbers and influence have increased dramatically. No ethnic or racial group has ever been as proportionally large in U.S. Catholicism as Latinos are now. No group will have a greater impact on the future of American Catholicism in the twenty-first century. Yet, unlike European émigrés from the great century of migration between 1820 and 1920, today's Hispanic newcomers tend to have not only ethnic but also class and educational differences with the descendants of previous immigrant groups. They are not just the mainstay of the "new immigrant church," as David Badillo has rightly deemed them. In large part they are also, as the late Joseph P. Fitzpatrick, S.J., so aptly put it, the "Hispanic poor in a middle-class church."[4]

Observers of the U.S. Catholic Church usually presume it is largely composed of former immigrants who have now become Americanized, often examining U.S. Catholics through the lens of a split between conservative and progressive factions that have emerged in the half-century since the Second Vatican Council. The Hispanic presence reveals that the U.S. Catholic Church is not solely an "Americanized" church, nor is it exclusively comprised of the right and left camps that dominate contemporary media coverage and debates about U.S. Catholicism. Rather, it is a church whose leaders at every level are largely European-descent Catholics, but whose members are now in the majority not Euro-Americans: growing numbers of Latino, Asian, and African immigrants, along with sizable contingents of native-born Latino and African American Catholics and some Native Americans. The Hispanic influence on Catholic parish life, public policy stances on immigration, and the collective challenge of passing on the faith to young people illustrate the significant ways that Latinos are shaping and shaped by U.S. Catholicism and its public role in American society.

FROM NATIONAL TO SHARED PARISH

Hispanics' participation in parishes exerts its greatest influence on the internal dynamics of U.S. Catholicism. This is not surprising, given that the congregation or parish has long been the locus of religious life and experience in the United States and that the general U.S. trend over recent decades has been away from denominational and toward congregational or other local attachments. Commenting on the more than 300,000 religious assemblies in the United States, a figure that ranks them as the most widespread institution in the country, sociologist of religion R. Stephen Warner succinctly summed up the status of the congregation as the "bedrock of the American religious system . . . an unofficial norm in American religious life."[5] Many Catholics and those who observe the Roman Catholic Church recognize it is a universal body with a centralized hierarchy overseeing everything from core beliefs to liturgical rubrics. Latin American immigrants often bring a tradition of home-based religion. But in the United States, Catholicism and other religions have adapted to a religious milieu marked by a decidedly congregational polity. The national parish that served numerous European immigrant Catholics declined concurrently with the rise of Latino immigration and the multicultural or shared parish. Intercultural encounters between Hispanics and their coreligionists in shared parishes alter the day-to-day congregational experience for numerous Catholics in the United States.

The integrative role of the ethnic or national parish for European Catholic immigrants is well known. Initially havens where émigrés nurtured their faith and felt a sense of ownership and belonging in a strange new land, over time national parishes enabled the descendants of immigrants to integrate into U.S. society and ecclesial life from a position of strength.[6] Today a number of Catholic congregations are in effect national parishes, such as those that serve overwhelmingly Asian or Hispanic communities. The impulse to found and support such faith communities is extant among all Latino groups, as is evident in the predominantly Puerto Rican parish of Santa Agonía (Holy Agony) in New York, the Cuban parishioners of San Juan Bosco in Miami, the largely Mexican congregation of St. Pius V in Chicago's Pilsen neighborhood, and the multiethnic Latino community of the Misión Católica de Nuestra Señora de las Americas on the outskirts of Atlanta. Congregations like these engage parishioners at multiple levels, providing social services and sacraments, English classes and traditional devotions, religious education and legal aid, parenting classes and prayer groups.

Yet Latino parish congregations are increasingly more the exception than the rule. On the whole, Catholic congregations are the most internally diverse of all Christian congregations in the United States and are becoming increasingly so because of the heterogeneity of the Catholic population, trends toward larger parishes, the geographic dispersion of Hispanics across the United States, and the growing Catholic population in the western region of the country, where churches of all groups tend to be more integrated. Michael Emerson's 2006 study on multiracial congregations in the United States found that, despite the relative paucity of instances in which no single racial group comprises more than 80 percent of a congregation, the percentage of multiracial Catholic parishes is three times higher than among Protestant congregations. The 2014 National Study of Catholic Parishes with Hispanic Ministry found that one-fourth of all Catholic parishes in the United States intentionally serve Hispanics. Nationally, and particularly outside of areas with more concentrated Hispanic populations like the Southwest, Florida, New York, and Chicago, an increasingly frequent scenario in Catholic parishes is that Latinos are migrant newcomers in established, predominantly Euro-American congregations.[7]

Historically, the reasons for the shift away from national parishes include the depleted congregations and aging church buildings of previous immigrant groups, the loss of faith among some immigrant descendants who identify Catholicism with the "archaic" practices of their national parish community, increasing shortages of priests and fiscal resources, and the contention that national parishes lead to segregation and disunity. Today, the customary practice or stated norm in most dioceses is for integrated or multicultural parishes. Brett Hoover argues that naming such parishes "integrated" or "mixed" parishes can tend to exaggerate the unity between groups or impose a predetermined prescription for rapid and often superficial acculturation in intergroup relations. At the same time, the designation "parallel congregations," a phrase synonymous with segmented parishes, is structurally accurate but does not focus sufficient attention on the cultural interactions that are typical of such communities. Hoover prefers the term "shared parish" in order to highlight "the art of the ongoing negotiated arrangement created by the presence of multiple cultural groups in the same parish space."[8]

When a parish includes two or more language groups worshiping under the same roof, they often coexist in isolation or even in conflict. After more than half a century as a parishioner, when the number of Hispanic parishioners increased one woman began to feel "my church isn't my church anymore." The large number of Latino newcomers in many parishes can exacerbate tensions. When Hispanics attempt to make a parish feel more like home by placing one of their own sacred images in the worship space or scheduling a Spanish Mass in a "prime time" slot on Sunday morning, for example, established parishioners frequently rebuff them with the claim that "our ancestors built this church" or "we were here first." As one lay leader lamented, "I am discouraged by the fact that we, Hispanics, don't count here in this parish. We come to Mass in great numbers and our Masses are really filled with the spirit. But all the power is in the hands of a small group of [non-Hispanic] old-timers who contribute a lot of money to the Church." If Latinos respond with protest or complaint, their Euro-American coreligionists may perceive them as being unappreciative of the welcome offered to them. Like their non-Catholic neighbors, many European-descent U.S. Catholics presume that newcomers who do not adopt U.S. customs and speak English in public are ungrateful or even not qualified to remain in the United States. Critics also claim that the practice of distinct language Masses creates "parallel parishes" that have virtually no relationship with one another, leading to fragmentation within the body of Christ. Leaders in Hispanic ministry like Father Chuck Dahm, O.P., counter that "the promotion of multicultural parishes is often little more than a veiled attempt to assimilate the minority culture into the dominant one."[9]

Tensions also arise in shared parishes with significant Hispanic and African American contingents. A 1997 joint statement of the Bishops' Committee on African American Catholics and the Bishops' Committee on Hispanic Affairs promoted reconciliation and collaboration between their communities. The prelates noted that division and mistrust often mark African American and Latino intergroup relations, even though they have common struggles with discrimination, poverty, and a lack of opportunity that could potentially unite them as allies. A particular challenge frequently occurs "when our people worship in the same parish and compete for liturgical resources." Concretely, the more prominent group in the parish tends to dominate the smaller group, efforts to celebrate joint liturgies are difficult because of differences in language and faith expressions, and both groups are prone to "negative forms of religious and ethnic pride" that deepen antagonisms. The bishops urged that parishioners strive to worship together in harmony, especially on major liturgical feasts that are prime occasions for the whole parish to gather. They also recommended that African Americans and Hispanics in shared parishes sustain systematic efforts to examine and appreciate each other's histories, faith experiences, music, art, and cultural heritages.[10]

A 2005 survey of the National Pastoral Life Center confirmed the difficulties in shared parishes. In response to the prompt "parishioners appreciate and encourage the multicultural diversity of our parish," pastoral leaders from 928 parishes rated their congregations exceedingly low—twenty-ninth out of thirty-two parish-vitality indicators. John Andrews of the San Bernardino, California, diocese noted the need for a pastoral response to parishioners in communities undergoing a rapid influx of newcomers: "Somebody who feels that way [uneasy about changing parish demographics] should not be ignored or dismissed. They should be ministered to." But he also added that "the church belongs to everyone who calls themselves a Catholic, and we need to pay attention to the needs of all people coming to the church." Through passive resistance or overt confrontation, it is not unusual for parishioners to criticize or flatly reject admonitions toward charity and "integration without assimilation," whether they emanate from their pastor, bishops, or the pope. When Bishop Edward Slattery of Tulsa held a meeting with parishioners angry at him for celebrating a confirmation service mostly in Spanish, he was stunned to hear that some practicing Catholics preferred that no Masses in the diocese be conducted in Spanish. One man even offered to "drive a bus" to evict undocumented immigrants from the country.[11]

Pastoral leaders can easily feel conflicted in such situations, not wanting to antagonize the parties involved, yet desiring to lead their flock to enact papal and episcopal pleas for unity rooted in Christ, not in cultural uniformity. They are aware that offending the wrong parishioners may lead to a loss in donations needed to keep the parish viable for the good of all, but they are also concerned that financial matters not drive their decision between what is right and wrong. The strident emotions of ethnic tension can exact a large toll on parish leadership. As one pastor who asked to remain anonymous put it, "I am called to be a bridge builder between the groups in my parish. Unfortunately, bridges get walked on."

Such observations suggest that building unity within a diverse congregation is not merely a matter of tolerance or "celebrating differences," as is often imagined. Frequently at stake are the issues of how decisions are made and by whom, including the decision of marginal groups to vote with their feet when they perceive existing ecclesial life is unwelcoming or irrelevant. Many of the difficulties in developing shared parishes stem from a lack of attention to power relations in parochial life and ministries, what Michael Emerson deems "the nightmare of misused power."[12] Intentionally or not, even many Euro-American Catholics who welcome their Hispanic sisters and brothers and practice "cultural sensitivity" frequently embody the message that Latinos are guests and that Euro-American Catholics are the owners of the house. While hospitality and "cultural sensitivity" are an essential first step in ministry with newcomers, often implicit is the notion that those in power will remain in power, although they may choose not to exercise it autocratically. At best, Hispanic traditions and religious expressions will be tolerated, but the established group will control and limit the conditions of this pluralism and diversity. It is as if Latinos are told, "Welcome to the home of God's family, but please don't touch the furniture without permission."

Hispanics frequently respond to shared parishes with what could be deemed the "national parish dynamic," which is arguably the most significant trend underlying Hispanic ministerial efforts and participation in U.S. Catholic parishes over the past half-century. Consciously or not, like European immigrants who built national parishes, Latinos attempt to establish and nurture feast-day celebrations, renewal movements, pious organizations, and other structures of Catholic life that enable them to move from at best feeling hospitality in someone else's church to a sense of homecoming in a faith community that is their own. These widespread initiatives reflect Latinos' desire to stake out their own turf within U.S. Catholicism, just as Germans, Poles, Italians, Slovaks, Czechs,

Ukrainians, and others did previously in their national parishes. Not surprisingly, Hispanic ministry initiatives in the U.S. Catholic Church tend to be strongest among immigrants who respond enthusiastically to the national parish dynamic: their traditional rituals and devotions, recognizable spiritual and material needs, preference for Spanish, and deep resonance with pastors who express solidarity with them make them relatively easier to form into vibrant faith communities. The preponderance of foreign-born Latino clergy—five of every six among some three thousand Latino priests in the United States are foreign born[13]—undergirds the prominence of an immigrant-focused, Spanish-language approach in Hispanic ministry.

Hoover's research illustrates well the group dynamics in a shared parish. He conducted a ten-month ethnographic study at a Midwest parish he gives the pseudonym All Saints, founded in 1860 and still the only Catholic church in a majority Protestant town. Waves of working-class Mexican immigrants arriving since around 1990 changed the demography of the small town considerably and led the parish staff to initiate Spanish-language ministries. Currently, a Euro-American priest serves as pastor and a Mexican émigré priest as associate pastor. Hispanic Catholics have two Sunday Masses in Spanish, approximately twenty ministry programs, and an attendance that often exceeds five hundred at their most populous Mass, while Euro-American Catholics have three Sunday Masses in English, about thirty ministry programs, and a high Mass attendance of nearly four hundred. Yet an "asymmetrical power situation" in the parish reflects the lower social status of Mexican immigrants in the local populace: Euro-American Catholics hold most positions on the parish council and the stewardship committee, their Masses are in the earlier and generally more preferred time slots on Sunday morning, and the priest of their background is the pastor.[14]

As is largely the case in the town around them, the "avoidance" between Hispanics and Euro-Americans in the parish was "rampant." This was evident in important areas of parish life like the religious education programs. The English program addressed the needs of Catholic young people whose varied schedules and "multiple extracurricular activities" required flexibility. The much larger Spanish program addressed the pressing need of literally hundreds of baptized Catholic children who had not received the sacraments of first communion and confirmation. It addressed what

Hispanic leaders deemed "people's lukewarm commitment" to the church with a strict policy of children's attendance at catechism classes and Sunday Mass, parental involvement in bimonthly meetings, and weekly training sessions for catechists. The Euro-American pastor and religious education director both initially objected to the potential divisiveness of establishing a Spanish-language religious education track, but they relented in light of the large numbers and the obvious pastoral need. Recurrent tensions surfaced when Hispanic children began to transfer to the English-language program. The religious education director contended this was a natural and desirable adjustment to life in the United States, while the Mexican priest protested that children and their parents had made the switch to undermine his authority and avoid the more stringent requirements of the Spanish-language program.[15]

Hoover found that, despite good faith efforts on both sides, disagreements and ill feelings inevitably arise. Congested parking lots are one source of strain, as when a Euro-American woman went with frustration to the Spanish-language religious education classes seeking someone who spoke English to help locate the person who had double-parked behind her car. Another Euro-American woman had a scheduled meeting in the church basement but found that Hispanics had occupied the entire space. She stated that the fellow parishioners she approached responded that they could not speak English, until finally she located one who translated her concern to the others. Though the people graciously accommodated her once they understood the situation, when she later recounted the incident to Hoover it still annoyed her that she had to ask that meeting space be relinquished to her.

Given language and cultural divides, it is not surprising that "avoidance" remained a common pattern between Hispanics and Euro-Americans in the parish. Both Euro-American and Hispanic parishioners told Hoover they intentionally parked for Mass on Sunday in a place that reduced contact and potential conflict to a minimum. Some confessed that they left Mass quickly to avoid contact with the incoming parishioners for the following Mass. When parish school teachers complained about disorder in their rooms following Spanish-language religious education classes conducted there, both the Mexican priest and the volunteer director of the Spanish religious education program were annoyed at what they considered picayune charges that sullied their community's reputation with

Euro-American parishioners. They felt that school personnel held the Hispanic community to an "unfair standard" and relentlessly asked "about the whereabouts of every pencil." Yet they did not generally voice their protests directly to the accusers, choosing instead to encourage the Spanish-speaking catechists to be diligent in keeping order and even keeping an extra supply of pencils to replace any missing ones proactively. Their simultaneous sentiments of gratitude for the space afforded them in the parish and resentment over such conflicts typify the response of many Hispanics to shared parishes. Hoover concludes his frank assessment with the theological claim that the challenge for parishioners in shared settings is not to deny or minimize the significance of difficulties and conflicts, but to "reimagine intercultural negotiations not as tension-filled ordeals but rather as the ordinary work of the Church. This is communion enacted on an everyday basis in a complex, culturally diverse parish context."[16]

The National Study of Catholic Parishes with Hispanic Ministry provides an excellent statistical snapshot of structures, leadership, and faith formation in parishes with significant Hispanic membership, but there are no detailed statistical studies of group relations between Hispanic and other Catholics in shared parishes. Nonetheless, ethnographic analyses like Hoover's suggest that they are one of the most frequent causes of internal tension within U.S. Catholicism. In some locales they are even more divisive than the much-commented-upon disagreements between conservative and progressive Catholics. James Rutenbeck's film *Scenes from a Parish* explores communal dynamics in "a Catholic parish struggling to reconcile the ideals of faith with the cultural realities of a globalized United States." Filmed over a four-year period at St. Patrick parish in Lawrence, Massachusetts, the documentary examines the lives of new pastor Father Paul O'Brien, recent Hispanic arrivals to his parish, and established, predominantly Irish-descent parishioners. Some established congregants were "resentful of a new generation of immigrants," while others dedicated themselves to assisting new émigrés "but faced cultural entanglements that grew more complicated with the passage of time." Rutenbeck's series of vignettes on select parishioners illuminates the various transformations that interethnic contact provoked among them. He poignantly contends that "life at Saint Patrick's anticipates what lies ahead for all Americans: how [we] perceive each other, whether we choose to withdraw or whether we can forge community from disparate consistencies, are matters [of] consequence that will shape the future of our country." The provocative title of a *Boston Globe* film review of *Scenes from a Parish* summed up Hispanics' dramatic significance for Catholic faith communities like St. Patrick: "In One Parish, the State of the Church."[17]

IMMIGRATION ACTIVISM

The expanding Latino presence has also shaped the public activism and policy stances of U.S. Catholics, most notably the U.S. bishops' growing solidarity with immigrants. A number of historical events have fueled debates about Hispanic immigration to the United States: the massive and often illegal deportations of Mexican residents during the Depression years of the 1930s and "Operation Wetback" during the 1950s; the Bracero Program that brought in some five million guest workers between 1942 and 1964; Operation Peter Pan and other efforts to assist Cuban exiles fleeing the socialist revolution in their homeland; the major national immigration legislation of 1965 and 1986; the Central American civil wars and the Sanctuary movement of the 1980s; the influence of NAFTA and other international trade agreements on immigrant flows; anti-immigrant backlash like the 1994 passage of Proposition 187 in California; the notorious 2000 custody battle for Elián González after his mother drowned in her attempt to flee Cuba with him; and the current immigration furor prompted by President Donald Trump's campaign promises to build a wall on the U.S.-Mexico border and ban or seriously curtail Muslim entry into the United States. Catholic bishops have increasingly defended Hispanic immigrants, from their lackluster response during the Depression-era deportations to their noteworthy advocacy on behalf of immigrants in their 2003 joint pastoral letter with the bishops of Mexico and their subsequent Justice for Immigrants campaign and lobbying efforts for comprehensive immigration reform.[18]

The 2003 pastoral letter illuminates developments in the bishops' approach to immigration since their response to the Bracero Program a half-century earlier. Archbishop Robert Lucey, chair of the Bishops' Committee for the Spanish Speaking, was the foremost Catholic episcopal spokesperson on the Bracero issue. Reflective of views held among his contemporary Catholic clergy in Hispanic ministry, organizations like the League of United Latin American Citizens (LULAC) and the American

G.I. Forum, and labor activists such as Ernesto Galarza, Lucey charged that farm owners lobbied heavily for guest worker contracts in order to undercut the salaries and rights of Mexican Americans and other U.S. citizen workers. Thus he urged that Congress enact legislation to "control the traffic in 'wetbacks'" and to even allow U.S. immigration officials greater latitude to search for undocumented workers on farms. While Lucey recognized the plight and pastoral needs of immigrants, until Congress abolished it in 1964 he consistently cast the Bracero Program as primarily a controversy over workers' as opposed to immigrants' rights. In contrast, the 2003 pastoral letter *Strangers No Longer: Together on the Journey of Hope*, the first such collaborative effort between the bishops of Mexico and the United States, examines migration as a hemispheric and global phenomenon and as a long-standing concern in the Bible and in Catholic social teaching. That teaching undergirds the vision the bishops articulate for the church's multifaceted pastoral response to contemporary migrants. It is also the foundation for the broad range of public policy recommendations they make in major areas of concern: addressing the root causes of migration, protecting family unity, providing pathways to legalization, ensuring just treatment for both permanent and temporary immigrant workers, and following humane enforcement policies.[19]

Archbishop José Gomez of Los Angeles (formerly of San Antonio) gave a speech in 2008 that illuminates the faith and moral convictions of many Catholic leaders about the contemporary immigration furor in the United States. Gomez asserted that immigration is "one of the critical challenges the church faces in our hemisphere" and "the greatest civil rights test of our generation." He professed that "in Catholic teaching the right to migrate is among the most basic human rights," one "very close to the right to life . . . because God has created the good things of this world to be shared by all men and women—not just a privileged few." While recognizing government's right to regulate immigration, Gomez reminded his hearers that "the church also insists that no country can deny this basic human right [to migrate] out of exaggerated fears or selfishness." He articulated the tragic human cost of negative responses to immigrants among U.S. citizens: it "is bad for the soul of America. And it's bad for the souls of Americans. There is too much anger. Too much resentment. Too much fear. Too much hate." Noting that the lack of comprehensive immigration reform at the federal level had led to at least two hundred new laws in more than forty states during each of the previous two years, Gomez called for "a moratorium on new state and local legislation," which too often is "so clearly vindictive, so obviously meant to injure and intimidate" that it creates new problems without resolving existing ones. For similar reasons, he urged "an end to federal worksite enforcement raids." "Most troubling" to Gomez as a pastor "is that these deportations are breaking up families," since "a fundamental dimension of Catholic social teaching on immigration is that our policies should be aimed at reuniting and strengthening families—not tearing them apart." He called on church leaders to be instruments of reconciliation, not excusing those who entered the country illegally, but seeking "more suitable penalties" for them such as "intensive, long-term community service" as a "far more constructive solution than deportation." His concluding appeal was that Catholics be faithful to Christ: "We will change the hearts and minds of our countrymen on this issue only if we ourselves become living examples of the Gospel we proclaim."[20]

Archbishop Gomez was elected vice president of the United States Conference of Catholic Bishops just weeks after the election of President Trump. On the eve of the inauguration, Gomez gave a keynote address in which he proclaimed that "people do not cease to be human—they do not cease to be our brothers and sisters—just because they have an irregular immigration status." He went on to add that "tonight—in this city and in immigrant neighborhoods all across this country—there is a lot of fear, a lot of uncertainty and a lot of anger because our new president campaigned with harsh rhetoric about foreigners and sweeping promises to deport millions of undocumented immigrants." Gomez observed that more immigrants had been deported under President Barack Obama than under any previous administration, and stated that "we know that both political parties are exploiting the immigration issue for their own purposes." He avowed that building walls "won't solve anything" and renewed his plea for family unification as a necessary principle for any humane immigration policy. When Pope Francis visited Mexico and celebrated Mass on the border near El Paso the year before, he famously entered into a war of words with then candidate Trump over immigration. Trump charged that "I don't think he [Francis] understands the danger of the open border we have with Mexico. And I think Mexico got him to do it because Mexico wants to keep the border just the way it is, because they're making a fortune and we're losing." For his part, in response to a journalist's query, Francis stated "a person who thinks only about building walls—wherever they may be—and not building bridges, is not Christian. This is not in the Gospel." Both sides then debated whether the pope was meddling in U.S. politics and the appropriateness of Trump's response to what Vatican official claimed were moral teachings that Francis proclaims all over the world.[21]

Dioceses, religious communities, and the national bishops' conference sustain numerous immigrant outreach efforts, most notably the bishops' Migration and Refugee Services office and the Catholic Legal Immigration Network (CLINIC), a network of nearly three hundred field offices in forty-eight states whose mission is "to enhance and expand delivery of legal services to indigent and low-income immigrants principally through diocesan immigration programs and to meet the immigration needs identified by the Catholic Church in the United States." The bishops also address immigration legislatively at the state level, an arena of increasing importance as the "New Federalism" that has emerged under presidential administrations dating back to Richard Nixon places more governance responsibilities on state officials. State Catholic conferences give the U.S. Catholic Church an organizational strength in state-level politics that is matched among few other national institutional bodies. Two-thirds of states and the District of Columbia have state conferences. For most, the state's bishops serve as the board of directors, though nearly a dozen have members besides bishops, and all employ staffs that carry out daily operations. State Catholic conferences across the country have issued numerous statements on immigration that reinforce the bishops' principles and policy positions, both in states with large Hispanic populations and in those with growing numbers of Latinos such as Washington, Nebraska, Indiana, Ohio, Kentucky, Georgia, Virginia, and Connecticut, among others. A Maryland bishops' 2007 statement, "Where All Find a Home: A Catholic Response to Immigration," presents a typical admonition, urging that "as Catholics, we must move past divisions and remain focused on the dignity of the human person and the welfare of families." The Maryland Catholic Conference posts further resources on its website and also advocates for specific policy decisions regarding émigrés, such as their unsuccessful support for state legislation to allow undocumented residents to obtain a driver's license. Collaboration between Catholic leaders reinforces a number of state and local efforts, as in 2010 when Bishop John Wester, chairman of the United States Conference of Catholic Bishops (USCCB) Committee on Migration, expressed the strong support of the USCCB for the Arizona Catholic bishops' opposition to a new state law criminalizing undocumented immigrants and those who assist them.[22]

Even those who criticize the bishops' immigration stance acknowledge their collective resolve on the issue, though some question the prelates' motives. The late Father Richard John Neuhaus, founding editor of the journal *First Things*, attested in its editorial pages that "immigrants continue to be a revivifying force in our national life" and that "the largest immigrant group, the Hispanics, is in fact many distinct groups, almost all of whom enthusiastically embrace the chance to enter into the mainstream American experience." But in a subsequent editorial he quipped that "on immigration the U.S. bishops take pretty much the position of the *Wall Street Journal*, which, only half tongue in cheek, calls for a constitutional amendment abolishing national borders." He concluded: "The Catholic Church is the largest, and possibly the most effective, pro-immigration organization in the country. This has everything to do with strategic and pastoral planning, reflecting the fact that Latinos constitute a growing number of U.S. Catholics, bolstering the bishops' conviction "that a generous immigration policy is good for poor people seeking opportunity, good for America, and good for the Catholic Church."[23]

A sizable group of U.S. Catholics disagree with all or at least significant parts of the bishops' stance on immigration. Some Catholic political officials and activists have even taken the lead in enacting punitive laws aimed at inducing the departure of undocumented immigrants. Several detractors are so incensed at the bishops' teaching and advocacy that they have left the church, such as Californian Raymond Herrera, who avows "a church that rails on behalf of the criminal [undocumented] elements in our society is a church that's un-American and against the rule of law. They [the bishops] should be ashamed of themselves." But a number of Catholics promote education on the church's teaching and on policy debates, devote attention to the human struggles and life stories of immigrants, and engage in conversation about responding in faith. Numerous Catholic pastors, activists, and scholars have also endeavored to enhance the church's immigration work; notable among them is Father Daniel Groody, C.S.C., whose writings, presentations, and video productions on the theology of migration and on the perilous experience of border crossing and life as an undocumented immigrant have engaged large audiences among Catholics and their fellow citizens. Catholic institutions have launched initiatives like the Theology of Migration Project, with research centers at Fairfield University and Georgetown University, CLINIC, and other partners organized to address a range of topics centered on "immigration as an issue for those of the Catholic faith."[24]

The most widespread form of Catholic public presence on immigration is the compassionate outreach to émigrés in local faith communities. Many parishes represent a "safe haven" for immigrants, such as St. Pius V in Chicago, where an impressive array of ministries empower émigré parishioners to learn and act on their faith and provide for one another's everyday needs like food, shelter, clothing, parenting skills, family counseling, refuge from spousal abuse, employment, safe neighborhoods, English language classes, and legal defense. When federal authorities raided the Agriprocessors factory in Postville, Iowa, on May 12, 2008, and arrested nearly four hundred undocumented workers, most of them Guatemalan and Mexican men, their wives and children fled to St. Bridget's parish. Parish life coordinator Sister Mary McCauley, B.V.M., pastor emeritus Father Paul Ouderkirk, and lay Catholics, many the descendants of earlier Irish and Norwegian immigrants, served food to the frightened families, compiled a list of the detained workers, and stood watch at the church door. Immigration officials placed electronic homing devices on the ankles of about forty mothers they had detained and allowed them to reunite with their children, but the other workers faced deportation. Father Ouderkirk mourned on behalf of all. The raid, he said, "has ripped the heart out of the community and out of the parish. Probably every child I baptized has been affected. To see them stunned is beyond belief." Irma López, who was arrested along with her husband Marcelo but released to care for their two-year-old daughter, stated, "I came to the church because I feel safe there, I feel secure. I feel protected. I feel at peace." A *New York Times* reporter concluded that the "only redemptive thing that can be said, perhaps, is that in the crisis of Postville . . . the beacon of the Roman Catholic Church to immigrants has rarely shone more brilliantly."[25]

Numerous grassroots Latinos have advocated for the rights of émigrés and immigration reform. Hispanic leaders have contested the views of fellow Catholics who claim to be adamantly pro-life but object to bishops' stances on social concerns like immigration. As one undocumented Catholic mother put it, "They say our children in the womb are 'innocent life,' but the day the children are born they call them 'illegals' who have no rights and should 'go home' [to their mothers' country of origin]." In the wake of massive pro-immigrant rallies across the nation that rancorous immigration debates incited during spring 2006, the 2007 Pew Latino religion survey found that slightly over a fourth of Latino Catholics said their congregation had participated in an immigrant rights protest or boycott during the previous twelve months, a substantially higher percentage than mainline Latino Protestants and more than double that of Latino evangelicals. Reflecting in part the higher percentage of immigrant Latinos who are Catholics, Hispanic Catholics were also more likely than Protestants to have personally participated in an immigrant rights demonstration and to report that their parish clergy had spoken out on immigration. Father Claudio Díaz, director of Hispanic ministry for the Archdiocese of Chicago, commented on the feverish activity—rallies, protests, voter registration drives, and public prayer—among Latino and other area Catholics in response to the immigration debates: "it's been like a jolt of energy to really have a group of people be updated, get informed, be organized."[26]

Hispanic efforts have had greater resonance within the U.S. Catholic Church than in advancing federal legislation on immigration reform, which after the election of Donald Trump heavily focused on deportation and border defense. The presence and activism of Hispanics have elicited debates about immigration among their coreligionists, but they have also inspired extensive pro-immigrant initiatives from a wide range of their fellow Catholics. Among Catholic bishops, immigration is the social issue that draws the most consistent public response across regions and theological perspectives, complementing the bishops' more frequently noted stance on the right to life and perceptibly supporting the contention that the Catholic defense of life extends, in the words of many Catholic leaders like Archbishop Gomez, from "conception to natural death." Immigration is also the issue that has most prompted Latino Catholic leaders to publicly address the link between faith and politics, as they have sought to integrate Catholic teaching with the complex challenge of formulating just and effective immigration policies. Latinos shape public Catholic witness through their ongoing attempts to convince U.S. citizens that immigration is not merely an ethnic Hispanic nor solely a legal or a U.S. issue but a human and, for their coreligionists, ultimately a profoundly Catholic issue.

PASSING ON THE FAITH

Immigrant concerns remain strong among many Hispanics, but the inevitable demographics of generational transition are changing the face of Latino and U.S. Catholicism. Despite misconceptions about the Hispanic population exacerbated in public debates about immigration, the majority of Latinos—some two-thirds—are not immigrants. While more than half of Latino adults speak exclusively or primarily Spanish in their home, two-thirds of Latino teens speak exclusively or primarily English among their friends. These statistics are just some of the indicators that an analysis of Latino Catholicism that solely emphasizes immigrants is deficient. Indeed, forming young Hispanics in the faith is a greater and far less acknowledged challenge in U.S. Catholicism than preserving the faith allegiance of immigrants. Moreover, collectively, young Latinos are a vital population for the future of the United States: one-fifth of schoolchildren and one-fourth of newborns in the United States are Hispanic. A 2009 Pew Hispanic Center study on young Latinos coming of age in the United States avows that Hispanics are currently "the youngest minority group in the United States" and that "never before in this country's history has a minority ethnic group made up so large a share of the youngest Americans."[27]

Christian Smith's acclaimed National Study of Youth and Religion (NSYR) and other surveys reveal that Hispanic young people participate in Sunday worship and Catholic devotional practices as least as regularly as their Euro-American peers. The research of Robert Putnam and David Campbell even concludes that Latinos comprise as many as two-thirds of all regularly practicing Catholics between the ages of eighteen and thirty-four. Nonetheless, like their peers, young Hispanics' level of participation is relatively low compared to that of other Latino age groups. Likewise, studies of self-reported religious affiliation indicate that, as with their non-Latino counterparts, the U.S. Catholic Church faces an immense pastoral challenge of declining allegiance across Hispanic generations. The 2000 Hispanic Churches in American Public Life (HCAPL) survey showed that the self-reported Catholic affiliation of U.S. Latinos drops from 74 percent among the first generation to 62 percent among the third generation. Subsequent studies concur with the HCAPL findings and conclude that adoption of the English language correlates closely with decreased Catholic affiliation. Thus the key factor in generational transition for Latinos is the increasing numbers of those born in the United States who speak English and, presumably, become more enmeshed in the U.S. social milieu. Ken Johnson-Mondragón provides analysis based on the NSYR consistent with these findings. He asserts that "the large gap between the 74 percent of Spanish-dominant teens who are Catholic and the 57 percent of English-dominant Hispanic teens who are Catholic indicates that more acculturated Hispanics are more likely to be Protestant and less likely to be Catholic." These figures also reflect the growing number of Hispanics who reply "no religion" to survey questions about religious affiliation.[28]

No factor affects efforts to form young Hispanics in the Catholic faith more crucially than the dynamics of generational transition, through which most Hispanics pass amidst the accompanying process of adapting to life in the United States as immigrants or the children of immigrants. Instituto Fe y Vida estimated that as of 2007, among the nine million Hispanic Catholics between the ages of thirteen and twenty-nine, 45 percent were immigrants, 32 percent the children of immigrants, and 23 percent the children of U.S.-born parents. Tomorrow's Hispanic teens and young adults— those currently twelve years old or younger—encompass a far higher ratio of second- and subsequent-generation children. These trends illuminate the staggering demographic reality of generational transition; over the next three decades, the number of third-generation Latinos will triple, the second generation will double, and the overall percentage (though not necessarily the raw number) of first-generation immigrants will decline.[29]

Johnson-Mondragón's insightful categorization of young Latino Catholics provides a helpful template for assessing present and future efforts to hand on the faith to them.[30] The first of the four categories of young Hispanics he distinguishes are immigrant workers who came to the United States after age fifteen—that is, after the age at which they might have received some of their education in English-speaking U.S. classrooms. According to Johnson-Mondragón, they comprise some 25–45 percent of young Hispanic Catholics. They tend to have lesser economic means and formal education, prefer to speak in Spanish, and work in a number of service sector, agricultural, and manual labor occupations within the U.S. economy. Though generally industrious and focused on supporting their families back home and building a brighter future, isolation and the drudgery of their labors exacerbate instances of binge drinking, drug use, and unintended pregnancy. Some are attracted to Spanish-language Protestant youth groups and congregations. Others are so focused on work and survival that they rarely participate in formal worship. Yet among their young Hispanic peers, immigrant workers are statistically more likely to practice traditional Hispanic devotions and to retain a Catholic affiliation. Many live in the United States apart from their families back home, leading them to engage Catholic parishes and apostolic movements as means to build networks of friendships and faith. Their willingness to work at almost any job is parallel to the energetic desire many of them bring to their church involvement. As with Hispanic ministry in general, ministries that engage predominantly immigrant youth in a language and style that is familiar draw the most dynamic results of any initiatives among young Latinos.

Mainstream movers are at the other end of the spectrum in terms of their knowledge of the English language and their acclimatization to life in the United States. They comprise a smaller group that Johnson-Mondragón estimates to be about 15–25 percent of young Latinos. The overwhelming majority are U.S. citizens. Most speak English fluently and little or no Spanish, although those who do speak it tend to learn it well and eventually employ their language ability advantageously in their professions. A more privileged family background, parental sacrifice, personal initiative, or the benefit of a mentor or a quality education enables them to achieve an educational level and socioeconomic status that enhances their advancement in U.S. society. Some give back to their Hispanic community in professional work, service, or philanthropy. Others see their Latino counterparts as lacking initiative or as barriers on their own pathway to success. Some even dissociate themselves from what they perceive as the lowly status of being Hispanic, or criticize Hispanic cultures and communities as inhibiting the progress of Latinos. These attitudes can shape their views of Catholicism, especially if they perceive the religious practices of Hispanic Catholics as vestiges of an outmoded immigrant heritage. Mainstream movers with these perceptions are more susceptible to joining Protestant churches or not practicing any religion. Like youth of other ethnic and racial groups, their busy lives, professional success, and focus on other concerns can also tempt them to drift away from practicing their faith. Those among them who are involved in Catholic youth ministries tend to fit more easily into English-speaking parish youth and young adult groups and into outreach in Catholic schools, campus ministry, and youth retreats like Teens Encounter Christ and Kairos.

Identity seekers comprise some 25–45 percent of young Latinos. They are similar to mainstream movers in terms of generation, but they tend to struggle more with being caught in between the homeland of their elders' often nostalgic views and the new home of the land in which they were raised. Perceiving themselves to be fully a part of neither the Hispanic immigrants' world nor the U.S. cultural mainstream, their primary quest is for identity and self-esteem. Many are bilingual, though they tend to speak English among their peers. The sting of prejudice and their tendency to enroll in public schools with high dropout rates stifle the energies of advancement through self-initiative. When they don't receive support and guidance to motivate themselves, they can easily become busy with seeking immediate gratification in activities like playing video games, watching television or movies, chatting online, gossiping, listening to music, or dancing. A downward cycle of boredom, blaming society or themselves for their sense that their lives are not progressing, and little hope for setting and realizing personal goals can eventually lead to more destructive behaviors such as drinking, drug use, and sexual promiscuity. English-language parish youth ministry and Spanish-language *pastoral juvenil* groups potentially can address the longing to belong that these youths confront in their daily existence, depending on the availability of a welcoming group and the young person's capacity to identify with a group's leaders and members. But many don't encounter such a group within Catholic circles or fail to participate because they feel they are being judged or that they don't belong. The U.S. bishops assert in their 2002 document *Encuentro and Mission: A Renewed Pastoral Framework for Hispanic Ministry* that one of the most "vital" needs in Hispanic ministry is "to develop ministerial models that respond to the specific needs and aspirations of U.S.-born Hispanic youth."[31]

Johnson-Mondragón's fourth category, gang members and high-risk youth, tend to be born in the United States or to have come here at a young age. Media coverage of Latino gangs notwithstanding, the vast majority of Latino youth are not gang members, a number of them despite ample temptations and pressures to choose this pathway. Still, Latino gang activity represents a considerable number of lives adversely influenced: young Hispanics, their families, neighbors, and victims of their criminal acts. When the Latino young who are at high risk for possible drug abuse, violence, or other criminal activity are also considered, Johnson-Mondragón estimates they comprise the smallest group among his four categories, but nonetheless a tragic and unacceptable proportion of around 10–15 percent of young Hispanics. The common denominators for most of them are that they were raised in poverty, lack formal education, are exposed to various negative role models and destructive peer pressures, and are prone to a level of hopelessness or anomie that enhances the possibility they will turn to gangs, drugs, and other antisocial behavior. Father Greg Boyle and his Jesuit confreres at Dolores Mission in East Los Angeles began a ministry among Latino gang members in 1988 that evolved into Homeboy Industries, a nationally renowned effort to offer young people a way out of gangs and accompany them as they transition to new lives.[32] In Los Angeles and other locales, former gang members and prisoners who have had profound faith conversion experiences are the most effective ministers to high-risk Latino youth and those already caught in the web of criminal and gang activity. Yet such efforts are sporadic; most parishes, dioceses, and pastoral leaders have scarcely begun to address Latino youth in these situations.

Johnson-Mondragón concludes that the lack of ministries tailored to the range of life situations among Latino youth is a major detriment to nurturing their Catholic faith and practice. Delegates from the landmark First National Encuentro for Hispanic Youth and Young Adult Ministry and the U.S. bishops' *Encuentro and Mission* document concur that "generally speaking, the majority of parish youth ministry programs serve a population that is mostly European white, mainstream, middle-class, and English-speaking" and, conversely, do not reach many young Hispanics because of differences in cultural, educational, and economic backgrounds. NSYR data confirm that Hispanic involvement in U.S. parish youth groups is greater as family income increases and is notably higher for English-dominant Latinos. In Johnson-Mondragón's terminology, when they engage young Hispanics at all, extant ministries tend to resonate with the demographic minority of Hispanic mainstream movers more than with the other three categories of young Hispanics.[33]

Efforts to address this limitation are considerable, though they pale in comparison to the need. Catholic schools have fostered the faith and education of literally millions of previous working-class and immigrant Catholics. Today, however, less than 3 percent of Hispanic children and teens are students in Catholic parochial and high schools, a paltry figure compared to the heyday of these institutions during the 1950s, when nearly half of Catholic elementary school students were enrolled in parochial schools and a fourth of Catholic high school students were. Tuition costs and selective admissions standards also tend to make Catholic colleges and universities less accessible for Hispanics. Moreover, there are only eleven two-year Catholic colleges in the United States, and cumulatively their enrollment is just over five thousand, while nationally 40 percent of Latino college students attend two-year institutions. In many instances, bishops and dioceses are hard-pressed to even assign campus ministers to community colleges with a large number of Hispanic Catholic students. According to a 2005 report of the Center for Applied Research in the Apostolate (CARA), students at as many as 70 percent of the 4,453 degree-granting institutions of higher education in the United States have little or no access to Catholic campus ministry. Another CARA report found that fewer than 10 percent of the students participating in Catholic campus ministries were Hispanic.[34]

Various initiatives to increase Catholic education among Hispanics exist. There are no Hispanic institutions parallel to historically African American colleges and universities like Xavier University in New Orleans, but in 2008 the Association of Catholic Colleges and Universities (ACCU) listed ten Catholic institutions with at least one-fourth Hispanic enrollment. A growing number of the nearly 250 Catholic institutions of higher education in the United States have initiatives to recruit and retain Latino students. Voucher and tax-credit programs have enabled parochial schools in several states to expand their outreach to Latinos, most notably St. Anthony School in Milwaukee, which has expanded its facilities to serve more than a thousand Latino children and become the largest Catholic elementary school in the United States. In many dioceses, bishops and educational leaders have conducted campaigns to build endowments for school tuition scholarships, such as the Catholic Education Foundation in Los Angeles, the Seeds of Hope Charitable Trust in Denver, and the Big Shoulders Fund in Chicago. Jesuits, Christian Brothers, and lay colleagues have built a national network of Cristo Rey high schools and Nativity Miguel middle schools for students from predominantly poor and working-class families, a total of eighty-eight schools with more than nine thousand students, nearly half of them Hispanic. Fourteen Catholic institutions of higher education have established programs to enlist recent graduates as teachers in under-resourced Catholic schools for a period of postgraduation service. A 2009 report of the fifty-two national leaders who formed the Notre Dame Task Force on the Participation of Latino Children and Families in Catholic Schools articulated a strategy to double the percentage and triple the number of Hispanic students in Catholic parochial and high schools to one million by the year 2020. The Roche Center for Catholic Education at Boston College launched its Two-Way Immersion (TWI) project in 2012 to promote dual language learning in Catholic schools.[35]

Despite such initiatives, the vast majority of Hispanic children, teens, and young adults will not receive faith formation in Catholic schools, amplifying the vital importance of catechetical efforts among Latinos. The longest-standing efforts among Hispanics themselves are those of numerous grandmothers, parents, other family members, and catechists to pass on their faith. The National Study of Catholic Parishes with His-panic Ministry revealed that 95 percent of parishes with Hispanic ministry have religious education programs that meet weekly. On average, some 265 children are enrolled in these programs. Significantly, two-thirds of the parishes have initiatives to involve parents in their children's faith formation. Yet no study has estimated the number of young Hispanics who fail to participate in parish catechesis. Like Catholics of other back-grounds, many Hispanics send their children for first communion classes when they reach the age of seven or eight. A significant but lesser number have their children prepared for the sacrament of confirmation, usually received during the teenage years. But participation in religious education not directly related to sacramental preparation is less frequent. Martha Nuñez, who directs a Spanish-language Bible institute for the Los Angeles archdiocese, reports that in Los Angeles alone several hundred Hispanics complete their training and are commissioned as catechists annually. The archdiocese forms new catechists through initiatives like their catechist formation programs, run in both Spanish and English, and their annual multilingual Religious Education Congress, the largest event of its kind in the United States. Nuñez also attests that approximately 100,000 Hispanic children are baptized in the archdiocese each year, presenting parishes with numerous new members and the accompanying opportunity and challenge to assist parents in evangelizing them and forming them in the Catholic faith.[36]

A number of young Hispanics and their adult supervisors have initiated and sustained ministries to advance catechesis and evangelization, often in locales where the structures of U.S. Catholic parishes and dioceses do not engage Hispanic young people effectively. The scores of apostolic movements and youth groups that participated in the diocesan and regional gatherings of the First National Encuentro for Hispanic Youth and Young Adult Ministry reveal the wide range of these ministries among the young. Entities represented in the Encuentro process included those with a presence among the young in various regions and dioceses, such as the Catholic Charismatic Renewal, Jóvenes para Cristo, and *Cursillo*, as well as numerous groups distinctive to particular locales, such as Cristo y Yo (Christ and I), Disciples in Mission, Ministerio Alianza Nueva (New Covenant Ministry), and Youth to Youth.[37]

Hispanic ministry leaders and organizations have supported young people in their efforts, most notably Instituto Fe y Vida, where Carmen Cervantes has served as director since its establishment in 1994 and which the De La Salle Christian Brothers have generously supported. The Instituto has advanced ministry with young Hispanics through its national leadership training programs for young Latinos and those who work with them, development of ministerial resources, and the research of its National Research and Resource Center for Hispanic Youth and Young Adult Ministry. The work of Instituto Fe y Vida complements that of the National Catholic Network de Pastoral Juvenil Hispana—La Red, which Latino young people established in 1997. La Red convoked the First National Encuentro for Hispanic Youth and Young Adult Ministry and is now engaged in efforts to implement its conclusions. La Red initiatives focus on promoting formation and leadership among young Hispanics as well as on developing pastoral models, practices, strategies, and resources that enable them to live as active disciples.[38]

The status of La Red as a volunteer organization with no paid staff, along with the lack of paid personnel in most parishes and dioceses, inhibits progress on the organization's daunting but crucial ministerial agenda.

The National Study of Catholic Parishes with Hispanic Ministry found that only four of ten parishes surveyed "have formal programs to minister specifically to Hispanic youth." Johnson-Mondragón notes that La Red's mission encompasses half of young Catholics in the United States and that the bulk of resources for youth ministry in U.S. Catholicism support parish programs in which Hispanics "are significantly less involved, less likely to persevere, and less likely to be leaders." Thus Johnson-Mondragón and other Hispanic ministry leaders call for "greater institutional and philanthropic support for its [La Red's] ministry."[39]

Commitments of resources, pastoral ingenuity, and Latinos' own efforts to pass on the faith to their young are as vital a determinant of Catholicism's future in the United States as any other initiative or ministry. Hispanic pastoral leaders implicitly call for a U.S. Catholic response to this pressing need that is parallel in scope to the building up of Catholic schools in the nineteenth and twentieth centuries. While sometimes denoted as a national school system, Catholic schools in fact emerged as a diverse array of local institutions with a variety of administrative structures, instructional approaches, and ethnic populations. Their commonality was the broad mission of education and Catholic faith formation. Today's efforts to nurture faith among young Latinos range from catechesis within families to national initiatives such as those of La Red, the Notre Dame Task Force, and the TWI project at Boston College. These largely nascent efforts are not yet generally perceived as a communal attempt to address the massive transition of second- and subsequent-generation Hispanics into church and society. Like the expansion of Catholic schools in previous eras, the capacity of U.S. Catholic leaders and Latinos themselves to meet the current challenge hinges not only on the effectiveness of particular initiatives but also on a more widespread conviction that passing the faith to young Latinos is an urgent priority for the entire U.S. Catholic Church.

LATINOS IN U.S. CATHOLICISM

Latinos have much to offer their fellow Catholics and the U.S. Catholic Church. In their 1983 pastoral letter on Hispanic ministry, the U.S. bishops noted that Latinos accentuate salutary values such as respect for the dignity of each person, profound love for family life, a deep sense of community, an appreciation of life as a precious gift from God, and pervasive and authentic devotion to Mary, the mother of God. Hispanics' ritual and devotional traditions mediate embodied prayer and faith in numerous parishes and dioceses. Their historical and contemporary links with Latin America are a vital connection to the most populous Catholic region in the world and enhance the prospects of greater solidarity and common purpose among Catholics across the American hemisphere. Their desire for faith formation and to serve in ministries provides a new cadre of pastoral leaders. Their youthfulness is a potential source of revitalization for the whole church. With the 2013 election of Pope Francis, many Latinos have felt a sense of pride and solidarity as Francis clearly supports the poor, immigrants, and the everyday piety of Latino and other Catholic faithful. Leaders like Bishop Ricardo Ramírez, C.S.B., of Las Cruces, New Mexico, note that Francis's papacy has not inspired a massive return to the Catholic Church among Latinos who have left for another religion or no religion at all. Yet because of Francis many observant Latino Catholics "are becoming stronger in their beliefs and practices."[40] As the first Latin American pope, Francis reminds Latinos of all they can contribute to the church with their dedication and leadership.

Hispanics can also receive much from their participation in the U.S. Catholic Church. A strong emphasis in the United States on the congregation encourages Latinos to strengthen their cultural and familial Catholic traditions with a deeper commitment to the parish community, especially the sacraments that are at the heart of Catholic life and faith. The considerable array of ethnic and racial groups in the U.S. Catholic Church invites Latinos and their coreligionists to seek a unity rooted in faith that can be a countersign to human divisions in society and even in churches. Collaboration with other Catholics who are not from the majority culture is another possible source of enrichment, particularly with African Americans who have many social and ecclesial concerns similar to those of Hispanics. The support of U.S. Catholic leaders provides allies in advocacy for Hispanics on immigration and related issues, such as education and health care. Catholic schools are among the most effective pathways for Latino children and teens to receive faith formation and a brighter future. Faith and leadership formation programs in U.S. Catholicism provide opportunities for Latino Catholics to expand their knowledge of their faith and pass it on to young people as catechists, youth ministers, deacons, and more.

Yet various factors militate against mutual enrichment between Hispanics and their fellow Catholics in the United States. Ethnic tensions, suspicions between English- and Spanish-speaking parishioners, the anti-immigrant attitudes among some Catholics, the financial inaccessibility of Catholic education for numerous Hispanics, and many Latinos' lack of participation in parish life are but a few of these potential drawbacks. The political climate of the nation since the election of Donald Trump has exacerbated the fears and frustrations of many Hispanic Catholics, as well as the animosity that even many of their coreligionists have toward Latinos who are undocumented. One of the greatest pitfalls is the tendency to equate unity with uniformity in core areas of Catholic life, ranging from parish participation to political perspective.

Authentic unity entails not only Hispanic involvement in parishes and dioceses, but also considering Hispanic viewpoints in wider conversations and decision-making processes that shape Catholicism in the United States. These viewpoints reveal a fundamental gap between many Hispanic Catholics and their coreligionists of European descent. Over the past four decades, Euro-American Catholics have tended to give most attention to the internal dynamics of the church: liturgical reform, the voice and role of the laity, dissent from or obedience to sexual ethics and other church teaching, the proper exercise of authority, the question of who is called to ordination. The focus on these issues tends to produce debates along a liberal-conservative continuum, an approach so familiar that its application to public discourse about events such as the clergy sex-abuse crisis or the selection of a new pope is as much reflex as it is a conscious choice. Such debates are even deemed the "Catholic culture wars." Media outlets reinforce the dialectical approach with their tendency to cover nearly all stories that deal with the Catholic Church with comments from Catholics on the "right" and the "left," but rarely from Hispanics, whom we are left to presume fit into one camp or the other, or soon will, or are simply not significant enough to matter for the issue at hand.

Conversely, Hispanics have been more inclined in recent decades to accentuate the mission of the church, frequently calling for more funding for Hispanic ministry offices, youth initiatives, outreach efforts, and leadership training and formation programs, as well as an increase in Spanish Masses, Hispanic bishops, celebrations of feast days that are part of their Hispanic traditions, and culturally sensitive formation programs for seminarians and other ecclesial leaders. While these efforts encompass attempts at internal reform in areas like liturgy and participation in church leadership, they are primarily directed at the larger concern of equipping the church to serve and accompany its Hispanic members in their faith and daily struggles. In a word, while Hispanic Catholic leaders frequently perceive the U.S. Catholic Church as a significant institution that could do much to uplift their suffering sisters and brothers, Catholic leaders of European origin or descent tend to be more concerned with democratization and the adaptation of the church to the U.S. milieu or, conversely, with the alarming worry that U.S. Catholicism has in fact already progressed much too far along the road to becoming more American than Catholic.

One of the most hopeful possibilities of transformation that Hispanics bring to the U.S. Catholic Church is their potential to help transcend the conservative-progressive impasse, which Hispanic ministry leaders contend impedes efforts to identify and address the key issues for the present and future of the U.S. Catholic Church. They further contend that engaging Hispanics is necessary in all areas of church life, from parish communities to church involvement in national public policy debates to the core Catholic mission of evangelizing the young. Such engagement requires breaking old habits of assuming that Latino views are subsumed in existing perspectives and paradigms. Hispanic ministry leaders insist this inclusiveness is neither merely a pragmatic challenge to retain Hispanic members, nor a sociological strategy for group cohesion. More fundamentally, Hispanic leaders avow that U.S. Catholics face an ecclesial challenge to be a church that unites people of all backgrounds in common faith and mission. Only then can Catholics in the United States address the present and the future comprehensively.

NOTES

1. *America* 12 (October 17–December 19, 1914): 7, 66.
2. *America* 12: 246; Rudolph J. Vecoli, "Prelates and Peasants: Italian Immigrants and the Catholic Church," *Journal of Social History* 2 (1969): 243–244.
3. For usage of Latino/a, Latinx, and Hispanic, see note 6 in chapter 1.
4. David A. Badillo, *Latinos and the New Immigrant Church* (Baltimore: Johns Hopkins University Press, 2006); Joseph P. Fitzpatrick, "The Hispanic Poor in a Middle-Class Church," *America* 159 (July 2, 1988): 11–13.

5. R. Stephen Warner, "The Place of the Congregation in the Contemporary American Religious Configuration," in *American Congregations*, ed. James P. Wind and James W. Lewis, 2 vols. (Chicago: University of Chicago Press, 1994), 2:54–99, at 54, 73.

6. Silvano Tomasi's landmark study of Italian immigrants in New York is a frequently cited work on this influential thesis. Silvano M. Tomasi, *Piety and Power: The Role of Italian Parishes in the New York Metropolitan Area, 1880–1930* (Staten Island, NY: Center for Migration Studies, 1975).

7. James D. Davidson, *Catholicism in Motion: The Church in American Society* (Liguori, MO: Liguori/Triumph, 2005), 69; Kevin J. Dougherty, "How Monochromatic Is Church Membership? Racial-Ethnic Diversity in Religious Community," *Sociology of Religion* 64 (Spring 2003): 65–85; Michael O. Emerson with Rodney M. Woo, *People of the Dream: Multiracial Congregations in the United States* (Princeton, NJ: Princeton University Press, 2006), 35, 39; Hosffman Ospino, *Hispanic Ministry in Catholic Parishes: A Summary Report of Findings from the National Study of Catholic Parishes with Hispanic Ministry* (Chestnut Hill, MA: Boston College, 2014), 5.

8. Brett C. Hoover, *The Shared Parish: Latinos, Anglos, and the Future of U.S. Catholicism* (New York: New York University Press, 2014), 12. See also John Francis Burke, *Building Bridges, Not Walls: Nourishing Diverse Cultures in Faith/Construyamos puentes, no muros: Alimentar a las diversas culturas en la fe* (Collegeville, MN: Liturgical Press, 2016).

9. Stephen Wall, "Schism Hits Church: Some Feel Left Out by Latino Culture Shift," *San Bernardino County Sun*, March 13, 2010; Bishops' Committee on Hispanic Affairs, *Hispanic Ministry at the Turn of the New Millennium* (Washington, DC: United States Conference of Catholic Bishops, 1999); Charles W. Dahm, *Parish Ministry in a Hispanic Community* (Mahwah, NJ: Paulist Press, 2004), 294.

10. Committee on African American Catholic Affairs and Committee on Hispanic Affairs, National Conference of Catholic Bishops, *Reconciled Through Christ: On Reconciliation and Greater Collaboration Between Hispanic American Catholics and African American Catholics* (Washington, DC: United States Catholic Conference, 1997), 39, 45.

11. Ken Johnson-Mondragón, "Ministry in Multicultural and National/Ethnic Parishes: Evaluating the Findings of the Emerging Models of Pastoral Leadership Project," report and presentation to the National Ministry Summit: Emerging Models of Pastoral Leadership conference, April 2008, accessed June 2009, http://www.emergingmodels.org/doc/Multicultural%20Report%20(2).pdf, 23; Wall, "Schism Hits Church"; Marilyn Duck, "Bishop Meets with Parishioners Angry Over Perceived Slight," *National Catholic Reporter*, July 26, 2006, http://www.nationalcatholicreporter.org/update/nt072606.htm.

12. Emerson, *People of the Dream*, 147–55.

13. United States Conference of Catholic Bishops, Hispanic Affairs, "Hispanic Ministry at a Glance" (accessed June 2008, now in possession of author).

14. Hoover, *The Shared Parish*, 121.

15. Hoover, *The Shared Parish*, 129–131.

16. Hoover, *The Shared Parish*, 130, 208.

17. Synopsis, *Scenes from a Parish* (2009), a film by James Rutenbeck, http://scenesfromaparish.com/synopsis.html; Ty Burr, "In One Parish, the State of the Church," *Boston Globe*, 8 April 2009, http://www.boston.com/ae/movies/articles/2009/04/08/in_one_parish_the_state_of_the_church/.

18. Bishops' statements on immigration prior to 1988 are in National Conference of Catholic Bishops, *Pastoral Letters of the United States Catholic Bishops, 1792–1988*, 5 vols. (Washington, DC: United States Catholic Conference, 1983–1989). See also U.S. Catholic Bishops, *Welcoming the Stranger Among Us: Unity in Diversity* (Washington, DC: United States Conference of Catholic Bishops, 2000); Catholic Bishops of Mexico and the United States, *Strangers No Longer: Together on the Journey of Hope* (Washington, DC: United States Conference of Catholic Bishops, 2003); Justice for Immigrants, http://www.justiceforimmigrants.org/.

19. Gina Marie Pitti, "To 'Hear About God in Spanish': Ethnicity, Church, and Community Activism in the San Francisco Archdiocese's Mexican American *Colonias*, 1942–1965" (Ph.D. diss., Stanford University, Stanford, California, 2003), 301. See esp. chap. 8, "'At the Cost of the Poorest of Our Own Citizens'? Catholic Migrant Ministry and the Bracero Program, 1942–1955," and chap. 9, "'A Ghastly International Racket': Catholic Opposition to the Bracero Program in California, 1954–1964"; Catholic Bishops of Mexico and the United States, *Strangers No Longer*.

20. José Gomez, "Immigration Reform After the Election," *Origins* 38 (November 13, 2008): 363–366.

21. "Archbishop Gomez Emphasizes Dignity of Immigrants on Eve of Inauguration," *Crux*, January 20, 2017, https://cruxnow.com/cns/2017/01/20/archbishop-gomez-emphasizes-dignity-immigrants-eve-inauguration/; Joshua Partlow and Julie Vitkovskaya, "This Is How the Pope Francis–Donald Trump Argument Has Played Out," *Washington Post*, February 18, 2016, https://www.washingtonpost.com/news/worldviews/wp/2016/02/17/vatican-its-not-all-about-you-trump/?utm_term=.c63413d7835d.

22. USCCB Migration and Refugee Services, http://www.usccb.org/mrs; Catholic Legal Immigration Network, Inc., http://www.cliniclegal.org; David Yamane, *The Catholic Church in State Politics: Negotiating Prophetic Demands and Political Realities* (Lanham, MD: Sheed and Ward, 2005), 9–13, 41, 62–69; Maryland Bishops, "Where All Find a Home," *Origins* 37 (December 6, 2007): 418–419, at 418; Maryland Catholic Conference immigration page, http://www.mdcathcon.org/Immigration; Gerald Kicanas, "Arizona Immigration Law Is Flawed," *Origins* 40 (May 13, 2010): 3–5; "USCCB Migration Chairman Joins Arizona

Bishops in Decrying Anti-Immigrant Measure, Calls for Comprehensive Reform," USCCB news release, April 27, 2010, https://adw.org/news/usccb -migration-chairman-joins-arizona-bishops-in-decrying-anti-immigrant -measure-calls-for-comprehensive-reform/.

23. Richard John Neuhaus, "Immigration and the Aliens Among Us," *First Things*, August/September 1993, 63–65, at 64; Richard John Neuhaus, "When Bishops Speak," *First Things*, February 2001, 60–64, at 63.

24. Stephen Wall, "Bishops Begin Campaign," *San Bernardino County Sun*, January 10, 2010; Daniel G. Groody, *Border of Death, Valley of Life: An Immigrant Journey of Heart and Spirit* (Lanham, MD: Rowman and Littlefield, 2002); Daniel G. Groody and Gioacchino Campese, eds., *A Promised Land, a Perilous Journey: Theological Perspectives on Migration* (Notre Dame, IN: University of Notre Dame Press, 2008); Daniel G. Groody and Bill Groody, *Dying to Live: A Migrant's Journey* (videorecording), Groody River Films in collaboration with the University of Notre Dame Center for Latino Spirituality and Culture, 2005; Donald Kerwin and Jill Marie Gerschutz, eds., *And You Welcomed Me: Migration and Catholic Social Teaching* (Lanham, MD: Lexington, 2009); Theology of Migration Project, http://woodstock.georgetown.edu/programs/Theology-of -Migration.html.

25. Dahm, *Parish Ministry*, 61; Samuel G. Freedman, "Immigrants Find Solace After Storm of Arrests," *New York Times*, July 12, 2008.

26. Hispanic ministry leader, comment during group discussion, National Catholic Council for Hispanic Ministry Raíces y alas/Roots and Wings National Hispanic Leadership Congress, University of Notre Dame, May 2003; Pew Research Center, "Changing Faiths: Latinos and the Transformation of American Religion," 2007, http://www.faithformationlearning exchange.net/uploads/5/2/4/6/5246709/changing_faiths_-_pew.pdf, 62–64; Kim Lawton, "Immigration Fuels Hispanic Church Activity," *Christianity Today*, November 2, 2006, http://www.christianitytoday.com/ct/2006 /novemberweb-only/144-42.0.html.

27. Ken Johnson-Mondragón, "Socioreligious Demographics of Hispanic Teenagers," in *Pathways of Hope and Faith Among Hispanic Teens: Pastoral Reflections and Strategies Inspired by the National Study of Youth and Religion*, ed. Ken Johnson-Mondragón (Stockton, CA: Instituto Fe y Vida, 2007), 24; Pew Hispanic Center, "Between Two Worlds: How Young Latinos Come of Age in America," 2009, http://pewhispanic.org/files/reports/117.pdf, 1.

28. Lynette DeJesús Sáenz, "Church and Youth Ministry Participation: Creating a Welcoming Environment for Latino/a Teenagers," in *Pathways of Hope and Faith*, 86; Ken Johnson-Mondragón, "The Second Wave of the National Study of Youth and Religion," in *Pathways of Hope and Faith*, 281; Christian Smith with Melinda Lundquist Denton, *Soul Searching: The Religious and Spiritual Lives of American Teenagers* (New York: Oxford University Press, 2005); Christian Smith with Patricia Snell, *Souls in Transition: The Religious and Spiritual Lives of*

Emerging Adults (New York: Oxford University Press, 2009); Dean R. Hoge, William D. Dinges, Mary Johnson, and Juan L. Gonzalez, Jr., *Young Adult Catholics: Religion in the Culture of Choice* (Notre Dame, IN: University of Notre Dame, 2001), 51; David E. Campbell and Robert D. Putnam, "The Changing Face of American Catholicism," memorandum prepared for the United States Conference of Catholic Bishops, 2008; Gastón Espinosa, Virgilio Elizondo, and Jesse Miranda, "Hispanic Churches in American Public Life: Summary of Findings," Interim Report, Institute for Latino Studies, University of Notre Dame, 2003, 15; Paul M. Perl, Jennifer Z. Greely, and Mark M. Gray, "What Proportion of Adult Hispanics Are Catholic? A Review of Survey Data and Methodology," *Journal for the Scientific Study of Religion* 45 (September 2006): 419–436, at 428; Juhem Navarro-Rivera, Barry A. Kosmin, and Ariela Keysar, "U.S. Latino Religious Identification 1990–2008: Growth, Diversity, and Transformation, A Report Based on the American Religious Identification Survey 2008" (Hartford, CT: Trinity College, 2010), http://commons.trincoll.edu/aris/files/2011/08/latinos2008.pdf, 16–17; Pew Hispanic Center, "Between Two Worlds," 64; Johnson-Mondragón, "Socioreligious Demographics of Hispanic Teenagers," 21.

29. National Catholic Network de Pastoral Juvenil Hispana—La Red, *Conclusiones: Primer Encuentro Nacional de Pastoral Juvenil Hispana, PENPJH* (Washington, DC: United States Conference of Catholic Bishops, 2008), 92; Johnson-Mondragón, "Socioreligious Demographics of Hispanic Teenagers," 16; Gregory Rodriguez, *Mongrels, Bastards, Orphans, and Vagabonds: Mexican Immigration and the Future of Race in America* (New York: Pantheon, 2007), 254.

30. Johnson-Mondragón, "Socioreligious Demographics of Hispanic Teenagers," 33–39; Ken Johnson-Mondragón, *The Status of Hispanic Youth and Young Adult Ministry in the United States: A Preliminary Study* (Stockton, CA: Instituto Fe y Vida, 2002), chap. 1, "The Pastoral Reality of Hispanic Youth and Young Adults."

31. United States Conference of Catholic Bishops, *Encuentro and Mission: A Renewed Pastoral Framework for Hispanic Ministry* (Washington, DC: United States Conference of Catholic Bishops, 2002), no. 70.

32. Celeste Fremon, *G-Dog and the Homeboys: Father Greg Boyle and the Gangs of East Los Angeles*, updated ed. (Albuquerque: University of New Mexico Press, 2004); Gregory Boyle, *Tattoos on the Heart: The Power of Boundless Compassion* (New York: Free Press, 2010).

33. United States Conference of Catholic Bishops, *Encuentro and Mission*; National Catholic Network de Pastoral Juvenil Hispana—La Red, *Conclusiones*, 14, 33; Ken Johnson-Mondragón, *Youth Ministry and the Socioreligious Lives of Hispanic and White Catholic Teens in the U.S.* (Stockton, CA: Instituto Fe y Vida, 2005), 9.

34. Notre Dame Task Force on the Participation of Latino Children and Families in Catholic Schools, *To Nurture the Soul of a Nation: Latino Families, Catholic Schools, and Educational Opportunity* (Notre Dame, IN: Alliance for Catholic Education

Press, 2009), 9; Hosffman Ospino and Patricia Weitzel-O'Neill, *Catholic Schools in an Increasingly Hispanic Church* (Chestnut Hill, MA: Boston College, 2016), 6; Bryan T. Froehle and Mary L. Gautier, *Catholicism USA: A Portrait of the Catholic Church in the United States* (Maryknoll, NY: Orbis, 2000), 68–73; Richard Fry, *Latinos in Higher Education: Many Enroll, Too Few Graduate* (Washington, DC: Pew Hispanic Center, 2002), 5, http://pewhispanic.org/files/reports/11 .pdf; Center for Applied Research in the Apostolate, "The Impact of Catholic Campus Ministry on the Beliefs and Worship Practices of U.S. Catholics," Fall 2005, 6–8, https://cara.georgetown.edu/publications/USCCB_Campus Min_final.pdf; Mark M. Gray and Mary E. Bendyna, "Catholic Campus Ministry: A Report of Findings from CARA's Catholic Campus Ministry Inventory," (Washington, DC: Center for Applied Research in the Apostolate, 2003), 12, https://cara.georgetown.edu/Publications/edandcminsitry .html.

35. Association of Catholic Colleges and Universities, "Catholic Higher Education and Hispanic Students," August 11, 2008, http://www.accunet.org /files/public/NP_8-11-08.pdf; Notre Dame Task Force, *To Nurture the Soul of a Nation*, 6, 11, 13, 25, 39, 51; Ospino and Weitzel-O'Neill, *Catholic Schools in an Increasingly Hispanic Church*, 19–20.

36. Ospino, *Hispanic Ministry in Catholic Parishes*, 33–34; Catholic News Agency, "Hispanic Outreach and Faith Formation Considered at National Meeting," December 9, 2008, http://www.catholicnewsagency.com/news/hispanic _outreach_and_faith_formation_considered_at_national_meeting/.

37. National Catholic Network de Pastoral Juvenil Hispana—La Red, *Conclusiones*, 96–106.

38. National Catholic Network de Pastoral Juvenil Hispana—La Red, *Conclusiones*, 21–22, 27–28.

39. Ospino, *Hispanic Ministry in Catholic Parishes*, 36; Johnson-Mondragón, *Youth Ministry and the Socioreligious Lives of Hispanic and White Catholic Teens*, 8; Ken Johnson-Mondragón, *Hispanic Youth and Young Adult Ministry in the United States: Bridging Hispanic and Mainstream Ministry to Forge the Church Anew in Twenty-First Century America* (Stockton, CA: Insitituto Fe y Vida, 2010), 10.

40. National Conference of Catholic Bishops, *The Hispanic Presence: Challenge and Commitment* (Washington, DC: United States Catholic Conference, 1984); Ricardo Ramírez, *Power from the Margins: The Emergence of the Latino in the Church and in Society* (Maryknoll, NY: Orbis, 2016), chap. 11, "The Francis Effect on Latinos," 180.

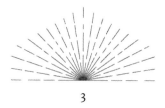

Since Vatican II

AMERICAN CATHOLICISM IN TRANSITION

Steven M. Avella

In the daily exercise of our pastoral office, we sometimes have to listen, much to our regret, to the voices of persons, who though burning with zeal, are not endowed with too much of a sense of discretion or measure. In these modern times they can see nothing but prevarication and ruin. They say that our era, in comparison with past eras, is getting worse and they behave as though they had learned nothing from history, which is nonetheless, the teacher of life.

—Pope St. John XXII, Opening Address,
Vatican Council II, October 11, 1962

By the time the Church got its windows open in the mid-1960s there were all sorts of toxins in the air. In high culture, and especially in intellectual life, the bright hopes of "modernity" were being dashed on the rocks of irrationality, self-indulgence, fashionable despair and contempt for any traditional authority.

—George Weigel, *The Courage to Be Catholic*, 62

Between 1965 and 2017, the Catholic Church in the United States underwent significant change and transition. A period of early enthusiasm gave way to a period of retrenchment and then a new opening for an agenda of change. In some ways this paralleled and in other ways it diverged from shifts in American society at large as it moved from the era of civil rights, the Great Society, and the war in Vietnam, through the Reagan Revolution and the emergence of the religious right, and finally to the sharply contrasting presidencies of George W. Bush, Barack Obama, and Donald Trump. Church and American society were not synonymous but could not help influencing each other.

As the sixties began, American Catholics belonged to a growing and dynamic institution that was enjoying a dramatic increase in numbers and in institutional strength—"this confident church," as it was called. The election of a Catholic president, John F. Kennedy, was seen as a watershed in the acceptance of Catholics into the mainstream of American life. That sense of confidence carried them into the early years of Vatican II. Most Catholics embraced the changes wrought by the Second Vatican Council—the vernacular liturgy, the improved relations with non-Catholic Christians (our separated brethren) and the dropping of archaic practices and rules that no longer seemed to make sense. As Dominican theologian Yves Congar noted during the first session of Vatican II, "something irreversible" had happened.[1]

Yet the reforms of Vatican II left some in the church perplexed and the church unsure of itself—no longer a confident church, but one that had seemingly capitulated to modern culture. These disgruntled elements, along with sympathetic forces in Rome, created a backlash that explains much of what happened in the American church, especially during the pontificate of Pope John Paul II (1978–2005). This reaction, blessed and encouraged by the highest church authorities, held sway for more than three decades, until a new pope was elected in 2013 who had different ideas.

This essay sketches out the main lines of these developments.

THE POSTCONCILIAR PERIOD: THE POSITIVE APPRAISAL

Although the Second Vatican Council is sometimes discussed in the same vein as twenty-first-century people comment on hippies, bell-bottom pants, and pet rocks, there was a genuine excitement in the U.S. church in the wake of the Council. For many, Vatican II was a moment of liberation, and its aftermath brought an explosion of enthusiasm and expectation. On the burlap and felt banners that began to adorn churches, the words "Joy and Hope" (taken from *Gaudium et Spes*, the opening words of the *Constitution on the Church in the Modern World*) symbolized the exuberant mood. Likewise, words like "*aggiornamento*," "opening the windows," "relevance," and "renewal" became a familiar argot of progressive Catholics. The tenor of the times even affected members of the hierarchy. Bishop John King Mussio of Steubenville, Ohio, returned from the Council exulting in the freedom it gave him to pursue his ministry: "I can be the kind of bishop to my people that I want to be . . . formerly I was hedged by many outmoded regulations which hindered my pastoral care of the people . . . I feel much closer to the people because of the care I can give them."[2] Many other bishops felt the same. Even conservative commentators like James Hitchcock were initially enthusiastic for the changes of Vatican II.[3]

Most dioceses implemented new liturgical practices as soon as they could. After centuries of "hearing" a quietly whispered Latin Mass, clergy introduced a partially "vernacularized" service, along with alterations in the "liturgical environment," as it came to be called. The altar now faced the congregation, and lay lectors proclaimed the epistle of the Mass from a secondary pulpit. The Council's call to "full, active, and conscious participation" on the part of the laity inspired church musicians to produce an array of new music—set to guitars and drums and often quite jaunty. Subsequent reforms totally vernacularized the liturgy, introduced a new three-year cycle of scripture readings, reinvigorated the Rite of Christian Initiation of Adults (and all the other sacraments), and admitted more lay participation. Most American Catholics seemed to like the new form of Mass. Then other modifications came, including a new emphasis on Christian unity—a positive sign for many who had "mixed marriages" or who had many non-Catholic friends. Early ecumenical prayer services and discussions tried to stress what Catholicism and other Christian faiths shared, rather than what separated them. In a late December 1965 editorial written after the Council closed, the *National Catholic Reporter* expressed what many felt: "It has set a course toward new beginnings, toward becoming a church of service, fraternity and honesty. . . . Like Christmas itself, it is an irreversible event. . . . It has not achieved reform and renewal, but it is now possible."[4]

Equally momentous were changes in some of the traditional markers of Catholic culture. In 1966, for example, Rome and the U.S. bishops mitigated the Friday abstinence, a symbolic mainstay of Catholics for many years encapsulated in the phrase "fish on Fridays."[5] Although church leaders urged the faithful to find alternate ways of joining their lives to Christ's sufferings, the passing of this time-honored sacrifice, the nonobservance of which had once brought the penalty of mortal sin, was significant.

Likewise, U.S. Catholics began to rethink church teaching on artificial contraception, stimulated by the invention and marketing of the contraceptive pill. Pope John XXIII had initiated a new phase of discussion about the liceity of birth control when he appointed a commission of clerics to discuss and report on the issue. Later, Pope Paul VI expanded the commission to include laypeople.[6] Many expected a change in the teaching.

Vatican II documents encouraged new openings to the world, especially in *Gaudium et Spes*, which urged Catholics to become more engaged in serious social, economic, and international issues. Although action in the world had long been a motif of social-minded Catholics, the social activism of 1960s America, especially in civil rights and anti-Vietnam protests—had a special urgency. Priests and nuns began to shed their cloistered lifestyles, appearing more often in public in secular dress and attempting to relate with youth.

RELIGIOUS WOMEN

Renewal in religious life had been percolating for many years, inspired by the Sister Formation Movement in the 1940s and 1950s, which strongly urged sisters' communities to send young nuns on for advanced degrees, especially in theology.[7] Religious sisters had also been influenced by Cardinal Leon Joseph Suenens's work, *The Nun in the World* (1962), and the writings of Christian Brother Gabriel Moran. Eager to respond to the "signs of the times," they embraced the Vatican II decree on the renewal of religious life (*Perfectae Caritatis*). In 1968 and 1969, many convoked chapters of renewal that brought about major changes in their rules of life, governance structures, and ministries. Some communities instituted changes gradually: modest alterations in the religious habits, some revision of archaic rules, better policies for assigning work and placements. For others, the changes were quite dramatic: new constitutions (rules of life), the substitution of secular clothing for the religious habit, a rethinking of the structure of common life and the vow of poverty, and the importation of popular psychological and group dynamic methods to deal with issues of maturity and common identity in convents. Sisters were permitted to diversify their ministries, and many left the work of classroom teaching.

Social activism by clergy and "religious" (men in holy orders and women in vows) also created divisions. For many years, a relatively small cohort of Catholic clergy, religious, and laity had labored quietly on behalf of racial justice and the rights of farmworkers. The social activism of the

1960s drew even more priests and nuns, who marched with demonstrators in clerical attire and habits. Antiwar activism among clergy and religious grew significantly as Vietnam-era protests escalated. Priests often counseled young men who wished to use their Catholic faith as a rationale for conscientious objection to the war and the draft. The Berrigan brothers, Philip and Daniel, became the most prominent clergy war-protestors, burning draft files and dousing them with human blood.

LITURGICAL EXPERIMENTATION

As noted earlier, many embraced the liturgical changes of Vatican II, which began in many places on the first Sunday of Advent 1964. New music, new vesture, and greater informality at Mass became more commonplace, especially as young priests, fresh from the seminary, were assigned to parishes. Participants were urged to stand during the most sacred part of the Mass, the canon, and to receive Eucharist standing rather than kneeling. Sometimes priests invited participants to stand around the altar. Communion in the hand and from the cup were innovations that startled those who believed only a priest's hands could touch the Eucharist.[8]

In 1967, Pope Paul VI had restored the diaconate as a distinct order rather than just a way station to priestly ordination, opening it to married men. By the mid-1970s, many U.S. dioceses were ordaining men to this rank—creating a visible body of married clergy. Some thought that an end to mandatory celibacy for the secular clergy was not far off.

The Sacrament of Penance (confession), a mainstay of Catholic practice, also changed. Rebranded as the Sacrament of Reconciliation, it provided opportunities for face-to-face discussions with the confessor. Eventually, many Catholics began to rethink confession, seeing no need to ask forgiveness for every single peccadillo. New understandings of sin underscored the root causes of bad behavior rather than the individual sin itself. Popular penance services brought together scores of priests for confessions prior to Christmas and Easter and became an important part of the parish year. A shift also occurred in another staple of Catholic life, first confession before first communion, as input from religious educators created questions about whether children at the age of seven could really know what serious sin consisted of or if they had much understanding of conversion.[9] General absolution, the "emergency" form of official forgiveness given to soldiers going into battle, for example, was now offered more widely in certain circumstances. In 1976, one bishop, Carroll Dozier of Memphis, used it for a large assemblage of Catholics in Tennessee.[10]

CHANGES IN CATHOLIC INSTITUTIONS: CATHOLIC HIGHER EDUCATION

Changes in American Catholic higher education had been gestating for many years, especially as the neoscholastic philosophical and theological synthesis that had undergirded curricula for years began to unravel. Concern for the quality of Catholic higher education had been sounded by Catholic University of America historian Monsignor John Tracy Ellis, in his famous 1955 address "American Catholics and the Intellectual Life," and also by the demands of an increasingly better prepared professoriate. Administrators and professors, not interested in the deductive logic of the neoscholastic way, often insisted on using the inductive methodologies employed by their counterparts in academic life.[11] In fact, as Ellis often complained, many Catholic colleges were nothing more than glorified high schools with poorly trained faculty, woefully inadequate libraries and laboratories, and outdated facilities. Impelled by the demands of accreditation agencies and the desire to assure students of the best possible education, Catholic colleges and universities began to steadily upgrade their programs on every level.

In July 1967, at the invitation of Father Theodore Hesburgh, C.S.C., of Notre Dame, twenty-six educators and administrators gathered at a retreat in Land O' Lakes, Wisconsin, to discuss how Catholic education would respond to the changes of Vatican II. Their 1,500-word statement, described by historian Philip Gleason as "a declaration of independence from the American hierarchy," insisted on the same academic freedom their counterparts in the academy enjoyed:

> To perform its teaching and research functions effectively the Catholic university must have true autonomy and academic freedom in the face of authority of whatever kind, lay or clerical external to the academic community itself . . . institutional autonomy and academic freedom are essential conditions of life and growth and indeed survival for Catholic universities as for all universities.[12]

Catholic colleges and universities soon began to disaffiliate from their founding religious orders and form independent corporations managed by lay boards. Catholic scholars and intellectuals, particularly theologians, but also sociologists and others whose work impinged on Catholic doctrine, now had the freedom to pursue research and intellectual inquiry without worrying about the hand of a censor or a suspicious Catholic bishop. Catholic universities seemed to flourish under these new regimes.

THEOLOGICAL DISSENT:
THE CASE OF FATHER CHARLES CURRAN

Nothing underscored the new commitment to academic freedom more than the activities of Catholic theologians who now explored topics and ideas that might have been "off limits" before the Council or which may have earned a rebuke from the Holy Office, the Vatican dicastery that monitored theological "aberrations." The work of Catholic moral theologian Father Charles Curran, a priest of the Diocese of Rochester, New York, was perhaps the most famous case. Curran's struggle for academic freedom attracted considerable attention in the Catholic and secular media.[13]

Curran, a former professor at St. Bernard Seminary in Rochester, joined the faculty of the Catholic University of America in 1965. A protégé of famed Redemptorist theologian Bernard Haring, his writings on moral topics veered away from the traditional natural law emphases of his contemporaries. Well versed in the history of Catholic theological thought, Curran understood that over the centuries key church teachings had undergone significant change in some important ways. Moreover, he believed that some of them had actually been wrong or subject to revision in the light of new data. Carefully, and with more nuance than some of those who popularized some of his ideas, he suggested a rethinking of Catholic bans on artificial contraception, masturbation, homosexuality, and other moral issues. Curran thoughtfully argued that his writings derived from an appreciation, not a rejection, of some of the most profound sources of Catholic moral theology. A deeply committed priest and respected teacher, he offered his ideas believing that he was participating in the same dynamic that had produced the great theological insights of the church's past. Nonetheless, his speculations earned him the ire of some of his colleagues at the Catholic University and various bishops on its board, and in 1967 he was fired by Bishop William McDonald, the university's rector. In response, Curran and his supporters took to the airwaves and complained loudly about the lack of due process in his case and the lack of academic freedom—rights that would be articulated at Land O' Lakes that summer. After a campus strike at the Catholic University, and with strong faculty support and the help of legal counsel, he was reinstated.[14]

Curran's emphasis on historical development and his assertion of a right to dissent from noninfallible church teaching became newsworthy once again when he and several colleagues obtained an advance copy of *Humanae Vitae* and issued a strong dissent from the encyclical's most touted conclusion: that all forms of artificial contraception were forbidden by natural law and gravely evil. This placed Curran again in the spotlight as a number of priests of the Archdiocese of Washington also publicly dissented from the encyclical and incurred suspension from Archbishop Patrick O'Boyle. In the aftermath of *Humanae Vitae*, the American bishops issued a document, "Human Life in Our Time," endorsing and supporting Pope Paul's position but also laying out criteria for dissent. The ensuing standoff between O'Boyle and the nineteen priests who had remained in the active ministry was not fully resolved until 1971.

The Washington, D.C., fracas and other highly public feuds between priests and bishops in Los Angeles and San Antonio called for a new approach to episcopal appointments. What was required were men of a collegial temperament who could reduce the tensions. Within the next several years, the American hierarchy would be made over with a new crop of bishops who both pleased and offended the various camps of American Catholicism.

THE AMERICAN BISHOPS: COLLEGIALITY IN ACTION

In 1974, Belgian Archbishop Jean Jadot replaced Archbishop Luigi Raimondi as apostolic delegate to the United States.[15] The process of selecting U.S. bishops had evolved over the years, but by the twentieth century, the role of the delegate in identifying worthy candidates and recommending them to Rome increased substantially. Jadot's appointments reflected a desire for more pastoral bishops—men who were more personable and willing to eschew some of the traditional perks of episcopal life (mansions, elaborate ceremonies, austere distance from their priests and flocks). Vatican II's strong emphasis on episcopal collegiality meant that bishops had to be listeners as well as lawgivers. Jadot relied on the recommendations of the priests of a locality and also the advice of the newly restructured episcopal conference. Some of these prelates entered dioceses terribly polarized by postconciliar controversy and were able to still the tempests. Many arrived anxious to engage their local churches in the challenges of the times. Drawing inspiration from Vatican II's decree *Christus Dominus* on the role of bishops, bishops' conferences became a new vehicle of local collegiality. The devolving of a certain sphere of authority from Rome to the national bishops' conferences represented one of the important thrusts of the Council. In 1966, the National Catholic Welfare Conference (NCWC), the official organization of the American bishops since 1919, was divided into two parts: the National Conference of Catholic Bishops (NCCB) and a policy-making body, the United States Catholic Conference (USCC). The NCCB functioned as a collegial body envisioned and mandated by Vatican II under the direction of an elected president, the first being Cardinal John Dearden of Detroit. The USCC/NCCB worked in a number of critical policy areas formerly overseen by the old NCWC, but also engaged newer issues. An executive secretary, a cleric who exercised important influence over church policies and representation to the Vatican, oversaw both entities. Many of these secretaries later themselves became bishops of prominent dioceses: Joseph Bernardin (Cincinnati and Chicago), James Rausch (Phoenix), Thomas Kelly (Louisville), and Robert Lynch (St. Petersburg.)

The NCCB's presidents, especially Cardinal Dearden, ran the bishops' conference in a collegial and open fashion. His successors, Cardinal John Krol, Archbishop John Quinn, Archbishop John Roach, Archbishop John L. May, and Bishop James Malone continued in this manner. Both the NCCB and the USCC delved not only into internal church matters (such as the number of holy days in the American liturgical calendar) but also into a number of social and political issues.[16] The influence of Cardinal Dearden in particular set the collegial tone that became a hallmark of the organization.[17] Opportunities to serve on committees, to openly discuss certain issues, and to suggest courses of action for the American bishops were an important part of the mix. Not every bishop chose to participate actively or serve, but the votes of the body of bishops and the active work of the USCC underscored the church's desire to dialogue with, and at times challenge, contemporary American society. It also functioned as an important liaison with the Vatican, whose approval was necessary for its organization, statutes, and various policies the bishops adopted. Annual November meetings of the bishops became intense working sessions in which the prelates pored over reports and conducted votes on an array of matters. For nearly two decades, the USCC/NCCB was a force to be reckoned with in U.S. Catholicism.

Two of the bishops' most important statements came in the mid-1980s in reaction to the Reagan administration's defense and economic policies. The first addressed the issue of nuclear war, and particularly the morality of nuclear deterrence—a position the Reagan military buildup and major increase in defense spending aggressively advanced. The second concerned Reagan's embrace of laissez-faire economics and the impact of his policies on the poor and middle class. A careful and systematic process of hearings, revisions, and public debate resulted in two major letters (pastorals): *The Challenge of Peace* (1983) and *Economic Justice for All* (1986). The drafts of both letters were submitted to all of the bishops and to a wide array of supporters, critics, and experts who had a chance to argue and challenge data and conclusions. These letters underwent significant modification, including Vatican input, before their ultimate approval. They were, to many, a model of the collegiality inspired by Vatican II.

LAY MINISTRY

Church leaders also embraced a renewed ecclesiology that stressed the significance of baptism, resulting in a proliferation of new ministries for lay Catholics, especially women. Lay ministry became a regular feature of parish life as women read at Mass, distributed communion, and accepted positions of leadership in local parishes—often as directors of music, liturgy, religious education, and pastoral ministry. Sometimes these efforts were the result of the steady decline in the number of priests. However, their strongest advocates insisted that lay ministry was rooted in the baptismal call to serve and advance the kingdom of God—not just as an auxiliary to the "real" ministry of priests or deacons. This emphasis on baptism also implied an elevated role for women as the logical next step in the full realization of the ecclesiology of Vatican II.

A high-water mark of sorts for the role of the laity was the Call to Action (CTA) Conference convened in response to Pope Paul VI's request that laity take their part in the renewal of the temporal order and to celebrate the U.S. Bicentennial. The bishops held a series of discussions with some eight thousand people around the country, soliciting input from the laity, clergy, and religious. The plenary session held at the Detroit conference brought together nearly three thousand people, delegates and observers, who called for the end of mandatory celibacy; more compassionate ministry to homosexual, divorced, and remarried Catholics; and the ordination of women. The trend of the votes, especially as they pertained to internal church issues, created discomfort among the bishops in attendance and the American hierarchy in general, who backed away from the entire project.[18] The CTA later institutionalized itself as a distinct organization to press for liberal reform in the church, but very few bishops supported it. Its ongoing existence made it the *bête noire* of conservative Catholics, the epitome of everything that had gone wrong in the aftermath of Vatican II.

THE CRASH

Almost from the start, there was unhappiness with the changes wrought by Vatican II in the American church. Some pointed to the precipitous decline in Mass attendance as a sure sign the new liturgy had failed to attract and hold young people. In fact, young Catholics seemed to drop away from the faith as soon as they could. Catholic teaching on the sanctity of marriage and the exclusivity of sexual relations seemed to be discarded as premarital sex, cohabitation, and toleration of homosexuality became increasingly regular phenomena. Others took umbrage at open dissent not only by theologians, who were apparently questioning every aspect of the faith, but also by parish priests, who did strange things at liturgy or preached sermons offensive to parishioners' religious, political, or social ideas.

Among progressives, "Joy and Hope" gave way to gloom and despair. The exhilaration of change bred the desire for more, and when it did not come, or was seemingly thwarted by authority, people became frustrated. For example, those (including some bishops) who had hoped that mandatory celibacy for diocesan clergy would be abolished were crushed when Pope

Paul VI upheld the discipline in the 1967 encyclical *Sacerdotalis Celibatus*. An even more crushing blow came in July 1968, when Pope Paul reaffirmed the ban on all forms of artificial contraception in the encyclical *Humanae Vitae*. After it was revealed that the pontiff had gone against the recommendations of his own committee, anger erupted among theologians, priests, and laity for this seemingly egregious disregard of collegiality.[19] This provoked a serious upheaval among priests, even as surveys indicated that laypeople quietly rejected the papal directive and used banned birth control methods while continuing to practice their Catholic faith.[20]

Catholics unhappy with the results of Vatican II compiled a number of grievances, many of which centered on the behavior of priests and sisters. Most Catholics, reared with a deep respect for the clergy and religious, were taught to admire their steadfast devotion to a very difficult vocation. Hence the exodus of priests and sisters in the period after the Council shook the church to its foundations. These departures were for many reasons. Some discovered that they had made the "decision" to enter the seminary, convent, or religious house at an early age, only to discover that their adolescent dreams did not persist into adulthood. Others left, sometimes quite angrily, impatient at the seemingly snail-like pace of postconciliar reform; church teaching on mandatory celibacy and birth control were most frequently cited. Still others left because they felt in conscience they could no longer uphold certain church teachings or were harassed by pastors and bishops beyond their emotional breaking points. At the same time, seminary enrollments began to dip. Between 1965 and 2016, the number of U.S. priests sank from 58,632 to 32,192.[21]

The number of religious sisters plunged even more. In 1965, there were nearly 180,000 religious women in the United States. In 2016, there were 47,170.[22] Generational differences and mistrust for authority bled from secular into religious culture and manifested themselves in differences between the older and younger clergy and between priests and bishops. Older styles of episcopal governance, especially the placement of clerics, clashed with Council-inspired demands for collegiality. Priests in some places like Chicago formed an Association of Priests to resist Cardinal John Cody.[23] Individual priests made headlines in public clashes with their bishops.[24] It seemed as though the polarizations and divisions of secular society had implanted themselves inside the sacred precincts of the church. Catholics now referred to themselves as liberal or conservative.

Liberal Catholics grabbed most of the headlines, but for those on the right, there were moments of anger and resistance. Some complained loudly about liturgical reforms and excesses. Among the first to organize resistance to the new liturgy was Father Gommar DePauw of the Archdiocese of Baltimore, who formed the Catholic Traditionalist Society. The Belgian-born and Leuven-educated DePauw continued to celebrate the traditional Tridentine Mass and resisted efforts by his archbishop, Cardinal Lawrence Shehan, to rein him in. DePauw's resistance, though not widely emulated, was an early harbinger of discontent over some aspects of Vatican II implementation in the United States.[25]

Some parents and religious educators took exception to the changes in catechetics—formal religious teaching—they believed undercut the transmission of orthodox Catholic teaching. Other Catholics reacted badly to changes in music and church renovations. Some lamented the loss of devotional life—rosaries, novenas, processions, and benediction of the Blessed Sacrament—often summarily done away with by priests who insisted that Vatican II demanded it.[26] Added to a sense of change for the worse was the ongoing demographic shift of Catholics to the suburbs, which left behind the old immigrant churches with their majestic church buildings, schools, convents, and rectories.

THE LOSS OF CLARITY

Conservative Catholics reacted negatively to the decline of the neoscholastic theological method, with its clarity and rationality, and regarded historical and critical approaches to scripture and church teaching with suspicion and even cries of heresy. They regularly scorned the heralds of the new order: liturgists, moral theologians, catechetical "experts," feminist nuns, and disobedient priests.[27] To stem the tide of decline they saw in parishes, seminaries, convents, and other bastions of Catholic life, they argued for a stronger response from the Holy See and for firmer bishops to turn back the tide of secularism and dissent that had crept into the church. By the time Cardinal Karol Wojtyla became Pope John Paul II on October 16, 1978, there was a clear perception that the American church was somewhat out of control.

American political and social conservatives found much to admire in Pope John Paul. Conservatives who still fed on the militant anticommunism of the Cold War Era made much of the pope's own struggles with the communist government of Poland. His triumphant return to his homeland in 1979 and his endorsement of the Solidarity movement gave a nudge to the decline of Soviet hegemony over Eastern Europe. All this seemed to dovetail with the militant cold war rhetoric of the Reagan administration, which came to power in the 1980s. The president and the pontiff, both of whom escaped assassination attempts in 1981, were yoked to each other as counterparts of a conservative revival that seemed to link the Catholic Church with the thrust of the so-called Reagan Revolution. On another front, Catholics and Evangelical Protestants, usually at odds over doctrinal issues, found themselves in an actively brokered alliance to resist the perceived cultural decline of America, epitomized by the legalization of abortion. U.S. Catholics themselves fed into the conservative ethos of the later twentieth century, moving away from their traditional allegiance to the Democratic Party. Although Latino/a Catholics continued to vote strongly Democratic, the white Catholic vote broke in favor of the Republicans in 2000, 2004, 2008, 2012, and 2016.[28] Although the marriage of the Catholic Church and the GOP was not perfectly harmonious or stable, some Catholics shared the passion of political and social conservatives to purge both church and nation of the curses of those damnable sixties and their aftermath.

VOICES OF "ORTHODOXY"

Individuals and groups often claiming the mantle of "orthodoxy" opposed the trends and people in the church whom they felt had undermined the institution and radically misinterpreted Vatican II. Some actually broke with Rome, inspired by schismatic Archbishop Marcel Lefebvre, who founded the Society of St. Pius X. Rejecting some of the decisions of Vatican II, Lefebvre ordained his own priests and bishops, who offered Mass in hotels and other buildings. Rome would spend a lot of time trying to get these schismatics back in the fold. However, most critics could not bring themselves to blame the Council itself for the problems, but rather tagged the interpretation of the Council as defective.

An important mouthpiece for Catholic traditionalists was the *Wanderer*, a St. Paul-based Catholic periodical established in 1867 as a German-language newspaper. Edited after Vatican II by Alphonse Matt Sr. and then his son Alphonse Matt Jr., its pages were a densely packed blend of theological traditionalism and political conservatism that gave equal time to abuses in the postconciliar church and stoking cold war fears of communism at home and abroad. The opposition to artificial contraception became the touchstone of Catholic faith and identity, and the Matts stoutly defended *Humanae Vitae* while chastising those who did not. Although the *Wanderer* loyally supported the right of the pope to make liturgical changes (losing seven thousand subscribers in the process), its subscribers were treated weekly to horror stories about odd liturgies, pro-homosexual groups meeting in Catholic facilities, or dilly-dallying bishops. The *Wanderer* also held annual forums at which conservatives spoke out against the "havoc" Vatican II renewal was wreaking on every aspect of church life: morals, sacramental practices, especially the Mass, old-time devotions, and church renovations and modern architecture. The *Wanderer* often urged its readers to communicate their displeasure to various Roman officials known to be concerned about the church in the United States.[29]

Lyman Stebbins, a retired stockbroker, founded Catholics United for the Faith (CUF) in 1968 "to support, defend, and advance the efforts of the teaching church." Utterly dismayed by the dissent against *Humanae Vitae*, Stebbins mobilized supporters in various affiliates all over the nation to keep a watchful eye on catechetical texts, sex education programs, liturgical errors, and other matters that seemed to diverge from papal directives. Touting its motto, *Ubi Petrus, Ibi ecclesia; Ubi ecclesia ibi nos"* (Where there is Peter there is the church; where there is the church there are we")—CUF put out a bimonthly newsletter, *Lay Witness*, and other publications. CUF encouraged letter-writing campaigns to friendly or receptive sources in the Vatican and to the apostolic delegation. Among their first major "victories" was having the imprimatur stripped from former Paulist Anthony Wilhelm's *Christ Among Us*, an adult catechism they accused of lacking "doctrinal precision" in matters of sexual morality. Other groups with focused agendas appeared on the scene, including the Orthodox Roman Catholic Movement (1973), the Catholic League for Religious and Civil Rights (1973), and Women for Faith and Family (1984). In addition, popular magazines and newsletters, including *Crisis*, the *National Catholic Register*, *Challenge*, *Fidelity*, and *Triumph*, broadcast accounts of theological dissent, liturgical aberrations, advocacy of women's ordination, and stories of erring priests, unsympathetic bishops, and other horror stories of unorthodox behavior and teaching. In due course, social media would further amplify their reach and organizational ability.

Some academics and church officials joined the chorus of discontent. Early on, St. Louis University history professor James Hitchcock, who asserted he was a disillusioned progressive Catholic, offered an articulately written critique of the postconciliar church, *The Decline and Fall of Radical Catholicism*.[30] Drawing heavily from articles in the Kansas City–based *National Catholic Reporter*—an independent Catholic weekly that took a strong liberal line on church reform—Hitchcock frequently called out so-called liberal Catholics who could often be as authoritarian as any bishop or curial official. He noted that often those who were loudest in calling for church reform were either about to leave the ministry or even the church or, worse yet, had given up on the faith altogether.

One of the most hard-hitting tracts on the decline of U.S. Catholicism after the Council was penned by Monsignor George A. Kelly. A priest of the Archdiocese of New York and ordained in 1942, Kelly had been a protégé and friend of Father John P. Monaghan, a well-known New York labor priest. He attended the Catholic University of America, where he earned a doctorate in sociology and headed the Catholic Family Life office. An early advocate of a vernacular liturgy, he was later appointed as Cardinal Francis Spellman's secretary of education in New York and eventually joined the faculty of St. John's University in Queens. One priest described him as a "former progressive . . . who thought that the church was coming apart at the seams." In 1977, alarmed by the liberal orientation of the Catholic Theological Society of America and its sponsorship of a controversial report on human sexuality, Kelly helped form the Fellowship of Catholic Scholars at a meeting in St. Louis, with Ronald Lawler, O.F.M. Cap., Father Joseph Fessio, S.J., and Hitchcock as officers and Kelly as executive secretary.[31] The group began holding conventions dedicated to upholding orthodox Catholicism and loyalty to the authentic teaching authority of the church—the Magisterium. Blessed by Cardinal John Carberry of St. Louis, they invited Cardinal Joseph Ratzinger as their first major lecturer. When he could not come, Cardinal William Wakefield Baum of Washington, D.C., replaced him.

In 1979, Kelly produced his blockbuster, *The Battle for the American Church*, the first of several publications explaining what went "wrong" with Catholicism in America. Kelly laid blame at the door of scripture scholars, theologians, and weak bishops who had sown confusion and disarray. With a take-no-prisoners rhetorical style, Kelly indicted the immediate postconciliar era for disobedience, dissent, and questionable scholarship and mourned the end of a golden era of American Catholicism.[32] This kind of conservative discontent within Catholicism grew in tandem with the rising tide of conservative discontent in the wider culture.

THE WATERSHED:
THE ELECTION OF JOHN PAUL II

Pope Paul VI died peacefully on August 6, 1978, the Feast of the Transfiguration. His immediate successor, the smiling Venetian patriarch Albino Luciani, elected later that month, passed away unexpectedly at the end of September, and the cardinals turned to the relatively youthful fifty-eight-year-old Cardinal Karol Wojtyla of Krakow, who took the name Pope John Paul II. Although his twenty-eight-year pontificate is only now being critically evaluated, there is no doubt that John Paul II dramatically changed the papacy and the church, and even had a defining role in the collapse of Soviet domination of Eastern Europe. Telegenic and charismatic, the pontiff traveled abroad and won large, admiring crowds wherever he went—taking the modern cult of the papacy to new heights. His institution of World Youth Day turned out millions of young people, and his speeches and addresses, which fill hundreds of volumes, left a corpus of papal teaching that will take many years for scholars and theologians to digest.

While he projected a benign and personable presence to the world, his internal administration of the church showed a much sterner and more authoritarian face. Although he had been a father of Vatican II, he too (and those who elected him) felt the church had strayed from the path of true renewal. He was determined to arrest the seeming decline of the church by removing dissenters and demanding ironclad obedience to papal and episcopal authority. His curial appointments, particularly Munich's Cardinal Joseph Ratzinger—an important *peritus* (theological adviser) at Vatican II and a theologian of some renown—to the Congregation for the Doctrine of the Faith (CDF) in 1981, reflected a harder stand against the theological excesses of the postconciliar period. Among the targeted areas were the states of Western Europe, where Catholicism was on the decline; Central and South America, a hotbed for "Marxist-inspired" liberation theologians; and the United States, from where continual reports of disobedience, dissent, and permissiveness flowed to the Vatican.

The list on the United States was long and depressing: weak or dangerously liberal bishops, unhealthy and nearly empty seminaries, liturgical aberrations (especially the growing use of general absolution), emptying convents, a growing feminist movement in religious communities and among laywomen, and Catholic institutions of higher learning that welcomed dissenters on their theological faculties and hosted anti-Catholic artists and speakers. Something had to be done.

THE CRACKDOWN

As Cardinal Wojtyla, Pope John Paul II had visited the United States in 1976 and may have observed firsthand the conditions among Catholics and heard the complaints of disaffected bishops. When he returned to the United States as pope in the fall of 1979, he may have tipped his future strategy for the United States by visiting the see of every cardinal east of the Mississippi except Cardinal Dearden's Detroit. Hundreds and thousands greeted him warmly and turned out to celebrate Mass with him or tramp with him in the cornfields of southwestern Iowa. President Carter welcomed him at the White House, and he gave a speech to the United Nations. But a dramatic moment of his visit occurred during a meeting with religious in the National Shrine of the Immaculate Conception when Sister of Mercy Theresa Kane asked that he be open to the possibility of admitting women to holy orders. The audience applauded Kane, while the pontiff, on a throne, looked pained. The American church needed cleansing.[33]

Progressives in the U.S. church reacted with alarm in December 1979 when the pope removed theologian Hans Kung's authorization to teach Catholic theology at the University of Tübingen. Under the direction of Cardinal Joseph Ratzinger, investigations were launched into the writings of theologians Edward Schillebeeckx, Leonardo Boff, and others.[34] This crackdown reached American shores in 1986, when the Vatican resumed efforts to remove Father Charles Curran from the faculty of the Catholic University of America. Curran refuted accusations of dissent by stating that he had scrupulously followed the guidelines for dissent laid down by the American bishops in 1969. Archbishop James Hickey of Washington, D.C., the chancellor of the Catholic University, simply swept away the guidelines and demanded that Curran be dismissed. Efforts to work out a compromise failed, and in 1987 Curran departed.[35] He eventually accepted a position at Southern Methodist University, but his dismissal and subsequent attacks on so-called dissident theologians created divisions among Catholic theologians. It was clear to many that a new regime was in place, with a clear definition of what constituted authentic Catholic teaching—and what did not.

Insistence on sound doctrine led to a reevaluation of catechetics in the universal church. At a synod in 1983, Archbishop (Cardinal) Bernard Law of Boston proposed the development of a new catechism to stipulate the baseline of authentic Catholic teaching and provide some clarity about official church teaching amidst the perceived theological babel that had developed after the Council. Pope John Paul gave his approval, and a new *Catechism of the Catholic Church* was published in English in 1986. This soon became a popular tool for priests, catechists, and teachers not only to correct the deficient catechetical texts of the postconciliar period, but also to challenge those who appeared to stray from the authentic teaching of the church—whether degreed theologians or parish catechists. Various papal addresses, exhortations to bishops on *ad limina* visits to Rome, and especially the encyclical *Veritatis Splendor* (1993) established bright lines of orthodoxy for theologians and the faithful while narrowing the possibilities for dissent from even noninfallible magisterial teaching.

THE END OF THE JADOT BISHOPS

Changing the composition of the American episcopate became another high priority of Wojtyla's papacy. Already in 1979, plans were afoot to replace apostolic delegate Archbishop Jean Jadot. Jadot had been the object of a great deal of criticism from conservatives for his "neglect" of the "deteriorating" American church. In 1980, Rome summoned him to take over a Pontifical Council for Interreligious Affairs there. In what was considered a deliberate snub, he was not created a cardinal, the traditional "reward" given to former apostolic delegates; he retired in obscurity. With his removal, Vatican authorities had sent a clear signal that important changes were in motion for the American church.[36]

In his place, Pope John Paul II sent Archbishop Pio Laghi. Ordained a priest in 1946, and a bishop in 1969, Laghi had served in the papal diplomatic corps, holding posts in Nicaragua, the Middle East, and Argentina. When he was appointed to the American apostolic delegation in 1980, George Kelly related that former apostolic delegate Egidio Vagnozzi had confided to him already in 1979 that Laghi was being brought up from Argentina to "clean up the American church." Kelly later bragged that Laghi had made his *Battle for the American Church* required reading for members of his staff.[37] Clearly, Laghi shared the views of Kelly and others: weak or liberal bishops in league with academic theologians, feminist nuns and laywomen, and political liberals had done damage to the church in the United States. Compliant bishops were needed to restore ecclesiastical order and once again make the American Church an obedient daughter.

Rome meant business, but its efforts to "crack down" often blew up. Such was the case in 1987, when the Vatican launched an investigation of the pastoral administration of Archbishop Raymond Hunthausen of Seattle, a well-known peace activist and frequent target of abuse by Catholic conservatives. In addition to his opposition to the federal government (he refused for a time to pay taxes), his "failures" included being unwilling to crack down on liturgical abuses in his diocese and permitting the gay-ministry organization Dignity to operate on church property. The investigation of Hunthausen resulted in an unworkable administrative split after Bishop Donald Wuerl was appointed to take over some critical aspects of Seattle's governance. A huge public relations fiasco ensued as Hunthausen, Wuerl, and the apostolic delegate were publicly at odds until Cardinal Joseph Bernardin of Chicago intervened and resolved the situation. Hunthausen regained control but was compelled to accept a coadjutor bishop with an implicit deadline for retirement. At a meeting of the bishops, Hunthausen sought support against this encroachment on his episcopal prerogatives, but only a few of his peers were willing to stand with him—even those who shared his pastoral views. His case was a clear warning to other "liberal" bishops.[38]

Steadily and systematically, in conjunction with curial officials in Rome, Laghi shifted the character of the episcopal college in the United States. Retirements (some of them before the required age of seventy-five) gave him and his successors the opportunity to replace a substantial portion of the American episcopate. The new prelates were a mixture of personalities and backgrounds, but the primary criteria for appointment were loyalty and obedience to the Holy See, particularly on issues the pope himself stressed in his public addresses: the intrinsic evil of abortion, birth control, homosexuality, and opposition to women's ordination. Priests who publicly questioned the Holy See's positions on these issues, or wondered about the fate of episcopal collegiality, would not be seriously considered for the miter and crosier. The old collegial style of prelates like John Dearden, Joseph Bernardin, and Milwaukee's Rembert Weakland gave way to the more authoritarian style of Boston's Bernard Law, Washington's James Hickey, and New York's John J. O'Connor—all of whom became cardinals. The new bishops were for the most part not autocrats in the styles of Cardinals William Henry O'Connell (Boston), Francis Spellman (New York), or James Francis McIntyre (Los Angeles)—in fact, many were very popular and personable figures—and they all retained the collegial bodies created by the Council. But like John Paul II, they established stricter controls over clerical conduct and insisted on more orthodox catechesis and proper liturgical observance. They also spoke out publicly on issues like abortion and homosexuality more often than their more irenic predecessors. Law would later stumble badly over the issue of sexual abuse by clergy.

What Laghi began was carried on by his successors—Agostino Cacciavillan, Gabriel Montalvo, Pietro Sambi, and Carlo Maria Vigano—and the character of the American hierarchy shifted substantially to the right. The new bishops brought a different tone to the conference.

WEAKENING THE BISHOPS CONFERENCE

The pastorals on peace and economic justice represented the fullest flowering of episcopal collegiality embraced by Cardinal Dearden and the bishops appointed in the aftermath of Vatican II. As important as the content of the letters was the use of a collegial process to assemble them—relying on testimony from invited experts, witnesses, and others who felt they had something to say. Since President Reagan had made strident anti-Soviet rhetoric a part of his political appeal, military and administration officials expressed fears to the Vatican that the *Challenge of Peace* might complicate America's ability to defend itself from a potential Soviet missile strike. Wealthy Catholics like former Treasury secretary William Simon and shipping magnate W. Peter Grace believed the questions raised about capitalism in *Economic Justice for All* constituted a form of backdoor socialism. As with other liberal issues that challenged conservative "doctrine," conservative Catholics were drafted to offer contrary opinions that could be widely circulated. Hence, in response to the "dovish" thrust of the pastoral on peace, conservative polemicist George Weigel dusted off a defense of the just-war theory.

Michael Novak, a brilliant philosopher and freelance theologian, social commentator, and popular enthusiast for Vatican II–inspired change, also migrated to more conservative positions over time. He offered a strong apologia for the beneficence of capitalism, celebrating its ability to create wealth and employment.[39] Novak issued a refutation of *Economic Justice for All* before it was formally released to the public and, with substantial financial support, circulated it far and wide. He also managed to have inserted an encomium to this aspect of capitalism into Pope John Paul II's encyclical *Centesimus Annus* (1991).[40] Later, any attempt by bishops to speak to issues of public concern (international relations, armaments, the economy, or environmental issues) would be chastised by pundits or others for going beyond their sphere of expertise.[41]

While Weigel and Novak questioned the intellectual underpinnings of the two pastorals, others raised doubts about the process used to draft them. The extensive listening sessions, argued some, gave the impression that church teaching emerged from some sort of compromise among diverse points of view rather than proceeding deductively from divinely revealed truths. Others suggested that the bishops were naive and even ignorant. Catholic author Dinesh D'Souza of the Heritage Foundation accused the bishops of being "pawns" of American liberals and of knowing "little or nothing about the ideas and proposals to which they are putting their signature and lending their religious authority."[42] Despite the criticism, the American bishops overwhelmingly approved both documents. The Reagan administration opposed them and made its complaints known to the Vatican.

U.S. bishops backed away from comment on controversial public issues, restricting most of their public comment to the abortion issue or government support for contraception. No more efforts were made to produce documents of the size and sophistication of the pastorals—including on issues of purely Catholic concern. A decisive moment came in 1992 when Laghi-picked bishops, and Pope John Paul II himself, short-circuited a proposed letter on the role of women in the church, which used the same collegial information-gathering and writing strategies deployed in the pastorals.[43] Cardinal Joseph Ratzinger of the CDF openly expressed reservations about the teaching authority of episcopal conferences. In 1998, the Holy See issued *Apostolos Suos*, which restricted the ability of episcopal conferences to issue statements on certain matters by requiring a nearly impossible two-thirds vote of the bishops and the approval of the Holy See. In July 2001, the NCCB and the USCC merged into the United States Conference of Catholic Bishops (USCCB). The agencies of the USCC were subsumed under the new agency with a bishop at the head of each committee that had formerly been an office. Staff reductions and the rules governing policy assured that, with a few exceptions, the priority of work done by the American bishops would be related to internal church affairs. A moment of triumph came in 2010 with the unexpected election of Archbishop (Cardinal) Timothy Dolan of New York, a protégé of Laghi, to the presidency of the conference, "upsetting" the presumed selection of Bishop Gerald Kicanas, a former auxiliary of Cardinal Bernardin and conference vice-president. In a gloating article in the conservative Catholic journal *First Things*, George Weigel could barely contain his glee that the so-called "Bernardin Machine," which had "dominated the affairs of the American hierarchy for more than two decades" and presided over "a culturally accommodating Catholicism," was now done.[44] So he thought.

THE THEOCONS:
BRIDGES WITH CONSERVATIVE POLITICS

The severe weakening of the bishops' conference not only derived from arcane issues of ecclesiology, but also in reaction to the so-called liberal documents that had come out of the conference. Opponents of these letters sought to refute and diminish the impact of episcopal statements they viewed as favoring liberal causes: the protections of the social safety net, a less hawkish foreign policy, and an emphasis on the common good that relied on government activism. All of these were anathema to the increasingly conservative Republican Party—and perhaps also to "mainstream" white Catholics, who felt more and more affinity with conservative politics. Conservative think tanks reached out to thoughtful Catholic conservatives to frame a counter-narrative that would cut the ties between the church and the Democratic Party. This cohort of bridge builders came to be known as theocons (a play on the neocon moniker given to many of the intellectual of the George W. Bush era).

Stepping into this moment of flux were two key figures who had once been 1960s-era radicals and liberals: Richard John Neuhaus and Michael Novak.[45] Neuhaus, a Missouri Synod Lutheran pastor and former anti-war radical who had once marched with Martin Luther King, had become disenchanted with liberal causes—alarmed, in particular, over the left's support for abortion. He felt more and more affinity with the various evangelical groups that, with increasing militancy, insisted on repeal of the Supreme Court's 1973 *Roe v. Wade* decision legalizing abortion.

In 1984, while still a Lutheran, Neuhaus published *The Naked Public Square: Religion and Democracy in America*.[46] Neuhaus insisted that religion had a role in shaping public life and policies and rejected the privatization of belief and the "religion of secularism" that seemed to be dominating American public discourse. He strongly urged a renewed effort to insert religious faith into the national dialogue and made strategic alliances with the growing neo-conservative movement that flourished after the Reagan election. Conservatives looking for a religious voice to counter the perceived liberalism of mainline churches warmly welcomed his efforts. Neuhaus plugged himself into the financial resources of millionaire-funded think tanks. First landing a spot at the Illinois-based Rockford Institute, he opened the Center for Religion and Society under its auspices in Manhattan, flush with cash from the conservative Bradley and Scaife foundations. When a dispute in 1989 literally pushed him out the door, Neuhaus formed a new think tank called the Institute on Religion and Public Life. In 1990, with money from the conservative Olin Foundation as well as Bradley and Scaife, he began publishing the premier theocon journal, *First Things*.

Neuhaus had alluded to the possibility of a Catholic-Evangelical alliance at the end of *Naked Public Square*, and in 1987 he fleshed it out more substantially in *The Catholic Moment*.[47] In 1990, he seized the moment himself and became a Catholic. The next year, Cardinal John O'Connor of New York ordained him to the Roman priesthood. In 1994, Neuhaus and former Nixon staffer and Watergate felon Charles Colson issued "Evangelicals and Catholics Together," a manifesto that signaled the beginning of a fruitful relationship between the Republican Party and the Catholic Church.[48] If the alliance overlooked serious differences in the interpretation of scripture and theology, it undergirded the GOP's embrace of pro-life rhetoric in its platforms and from its candidates for high office. This alliance would later come under scrutiny and critique during the pontificate of Pope Francis.

Perhaps the most visible impact of the alliance was the enthronement of the abortion issue as the Catholic Church's paramount concern. Encouraged by Pope John Paul II, Vatican officials and theologians who prioritized the defense of fetal life over and above any other life issue, Neuhaus and his followers plunged into U.S. politics. Their gift to the Republican Party was the exhortation that Catholics could only legitimately vote for pro-life candidates. Although careful not to insist on ecclesiastical sanctions for "dissenters," the pope encouraged bishops to penalize Catholic politicians who took pro-choice positions, suggesting they were not fit for communion or heaven. Pro-life groups, individual priests, and even some bishops took this exhortation quite literally and denounced Democratic candidates from the pulpit, in printed flyers placed on the windshields of worshippers at Sunday Mass, or in their diocesan newspapers. The use of Catholic venues for political rallies and the banning of Catholic legislators who did not toe the line on abortion created intense controversy. In 2000, Neuhaus became the Catholic tutor of George W. Bush, and he met periodically with the president and his political advisers to shape the administration's Catholic strategy and other religious initiatives.

George Weigel, a former seminary professor, helped to found the Ethics and Public Policy Institute, heavily funded by conservatives, including the Olin and Bradley foundations. Weigel enjoyed a special relationship with Pope John Paul, whose biography he wrote in two massive volumes.[49] Weigel enjoyed hours of face time with the pontiff and never failed to assert the pope's strong leadership, not only of the church but also of the Western world. Weigel's speculations on just-war theory—and his justification of America's nuclear buildup in the eighties—won the attention of Republican strategists, with whom he worked to both attack and neutralize liberal Catholic positions, even when they came from the pope. Indeed, in a strategy curiously similar to Curran's, he suggested that people could exercise "prudential judgment" on noninfallible teaching—a rhetorical/theological device conservative Catholic politicians frequently used to distance themselves from official church positions on economics, immigration, and the environment.

Novak and especially Weigel put themselves at the forefront of efforts to justify George W. Bush's invasion of Iraq in 2003. Even when Pope John Paul publicly lamented the prospect of war and Cardinal Ratzinger questioned the morality of a preemptive invasion, the two defended the war and the erroneous belief that there were weapons of mass destruction in Iraq. To pressure the Vatican, the American government, at the urging of its ambassador to the Holy See James Nicholson, flew Novak to Rome to intercede personally with the pontiff. Weigel spoke of a "charism of political discernment" enjoyed by politicians and not by churchmen, and urged Catholic leaders to be "modest" in their comments on the war.[50] The pope refused to meet with them.[51] Nonetheless, Neuhaus, Weigel, and Novak all found themselves on the Rolodexes of the media, where they were often quoted as "Catholic experts."

CATHOLIC SEMINARIES AND COLLEGES

Concerned about the obedience and loyalty of U.S. priests, Pope John Paul II mandated at least two studies of American seminaries to inspect programs of priestly formation, especially instruction in celibacy, the quality of doctrinal teaching, and the relationship between clerical students and lay formation programs. In 1990, a synod on priestly formation held in Rome reviewed the recommended revisions of priestly formation programs. In March 1992, Pope John Paul issued the postsynodal apostolic exhortation *Pastores Dabo Vobis*, which laid out his expectations of seminary education and formation. In response, American seminaries revisited their basic curricula, placing more emphasis on instruction in doctrine as well as insisting on better spiritual formation—Mass, common prayer, devotional life, Eucharistic adoration. They also emphasized priestly identity: clerical attire, common prayer, and communal living. Symbolic of these changes, the North American College underwent a major transformation under the rectorates of future archbishops and cardinals Edwin O'Brien and Timothy Dolan, creating a "vibrantly orthodox" environment for young seminarians, who lived and studied in the shadow of St. Peter's. A Roman education, once questioned for its practical pastoral value to American seminarians, became an important step for those who aspired or were slated to become bishops or hold positions of authority in the local church.

A new set of seminarians began to apply to seminaries, often citing the example of Pope John Paul whose international travels and sponsorship of World Youth Day genuinely inspired them to seek a priestly or religious vocation. A growing number of young priests, who proudly identified themselves as "John Paul II priests," sometimes set themselves apart from their clergy colleagues who had been formed and ordained in the period right after the Council. Similarly, a new type of conservative Catholic college evolved in response to the perceived decline in Catholic identity in existing Catholic colleges and universities. One popular site of dynamic Catholic conservatism was the College of Steubenville, a small liberal arts college in Ohio, founded in 1946 and run by the Third Order Regular Franciscans. Nearly defunct in 1974, the campus received new life when Father Michael Scanlan became president and brought the Charismatic Renewal to the college, making it a major site for conferences for priests, young people, and laity. Scanlan welcomed an array of conservative faculty and eloquent speakers who strongly urged utter loyalty to papal utterances, including popular charismatic preachers Father John Bertolucci, former Trappist Francis Martin, and laymen Ralph Martin and Scott Hahn, the last a convert from Presbyterianism. Hahn in particular became a popular author and speaker.

In 1985, to accentuate the college's Catholic identity and loyalty to the Magisterium, Scanlan transformed the campus into a virtual mecca of orthodoxy for young people and, inspired by the example of Pope John Paul II, built adoration, rosary, and other aspects of traditional Catholic devotion into the regimen of student life. Steubenville's graduates entered the Catholic workforce as catechists and directors of diocesan religious education offices.[52] The college renamed itself the Franciscan University of Steubenville in 1986.

During his visit to the United States in 1979, Pope John Paul had urged Catholic colleges and universities to enhance their Catholic identity. In 1983, the revised code of canon law carried eight canons relevant to Catholic universities and other institutes of higher studies—most importantly Canon 812, which required those who taught theological subjects to have a mandate from "competent ecclesiastical authority" and profess loyalty to the Magisterium. In 1985, the Holy See sent out for comment the first draft of the apostolic constitution for Catholic higher education that would become *Ex Corde Ecclesiae*. The Association of Catholic Colleges and

Universities offered objections and called for clarifications. Key among them was a fear of transgressing on academic freedom and reversing years of progress in bringing Catholic institutions into conformity with secular higher education. After difficult discussions and revisions, Rome promulgated *Ex Corde Ecclesiae* in 1990, and pontifical universities like the Catholic University of America implemented the provisions in their theological faculties. Other colleges and universities entered into delicate negotiations with local bishops, who handled the mandates in various ways.[53]

CATHOLICS WADE INTO THE CULTURE WARS

The ascendancy of the religious right in American politics propelled social and cultural issues to the forefront. Still angry with the excesses of the 1960s, powerful evangelical Protestant leaders pushed hard against an array of enemies to family and faith: pornography, homosexuality, premarital sex, and especially abortion. Under Bernardin's leadership, opposition to abortion had been linked to support for a "consistent ethic" or "seamless garment" of Catholic concern for life that extended to capital punishment and advocacy for the poor, the availability of health care, and education. Bernardin never minimized the importance of preborn life, but by yoking it with wider concerns, he removed the possibility that the church could be co-opted by either political party.[54]

However, Republican operatives, anxious to weld Catholics to their base, made opposition to abortion a key plank in their party platform and drove out any who dissented. The growing militancy of the pro-life movement had been fanned by Pope John Paul II, who repeatedly insisted there should be no compromise on the issue of abortion because it was an intrinsic evil. Father Neuhaus became an important bridge between the church and the Republican Party, working closely for a time with Bush adviser Deal Hudson, a Catholic convert.[55] Neuhaus, distressed by the reelection of President Bill Clinton in 1996, openly supported Republican pro-life candidates, suggesting that this was only real option for faithful Catholics. His support of Republican candidates was replete with claims that there was no other way for true Catholics to vote. This sentiment was echoed by others, especially certain bishops such as LaCrosse's Bishop (now Cardinal) Raymond Burke, who at one point referred to the Democrats as the "Party of Death" (as conservative author Ramesh Ponnuru labeled them) for refusing to give pro-life Pennsylvania governor Robert Casey a speaking role at the 1992 Democratic convention. George Weigel supported Bush for reelection in 2004 over Catholic John Kerry, declaring that, because of his antiabortion views, "this Texas Methodist has a clearer understanding of the Catholic vision than his Catholic opponent."[56]

When antiabortion absolutism replaced Bernardin's consistent ethic or seamless garment, certain American bishops began interpreting a controversial provision in the Code of Canon Law as the reason to refuse communion to pro-choice Catholic politicians. Thus in 2003, William K. Weigand, bishop of Sacramento, publicly urged Catholic Democratic governor Gray Davis in 2003 not to present himself for Eucharist. Archbishop Charles Chaput of Denver singled out Kerry's pro-choice views and his support of embryonic stem cell research as reasons to vote against the Democratic candidate. Other bishops, including Bishop Michael Sheridan of Colorado Springs, Archbishop (later Cardinal) Raymond Burke of St. Louis, and Archbishop John J. Myers of Newark echoed that sentiment.[57] Bishop Thomas Tobin of Providence threatened the same against Rhode Island representative, Democrat Patrick Kennedy.

Not all bishops chose this draconian sanction, but the voices of those calling for it picked up steam, led by Archbishop Charles Chaput of Denver, who was later moved to the cardinalatial see of Philadelphia. Although Chaput did not favor using communion as a weapon against erring politicians, he lamented that there was not unanimity among the bishops over the imposition of penalties for pro-choice Catholic politicians.[58] Chaput, perhaps the most publicly critical of the Democrats, took aim at the policies of the party and particularly President Barack Obama. A skilled pastor and a capable administrator, Chaput fully embraced the notion that the nation was on a steep moral decline and that it needed the corrective of a strong orthodoxy and—echoing Pope Benedict—a smaller, more purified Catholic Church. Chaput's thoughtful, if sometimes trenchant, articles and public addresses made him a favorite in conservative Catholic circles, including the Napa Institute in California.[59]

CATHOLIC CONSERVATIVE MEDIA

Theocons enjoyed generous support from conservative think tanks that challenged "liberal" Catholic positions on a variety of issues. For example, the Bradley Foundation underwrote Neuhaus's *First Things*.

But as important as the print media have been, the power of cable television and radio has far outstripped them. Catholics had long been in television. The famous *Life Is Worth Living* was a popular, Emmy-award winning show hosted by the handsome and articulate Bishop J. Fulton Sheen in the 1950s. A lack of funds and organizational initiative deterred efforts of U.S. bishops to mount a more serious Catholic presence on the airwaves. Finally, Mother Angelica Rizzo, a Poor Clare of Perpetual Adoration, managed to tape and distribute religious broadcasts from her monastery in Irondale, Alabama.[60] With grit, determination, and the ability to use her identity as a nun to cajole donations for her project, she procured a broadcasting license from the FCC in January 1981 and inaugurated the Eternal Word Television Network (EWTN), which began broadcasting on August 15, 1981, from a garage of the monastery. By 1987, she was broadcasting twenty-four hours a day as she steadily improved her equipment and facilities. She began a shortwave station in 1992, and by 1996 was broadcasting on AM and FM stations. Indeed, Mother Angelica was a "force of nature." She cultivated powerful friends in Rome, and at her urging (and provision of contact information), many "abuses" in the U.S. church found their way to the desks of curial officials. She managed to charm benefactors and extract hundreds of millions from them for a state-of-the-art radio and television studio, satellite hookups, and worldwide coverage. She also found millions to build an imposing new convent for her community in nearby Hanceville.

EWTN's programming included the daily Mass from the chapel of her monastery each morning, led by various priests and later by members of the male religious community she founded, the Missionaries of the Eternal Word. Mother Angelica also broadcast devotions such as the rosary and the Chaplet of Divine Mercy on both television and radio. She included doctrinal programs offered by an array of orthodox figures, including professors from Steubenville, Marist Father Thomas Dubay, and Father John Trigilio, a priest of the Diocese of Harrisburg. Until a series of strokes felled her in 2001 (she died in March 2016), Mother Angelica herself hosted a freewheeling talk program called *Mother Angelica Live*, during which she sat on a chair and dispensed bits of grandmotherly advice. She also interviewed popular Catholic figures, including Franciscans of the Renewal cofounder Father Benedict Groeschel, Lincoln Bishop Fabian Bruskewitz, and even the scholarly Father Richard John Neuhaus, all of whom treated her with great deference.

Mother Angelica's wit and humor endeared her to many, and she traded actively on her religious identity; for example, she and her sisters returned to the older Poor Clare habit sometime in the 1990s. Her televised exhortations soon turned from pieties and grandmotherly advice and took on a sharper edge. She had no use for liberals, feminists, and other "dissenters," many of whom she characterized as "kooky," "daffy," and outright disloyal. Her periodic outrage at issues or behavior she considered unacceptable became part of her appeal.[61] Her most famous public eruption came during the 1993 World Youth Day in Colorado, where planners of a mimed outdoor Stations of the Cross used a woman as the person of Jesus. Enraged by the use of a woman for Jesus, she launched into what can only be described as an unhinged rant, denouncing the Denver program as "blasphemous" and called out everything she felt was wrong with the church. She punctuated every blast with the refrain "I'm sick of you liberals." When Archbishop Rembert Weakland of Milwaukee criticized her performance, she crudely retorted, "He can go put his head in the back toilet as far as I'm concerned."[62] In 1997, she accused Cardinal Roger Mahony of Los Angeles of liturgical error in his diocesan instruction "Gather Faithfully Together." Mahony reported her actions to Rome, prompting an investigation of her Eternal Word Television Network (EWTN).[63]

In 2008, Mother Angelica transferred control of the network from the Poor Clares to a lay board of trustees, out of the reach of the American bishops. Her stroke removed her from the air, and although the network still has a wide reach, especially through radio, without "Mother" it has not been the same. (She does appear in reruns). The network offers prime coverage of papal events and the annual meetings of the American bishops and devotionals; it also keeps up a steady flow of comments on culture-war issues, especially from Angelica's friend and biographer Raymond Arroyo, who anchors a news program on the network.

THE RATZINGER HIATUS

The long papacy of John Paul II ended in April 2005. Millions of mourners descended on Rome to pay their last respects. At the papal funeral, Cardinal Ratzinger gave an eloquent and touching homily, paying tribute to the pontiff and winning the attention of the cardinals who would soon be gathering for the papal conclave. Ratzinger's actions as head of the Congregation for the Doctrine of the Faith (CDF) had given this gentle and somewhat fragile prelate a bad reputation among some. No less well connected a Vatican pundit than John Allen of the *National Catholic Reporter* had been critical of then Cardinal Ratzinger in a book about him as the head of the CDF. Allen noted the observation of some that he carried "too much baggage." But to Allen's shock while he was covering the papal announcement on CNN, Ratzinger was declared the winner of the papal election and had taken the name Benedict XVI. Benedict would sit on the papal throne (it literally was a throne) until the end of February 2013. His pontificate was marked by difficult moments, including a misunderstood statement about Muslims at an address in Regensburg, the theft and dissemination of private documents by his butler from his personal quarters, and a perceived mishandling of the rising number of clerical sex abuse cases while he was head of the CDF. As he had shaped the theological directives of John Paul's papacy, so he continued in his own writings the beautifully written encyclicals on doctrinal subjects and virtues. His audience discourses were rich gems of theological and spiritual reflection on the gospels and the saints.[64]

Perhaps his most significant act came in July 2007, when he advanced the efforts of Pope John Paul to reconnect the schismatic followers of Archbishop Marcel Lefebvre and also to satisfy his own liturgical tastes by issuing the motu proprio *Summorum Pontificum*. The apostolic letter, did not, some claimed, restore the old Tridentine Mass (now called the Extraordinary Rite)—that had already been done under John Paul. But it extended permission for all priests to celebrate the Mass and permitted the formation of groups to have it said. Although Benedict's accompanying letter indicated that this was not meant to challenge the liturgical reform of Vatican II, the decree, along with Benedict's predilection for older papal garb and the former trappings of the papal office (much of which had been simplified or abolished under previous pontiffs) aroused serious concern that Benedict was doing exactly that.

In a Christmas address of December 2010, Benedict weighed in on a discussion that had been raging among historians of Vatican II, inspired by the schism of the Lefebvrites: Was Vatican II a council that was in the tradition of other councils, or did it radically go beyond the boundaries of tradition? Benedict of course rejected the simply binary, a hermeneutic of continuity versus a hermeneutic of discontinuity, but he took pains to remind the schismatics that they could not ignore Vatican II and to warn those who used the Council for purposes that had nothing to do with its letter or spirit.[65] The oversimplification of this discussion however, pitted "advocates" of the Council against those who challenged the use of Vatican II as a means of ongoing reform—not only liturgically, but also in ecumenism, social justice, and ethics.

Benedict visited the United States in 2008 and was warmly received by President George W. Bush. He addressed a session of the General Assembly at the United Nations. He celebrated public Masses in Washington and New York. He also visited Ground Zero, the site of the dastardly 9/11 attack in Manhattan, praying for healing and peace. Looming over the visit was the escalating sex abuse scandal, which continued to make headlines and embroiled the church in costly litigation. In New York, Benedict met with victims and spoke about the scandal during a homily at St. Patrick's Cathedral.[66]

There was continuity in episcopal appointments. Two cardinals, very different in temperament but both quite traditional in their own ways, became significant figures in the U.S. hierarchy. Timothy Dolan, the former rector of the North American College and archbishop of Milwaukee, had been promoted to New York and given the red hat of a cardinal. Raymond Leo Burke, a canonist, who went from bishop of LaCrosse, Wisconsin, to archbishop of St. Louis, Missouri, to head of the Vatican Supreme Court, the Apostolic Signatura, was also promoted to the cardinalate and given a seat on the Congregation for Bishops. Burke's influence (and that of other conservative cardinals and prelates) would be felt in several important American sees. Under Benedict, two investigations of American sisters were launched. The first, launched by the Congregation of Religious, ended quietly. The other, under the CDF, threatened sisters over the theological dissent of some of their members. Both created an atmosphere of anger among many women religious as sisters decried this attack on their service and fidelity.

American bishops also took a dim view of Barack Obama, the Democrat who was elected president in 2008. While Obama's pro-choice position was the presenting issue, his efforts to create a long-needed national health-care program, nicknamed "Obamacare," raised their hackles even more by mandating that insurance plans provide women with free contraceptive coverage. Obama had tried to work with the bishops but was rebuffed. Official Catholic efforts to stop Obamacare, coordinated by the bishops' conference, were intense—especially on Catholic members of Congress. Religious sisters and the Catholic Health Organization pulled out all the stops to reassure skittish Catholic legislators that they would not go to hell if they voted for the legislation.

After the bill was signed, opposition to the Obama health policy shifted to religious liberty—that somehow the law undermined the freedom of conscience of faithful Catholics. Linking up with hard-core Republican leaders, who detested the bill because it was yet another entitlement that offended their philosophy of government, Catholic leaders, funded by the Knights of Columbus and under the guidance of Archbishop William Lori of Baltimore, organized and directed dioceses to host a "Fortnight of Freedom" as a way of mobilizing opposition to the law and, indirectly, to Obama himself. The advance of same-sex marriage in states and ultimately by the Supreme Court also provided a casus belli for certain American churchmen. Some blamed Obama for these developments. The president got a taste of conservative Catholic ire in May 2009, when he accepted an invitation to give the commencement address at the University of Notre Dame. Condemnations by the local bishop of Fort Wayne–South Bend, conservative members of the Notre Dame faculty, the Cardinal Newman Society, and various and sundry American prelates made sure the visit came off with much contention. Obama never visited another Catholic site during his presidency.

On February 11, 2013, Benedict shocked the world by announcing to a meeting of cardinals that he would step down from the See of Peter on February 28. His pontificate had been full of controversy. There was an embarrassing breach of his private quarters with personal papers given to journalists, infighting among the Curia, and growing public discomfort with the church's handling of child sex abuse cases, not only in the United States but also in Germany, Ireland, and elsewhere. These had made the job unbearable for the aging pope, who had earlier longed to return to his native Germany and live out his days in peace. He kept the title of Pope Emeritus and moved into a recently vacated convent in the Vatican Gardens, attended to by his faithful secretary (now prefect of the papal household), Archbishop Georg Ganswein.[67]

On the rainy evening of March 13, 2013, the papal announcement was made against the backdrop of an eerily lit Vatican loggia. The new pontiff was Cardinal Jorge Bergoglio of Buenos Aires, Argentina. He had taken the name Francis, after the most beloved of all Catholic saints, Francis of Assisi. Pope Francis greeted the waiting crowd with a simple "buona sera" and humbly bowed as he asked them to pray for him. Immediately, a series of actions taken by the new pope set the media on fire. He made a public trip back to the hotel where he had been staying to personally pay his bill. He refused to move into the papal palace, choosing instead to reside in two comfortable rooms in the Casa Santa Marta on the Vatican grounds. He walked with other cardinals to meetings, for a time took his place in line at the Santa Marta cafeteria, eschewed much of the pomp and ceremony of regal vesture, and kept his public ceremonies and homilies mercifully short.[68] He even bought his own shoes.[69]

Pope Francis's gestures and his obvious comfort with the public aspects of pastoral ministry won him warm admiration from Catholics in the United States. In a June 6, 2013, address to aspiring papal diplomats in Rome, he spoke candidly about the appalling careerism, declaring it a "leprosy."[70] In an address to new bishops, he referred to careerism as a cancer and urged the new prelates to stay home and resist being "airport bishops" who traveled hither and yon seeking publicity and a "better" job.[71] Some U.S. bishops were wary and privately critical of the pontiff. "When is he going to start acting like a pope?" one groused (reminiscent of one American prelate's critique of John XXIII: "he's no pope, he should be selling bananas"). The lavish lifestyles and residences of some began to come under close scrutiny. Cardinal Raymond Burke reinvested himself with the older vesture of cardinal—the huge cappa magna, red shoes, and even the broad-brimmed galero (no longer given at the consistory, but a gift of admirers). In his cardinalatial finery, he often presided over very elaborate pontifical high Masses in the Extraordinary form.

Pope Francis pursued his pastoral vision writing an exhortation on the *Joy of the Gospel* (November 2013)—an easy-to-read and very direct call to Christians to reinvest themselves in the work of the gospel, especially when it comes to those at the margins. His encyclical on the care of the Earth, *Laudato Si* (June 2015), represented a major advance in Catholic theological reflection on the environment. It also expressed a belief in climate science, which had been under attack from right-wing think tanks and politicians, especially in the United States. Francis's pontificate would go to the margins. It would cultivate leadership by those who had been close to the needy and the poor. It would advocate pastoral solutions to challenges, such as communion to the divorced and remarried, to the lesbian, gay, and transgender community, and to those who had become alienated. It would urge priests and bishops to abandon careerism and devote themselves to their flocks—not looking at their assignments as a mere means to a "better" parish or diocese. Above all, it would express the pope's hope for a rejuvenation of "synodality"—the return of a wider collegial approach to issues confronting the church. This was in contrast to the centralization of power in Rome—especially in the dicasteries—in critical areas such as liturgy, seminary instruction, and social comment under the previous pontificates.

Pope Francis was certainly well aware of ecclesiastical conditions in the United States even before his election. His first trip to the United States came in September 2015, when he accepted an invitation to address the World Meeting of Families that had been scheduled in Philadelphia. He added to this agenda visits to Washington and New York. In the nation's capital, he addressed the U.S. bishops, urging them to step back from the culture wars so favored by some of their number and to find ways to build bridges to American society. "Harsh and divisive language does not befit the tongue of a pastor," he said.[72] He also canonized the eighteenth-century Franciscan missionary to California, Junípero Serra. The high point was the pope's address to a joint session of Congress. Speaking in clear but accented English, Francis applauded American dreams and visions, defended immigrants, called for abolition of the death penalty, and upheld the figures of Abraham Lincoln, Martin Luther King, Dorothy Day, and Thomas Merton as role models for U.S. Catholics.[73] Remarkable not only for its historic setting but also for its evocation of figures on the margins of Catholic public life and thought, the speech sent a strong signal about his intentions. In New York, he was welcomed at a tumultuous Mass at Madison Square Garden in the company of Cardinal Dolan. In Philadelphia, he spoke to cassocked seminarians, who sang "God Save the Pope" in Latin, and to the huge crowds assembled for the World Meeting of Families. His reception everywhere was warm, including in Philadelphia, where Archbishop Chaput's frequent cultural pessimism had no doubt been a target of the pope's words to the bishops in Washington, D.C.

As different a pope as Francis was, he made it clear that he wanted a different set of voices in the United States. When Francis reached out for an American for his inner circle, he chose the irenic and pastoral Cardinal

Sean O'Malley of Boston (whom he had known before) rather than New York's Cardinal Dolan. His curial appointments (and the red hat) included the genial bishop of Dallas Kevin Farrell, who had made a strong public defense of immigration and also spoke out against the proliferation of guns in the United States. Eager to change the tone of the international hierarchy, he made appointments to the College of Cardinals that reflected his desire to have men from different areas of the world join the international body that would elect his successor. Joining these ranks were two surprising choices from the United States: Bishop Blaise Cupich of Spokane, a moderate voice, to succeed the erudite but also culturally negative Francis George as archbishop of Chicago; and Redemptorist archbishop of Indianapolis Joseph Tobin, whom Francis appointed to Newark, making him the next-door neighbor of Cardinal Dolan. As an official at the Congregation of Religious, Tobin had helped defuse the investigation of religious sisters. Cupich replaced Burke on the Congregation for Bishops. Now the Catholic press and pundits began to speak of the "Francis Bishops"—pastoral men who had actually worked in parishes (as opposed to chanceries or academic institutions), who were hopefully devoid of careerism, and who had (in Francis's own colloquial terms) "the smell of the sheep." A new apostolic nuncio, Archbishop Christophe Pierre, was appointed to replace Benedict's Archbishop Carlo Maria Vigano, who had been appointed in 2011.

As the nature of Francis's papacy sank in, an American critique of the pope gathered steam, thanks in no small measure to social media. Traditionalist bloggers, including some priests, describe the pontiff as ignorant, deluded, or heretical—even as the Antichrist. Using the theological category of "prudential judgment," conservative commentators airily dismissed aspects of Francis's teaching they disliked or that clashed with their positions. American bishops, with a few exceptions, were mostly silent about major public issues involving Catholic teaching: racism, war, income inequality, and the environment. Only the issues of abortion, contraception, and same-sex marriage seemed to raise their righteous indignation and calls to action.

But these developments did not go unanswered by Pope Francis. His desire for a new tone in the Unites States expressed itself through Antonio Spadaro, S.J., the editor of the Vatican mouthpiece, *La Civiltà Cattolica*, and Marcello Figueroa, a Presbyterian cleric. In early 2017, the two published

"Evangelical Fundamentalism and Catholic Integralism: A Surprising Ecumenism," a pungent article that took aim at the "marriage" of Catholics and Evangelicals brokered by Neuhaus and Colson in the 1990s and ratified by prominent bishops.[74] The article lashed the "prosperity gospel" so dear to certain Evangelical leaders and rejected their interpretations of biblical texts to extol American exceptionalism. He decried the Catholic/ Evangelical ecumenism that found common cause on "pelvic issues" but also encouraged a xenophobic and Islamophobic vision "that wants wall and purifying deportations." It singled out the rather extreme digital site *Church Militant* as an example of encouraging the disastrous religious warfare that extolled Republican Donald Trump as Constantine and Democrat Hillary Clinton as the evil emperor Diocletian. Spadaro and Figueroa argued that what undergirds these extremist ideologies and movements is the same kind of fear that motivated the church's embrace of the culture war in the 1990s and the rebranding of the Catholic Church (at least its white adherents) as the Republican Party at prayer. Of this article, Michael Sean Winters of the *National Catholic Reporter* exclaimed, "Finally, someone in a semi-official organ of the Holy See stated that there is something unchristian about the Manichean worldview adopted by too many political leaders in the United States."[75]

CONCLUSION

The patterns of reform, counter-reform (or "reform of the reform," as it is called) and counter-counter-reform sketched here necessarily leaves open the question: Will Pope Francis and his faction have the strength and clout to truly change the direction of the Catholic Church in the United States? The conservative counter-counter-reform was, as of this writing, still a force to be reckoned with. Francis will be able to appoint a number of bishops who will reflect his pastoral priorities. But younger Catholic priests are for the most part still adherents of the revived "priestly identity" (or clericalism) of the era of John Paul II. Some Catholic laity also are strong devotees of the reform of the reform. Indeed, Latin Mass parishes and priests proliferate around the United States, mostly staffed by the Priestly Fraternity of St. Peter, whose American seminary is bursting with seminarians. White Catholics gave a majority of their votes to Donald Trump in the 2016 election. Not everyone is unhappy with the marriage of Catholics with conservative Republican principles—especially regarding the social safety net.

However, the impact of nearly a generation of Catholic restoration under John Paul II and Benedict XVI is still mixed. Surveys indicate a serious leakage in U.S. Catholic membership.[76] Catholic growth is propped up by the large influx of foreign-born Catholics and priests (many of them Latino). Some of this is the result of the tsunami of clerical sex abuse cases that never seem to end. This ongoing tragedy, which has brought untold suffering to hundreds and thousands of victims, has also enmeshed the church in a web of litigation and public opprobrium that will be hard to shake. This alone has severely undercut the authority of the John Paul II and Pope Benedict XVI bishops and complicated efforts to dial back the perceived excesses of the 1960s and 1970s.

A common phenomenon among U.S. Catholics is derisively called "cafeteria Catholicism." Many U.S. Catholics condition assent to various church teachings and practices depending on their ideology. Both progressives and conservatives regard papal authority with some qualification, exercising "prudential judgment" depending on the issue being addressed by the Holy Father. As of 2018, it is hard to say whether the papacy of Pope Francis will succeed in reversing the direction of the church in the United States established in the John Paul–Benedict era. No doubt the longer Francis lives to appoint people to office, the better chance there is for his vision and direction. His call is to reengage issues that matter to Catholic people so that their religious community can do what it had always done best: help them make sense of their lives.

Perhaps the statute of limitations on blaming present Catholic woes on the 1960s has finally run out.

NOTES

1. Quoted in Mark Massa, *The American Catholic Revolution: How the Sixties Changed the Church Forever* (New York: Oxford University Press, 2010), 5.
2. *National Catholic Reporter*, October 27, 1965, 1.
3. Hitchcock establishes his progressive "credentials" by noting, among other things, his participation in the St. John's University strike of 1966 and his involvement in Eugene McCarthy's presidential campaign in 1968. James Hitchcock, *The Decline and Fall of Radical Catholicism* (New York: Herder and Herder, 1971), 9–10.

4. "Feast of New Beginnings," *National Catholic Reporter*, December 22, 1965, p. 3.

5. U.S. Conference of Catholic Bishops, "Pastoral Statement on Penance and Abstinence," November 18, 1966, http://www.usccb.org/prayer-and-worship /liturgical-year/lent/us-bishops-pastoral-statement-on-penance-and -abstinence.cfm.

6. The most comprehensive treatment of the twists and turns of the artificial contraceptive debate is Leslie Woodcock Tentler, *Catholics and Contraception: An American History* (Ithaca, NY: Cornell University Press, 2004).

7. Angelyn Dries, "Living in Ambiguity: A Paradigm Shift Experienced by the Sister Formation Movement," *Catholic Historical Review* 79 (1993): 478–488.

8. For a broad overview of developments in prayer and Catholic participation in the Eucharist, see Joseph P. Chinnici, "The Catholic Community at Prayer: 1926–1976," in *Habits of Devotion: Catholic Religious Practice in Twentieth-Century America*, ed. James M. O'Toole (Ithaca, NY: Cornell University Press, 2004), 9–88; and Margaret M. McGuinness, "Let Us Go to the Altar: American Catholics and the Eucharist, 1926–1976, in *Habits of Devotion*, 187–236.

9. James M. O'Toole, "In the Court of Conscience: American Catholics and Confession, 1900–1975," in *Habits of Devotion*, 131–186.

10. Kenneth A. Briggs, "Wholesale Absolution Signals a New Catholic Debate," *New York Times*, December 8, 1976.

11. John Tracy Ellis, "American Catholics and the Intellectual Life," *Thought* 30 (1955): 351–388.

12. Philip Gleason, *Contending with Modernity: Catholic Higher Education in the Twentieth Century* (Oxford: Oxford University Press, 1995), 317. The full text of the Land O'Lakes Statement can be found in Mark Massa with Catherine Osborne, eds., *American Catholic History: A Documentary Reader* (New York: New York University Press, 2008), 110–114.

13. Charles E. Curran, *Loyal Dissent: Memoir of a Catholic Theologian* (Washington, DC: Georgetown University Press, 2006).

14. Samuel Thomas provides a more definitive account of the end of this first effort to remove Father Curran. See "A Final Disposition . . . One Way or Another: The Real End of the First Curran Affair," *Catholic Historical Review* 91 (2005): 714–742.

15. John A. Dick, "Jean Jadot, Hero of Progressive Catholics Dies," *National Catholic Reporter*, February 6, 2009, 5–7.

16. Thomas J. Reese, S.J., describes the evolution of the episcopal conference in the United States, in *A Flock of Shepherds: The National Conference of Catholic Bishops* (Kansas City, MO: Sheed & Ward, 1992), 21–66.

17. On the influence of Dearden, see Rembert G. Weakland, *A Pilgrim in a Pilgrim Church: Memoirs of a Catholic Archbishop* (Grand Rapids, MI: Eerdmans, 2009), 294–297.

18. Even moderate bishops like Joseph Bernardin of Cincinnati and the host bishop Cardinal John Dearden expressed misgivings about the outcome of

the conference. Kenneth Briggs, "Catholic Bishops Stirred to Debate by Proposals of 'Call to Action,'" *New York Times*, November 11, 1976.

19. For the fallout over *Humanae Vitae*, see Tentler, *Catholics and Contraception*, 264–279; Journalist Robert Blair Kaiser, *The Politics of Sex and Religion: A Case History in the Development of Doctrine, 1962–1984* (Kansas City, MO: Leaven Press, 1985) covers the same material in a much more pointed way.

20. An April 2011 report from the Guttmacher Institute suggests that 98 percent of sexually active Catholic women use some form of artificial contraception. Because Guttmacher is linked to Planned Parenthood, their statistics on sexual behavior are often dismissed or qualified by Catholic sources. See Rachel K. Jones and Joerg Dreweke, "Countering Conventional Wisdom: New Evidence on Religion and Contraception," Guttmacher Institute, April 2011, https://www.guttmacher.org/sites/default/files/report_pdf/religion-and-contraceptive-use.pdf.

21. *Frequently Requested Church Statistics*, http://cara.georgetown.edu/frequently-requested-church-statistics/.

22. *Frequently Requested Church Statistics*.

23. "1,300 at Priests Group Start," *National Catholic Reporter*, November 2, 1966, 3.

24. Prominent priests who clashed publicly with their bishops include Los Angeles's William DuBay, Milwaukee's James Groppi, and Lansing's Jerome Kavanaugh.

25. William D. Dinges, "Roman Catholic Traditionalism," in *Fundamentalisms Observed*, ed. Martin E. Marty and R. Scott Appleby (Chicago: University of Chicago Press, 1991), 66–101.

26. Monsignor R. G. Bandas, writing in the *Wanderer* in 1966, expressed the frustration of Catholic conservatives with the liturgy: "We are continuously told that the Mass must become more and more 'the central point' in the liturgical updating. To attain this object the tabernacle is being arbitrarily removed from its central place on the main altar and placed in some remote place so that the Faithful sadly roam about the church complaining like Mary Magdalen, 'They have taken away my Lord and I know not where they have laid him.' Statues and side altars have been removed, thrown in a church yard and consumed in a bonfire. . . . When they enter their beloved parish church their eyes are met with the ugly device, the temporary altar facing the people." Msgr. R. G. Bandas, "Open More Windows," *Wanderer*, December 15, 1966, 4.

27. Michael W. Cuneo, *The Smoke of Satan: Conservative and Traditionalist Dissent in Contemporary American Catholicism* (New York: Oxford University Press, 1997), 21–30.

28. Although Catholics tended more and more to vote as the rest of the country, the statistics cited here were compiled in the wake of a concerted effort by the Republican Party to garner a bigger share of the Catholic vote. In 2000, Catholics in general narrowly favored Al Gore over George W. Bush, 50 to 47 percent, but the white Catholic vote broke decisively for Bush, 45–52. In

2004, when Bush was matched against Catholic Senator John Kerry, Bush won the total Catholic vote 52–47 and the white Catholic vote 56–43. In 2008, Barack Obama claimed 54 percent of the Catholic vote to John McCain's 45, but white Catholics voted 52 percent for McCain to 47 percent for Obama. Gregory A. Smith and Jessica Martínez, "How the Faithful Voted: A Preliminary 2016 Analysis," http://www.pewresearch.org/fact-tank/2016/11/09 /how-the-faithful-voted-a-preliminary-2016-analysis/.

29. George A. Kendall, *Witness for the Truth: The Wanderer's 130 Year Adventure in Catholic Journalism* (St. Paul, MN: Wanderer Press, 1997). In its typically pungent prose, this book lays out most of the complaints of "orthodox" Catholics against the changes in American Catholicism since Vatican II.

30. Hitchcock, *The Decline and Fall of Radical Catholicism*.

31. Also in attendance at the meeting were James Hitchcock and Fathers Joseph Mangan, S.J., of Loyola Chicago; Robert Levis of Gannon College in Erie, Pennsylvania; John Miller, Provincial of the Holy Cross Fathers; and Ronald Lawler, O.F.M. Cap., Catholic University of America.

32. George Kelly, *The Second Spring of the Church in America* (South Bend, IN: St. Augustine's Press, 2001), 10–11.

33. Although written after the "cleansing" had begun, this *Time* article summarizes John Paul's intentions regarding the American church: Richard N. Ostling, "Religion: John Paul's Cleanup Campaign," *Time* 128, no. 15 (October 13, 1986): 75ff.

34. Journalist and Vaticanologist John Allen provides a rather incisive account of these actions during Cardinal Ratzinger's tenure as the head of the Congregation for the Doctrine of the Faith. See John N. Allen, Jr., *Cardinal Ratzinger: The Vatican's Enforcer of Faith* (New York: Continuum, 2000).

35. Curran's version of these events is found in *Loyal Dissent*, 107–159.

36. Douglas Martin, "Jean Jadot, Papal Envoy Dies at 99," *New York Times*, January 22, 2009.

37. George Kelly, *Battle for the American Church (Revisited)* (San Francisco: Ignatius Press, 1995), 9.

38. Kenneth Briggs offers an extensive description of the Hunthausen episode in *Holy Siege: The Year That Shook Catholic America* (San Francisco: HarperCollins, 1992), 8, 14–18, 19, 65, 124–125, 132–133, 155, 282, 373, 451–452, 535, 571–572. See a capsule history in Timothy P. Schilling, "When Bishops Disagree," *Commonweal* 130 (September 12, 2003): 15–22. Joseph Sobran presents the conservative case against Hunthausen in "Bishop in the Doghouse," *National Review* 38 (December 19, 1986): 28–30. See also John A. McCoy, *A Still and Quiet Conscience: The Archbishop Who Challenged a Pope, a President, and a Church* (Maryknoll, NY: Orbis, 2015).

39. Novak provides an interesting account of his own journey from Catholic progressive to paladin of capitalism. See Michael Novak, "Controversial Engagements," *First Things*, April 1999, 21–29.

40. Damon Linker, *The Theocons: Secular America Under Siege* (New York: Doubleday, 2006), 76.
41. An example of this would be the comments of conservative pundit Ross Douthat and Acton Society leader Robert Sirico on a Fordham University panel offering a twenty-five-year retrospective on *Economic Justice for All*. Patricia Zapor, "Debate Fresh 25 Years After 'Economic Justice for All," *National Catholic Reporter*, December 9, 2011.
42. Dinesh D'Souza, "The Bishops as Pawns," *Policy Review*, Fall 1985, 50–57.
43. Peter Steinfels, "Catholic Bishops in U.S. Reject Policy Letter on the Role of Women," *New York Times*, November 19, 1992. The vote for the letter was 137 in favor and 110 opposed—short of the two-thirds necessary for passage.
44. George Weigel, "The End of the Bernardin Era," *First Things*, February 2011, 18–25. Weigel's posthumous assault on the late cardinal, fourteen years after his death, drew angry rebuttals from Eugene Kennedy. See "Weigel's Attack Is a Smokescreen," *National Catholic Reporter*, March 18, 2011, 22–23; and Peter Steinfels, "Rewrite: The Contested Legacy of Cardinal Bernardin," *Commonweal* 138, no. 10 (May 20, 2011): 11–17.
45. Linker, *The Theocons*. A former editor of *First Things*, Linker offers an interesting perspective on the movement in which he was a participant.
46. Richard John Neuhaus, *The Naked Public Square: Religion and Democracy in America* (Grand Rapids, MI: Eerdmans,1984).
47. Richard John Neuhaus, *The Catholic Moment: The Paradox of the Church in the Modern World* (San Francisco: Harper & Row, 1987).
48. Charles Colson and Richard John Neuhaus, eds., *Evangelicals and Catholics Together: Toward a Common Mission* (Dallas: Thomas Nelson, 1995).
49. George Weigel, *Witness to Hope: The Biography of John Paul II* (New York: Harper Perennial, 2005); *The End and the Beginning: Pope John Paul II—The Victory of Freedom, the Last Years, the Legacy* (New York: Image, 2011).
50. Weigel cites this in a lengthy article in the run-up to the Iraq War. See George Weigel, "Moral Clarity in Time of War," *First Things*, January 2003, 20–27.
51. On papal opposition to the war, see Frank Bruni, "Threat and Response: The Vatican; Pope Voices Opposition, His Strongest to Iraq War," *New York Times*, January 14, 2003.
52. Other new Catholic colleges dedicated to orthodoxy also began attracting substantial donations and a steady enough flow of students. Reacting with concern to the "damage" of the Land O' Lakes conference, a group of philosophy professors from St. Mary's in Moraga, California, planned a college based on loyalty to the Magisterium and the use of the "great books" curriculum. Financed by a grant from oil millionaire Henry Salvatori and other generous benefactions, and with the support of key figures in the American hierarchy, they opened Thomas Aquinas College in 1971 in an old Claretian seminary in Santa Paula, California, with thirty-three students. Christendom College in Virginia opened its doors in 1977. "Founded in response to the devastating

blow inflicted on Catholic higher education by the cultural revolution that swept across America in the 1960s," it advertised its loyalty to the Magisterium and the opportunity for students to "breathe Catholic." Pizza mogul Thomas S. Monaghan sponsored perhaps the most ambitious venture into orthodox Catholic education when he founded Ave Maria University in 1998 in Ypsilanti, Michigan (moved to a planned community in Florida in 2003). Its law school provides training for young lawyers dedicated to protecting Catholic rights, and its undergraduate programs and spiritual focus uphold traditional Catholic teaching.

53. Philip Gleason, "The American Background of *Ex Corde Ecclesiae*: A Historical Perspective," in *Catholic Universities in Church and Society: A Dialogue on Ex Corde Ecclesiae*, ed. John P. Langan (Washington, DC: Georgetown University Press, 1993), 1–19; Alice Gallin, ed., *Ex Corde Ecclesiae: Documents Concerning Reception and Implementation* (Notre Dame, IN: University of Notre Dame Press, 2006).

54. The text of the Gannon Lecture delivered December 6, 1983, can be found in Cardinal Joseph Bernardin, *The Seamless Garment: Writings on the Consistent Ethic of Life*, ed. Thomas A. Nairn (Maryknoll, NY: Orbis, 2008), pp. 7–14.

55. Deal W. Hudson, *Onward, Christian Soldiers: The Growing Political Power of Catholics and Evangelicals in the United States* (New York: Threshold, 2008). Hudson spells out the challenges and possibilities of a Catholic-Evangelical alliance. His acknowledgments include other well-known priests—Benedict Groeschel, Frank Pavone, Bishops Robert Vasa and Allen Vigneron, Archbishop Jose Gomez—and high-profile lay Catholics such as former senators Rick Santorum and Sam Brownback, Representative Henry Hyde, Governor Frank Keating, and former Republican National Committee chair and ambassador to the Holy See, Jim Nicholson.

56. George Weigel, "A Catholic Votes for George W. Bush," *America* 191 (September 27, 2004): 12–15.

57. David Kirkpatrick and Laurie Goodstein, "Group of Bishops Using Influence to Oppose Kerry," *New York Times*, October 12, 2004.

58. Ann Carey, "Chaput: US Bishops Agree Abortion Is Evil but Differ on Sanctions for Support," *Colorado Catholic Herald*, April 15, 2011, 19.

59. In his 2014 Erasmus Lecture "Strangers in a Strange Land," Archbishop Chaput lays out his beliefs on America's true identity, cites instances of societal and cultural decline, but also holds out hope for those who believe the nation can be saved. *First Things*, January 2015, 25–31.

60. Raymond Arroyo, *Mother Angelica: The Remarkable Story of a Nun, Her Nerve, and a Network of Miracles* (New York: Doubleday, 2005).

61. Paul Vitello, "Mother Mary Angelica, Who Founded Catholic TV Network, Dies at 92," *New York Times*, March 27, 2016.

62. Jacqueline L. Salmon, "Mother Angelica, Founder of Catholic TV and Radio Empire, Dies at 92," *Washington Post*, March 27, 2016; Paul Vitello, "Mother Mary Angelica."

63. Arroyo, *Mother Angelica*, 259–278.

64. Laurie Goodstein, "A Turbulent Tenure for a Quiet Scholar," *New York Times*, February 11, 2013; Rachel Donadio and Elisabetta Povoledo, "Successor to Benedict Will Have a Church at a Crossroads," *New York Times*, February 11, 2013.

65. For a thorough discussion of Benedict's understanding of this subject, see Stephen M. Fields, "Introduction: Benedict XVI and Conciliar Hermeneutics," *Nova et Vetera* (English edition) 15, no. 3 (Summer 2017): 705–727. An overview of the impact of these arguments on the U.S. church is in Tom Fox, "The New Spin on Vatican II," *National Catholic Reporter*, March 2, 2010.

66. "Official Itinerary of the Papal Visit," *New York Times*, April 11, 2008.

67. There are many commentaries on Benedict's resignation. Perhaps the best comes from a series of interviews given by Benedict to journalist Peter Seewald. See *Last Testament in His Own Words*, trans. Jacob Philips (London: Bloomsbury, 2016).

68. Jim Yardley, "A Humble Pope Challenges the World," *New York Times*, September 18, 2015. Perhaps the best coverage of Bergoglio's career and ideology is to be found in Austen Ivereigh, *The Great Reformer: Francis and the Making of a Radical Pope* (New York: Henry Holt, 2014).

69. Josephine McKenna, "A Frugal Pope Buys His Own Shoes," *Religion News Service*, December 21, 2016.

70. "Pope Francis Calls Careerism a 'Leprosy' on the Priesthood," *National Catholic Reporter*, June 21–July 4, 2013.

71. Carol Glatz, "Pope: Bishops Are Pastors Not Princes; Be Humble, Loving, Return Calls," *Catholic News Service*, September 19, 2013.

72. "Pope Francis' Speech to the Bishops of the United States of America" (full text), *New York Times*, September 23, 2015.

73. "Transcript: Pope Francis's Speech to Congress," *Washington Post*, September 24, 2015.

74. Antonio Spadaro and Marcello Figueroa, "Evangelical Fundamentalism and Catholic Integralism: A Surprising Ecumenism," *Civiltà Cattolica*, July 13, 2017, http://www.laciviltacattolica.it/articolo/evangelical-fundamentalism-and-catholic-integralism-in-the-usa-a-surprising-ecumenism.

75. Michael Sean Winters, "The Civilta article: FINALLY!" *National Catholic Reporter*, July 14, 2017; Rachel Zoll, "Confidant of Pope Francis Offers Scathing Critique of Trump's Religious Supporters," *Washington Post*, July 13, 2017.

76. Michael O' Loughlin, "Pew Survey: Percentage of U.S. Catholics Drops and Catholicism Is Losing Numbers Faster Than Any Denomination," CRUX, May 12, 2015; Pew Research Center, "America's Changing Religious Landscape," May 12, 2015, http://www.pewforum.org/2015/05/12/americas-changing-religious-landscape/.

4

Who Pastors

THE PRIEST, THE CONTEXT, AND THE MINISTRY

Katarina Schuth

Even twenty-five years ago, asking who pastors a parish would have been rhetorical for the answer was fairly clear: a priest with fifteen or so years of experience as an associate pastor. Today, the response is more complex as we consider who actually provides services of a spiritual nature to a group of people. No longer can the officially assigned ordained pastor begin to meet the spiritual needs of all parish members, so many others, including lay ecclesial ministers and deacons, serve in roles that extend traditional pastoring functions.

At the same time, almost every Christian community in the United States considers the role of pastor essential to its vitality, and has since Euro-American settlement began in the seventeenth century.[1] Because of the centrality of the Eucharist, Roman Catholics ascribe particularly high value to priests. In the church of the twenty-first century, the characteristics of those who serve as pastors, the sociocultural and ecclesial circumstances affecting their exercise of ministry, and the scope of the ministry they provide converge in unique ways. That convergence reveals various dynamics that challenge how we understand church, parish, priest, minister, and member. Priests are remarkably dissimilar across generations; they are more international in origin, and they take on the role of pastor after shorter periods of mentoring by senior pastors. Many other people are carrying out ministries previously reserved for priests. Demographic shifts in the United States reflect a more ethnically diverse Catholic population, increasingly made up of Latino and other immigrant groups. There is growing diversity as well in attitudes and convictions among Catholics, producing what seems a clear, identifiable divide between Catholics formed in the progressive theology and vision associated with Vatican II and those shaped by the charismatic and more conservative papacy of John Paul II. The continued growth of membership, unequally distributed across regions, and the decline in ordination candidates are changing the size and configuration of parishes that include mega-type suburban parishes and clusters of two or more parishes in rural, small-town areas. These social and cultural realities are the context in which priests sort out their roles as pastors. It is important to understand who the priests are now serving and who those being prepared to serve as parish pastors are, as well as the essential collaborative role of those who minister along with priests in parochial settings.

In light of the rapidly changing circumstances of the new century, pastors are paying attention to necessary adaptations of their ministry. In some parishes, generational needs for faith development are primary; in others, it is cultural diversity; and in larger parishes, it is learning to work collaboratively with paid pastoral ministers and volunteers. In rural areas, parish structures are adapting to the decline both in members and in the availability of priests. By contrast, expanding suburban populations mean the creation of huge congregations, while inner-city parishes find themselves merged or suppressed. Economic conditions vary by region and diocese, and even by parish, in some cases affecting the viability of parochial schools and other pastoral services. Yet the desire for basic spiritual ministry—celebrating the Eucharist and the sacraments, preaching and teaching about the faith, and maintaining a vital parish community—remains constant.

WHO PASTORS: PRIESTS AND THEIR COWORKERS

Of the 26,199 diocesan priests in the United States in 2016,[2] approximately half are pastors, with an additional 15 percent of pastors belonging to religious orders. It is estimated that at least half of all pastors are in charge of at least two parishes. In 2016, they led the 17,651 parishes and 2,622 mission churches listed in the *Official Catholic Directory*. Assisting them were many of the 18,792 permanent deacons, more than 40,000 lay ecclesial ministers, and even more volunteers. In only a few cases are associate pastors available to assist in large parishes, and these priests are almost always newly ordained. Being a pastor today necessitates working collaboratively to meet the needs of some seventy million Roman Catholics. Pastors have always had the dual role of providing for the spiritual life of parishioners and the administration of parish business. In the contemporary church, those two roles expand significantly in light of the number and diversity of parishioners and the complexity of the structures inherent in parish life. In the past ten years, considerably more of the administrative duties are accomplished by permanent deacons and lay administrators. This situation calls for pastors who appreciate the expertise required for effective administration of parishes and institutions, and who are able to collaborate effectively.

Profile of Priests

Various surveys estimate the average age of priests to be over sixty-five, with those who are diocesan priests slightly younger and religious priests a few years older.[3] The average age at ordination has increased by six or seven years over the past twenty years. At the same time, however, the average age of priests *who are pastors* is considerably younger, because they are commonly assigned to this role within five years of ordination, compared to at least twenty years after ordination in the 1980s. Besides an increase in age overall, the total number of priests has dropped from 59,892 in 1967 to 37,930 in 2016, a loss of 21,962. The reduction in numbers was shared almost equally between diocesan and religious priests, but the proportion of loss among religious is considerably higher. Researchers offer various reasons for the decline in the number of priests, with some attributing it to the discipline of celibate chastity required of Roman Catholic clergy[4] and others to the current social and cultural milieu with its emphasis on individualism and materialism. Whatever the cause, the decrease is noteworthy: In terms of generational differences, 5,536 priests, both diocesan and religious, were ordained between 2006 and 2016, for an average of 503 per year; between 1986 and 2005, some 8,600 diocesan priests were ordained, for an average of 430 per year, plus an estimated average of 210 religious per year; during the prior two decades (1966 to 1985), more than 14,000 diocesan priests were ordained, for an average of 700 per year, plus an estimated 360 religious per year.[5] This becomes significant because a person's ordination date tends to predict his attitudes, orientation, and approach to ministry.

Generational Differences Among Priests

The attitudes and inclinations of priests are wide-ranging, conditioned in part by their background, age, experience, and ideological preferences. In the past several years, extensive research and publication by and about priests as pastors have revealed the complexity of the conditions shaping the priesthood. Pastors share a background of intense formation designed to prepare them theologically, spiritually, and pastorally for their work while ensuring healthy personal development as well. More than 90 percent of those responding to a wide range of surveys over the past ten years indicate high satisfaction with their ministry. Yet they differ tremendously because of their family backgrounds, wide age span and resulting generational influences, experiences of church, cultural origins, and ethnic and racial heritages.

An issue of marked significance concerning the role of pastor is the ecclesial perspective of priests. Of particular interest are the differences in the profiles between the earler so-called Vatican II priests and the John Paul II priests of today. Though this nomenclature is not universally accepted because of its generalized and narrow construal in describing priests, it is nonetheless commonly understood and frequently used across generational lines. The sexual abuse crisis has significantly influenced the morale among all priests and differentiated the generations of clergy even more sharply. The clearest description of these two cohorts is found in *Evolving Visions of the Priesthood: Changes from Vatican II to the Turn of the New Century*,[6] which sheds light on ecclesiological differences among priests, emphasizing the divergent views between younger and older priests in their approaches to ministry. Older priests describe themselves using such terms as servants, servant leaders, instruments, facilitators, enablers, pastoral leaders, and liberals. By way of contrast, younger priests portray themselves as traditional, conservative, establishment, "unapologetically Catholic," and "ecclesiologically sound."[7] The choice of descriptors illustrates how dissimilar are the self-understandings of the two groups, especially as they pertain to their role as pastors. In *The First Five Years of the Priesthood*, 42 percent of recently ordained priests noted that disagreements with older priests about ecclesiology and ministry were a problem for them.[8] They see themselves as having different hopes and goals for the church of the future than their predecessors.

These divergent perceptions are troublesome, especially when considering how each group perceives the other. In his research, Dean Hoge found that "younger priests called the older priests liberals, leftist fringe, secularized, anti-establishment, a 'lost generation,' and priests with a social work model," while "older priests referred to the young men as inflexible, divisive, liturgically conservative, institutional, hierarchical, and believers in a cultic priesthood."[9] Many senior priests worry that younger priests are out of tune with many older parishioners, as well as with their lay contemporaries. Two studies spanning nearly a decade document the gap between young clerics and other young Catholics.[10] The views of the two groups diverge when it comes to the church's claims of authority pertaining to sexual issues, the necessity of regular worship, and the requirement of maintaining institutional structures, among many others. These contrasting perspectives have a bearing on the effectiveness of priests. Moreover, the impact on parishes and other ministries is often negative when a younger priest who succeeds an older pastor upends the congregation and its experience of Christian life by scuttling much of what his predecessor put in place. The transition from one mode of pastoring to another is often challenging for parishioners. For lay ministers caught between the divergent approaches, the consequences are even more stressful.

There are identifiable differences in the ways priests understand their role as pastor. The approaches or methodologies they use flow from the particular model of priesthood that shapes the thinking of the individual priest. Since Vatican II, church leaders and clergy have debated, defended, and rejected various models of what it means to be a priest. Among those most frequently cited are the "sacral model," sometimes identified as the cultic model; the "ministerial model," akin to the servant-leader model; and the "representational model," grounded in the priest's role in the celebration of the sacraments. The more recently ordained are more likely to subscribe to the cultic model and those longer ordained to the servant-leader model. The representational model has elements of both. In *Priesthood Today: An Appraisal*, Thomas Rausch evaluates these models in ways that relate directly to the exercise of ministry. He finds that the strength of the sacral model is in its emphasis on the relationship of priesthood to the "Eucharistic orientation of the church's ministry of leadership as well as the nature of the church itself as a Eucharistic community."[11] Rausch points to the limitations of the model as well:

> The sacral model also tends to separate the priest from the community, a separation reinforced by obligatory celibacy, special privileges, and clerical dress. Finally, its elitism is very much out of sync with the contemporary sense of the church as a community of disciples or even as an egalitarian community.[12]

The ministerial model, on the other hand, emphasizes the role of leadership within the community and the link between the community and its leader. Rausch says that this understanding helps recover the multiplicity of gifts that resides in the Christian community, a concept critical at a time when the number of priests has declined and the gifts of the whole community are vitally important. Nonetheless, criticism of this model focuses on its functional approach and the loss of identity for many priests.

Through the years, church leaders have raised objections to excessive stress on one model to the virtual exclusion of the other. Avery Dulles proposed the representational model, which takes into account both of the others. It goes beyond the functionalism of the ordained ministry to an ontology of priesthood. The priest is sacramentally authorized to act in the name of the church, but does not personally exercise all ministerial functions in the church.[13]

Differing models of priesthood have serious ramifications for the way pastoral services are provided. The rapid increase of lay ecclesial ministry, for example, is received less enthusiastically among the younger clergy who favor the cultic model. Many of the more recently ordained see themselves as representing both the cultic and servant-leader types, though parishioners often experience them exhibiting the former more than the latter. A more authoritarian style of leadership, more devotional practices, less emphasis on community participation, and a narrower understanding of the church's tradition characterize the pastoral style of many of the recently ordained. Older priests are likely to favor collaborative leadership, Vatican II liturgical practices, community outreach, and a broader interpretation of church teaching.

Yet hopeful signs of convergence are appearing. In the face of the decreasing numbers of clergy and religious, a driving force is the sheer necessity of incorporating the gifts of the laity. Contributors to a comprehensive effort, "The Emerging Models of Pastoral Ministry Project: The Theological, Sacramental and Ecclesial Context," spent five years researching the pastoral life and leadership of Catholic parishes in the United States.[14] Their findings touched on multiple-parish pastoring, multicultural diversity, leadership, human resources, the next generation of leaders, and characteristics of communities of the future. The group identified six marks of excellence in leaders: collaborative, ethical, inclusive, pastoral, prophetic, and welcoming. In the opening address of the conference at which the data were presented, Bishop Blase Cupich (now Cardinal, Archdiocese of Chicago) strongly affirmed the findings and emphasized the call to holiness, to communion, and to witness on the part of both laity and the ordained. Successful pastoring, he said, requires the involvement of laity and the encouragement and animation of their gifts on the part of the ordained.[15] Even if a more traditionalist style of pastoring appeals to those recently ordained, the course of events dictates another path. The aging and retirement of clergy and an inadequate number of replacements, coupled with an ever-growing Catholic population, are major concerns in every diocese and archdiocese in the United States. Extraordinary cooperation between all clergy and laity is the only way forward. Such cooperation will require that younger priests adapt, translate, or build a crosswalk between their own understanding of the role of pastor and the project of the parish, and the complex reality of the faith communities they are called to lead.

International Priests Serving as Pastors

With pastors whose cultural and/or ethnic origins are unfamiliar to a congregation, the complications about who the pastor is and how he leads increase. While in some sense the population of priests in the United States has always been international in composition, the current situation presents challenges different from those of the late nineteenth and early twentieth centuries. Historically, priests came with immigrant groups from Ireland, Italy, Germany, Poland, and other countries; in more recent years, bishops have actively recruited priests from Mexico, India, Poland,

Colombia, Nigeria, and other countries to fill positions.[16] The Vietnamese community with its many refugees has provided a large number of priests, far exceeding the proportion of Vietnamese church members. Estimates place the proportion of foreign-born priests at minimally 25 percent of the current U.S. presbyterate. With the exception of those who come from Mexico, few of these priests serve parishioners who share their country of origin. This intensifies the need for priests to become more cognizant of culture, both their own and that of the people whom they serve, and to incorporate that knowledge into their vision and practice of pastoring.

Further, seminarians from other countries, for whom figures are more precise, have increased considerably. In 2009–2010, a record high 963 seminarians in theology (30 percent) were foreign-born, an increase of 131 from the previous high in 2007–2008. In the most recent two-year period the number has declined to 15 percent of seminarians, with the numbers at new lows of 421 in 2015–2016 and 501 in 2016–2017. Currently, 58 percent of foreign seminarians are studying for a U.S. diocese. The distribution of non-Anglo seminarians, including those born in the United States, is as follows: 15 percent Hispanic/Latino, 11 percent Asian, 5 percent African or African American, and 6 percent other, for a total of 37 percent. CARA first collected data on racial and ethnic background in 1993, when non-Anglos were 21 percent of seminary enrollment.[17] Ten years before, the number was less than 10 percent. Most dioceses prefer to educate foreign seminarians in the United States to expose them to American culture and to ensure that their theological formation is more suited to the U.S. parish context. The increased number of priests coming from other countries and the higher proportion of international seminarians are transforming the face of the presbyterate.

The implications of this transformation are enormous for pastors and parishioners. Pastors need to welcome into their midst priests newly arrived from other countries, many of whom cannot speak English and are unfamiliar with the church and culture of the United States. Acculturation is a long, slow process, and many priests on both sides simply do not have or take the time to become acquainted. Too often the result is division and alienation among priests. Besides language and cultural misunderstandings, international priests experience problems based on differences in ecclesiologies, in managing finances, and in relating to parishioners and lay staff, especially women.

Consequences for parishioners are considerable, and they receive international priests with varying degrees of enthusiasm. On the one hand, parishioners who realize that their parishes would close without the services of priests from other countries appreciate their willingness to serve. On the other hand, parishioners often find it impossible to understand homilies or deal with the cultural disparity in how international priests exercise their roles. Despite the importance of bridging cultural differences to minister effectively, only half of the dioceses employing foreign-born priests enroll them in programs orienting them to American culture or English-language instruction.[18] In their eagerness to have the priests take up pastoral responsibilities, diocesan leaders often fail to take into account the extent of formational needs of the new arrivals in cultural and linguistic areas. A few programs serve priests on a broader scale, such as the Oblate School of Theology in San Antonio, which makes available an International Priest Internship; Loyola Marymount University in Los Angeles, which has a Cultural Orientation Program for International Ministers; and Maryknoll in New York, which offers a Cross-Cultural Services Acculturation Workshop. Most priests who are willing to participate in these programs report significant benefit from the experience. We do not have data on how what they identify as beneficial translates into their pastoral practice.

In a 2008 series of articles in the *New York Times*,[19] Laurie Goodstein documented the impact of priests coming from other countries. She reported on a priest who "sorts through e-mail and letters from foreign priests soliciting jobs in America." He is looking for someone who can serve in his diocese, which is experiencing a considerable shortage of pastors.[20] Without international priests, many dioceses would be closing parishes and requiring current pastors to administer even more parishes. In Goodstein's second article, she illustrates some of the difficulties encountered by priests who did not grasp the American experience, could not be understood in their homilies, had never counseled parishioners like those in American parishes, and had no idea how to raise funds. In such situations, some parishioners threaten to leave the church, but over time many of them are won over by these priests.[21]

Priests coming from other countries often struggle to adapt under less than ideal circumstances. As much as immigrant priests alleviate the pressing need for clergy, this strategy has its limits. The third Goodstein article reports on the view of bishops in countries with expanding pastoral needs of their own; they will require priests to meet those growing needs and will not be continuing indefinitely to send priests to the United States.[22] Current reports from parishioners corroborate many of these observations. So, while parishioners struggle with and appreciate foreign-born pastors, clergy from abroad represent a stopgap measure, not a solution to the need for priests in this country.

THE CULTURAL AND ECCLESIAL CONTEXT OF PASTORING

Contemporary cultural and ecclesial circumstances affect the role of pastors in profound ways. Some shifts are long term and will have an impact far into the future. First among them is the large number of immigrant Catholics, especially from Mexico and other Latin American countries, who are nearing majority status in the South and West. This increase alters not only the ethnic/racial composition of parishes but also other demographic features, such as younger average age, less formal education, and lessened economic potential. Effective pastoring requires an understanding of the culture and language of recent immigrants and their unique ministerial needs. These new members have a profound impact on religious education, faith formation, and social programs in established parishes.

A second ongoing development concerns relocation of Catholics within the United States. People are on the move. Some are leaving rural areas for suburbs and cities, as well as populating the South and Southwest in greater numbers than ever before. The rural-to-urban phenomenon touches most acutely the northern tier of states and the Midwest, as hundreds of rural parishes and schools are combined or abandoned. Rural parishes are clustered with one pastor because of a shortage of priests. Large cities are not immune to the decline in the number of priests. The original members of many inner-city ethnic parishes have vanished, and large parish churches stand empty as priests are reassigned to mega-size suburban parishes. These movements result in church resources being disproportionately distributed. Underutilized facilities, especially parish churches and schools, appear frequently in the North and Northeast, while the South, broadly speaking, suffers from a dearth of church infrastructure. Restructuring parish life is significantly different depending on location.

Other trends have immediate, and often powerful, impacts, some of which may be more enduring than others. Attitudes among Catholics, for example, differ mostly by generation and by the religious contexts in which people from various age groups were raised. Currently, the rift between generations has reached what most Catholics believe to be a point of serious concern. The divisions cut in many directions, including ecclesiological discord based on the experience of and esteem for Vatican II and on ethnic/racial differences and related spiritualities. Other attitudinal shifts, such as those related to life issues, a weakened economy, immigration, and various international hostilities and wars, exacerbate the rift. Since the election of Pope Francis in 2013, another potent force for change has entered into church life. From the beginning of his papacy, Francis's emphasis on becoming "a poor church for the poor" has had the potential to be transformative for those who hear his message and are willing to look at the world and the church in new ways. His writings have generated reasons for early divisions to fade into the background for those who are willing to create new contexts and look at new questions related to evangelization, the natural environment, and difficult life questions. For others, these new contexts and new methods have deepened the divide between priests and people oriented around a cultic view of priesthood and those more inclined to a servant leadership view. As in the past, these factors change from time to time; some will lessen in importance while others will grow, but all of them impinge on the pastoral life of the church at this time, as evidenced in the evolving characteristics of the leader.

Church Growth Through Immigration Accompanied by Changing Demographic Patterns

The long-term increase in church membership from forty-seven million in 1967 to seventy million in 2016 can be attributed largely to the continuous influx of immigrants arriving mainly from Latin America but also from Asia, the Pacific Islands, and Africa. This movement means that the Catholic population is growing in linguistic and cultural diversity, complicating contemporary ministry as new arrivals populate parishes throughout the country. These newly arrived people live and work and worship together with longtime residents and with established immigrants from the same backgrounds who are well integrated into American culture.

For newcomers, their religion is an important source of identity, and their ethnic and cultural backgrounds determine many of their choices. Immigrant Catholics are entering a church that is often unprepared to receive them; if the success story of the nineteenth century is to repeat itself in the years ahead, their pastoral care must be a high priority. Adapting the proclamation of the Gospel to their culture includes both respecting them and understanding their particular needs. Pastors are much more likely to succeed when they do not merely tolerate immigrants, but recognize and appreciate their contributions, their culture, and their aspirations. Developing this attitude requires education for all parishioners about immigration, the value of cultural pluralism, and the evil of prejudice. Strong communities evolve when pastoral leaders explain and suitably incorporate into regular worship services the spiritual traditions and practices of both old and new parish members. New immigrants often face another major issue: poverty. Large numbers of Latinos and others are suffering from the effects of educational deficiencies, language barriers, and problems of social adjustment. Effective pastoring takes these social issues into account as an integral part of ministering, which means both addressing the spiritual needs of immigrants and attending to the environment of poverty that often engulfs them, much in line with the desire of Pope Francis for movement in this direction.

While language and religious customs are obvious aspects of new immigrants to which pastoral ministry must respond, immigrants affect parishes in other ways. Their presence often means that people are younger, lower in educational levels, and employed in tenuous economic situations. These profiles differ from those of long-term members, who represent a greater proportion of the elderly with European ancestry who are economically well established. Instituting appropriate faith-formation programs for the new young congregants, facilitating cordial relationships, and developing shared goals between them and newer parishioners who are worlds apart are not easy tasks. They require considerable reflection and creativity on the part of pastors and their collaborators.

Pastors generally worry about the spiritual needs of young adults because pastoral services have tended to be family centered, providing faith formation and education for young children and parents, but little for those in between. Determining exactly how to attract young adults is a dilemma for many pastors. They are counting on younger priests, the newly ordained, to minister to parishioners who are closer in age to them. Yet these younger priests do not always share the views of younger, single Catholics on priesthood or the church. In situations where several parishes are located in close proximity or are cooperating for other purposes, pastoral staffs have successfully combined young adults into a single organization. Shared services of all kinds are becoming more accepted and have proven to be an effective pastoral strategy, especially for specialized ministries. In many cases, this practice is essential when the same pastor is responsible for more than one parish. Fortunately, pastoral training in seminaries and the interests of seminarians seem to recognize how essential it is to be moving in this direction.[23]

Survey responses about Catholic practices and attitudes reveal the effects of demographic changes on ministry. Data from the most recent comprehensive CARA research provide insights into how important it is to respondents to be a member of the Catholic Church, how meaningful they find the sacraments, and how significant it is that younger generations grow up as Catholics.

- Seventy-five percent strongly or somewhat agree that being Catholic is a very important part of who I am.
- Seventy-five percent strongly or somewhat agree that the sacraments of the church are essential to my relationship with God.
- Seventy-seven percent strongly or somewhat agree that it is very important to me that younger generations of my family grow up as Catholics.

This relatively positive profile is somewhat diminished by responses to the question about how often respondents attend religious services. Only 32 percent said they attend Mass once a week or more, 23 percent about once to three times a month, and 45 percent attend only a few times a year or never. These low attendance figures represent a significant challenge to pastors to find ways of engaging people in their faith beyond basic spiritual needs.[24] This problem becomes evident by comparing attendance with the degree to which Catholics value their membership (see table 4.1).[25]

The combined responses of those who said their membership was most important and among the most important thing in their lives (37 percent) parallels the number of Catholics who attend Mass once a week or more (32 percent). The level of importance had declined by 10 percent since the

TABLE 4.1
How important is being a member of the Catholic Church to you personally?

Level of importance	Percent
The most important part of your life	9
Among the most important parts of your life	28
Fairly important to you, but so are many other areas	40
Not terribly important to you	17
Not very important to you at all	5
Don't know/Refused	1

Source: William V. D'Antonio, Michele Dillon, and Mary L. Gautier, *American Catholics in Transition* (Lanham, MD: Rowman & Littlefield, 2013).

same question was reported in a 2008 CARA survey—the same survey that reported 57 percent saying if you miss Mass on Sunday it is not a sin.[26]

The importance assigned to various spiritual practices and religiously oriented activities also guides pastors as they make decisions about introducing or expanding programs to attract members. Respondents were asked about how important some beliefs and practices were to them (see table 4.2).[27]

In this survey of Catholics, helping the poor had the greatest importance at 68 percent, followed closely by the sacraments at 63 percent. Interestingly, the church's involvement with social justice ranks much lower at 34 percent, suggesting that it is not identified with the highly rated "helping the poor." Having a regular daily prayer life might indicate to pastors the usefulness of providing opportunities for parishioners to experience a variety of prayer forms. Pastoral leaders might help people reflect on the relationship between prayer and Scripture to increase Bible reading as a spiritual practice. Although this survey was conducted before the election of Pope Francis, commitment to the poor and needy fares well. Perhaps care for the environment would also appear as important, given the encouragement of Pope Francis through the 2015 publication of *Laudato Si' (Praise Be to You): On Care for Our Common Home.* Fidelity to church teachings related to abortion, same-sex marriage, and the death penalty rate only 30 to 40 percent as very important, but closer to 70 percent say

TABLE 4.2
As a Catholic, how important is each of the following to you?

Level of importance by % activity	Very important	Somewhat important	Not at all important	Don't know / Refused
Helping the poor	68	28	3	1
The sacraments, such as the Eucharist	63	26	10	1
Having a regular daily prayer life	47	38	15	1
The Catholic Church's teachings that oppose abortion	40	30	29	1
The Catholic Church's teachings that oppose same-sex marriage	35	26	38	<1
Church involvement in activities directed toward social justice	34	49	15	1
The teaching authority claimed by the Vatican	31	45	23	1
The Catholic Church's teachings that oppose the death penalty	30	41	28	1

Source: William V. D'Antonio, Michele Dillon, and Mary L. Gautier, *American Catholics in Transition* (Lanham, MD: Rowman & Littlefield, 2013).

it is very or somewhat important as a priority. While not the only source of insight, research of this nature offers information about the attitudes and perceptions of members that can be helpful in determining pastoral goals and planning ministerial programs.

Generational Differences in Attitudes Toward the Church

As the data above show, Catholics do not think alike, value the same things in the same way, or attach similar importance to accepted beliefs and spiritual practices. At this time in history, these divisions are especially sharp between generations. Based mostly on the religious contexts in which each was raised, these differences can seriously affect the vitality of the parish community and the type of pastoral services provided. In the 2013 study of American Catholics,[28] the authors divided the population into four generations:

- Pre–Vatican II—age seventy-one and older in 2011
- Vatican II—between ages fifty-one and seventy in 2011
- Post–Vatican II—between ages thirty-two and fifty in 2011
- Millennials—between ages eighteen and thirty-one in 2011

In 1987 (as shown in table 4.3, three right columns), 78 percent of adult Catholics had lived through Vatican II (31 percent pre–Vatican II plus 47 percent Vatican); in 2011, this combination yields only 43 percent. Relative to their familiarity with and understanding of the Council, just over 40 percent of Catholics have firsthand experience of Vatican II. The divergent experiences of the two groups result in conflicting views about many aspects of church life, including feelings about the importance of being Catholic and what it means to be identified as a Catholic.

- Pre–Vatican II—10 percent of adult Catholics, down 21 percent from twenty-five years ago
- Vatican II—33 percent, down 14 percent from twenty-five years ago
- Post–Vatican II—34 percent, up 12 percent from twenty-five years ago
- Millennials—23 percent, none of whom were adults, and some not yet born, twenty-five years ago

The strength of Catholic identity for each group (see Table 4.3, three columns on the left) is measured by level of agreement with statements such as "being Catholic is a very important part of who you are"; "it is important to you that younger generations of your family grow up as Catholics"; and "you can't imagine yourself being anything but Catholic."[29] According to these self-descriptions, older generations are much more highly identified with the church. The extremely low 7 percent of the youngest generation with a similar level of commitment is disquieting for pastors who even now need to look to the younger generation for leadership and support in their parishes. Because of the somewhat contradictory experiences of Catholics on either side of Vatican II, participation in parish life tends to be generationally defined. After only four years of the papacy of Pope

TABLE 4.3
Strength of Catholic identity by generation, 2005

	Strength of identity			Generational distribution (%)		
	Low (%)	Medium (%)	High (%)	1987	2005	2011
Pre–Vatican II	22	45	33	31	17	10
Vatican II	31	44	25	47	35	33
Post–Vatican II	27	50	24	22	40	34
Millennials	47	46	7	0	9	23
Total Catholics	29	46	24	100	100	100

Source: William V. D'Antonio, Michele Dillon, and Mary L. Gautier, *American Catholics in Transition* (Lanham, MD: Rowman & Littlefield, 2013).

Francis, some hope of emerging unity is evident, but even with such a charismatic leader, views on the teachings of the pope are not uniformly positive. To further complicate the pastoral challenge, the influx of new immigrants brings together young people who are infused with values from another culture with Americans in their own age bracket who have grown up differently.

Serving as Pastor of Multiple Parishes

For several generations, the declining number of priests has affected the ways pastors function. The erosion of the rural population, accompanied by a movement of people from cities to suburbs, is changing both suburbs and rural communities. Combined, these changes create a daunting problem of providing pastoral services—and indeed church buildings—in the places where they are most needed. In burgeoning suburbs, new parishes are building enormous churches for thousands of parishioners, unequaled in size in previous years. At the same time, small, far-flung parishes in rural areas are either clustering with nearby parishes or closing, as the number of parishioners declines and fewer priests are available to serve them. Although some rural dioceses have long had some priests staffing multiple parishes, it is fast becoming normative. Since priests may be assigned to a parish with ten thousand members or a cluster with three small churches, extraordinary flexibility is essential.

In 2005, the percentage of parishes being served by a priest with more than one parish stood at 44 percent (9,109); consequently, 20 percent (4,408) of the 22,302 active priests serving in parish ministry had multiple parish assignments.[30] In the past ten years, a considerable number of dioceses have increased their use of clustering parishes, with at least 55 percent of parishes now part of a cluster and 30 percent of priests pastoring several parishes. The use of clustering is happening in urban areas as well. With a larger, more condensed population, the tendency is to merge two or more parishes. Sometimes two worship sites remain open, but more often church property is sold and parishes consolidated into one facility. In situations where appropriate pastoral planning preceded these changes, people usually adapt fairly well. Experience shows that decisions made without adequate consultation almost always produce serious disruption.[31]

These three developments sample the cultural and ecclesial concerns defining the role of pastor. The growing immigrant population changes the composition of many parishes and thus demands attention to new issues of relationship, to the nature of liturgical experiences, and to the content of spiritual and educational programs. The movement of Catholics from rural to urban and especially suburban locations, together with the decrease in the number of priests, has caused massive reconfiguration of parish arrangements. Consequently, most pastors are now in charge of suburban mega-parishes or of several parishes, newly merged or clustered to respond to the lack of available priests. Further aggravating the situation is the retirement of a disproportionately large number of priests who are reaching the age of seventy. These factors are likely to have long-term consequences for the way pastors function. Finally, the current generational composition of Catholics and the variations in their commitment to the church further complicate the agenda for pastors.

ADAPTING TO NEW CONTEXTUAL AND MINISTERIAL CONCERNS

As pastors analyze their individual parishes, they usually find it necessary to adapt to changed circumstances. New patterns of relationships are developing as pastors find themselves in sometimes unfamiliar positions requiring new management and collaborative skills and fresh approaches to ministry. In some situations, more lay ecclesial ministers need to be hired; in other cases, the only answer to fewer priests is taking on additional parish assignments. Cognizant of these changes, both priests and bishops are taking actions to ensure the continuity of essential ministry for long-established parish members and for new arrivals.

Adapting to Structural Changes of Parishes

One of the major shifts identified above concerns the rearrangement of responsibilities for parishes. In rural areas, the continuing exodus has depleted the number of parishioners, leading to the formation of parish clusters or actual closing of churches. Today, more than half the parishes in the United States share a pastor. By contrast, the expanding suburban population requires mega-size parishes to accommodate the influx of parishioners. The fate of inner-city parishes depends on the density of the population, the proportion of Catholics, and local economic factors. Some are closed and the property sold; others are merged but sometimes keep two worship sites. As these changes occur, the viability of parochial schools and existence of other pastoral services can come into question or require dramatic rethinking.

Pastors may find themselves in any one of these situations, then be reassigned to another with quite different circumstances. They are expected to move readily from one setting to the next, usually without special preparation. In the study of priests serving multiple parishes, for example, only 10 percent reported participating in any formal program to prepare them for this type of assignment. The same could be said of those who move from a medium-sized parish to one with several thousand families. Priests generally use informal networks to prepare for the unanticipated challenges of new assignments, but many of them lament the absence of a more structured and informed transition. While the size of the parish, the number of staff, and access to resources vary widely, the desire for basic spiritual ministry remains constant—the celebration of the Eucharist and the sacraments, preaching and teaching about the faith, and maintaining the parish community. Even these foundational activities, however, manifest themselves differently in different settings. Active support for adjusting to new situations, especially by priests with little experience as an associate pastor, is becoming an urgent, and too often unaddressed, priority for continuing education. Moreover, virtually all the younger clergy are destined to be pastors, whether or not they are suited for the work. Diocesan priests rarely have the option of teaching or serving as an associate pastor for more than the first few years after ordination.

Since Vatican II, dioceses and parishes have put into operation some intermediary consultative bodies to assist with parish administration. A parish finance council, for example, is required by the Code of Canon Law, and bishops may mandate the establishment of parish pastoral councils. These advisory groups often provide considerable assistance to the pastor, especially to those who have limited administrative experience. Some lay organizations have come forward to assist with the development of these structures. Of particular note is the Leadership Roundtable,[32] a group that seeks to help further the mission of parishes. Toward that end, the organization has developed *Standards for Excellence* for parishes relative to management policies and procedures, human and financial resources, and financial and programmatic performance measures. Even with lay assistance, the implementation and effective use of councils vary widely. In some situations where mediating structures are most needed, pastors neglect them or allow them to collapse entirely, regardless of the bishops' mandates and lay assistance. By way of contrast, where parish consultative bodies are nourished and their responsibilities identified, where the *Standards of Excellence* are implemented, and where systems of accountability are in place, the positive effects on parish administration are readily visible and measurable.

Adapting to the Changing Composition of Parish Ministers

Closely associated with variations in types of parish assignments are the quality, number, and availability of staff. Generally, the larger the parish, the more staff are hired to fill specialized ministerial roles, including religious educators, liturgists, music ministers, pastoral care, and youth and adult education ministers. Medium-sized parishes and clusters of small parishes often have only a few staff who are responsible for general pastoral ministry; one-third of these smaller parishes have no hired staff but depend entirely on volunteers. According to a comprehensive study of lay parish ministers in 2005,[33] the composition of those working in parishes has changed rapidly in recent years. The proportion of women religious declined steeply from 41 percent in 1990 to 16 percent in 2005. In the 2012 CARA study,[34] the proportion was only 3 percent. From 1990 to 2005, the proportion of laywomen increased from 44 to 64 percent, but by 2012 it was reduced to 57 percent. Conversely, the proportion of laymen increased from 15 percent in 1990 to 20 percent in 2005, and by 2012 it was 31 percent. Deacons comprised 8 percent in 2012, and priests or religious brothers 4 percent.

These shifts can create challenges for pastors and the parishes they lead. Hiring more lay staff usually requires more salaries and benefits. Incorporating new staff also brings about changes in relationships, interpersonal dynamics, and the way a pastor organizes and carries out his work. As pastors move from a parish where they have one or two staff persons to a parish with ten or more staff members, the adjustment to a more administrative and supervisory role is challenging. Finding qualified staff in many rural areas adds to the difficulties, especially if the position involves travel to more than one parish.

The idea of collaboration, alien to or disliked by some younger pastors, creates even more awkward interactions. Yet the future will inevitably involve a significant amount of ministry carried out cooperatively with lay ministers. Several recent official documents on lay ecclesial ministry offer guidelines for programs and certification of lay ministers that will benefit lay ministers and clergy alike as they learn how to work together effectively in advancing the mission of the church.[35] Clearly, church leaders recognize an entirely different phase of availability of clergy. Collaboration with laity is not optional, because it is implausible that in the near future even minimally required numbers of priests will be available to fulfill all the pastoral needs that arise. Church policy as expressed in the Code of Canon Law concedes this position. Canon 517, part 2, states that the exercise of pastoral care may be entrusted to someone other than a priest.[36] In recent years, the number of parish life coordinators, who take primary responsibility for the pastoral care of a parish in the absence of a resident priest, has increased to 477, and this position is but one of many expanded roles for laity.

Adapting to the Changing Composition of Parish Members

Unlike fifty years ago, members in most parishes today come from a wide variety of backgrounds with diverse characteristics. No feature is more prevalent or more powerful a force than the ethnic/racial mix resulting from immigration. For most pastors, the multicultural parishes resulting from this movement require coping with cultural differences for which they received no specialized education. That situation is beginning to change, as seminaries increasingly require students to study Spanish, with the goal of acquiring sufficient proficiency to celebrate Mass and the sacraments for Spanish-speaking parishioners. Understanding other immigrant groups and their cultural practices, particularly those related to spirituality, is more complicated. Both pastors and seminarians would benefit from exposure to well-functioning multicultural parishes and continuing education programs designed to enhance this aspect of ministry, but few convenient opportunities exist. The USCCB office for catechesis and inculturation has tackled the problem and offers six suggestions to pastors for unifying a diverse parish:[37]

- Know the backgrounds of all parishioners and the differences in needs of various generations and cultures.
- Set up a multicultural advisory committee reflecting the diversity of the parish, and consult it before making decisions that affect each group.
- Work for the complementarity of cultures by establishing procedures that treat all people equally and fairly, with dignity and respect.
- Develop structures, with the help of the advisory committee, to deal with cultural tensions by airing difficulties and addressing them publicly.
- Encourage conversation and interaction outside of liturgy to help bridge cultural chasms.
- Listen without judging or comparing or offering solutions.

Recent USCCB statistics highlight the magnitude of ethnic/cultural diversification in parishes. In 2006, of the 69.1 million Catholics,[38] 26.4 million (38 percent) were Hispanic, 2.3 million (3 percent) were African American, almost half-a-million were Native American (1 percent), and somewhere between 2 and 5 percent were Asian (no hard data on numbers are available).[39] By 2013, there were 69.4 million Catholics,[40] and a new report by CARA showed the following estimates relative to ethnic backgrounds: 30.4 million (43.8 percent) were Hispanic; 3.0 million (4.3 percent) were African American; 0.55 million (0.8 percent) were Native American; and 3 million (4.3 percent) were Asian.[41] These four groups combined comprise about 50 percent of the Catholic population in both years, underscoring the urgent need to modify pastoral services to respond effectively to this diverse population.

Actions to Be Taken by Priests

Considering the manifold responsibilities of a pastor, certain changes in patterns and policies seem advisable for the sake of both the individual priest and the ministry. Research on priests serving multiple parishes and subsequent consultations with numerous presbyterates on the results surfaced some constructive ideas for coping with the demanding role of pastor. Though the causes of the pressures and tensions differ among pastors who serve in different settings, the recommendations have relevance for all pastors.

On a personal level, pastors universally agreed on the importance of taking time to pray, exercise, and relax, but this advice is not well heeded. Priests know they should make time for prayer and spiritual growth, health issues, and rest and relaxation, yet lacking adequate assistance makes it difficult to attend to these needs without limiting their response to demands for ministerial service, an option most pastors would not accept as viable. Some of them said that it was rare to get a good night's sleep even once a week and difficult to take a day off each week. Having a vacation of more than a few days was nearly impossible. An indefatigable worker-priest said he wanted to "add more hours to the day and more days to the week—though not realistic, it is truly a need. I would love to have preparation time, time for planning/visioning, and time to cultivate friendships, but all I do is work." Less experienced pastors believe they are not very effective at organizing their time and balancing what they do—a skill the long-term pastors usually develop at least to some degree.

One of the best antidotes to overworking is to delegate appropriate responsibilities to staff or volunteers. The status of lay ecclesial ministers varies widely, from full-time professionally trained ministers and financial managers to part-time janitors and unpaid volunteers. In rural areas, where priests often pastor more than one parish, only about two-thirds have even part-time staff, so organizing volunteers is essential. Finding persons with the necessary skills in relatively unpopulated areas is difficult. By comparison, pastors of very large urban parishes may have plenty of staff, but organizing the work and fostering collaboration among them challenges these priests. Some, but not all, pastors would like another priest or perhaps a deacon to serve with them so they would have additional help with sacramental ministry, someone to confer with on a daily or regular basis, and more companionship. Realistically, most pastors realize that laypeople are more likely to be their primary resource, for which most express gratitude and satisfaction.

Another strategy for pastors is to focus time and attention on ministries reserved to priests—in particular, preparing well for Eucharistic celebrations and the administration of sacraments. While that approach has merit, being a pastor still requires attention to countless other matters. Many pastors may desire to do less administration and attend fewer meetings, but that is unlikely because of either the cost or the availability of support staff. Priests serving multiple parishes would prefer to spend less time on the road so they could have more contact with parishioners, but when nearly half of them need to travel more than five hundred miles a month just to reach their parishes, that solution is not feasible. Given the difficulties in altering these basic realities, some pastors believe they have to renegotiate expectations, even when parishioners are reluctant or unhappy about embracing lay ministers who are prepared to carry out pastoral responsibilities. The demands of some parishioners remain unrealistic, and lowering expectations may happen only gradually over time. Eventually, they will realize the pastor's limitations and get used to sharing a priest with other parishes or to being part of a very large parish. In some instances, more direct intervention on the part of diocesan leadership will be necessary to speed the process of adapting expectations to the current reality.

Practices to Be Initiated or Improved by Bishops

Although pastors have reasonable control over the way ministry is exercised in their parishes, bishops and other diocesan leaders contribute significantly to their effectiveness as pastors. When asked about what bishops could do to assist them, the nearly one thousand priests who responded to an open-ended written survey, and hundreds of others who responded verbally, identified several issues. The primary task for bishops, they said, was to lead planning efforts for the diocese. In particular, they were concerned about the ways parishes are closed, combined, or merged for administrative purposes and pastoral care. In dioceses where extensive planning included widespread consultation, new parish configurations were much more readily accepted; the reverse was true when such care was not taken. The consequences of inadequate planning for pastors who need to work in these situations are often problematic. Pastors want bishops to offer encouragement, show appreciation, and get to know firsthand the dynamics of parish ministry.

Encouragement can take many forms. Some pastors expressed the need for clear guidelines so that parishioners can correctly understand what they can expect of a priest.[42] Expectations must be lowered, for example, in matters related to Mass schedules, attendance at meetings, and other pastoral services. Some ministries a priest must perform, and others can be delegated to lay pastoral ministers. Especially for pastors in rural areas who have least access to substitutes for weekend assistance, having a diocesan office organize priests who might be available for weekend help would ease the burden of multiple Masses on weekends. Many pastors would like to see greater efforts to recruit priests, including those from other countries, and to be more proactive about vocations. In either case, they offered a caution: find suitable priests and seminarians who will fit with the culture and needs of the particular diocese, not invite anyone willing to show up. Finally, because they recognize the value of lay ecclesial ministers, priests want dioceses to recruit and educate them, make opportunities available that are affordable and accessible, and help address the need for just salaries for lay staff members.

A long-neglected function at the diocesan level is to provide continuing education for priests. In 2001, the U.S. bishops prepared *The Basic Plan for the Ongoing Formation of Priests*, intended primarily for diocesan priesthood. The plan provides a general description of the kinds of ongoing formation needed to enhance the integration of priestly identity and the tasks of pastoral ministry; it also outlines formation at different stages of priesthood and discusses some of the practical possibilities for formation. In an article about the plan,[43] the author identifies reasons, already mentioned in this essay, for requiring ongoing formation: a diminishing number of priests and more complex circumstances; divisions in presbyterates, based especially on age and formational backgrounds; fluidity and polarization in the post–Vatican II church; priestly identity, with many ministries and many ministers; international priests and multiculturalism; social shifts and realignments of church resources; and the new evangelization. These and other realities of twenty-first-century church life make renewal and continuing education all the more urgent.[44]

While programs of ongoing formation take a variety of forms, bishops are sometimes unable or unwilling to provide needed human and financial resources so priests can take advantage of offerings. Finding temporary pastoral help is the key obstacle to pastors' being able to take a sabbatical or participate in extended formation activities. Beyond these organizational concerns is the more perplexing fact that priests vary in their interest in participating in ongoing formation, whether because of excessive workloads, lack of money, resistance to new learning, or other personal factors.

Finally, one of the most uncomfortable topics concerning bishops is their role in the evaluation of pastors. Taking into consideration the resistance of some priests to assessment, fair and evenhanded evaluations serve the good of the whole church. Even those bishops who see the value and express interest in the evaluation process find that lack of time prohibits effective implementation. Some bishops, however, make evaluation a priority. For example, Bishop Ricardo Ramirez of Las Cruces, New Mexico, writes:

> I now send forms to all those involved in parish leadership, including the pastor, and ask for a self-evaluation of their ministries. These are compiled at the pastoral center. During the parish visit I read them their self-evaluation and have an extended discussion on the various aspects of their parish life. I usually ask a lot of questions, and the people provide what then helps me formulate a fairly thorough assessment of the parish. I am sure many other bishops conduct their parish visits in their own dialogical manner.[45]

Priests who undertake various forms of self-evaluation and parish assessment are usually satisfied, even delighted, by the outcome of these activities. Rather than receiving unwarranted criticism, they learn of their parishioners' broad appreciation, and they discover areas for improvement that enable them to grow in and deepen their pastoral leadership. Sometimes those who could benefit most are fearful not only of negative feedback but also of the need to make changes they are unwilling or unable to make.

SUMMARY AND CONCLUSIONS

The basic facts about how much the church and parish life have changed in recent years escape almost no one who is an active Catholic or an observer of Catholicism. In the twenty-first century, Catholic ministry is fashioned by priests and their coworkers who serve as lay ecclesial ministers, by those who receive their services, by the decisions of bishops locally and nationally, and by the demographic, attitudinal, and other factors that affect the context within which they minister. It is impressive to see the positive way in which most parishioners, priests, and parish staffs have adapted to personnel changes, new parish configurations, demographic and cultural change, and the generational revolution. The grace and magnanimity with which pastors and parishioners open their hearts and their doors to new members of diverse cultural backgrounds, different religious tendencies, various educational levels, and all ages is encouraging news for the future of Catholicism in the United States.

Equally heartening is the willingness of many priests during this time of change and disorientation to live with an expectation of improvement in their lives and ministries, depending on parishioners and bishops to participate with them in a process of renewal. They believe, at minimum, that certain unpopular topics must be discussed, particularly the ordination of married men to the priesthood, but also the ordination of women to the diaconate. They are cognizant of the need to provide continuing education for priests so that they learn how to utilize more effectively the assistance of lay ecclesial ministers and deacons, become knowledgeable regarding methods to improve their pastoral service, and pay more attention to their own spiritual and personal needs. They understand that priests who are coming from other countries need to become acquainted in formal, structured ways with the spirituality and culture of the United States, and that bishops and priests must incorporate them more fully into the diocesan milieu. They aspire to be honored partners with their bishops and superiors, not branch managers of parishes. The committed, clear-eyed realism and steady hope of these priests are gifts to the church.

At the same time, there are reasons for concern about the future of pastoral ministry. During decades of rapid and disorienting change, many bonds of trust have been tested and even broken, sometimes resulting in polarization and acrimony in parts of the church. Culture wars, internal church squabbles, and taking sides on nonessential issues have eroded community and point to the need for reconciliation on many levels. Perhaps the most serious cause for alienation of priests results from the sexual abuse scandal. Not only has the misconduct of some priests tainted the reputation of all priests, but in some dioceses priests feel a lack of support from their bishops. The divide between younger and older priests in their views of priesthood and the church is destructive, sometimes preventing parishes and other ministries from thriving. The "larger than life" misconceptions each generation of priests holds of the other need to be dealt with directly in face-to-face, sustained conversations that foster a lived sense of fraternity and mutual understanding. As well, pastors are concerned about Catholics who are not practicing their faith on a regular basis or in fact may be "unchurched." They worry equally about how well future generations will understand the basics of their faith.

Responding to these challenges requires personal conversion, reconciliation, and actions at the institutional level. These must take place against a horizon taking into account the "bigger picture" of what the church is to be in the world—namely, bringing about God's kingdom by working against suffering and hatred, division and fear.

In the midst of all these challenges, many effective pastors have found successful ways to minister to a growing and diverse Catholic population. They live exemplary lives of prayer and service as they cope with unprecedented change. They minister to enormously diverse parishioners, some of whom are deeply committed to their faith while others scarcely identify themselves as Catholic and yet expect to be married, have their children baptized, and be buried in the church. More and more priests serve as pastors of several parishes, while others are being asked to administer expansive complexes with large staffs.

All of these changes suggest the idea of initiating a "summit on pastoring" where the new circumstances can be examined and creative thinking can help direct the development of guidelines for truly excellent pastoring attuned to the conditions of the times. It is a worthy task, for what is at stake is developing and maintaining vital Catholic communities of faith. As such, this task demands extraordinary relationships and informed decisions among bishops and parishioners, pastors and their coworkers.

In recent years, the election of Pope Francis has provided new encouragement for pastors to adapt their ministry according to his thoughts, which so closely resemble the concerns of thriving pastors. In his first statements as pope, Francis specified the key dimension of the ministry he desires: "This is what I want, a poor church for the poor." Since then, he has challenged leaders to be certain that they bring alive this aspiration in order to be effective evangelizers. He says that priests must be infused with this central message of care for the poor so as to be servant leaders for all the people of God. Especially in *The Joy of the Gospel* (*Evangelii Gaudium*), the pope has expressed in clear terms his expectations for change in the focus of pastoring:

> The parish is not an outdated institution; precisely because it possesses great flexibility, it can assume quite different contours depending on the openness and missionary creativity of the pastor and the community. . . . This presumes that it really is in contact with the homes and the lives of its people, and does not become a useless structure out of touch with people or a self-absorbed group made up of a chosen few. The parish is the presence of the Church in a given territory, an environment for hearing God's word, for growth in the Christian life, for dialogue, proclamation, charitable outreach, worship and celebration.[46]

Pope Francis specifies that some attitudes that represent "insidious worldliness" must change:

> In some people we see an ostentatious preoccupation for the liturgy, for doctrine and for the Church's prestige, but without any concern that the Gospel have a real impact on God's faithful people and the concrete needs of the present time. . . . The mark of Christ, incarnate, crucified and risen, is not present; closed and elite groups are formed, and no effort is made to go forth and seek out those who are distant or the immense multitudes who thirst for Christ. Evangelical fervor is replaced by the empty pleasure of complacency and self-indulgence.[47]

Pope Francis cuts through false piety and places the emphasis on a ministry of leadership that reaches out to the needs of Catholics in the church today. These ideas, if taken seriously, will transform pastors and will be a great grace for all the faithful.

NOTES

1. E. Brooks Holifield, *God's Ambassadors: A History of the Christian Clergy in America* (Grand Rapids, MI: Eerdmans, 2007), 348–349.
2. *Official Catholic Directory*, 2016.
3. Earlier published reports indicate the average age was sixty-one in 2002–2003. *Los Angeles Times* Survey of Priests, October 21, 2002, sec. A; Dean R. Hoge and Jacqueline Wenger, *Evolving Visions of the Priesthood: Changes from Vatican II to the Turn of the New Century* (Collegeville, MN: Liturgical Press, 2003), 19–21, 200.
4. Exceptions to the requirement of celibacy are rare, but may be made for those ordained in another tradition, usually Episcopalian, who are converts to Roman Catholicism. This relatively new policy took effect in 1980.
5. Data for earlier years for diocesan priests are from *Annuarium Statisticum Ecclesiae*. Estimated total ordination numbers for religious are 7,200 between 1966 and 1985 (360 per year) and 4,200 between 1986 and 2005 (210 per year). Between 2006 and 2016 an average of 503 priests were ordained, including both diocesan and religious. In sum, all priests ordained from 1966 to 1985 averaged 1,060 per year; from 1986 to 2005 averaged 640 per year; and 2006 to 2016 averaged 503 per year. CARA data on Catholic ministry formation enrollments show annual enrollment of diocesan seminarians averaged 1,575 fewer in the second two decades than in the first two. Annual enrollment of religious-order seminarians averaged 1,430 fewer in the second two decades than in the first two.
6. Hoge and Wenger, *Evolving Visions of the Priesthood*, especially chap. 3, "The Shifting Emphasis in Ecclesiology," 47–59.
7. Hoge and Wenger, *Evolving Visions of the Priesthood*, 113.
8. Dean R. Hoge, *The First Five Years of the Priesthood* (Collegeville, MN: Liturgical Press, 2002), 171. This study showed that 12 percent of diocesan priests found the disagreements to be a great problem and 30 percent found them to be somewhat of a problem.
9. Hoge and Wenger, *Evolving Visions of the Priesthood*, 113–114.
10. Dean R. Hoge, William D. Dinges, Mary Johnson, and Juan L. Gonzales, Jr., *Young Adult Catholics* (Notre Dame, IN: University of Notre Dame Press, 2001); and William V. D'Antonio, James D. Davidson, Dean R. Hoge, and Mary L. Gautier, *American Catholics Today: New Realities of Their Faith and Their Church* (Lanham, NJ: Rowman & Littlefield, 2007).
11. Thomas P. Rausch, *Priesthood Today: An Appraisal* (New York: Paulist Press, 1992), 21. See also Thomas P. Rausch, "Priesthood in the Church of Tomorrow," *Origins* 27 (1997): 369–375.
12. Rausch, *Priesthood Today*, 22.
13. Rausch, *Priesthood Today*, 26–33.

14. Marti R. Jewell and David A. Ramey, *The Changing Face of Church: Emerging Models of Parish Leadership* (Chicago: Loyola Press, 2010). The authors and other leaders gathered data by conducting eleven symposiums with some eight hundred people, surveying more than three thousand others in writing and by phone, meeting with bishops in focus groups, and carrying out diocesan consultations. The six organizations involved were the National Association for Lay Ministry, the Conference for Pastoral Planning and Council Development, the National Association of Church Personnel Administrators, the National Association of Diaconate Directors, the National Catholic Young Adult Ministry Association, and the National Federation of Priests' Councils.

15. Blase Cupich, "The Emerging Models of Pastoral Ministry Project: The Theological, Sacramental and Ecclesial Context," *Origins* 38 (2008): 1–10.

16. Dean R. Hoge and Aniedi Okure, *International Priests in America* (Collegeville, MN: Liturgical Press, 2006), 1–9.

17. Center for Applied Research in the Apostolate, *Catholic Ministry Formation Enrollments: Statistical Overview for 2007–2008*, 12–13.

18. Hoge and Okure, *International Priests*, 22.

19. Laurie Goodstein, "Serving U.S. Parishes, Fathers Without Borders," *New York Times*, December 28, 2008, https://www.nytimes.com/2008/12/28/us/28priest.html; Laurie Goodstein, "In America for a Job, a Kenya Priest Finds a Home," *New York Times*, December 29, 2008, https://www.nytimes.com/2008/12/29/us/29priest.html; and Laurie Goodstein, "India, an Exporter of Priests, May Keep Them," *New York Times*, December 30, 2008, https://www.nytimes.com/2008/12/30/us/30priest.html. http://www.nytimes.com/.2008/12/28/us/28priest.html?sq=Goodstein.

20. Goodstein, "Serving U.S. Parishes."

21. Goodstein, "In America for a Job."

22. Goodstein, "India, an Exporter of Priests."

23. See Katarina Schuth, *Seminary Formation: Recent History, Current Circumstances, New Directions* (Collegeville, MN: Liturgical Press, 2016).

24. William V. D'Antonio, Michele Dillon, and Mary L. Gautier, *American Catholics in Transition* (Lanham, MD: Rowman & Littlefield, 2013), question 16, 172.

25. D'Antonio et al., *American Catholics in Transition*, question 14, 171.

26. Mark M. Gray and Paul M. Perl, *Sacraments Today: Belief and Practice Among U.S. Catholics* (Washington, DC: Center for Applied Research in the Apostolate, 2008), 48.

27. D'Antonio et al., *American Catholics in Transition*, 167.

28. D'Antonio et.al., *American Catholics in Transition*, 166.

29. Gray and Perl, *Sacraments Today*, 102.

30. Katarina Schuth, *Priestly Ministry in Multiple Parishes* (Collegeville, MN: Liturgical Press, 2006), 3. The data for this study involved examining the role of

each priest in the United States. In 2016, only estimates are available for the proportion of parishes being served by a priest with more than one parish and the proportion of priests in such situations.

31. Among the many dioceses engaged in parish reorganization in the past few years are Boston; Camden, New Jersey; Manchester, New Hampshire; Portland, Maine; Chicago; Detroit; St. Cloud and New Ulm, Minnesota; and many California dioceses. Others, such as Dubuque, Iowa, and Green Bay, Wisconsin, have been moving in this direction for years.

32. The Leadership Roundtable (previously known as the National Leadership Roundtable on Church Management), established in 2005, "promotes excellence and best practices in management, finances and human resource development of the Catholic Church in the U.S. by incorporation of the expertise of the laity." It is dedicated to helping individual Catholic dioceses, parishes, and nonprofits.

33. David DeLambo, *Lay Parish Ministers: A Study of Emerging Leadership* (National Pastoral Life Center, 2005), 19.

34. Mark M. Gray, *Perspectives from Parish Leaders: U.S. Parish Life and Ministry*, August 15, 2012, https://cara.georgetown.edu/CARAServices/Parish%20Leaders%20Phase%20Two.pdf, 16.

35. Committee on the Laity of the United States Conference of Catholic Bishops (USCCB), *Co-Workers in the Vineyard of the Lord: A Resource for Guiding the Development of Lay Ecclesial Ministry* (USCCB, 2005). The publications *National Certification Standards for Lay Ecclesial Ministers Serving as Parish Catechetical Leaders, Youth Ministry Leaders, Pastoral Associates, and Parish Life Coordinators* and *The National Certification Standards for Pastoral Ministers* are other resources to assist in setting goals for the formation and certification of those who are completing formation programs.

36. Canon 517.2: "If, because of a *lack* of *priests*, the *diocesan bishop* has *decided* that *participation* in the *exercise* of the *pastoral care* of a *parish* is to be *entrusted* to a *deacon*, to another *person* who is not a *priest*, or to a *community* of *persons*, he is to *appoint* some *priest* who, *provided* with the *powers* and *faculties* of a *pastor*, is to *direct* the *pastoral care*."

37. Daniel Mulhall, "Building Inclusive Communities: How Do You Take Distinct Cultural Communities and Nationalities and Make Them Into One Parish?" *America* 196 (2007): 20–22.

38. *Official Catholic Directory*, 2006.

39. United States Conference of Catholic Bishops, *Catholic Information Project: The Catholic Church in America—Meeting Real Needs in Your Neighborhood*, August 2006.

40. *Official Catholic Directory*, 2013.

41. Mark Gray, *Cultural Diversity in the Catholic Church in the United States* (Washington, DC: Center for Applied Research in the Apostolate, October 2016), 6.

42. Many priests mentioned the need for a review of the Code of Canon Law as it pertains to parishes and pastors, especially as found in book II, part II, section II, title III: The Internal Ordering of Particular Churches.

43. J. Cletus Kiley, "Human Development and the Ongoing Formation of Priests," *Origins* 30 (2001) 644–647.

44. Both the National Federation of Priests' Councils (NFPC) and the National Organization for the Continuing Education of Roman Catholic Clergy (NOCERCC) have addressed the promise and problems of actualizing these plans. In a series of articles, priests addressed the reasons for supporting ongoing formation: (1) to develop the priest spiritually and intellectually; (2) to reinforce attitudes, values, and behaviors that form a healthy culture with and within the presbyterate as a whole; (3) to prepare priests for increasingly complex church structures, such as serving multiple parishes or megaparishes; (4) to assist priests coming from other countries to integrate successfully into American culture; (5) to attend to the life stages and the unique demands and needs accompanying them; and (6) to seek a balance of life in order to stay healthy physically, emotionally, and spiritually.

45. Bishop Ricardo Ramirez, "Dialogue in Diocesan Pastoral Life," *Origins* 36 (2006): 193.

46. Pope Francis, *The Joy of the Gospel* (New York: Image, 2013), 28.

47. Pope Francis, *The Joy of the Gospel*, 95.

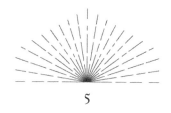

5

A Pluriform Unity

A HISTORIAN'S VIEW OF THE CONTEMPORARY CHURCH

Joseph P. Chinnici

INTRODUCTION

Now that the Council is over, the real work has begun: transmitting
the spirit and letter of the Council into reality in the life and structure
of the Church. Everyone who wants to have a serious part in that work
needs a steady supply of independent and reliable information in depth
about the events and ideas, both in Rome and around the world, which
shape the renewal and reform.

These words, written by the Jesuit Daniel O'Hanlon to a layman in
Baldwin, New York, one year after the closure of the Second Vatican
Council (1962–1965), capture in large part the task that lay before the
Catholic community in the United States in December 1966.[1] The author
refers to "events and ideas" that would "shape" the ensuing "renewal and
reform." He talks about transmission, the embodiment of "spirit and letter"
into "the life and structures of the Church." Sustaining the Council meant
changing attitudes and creating the ritual forms and social networks that
shaped people's lives. A communications officer at the Council, O'Hanlon
knew the challenges and opportunities of this implementation firsthand.
It was birthed in the religious experience of the Council, and he and his
cohorts believed that a fairly unified conciliar vision had emerged. The
Holy Spirit seemed to be acting in a new way, crossing boundaries, asking
people to open horizontal lines of communication, to risk the familiar
patterns of acting so as "to create new structures" that "used the full

talents of all, especially those of lesser rank." One expression of the new pathway would be an ecumenical spirituality, a unifying responsiveness to the Word of God so as to accomplish the "mission of Christ to the world." The new pathway of ecumenism and a new identity for Catholicism in the modern world had opened up. It did not quite turn out the way Daniel O'Hanlon expected.

Just over thirty years later, in the late summer of 1996, the American Catholic community and the public at large were exposed to a very unusual and intense disagreement between two ranking prelates in the church, Joseph Cardinal Bernardin of Chicago (1928–1996) and Bernard Cardinal Law of Boston (1931–2017). In many respects, they had similar career trajectories as administrators, bishops, archbishops, and cardinals. They were men of the same generation who helped implement the Council. Both were chosen to be bishops by Pope Paul VI; both were sensitive to and promoters of solid ecumenical relationships. Yet they disagreed as to the interpretation of the Council and its implementation; they disagreed about the state of the church in the United States; they disagreed about the methodology to be used to bridge the severe divides that had opened up not only within the church but within society as a whole. Cardinal Bernardin, the inheritor of a conciliar vision focused on lay participation, dialogue, and social engagement, saw one path forward in the midst of severe polarization: the "invitation to a revitalized Catholic common ground," an open public space that encompassed all—"whether centrists, moderates, liberals, radicals, conservatives, or neoconservatives—who are willing to reaffirm basic truths and to pursue their disagreements in a renewed spirit of dialogue." Cardinal Law, a man of different temperament and a different interpretation of the problems of polarization, responded: "The Church already has 'common ground.' It is found in sacred Scripture and tradition, and it is mediated to us through the authoritative and binding teaching of the magisterium. The disconnect that is so often found today between that Catholic common ground and faith and practice of some Catholics is alarming." Around the two cardinals stood companions among the bishops, priests, religious, and laity of the Catholic community committed to defending and promoting their public spokesmen. Each side marshaled for their causes networks of like-minded people, publications, and institutions.[2]

This open debate only foreshadowed other public disagreements that would occupy the church in the United States as it moved well into the first two decades of the twenty-first century. From 2000 to 2017, public arguments have surfaced in almost every field of church life: the amount of diversity that could be allowed in the church; the restoration of the Latin Mass; the reception of communion by politicians who in any way supported a woman's right to choose; the lifestyle and commitments of women religious; the legalization of gay marriage; the speech of an American president at a premier Catholic University; the interpretation of religious liberty in the "Fortnight for Freedom."[3] Most recent debates have centered around the pastoral policies and approaches of Pope Francis.[4] The bewildered observer can only ask: How did this all come about, and what does it mean for the church of the twenty-first century?

In what follows, I would like to outline a few of the fundamental transformations that have occurred in American Catholicism during the past forty-five years, and particularly those that have led to the current pluriformity in the church both in its internal life and in its external engagements. Because this historical field of inquiry is so vast, some methodological limits need to be mentioned. First, there will be no attempt here to present a complete picture of the postconciliar history that has led us to the present moment—no comprehensive analysis of the multitude of movements, people, and positions that have evolved in the past many decades. Instead, I would like to focus the argument by concentrating on one key conciliar theme, ecumenism, and how its development has exemplified the changing contours of Catholic identity. I believe that this ecumenical common story will in fact illuminate other analogous developments in the church's public life and internal pluriformity. But the interpretation presented here surely must be tentative because the research involved is still developing and there are no secondary studies encompassing the entire field.

Second, since the essay is focused on tracing change through a public institutional lens, it will assume as an illuminating historical parallel the interpretive framework outlined for the field of communications by Paul Starr. In *The Creation of the Media*, Starr notes how "triggering events" engender "constitutive moments" when significant new institutional choices are made and established "cultural patterns" are broken. Over time, these new choices create pathways of activity in law, technologies, networks of relationships, and constellations of power that branch out in numerous directions to influence other choices.[5] As applied to this essay, the ecumenical commitment of the Second Vatican Council triggered a "constitutive moment" that required choices to "encode" the event and its experience. These choices created significant new institutional pathways in the "constitutive period" from the close of the Council in 1965 to 1976. As the choices "branched out" into the church in the subsequent stages of the reception of the Council, they interfaced with new cultural, political, and economic forces. Another "constitutive moment," the legalization of abortion in 1973, engendered the rise of countermovements designed to limit the impact and balance the initial ecumenical moves toward similarity. As a result, the community publicly splintered in numerous divergent directions. It is the contention here that the ramifications of these choices, their establishment, their acceptance, and their splintering, will be felt well into the twenty-first century. It is this new pluriform reality that now calls for a new style of leadership under Pope Francis (2013–present) as he confronts a now globalized pluriform Catholic Church.

Third, in this essay I am particularly interested in changes within the church as they will continue to shape future developments in the "public" church in its relationship to American society.[6] For the historian, this demands that he be not simply analytic and interpretive, but also predictive. What is needed is not only a description of the immediate conciliar event, or simply an account of its contentious aftermath, but as much as possible an initial understanding of the fundamental trajectories of the *longue durée*.[7] How did the Council and its reception shift the deep structures, received organizational and ritual patterns, and basic attitudes of the community in such a way as to mark a new epoch in religious history, an epoch that has long-term social significance and lasting public impact?

It is within these defined orientations that I will concentrate in this essay on the shift in the balance between similarity and difference as expressed in the new religious and social practices associated with ecumenism. The essay will examine in chronological order, first, the constitutive phase of conciliar renewal, 1965–1976; second, the struggle for the control of public space, 1976–1988; and third, the advent of pluriformity, 1989–2013.[8] I will conclude with some comments related to the pontificate of Pope Francis and the challenge of both American and global pluriformity.

THE CONSTITUTIVE PHASE
OF CONCILIAR RENEWAL, 1965–1976

Beginning with a Religious Practice

Mary Carter approached the altar rail at her daughter's baptism and was startled to hear the priest ask, "Where's Bruce?" Her husband, an Episcopalian, had stayed in the pew, assuming he should not receive communion.

"Bruce belongs up here, too," said the priest.

"That was really quite a thrilling experience for me to feel called into that community in that fashion," remembers Bruce.[9]

This small vignette about a Catholic wife, her Protestant husband, and an accommodating priest, along with a host of similar stories, appeared in a prominent popular magazine in April 1984. The entire report became a *cause célébre*, dropping as it did into the contentious atmosphere created by the initial Roman investigation of pastoral practices in the Archdiocese of Seattle in November 1983. Even though Archbishop Raymond Hunthausen had already issued "extensive instructions" limiting the reception of communion by non-Catholics at Catholic services, technically referred to as "intercommunion," it appeared from the magazine article that the practice had come to be routine in many quarters of the church in the Northwest: at marriage encounters, a Catholic press convention, hospitals, Sunday Eucharists, baptisms, funerals, weddings, and first communions.

The practice could not help but be contentious; it symbolized the difficult course of the development of the church in the United States after the Council. On the one hand, following the initial conciliar emphasis, the Archdiocese of Seattle, like many others in the United States, established an Ecumenical and Inter-Religious Affairs Commission with an explicit goal of fostering "occasions for shared prayer and worship," theological dialogue, and education. One of its explicit goals was to stimulate "collaboration in whatever enables human development and a more just society."[10] Expanding a church in the great unchurched Northwest had called for a particular type of openness to social and ecclesial communion with others. In the spring of 1984, responding to the article about intercommunion, the archbishop reiterated in several letters that the practice should not be common but exceptional, allowed only under specific circumstances and with stated permissions. Still, in allowing intercommunion, he understood himself to be standing on solid ground as he appealed to the Vatican's *Directorium Oecumenicum* (May 14, 1967) and the June 1, 1972 Instruction, "On Admitting Other Christians to Eucharistic Communion in the Catholic Church."

On the other hand, for some in the archdiocese, intercommunion had become one of the many issues that deeply disturbed them about current church developments. They felt that a loss of public and specifically Catholic identity was at stake. What were the boundaries of what it meant to be Catholic? It was their local complaints about a host of pastoral practices that had initiated the original apostolic visitation of Seattle. For them, intercommunion had become subsumed into a larger pattern of postconciliar changes that seemed to imply the dissolution of a corporate public theological and juridical unity—the preferred role of individual conscience in moral decision making, the sequencing of first communion and first confession, general absolution in the rite of reconciliation, sacramental communion after divorce and remarriage, the more active and participative role of women in the church, the shaping of church doctrine and practice through democratic consultation.[11] Their interpretation appeared to be supported by the new emphasis on a distinctive Catholic doctrinal and pastoral integrity that was being encouraged by many others in the United States and throughout the world. On September 30, 1985, the Prefect of the Sacred Congregation for the Doctrine of the Faith in Rome wrote Archbishop Hunthausen and again called attention to the widespread practice of intercommunion: "The Catholic Church believes the Eucharist to be a sign of unity already achieved. Routine intercommunion on the occasion of weddings or funerals, wherever it is the practice, should be recognized as clearly abusive and an impediment to genuine ecumenism." The Sacred Congregation carefully called attention to abuses, but it did not completely reject the practice. Apparently, what was at stake in the controversy were many different assessments of the public boundary lines and internal church order separating Catholics from their neighbors.

Interpreting the Practice

The Catholic community in its authoritative pronouncements, rituals, pastoral practices, and social outreach—in the public embodiment of its identity—can position itself at various points along a spectrum stretching from similarity with one's neighbor to differences from one's neighbor, from religious identification to religious opposition, from social cooperation to social separation. Modern Roman Catholicism, from the time of the Reformation through the development of sixteenth-century tridentinism, seventeenth- and eighteenth-century state confessionalism, and nineteenth-century Protestant-Catholic exclusions, while not ignoring similarities, had organizationally privileged difference in its public self-definition: Catholic beliefs, rituals, behaviors, and institutions were different from others.[12] For the *longue durée*, what is remarkable about the controversy in Seattle is not the powerful institutional forces at play pitting local episcopal authority against papal centralization. Struggles between the local and universal poles of power and conflicts over conciliar interpretations have been a staple of church life for centuries. What is historically exceptional about intercommunion is that it embodied in ritual form a significant break from the public construction of Catholic doctrine, worship, and living that had prevailed for centuries. When compared to the public construction of post–World War II American religion along almost sectarian tripartite lines, this ecumenical crossover becomes that much more significant for the changing definition of Catholic identity.[13] The very fact that in some circumstances a non-Catholic could be given communion at a Catholic service indicated that the imaginative horizon of what was possible within the church had changed. The fulcrum of the community's ecclesial and social identity had moved in the direction of similarity.

This practice of intercommunion seems to have been occurring mostly at those key rites of passage marking community formation and human solidarity: baptism, first communion, weddings, Sunday liturgy, at times of sickness and death. A previous, less controversial move toward social solidarity had been manifest as early as 1954 when the American bishops approved a new ritual governing the use of English in the sacraments.[14] The Seattle practice presupposed that the wider social changes that had been occurring for years were now the established public pattern. Attempting to close the gap between faith and life, the ritual changes reflected a social world of personal mobility, mixed marriages, porous denominational boundaries, a shared consumer culture with its marketplace gatherings, common values of citizenship (personal rights, democratic participation, equality), and the unifying challenges (racism, poverty, war) of a society in mutation.[15] The form of praying, the form of believing, and the form of living between Catholics and Protestants now appeared to be similar; people argued for commonality and moved in the direction of dialogue, cooperation, mutuality, even the ritualizing of a common public space through shared Eucharistic eating. Intercommunion had become a possibility because of the emergence of a much wider and accepted ecclesial and public culture. It became contested precisely because the outer limits of this new socio-ecclesial identity begged for definition. Similarities and differences needed to be held in tension. In the world's largest and most pluralistic democracy, this shift toward shared religious space carried profound implications for the church's presence in society: intercommunion was only one symbol among many indicating a "constitutive change." Taking a longer view, it is possible to see how this broader change in the balance between similarity and difference has now become such an entrenched pathway as to be almost invisible. Twenty-first-century Catholicism will be shaped by the forces of this constitutive change.

Tracing an Ecumenical Consensus

Historically, within the Catholic community, this new social and religious culture of similarity expressed itself under the linguistic rubric of "spiritual" and "social" ecumenism. The Council issued its decree on ecumenism, *Unitatis Redintegratio*, November 21, 1964. The decree addressed the church's renewal in ecumenism in the biblical and liturgical movements, preaching, catechetics, apostolic works, and cooperation in social matters. Paragraph 4 read in part, "In addition, these communions engage in that more intensive cooperation in carrying out any duties for the common good of humanity which are demanded by every Christian conscience." This path of ecumenism required interior conversion: "This change of heart and holiness of life, along with public and private prayer for the unity of Christians, should be regarded as the soul of the whole ecumenical movement, and merits the name, 'spiritual ecumenism.' " Just six years later, the Roman Secretariat charged to direct the Council's implementation issued dual decrees, one on ecumenism in higher education (April 15, 1970) and one on ecumenical dialogue (August 15, 1970).[16] Spurred on considerably by the conciliar decree *Nostra Aetate*, such "spiritual ecumenism" extended into the relationships between Catholicism and Judaism and between Catholicism and Islam, thus helping to change the inherited religious images of intergroup relationships in North America.[17] It took concrete shape in the numerous programs and organizations established at the grassroots and institutional levels of all the major religious bodies. A mention of only a few of the developments within Roman Catholicism will indicate how this culture of similarity came to be institutionalized in both the internal and external life of the church.[18]

While the Council was still in session, one of the most popular programs to emerge immediately was that of *Living Room Dialogues*, small groups of Catholic, Orthodox, and Protestant laity gathering to pray and discuss questions of unity. Begun in Worcester, Massachusetts, in January 1965, "100 groups of twelve to fifteen people representing more than 100 Catholic and Protestant congregations participated." Each meeting began with a Bible reading and prayers for Christian unity. The dialogues centered on prayer, conversation in Christ, worship, common Christian heritage, renewal, Christian witness, and "Why We Don't Break Bread Together." Within one year of the Council, fifteen dialogue programs were being organized throughout the United States; by the following year, more than five thousand groups had gathered.[19] While the Living Room Dialogues were taking place, this same creation of shared spiritual and social space was becoming institutionalized in the educational sphere. In 1966, the Catholic Bishops' Commission on Ecumenical Affairs issued guidelines for education in ecumenism, setting up a trajectory of catechetical instruction that would have a long-term impact on the church. The fifth guideline proposed "person-to-person experience in a religious context. Because of the teacher's vital role in ecumenical education, they must seek out such encounters. Furthermore, education should have as an important part of this encounter ecumenical prayer gatherings or ways suggested in the Interim Guidelines for Prayer in Common and *Communicatio in Sacris* [participation in sacramental worship] of the Bishops' Commission for Ecumenical Affairs." All of the practices associated with ecumenism—the "knowledge of and respect for the beliefs and practices of other confessions," the awareness of prejudices, the move toward "common witness and service"—"must be internalized through meditative prayer for unity which transforms the Catholic."[20]

These rather abstract goals took clear institutional and quasi-legal shape in the numerous "ecumenical directories" published after the Council. For example, the Diocese of Richmond, Virginia's Synod of 1966, published a series of eight guidelines, among which were various recommendations regarding education, parochial programs, discussion clubs, catechetics, and public and private prayer for Christian unity.[21] The Vatican issued its first Directory May 14, 1967, calling for the creation of diocesan ecumenical commissions and drawing special attention to the fostering of "spiritual ecumenism," expressed both in prayers for unity throughout the liturgical year and in the reciprocal sharing of spiritual activity ("common use of sacred places and objects, as well as all sharing in liturgical worship").[22] The Diocese of Superior, Wisconsin, issued its *Guidelines for Ecumenism* the same year. It included specific recommendations for parishes, colleges, seminaries, and hospitals. Six major initiatives were included under the rubric of "reciprocity": "The principle of reciprocity will need constant application in the area of prayer in common with other Christians." While excluding participation by Catholics in the "official formal worship of other Christian churches," the *Directory* mentioned reciprocal activities such as Bible services, Lenten devotions, civic and patriotic occasions, joint prayers for Christian unity, and the mutual sharing of pulpits "outside of the format of official liturgical worship."[23]

In the summer of 1966, *America* magazine released a survey of the 150 chancery offices in the United States. A small sampling of responses (table 5.1) indicates the wide number of ecumenical programs being conducted, a new pathway of both praying and social action, and the massive change in both infrastructure and mentality that this implied.[24]

The extent and long-term importance of these grassroots, educational, and institutional pathways of shared spiritual and social space becomes even more significant when official developments in the liturgy are examined. The gradual transition in the United States to English in the Eucharistic prayer is only the first example.[25] In mid-October 1963, the English Liturgical Committee held its first meeting and marked the beginning of what was to become, the following year, the International Commission on English in the Liturgy (ICEL). The model of other churches and their use of the vernacular was always to be taken into consideration.[26] Members of ICEL also participated in the unofficial group of Roman Catholic, Anglican, Lutheran, and Reformed liturgists who established the (North American) Consultation on Common Texts. In the course of the following years, this group would produce common texts for the psalter (1976),

TABLE 5.1
Sample of ecumenical programs, 1966

Diocese	Programs
Portland, OR	Living room dialogues; clergy discussion between priests and ministers; cooperative Christian Center on campus of state university
Bismarck, ND	Meetings with ministers and members of non-Catholic church groups to explain Vatican II
Philadelphia, PA	Commission on Human Relations; ecumenical activities; work for racial justice
New Ulm, MN	Episcopal participation in interfaith Church Unity Octave; participation in ministerial associations
Spokane, WA	Clergy conferences on ecumenism
Brooklyn, NY	Ecumenical Commission formed; ecumenical committee in each parish
Croookston, MN	Theological conferences on Decree on Ecumenism
Lincoln, NE	Expansion of ecumenical contacts, lectures, educational, social programs
Cleveland, OH	Notable expansion of ecumenical contacts; publication of *Directives for the Practice of Ecumenism*
Kansas City, MO	Ecumenical library established
Baton Rouge, LA	Commission for Ecumenical affairs established
Los Angeles, CA.	Commission on Ecumenism: clergy conferences, convention of Episcopal Church, sponsored talks
Worcester, MA	Commission on Ecumenism; Interfaith Clergy Committee
Madison, WI	Ecumenical groups of priests and ministers have met once a month for two years
Wheeling, WV	Ecumenical programs held in Protestant and Catholic churches; common community vespers services
Pittsburgh, PA	Diocesan Ecumenical Commission directs ecumenical meetings, institutes

Source: "*America*'s Survey of Diocesan Post-Conciliar Programs," *America*, June–September 1966.

services of prayer (1983), and the sacraments of marriage (1987) and baptism (1988).[27] The International Consultation on English Texts, an ecumenical group established in 1969, produced *Prayers We Have in Common* (1970, 1971, 1975), the major texts of which (e.g., Our Father, *Gloria, Sanctus* and *Benedictus, Agnus Dei*) were adopted "into the revised prayer books of all English-speaking Churches."[28] The new text of the Roman Mass and the first *General Instruction of the Roman Missal* were issued in April 1969; the approved English version for the United States of the *Roman Sacramentary* came in February 1974.[29] This revision had a major impact in creating an "ecumenical consensus" about the order and importance of the Eucharistic celebration in Word and Sacrament in the Episcopal, Methodist, Presbyterian, Lutheran, and Disciples of Christ churches, each of which revised its common prayers during this same period. As one author puts it, "common to the different churches is the deepest structure of the *ordo* of Christian worship, the received and universal pattern or shape and scheduling of the Christian liturgy."[30] Paul VI approved the adoption of two or three more Eucharistic prayers for the Roman Church in June 1966; the Roman Missal of 1970 incorporated three in addition to the Roman canon. The other major churches followed suit, with the Lutheran, Reformed, and Episcopal churches offering a variety of choices. The hymnology furnished for the official liturgies of all the churches also came to take on a common tonality.[31]

The growing shift toward similarity between Catholics and Protestants perhaps took on its most visible shape in the convergence of the major religious bodies around a common Word of God. Within Roman Catholicism, a revitalized emphasis on Scripture as a norm of faith had been developing for many years, but it received decisive institutionalization in commentaries on the Council's Dogmatic Constitution *Dei Verbum,* changes in catechetics, new translations of the Bible, the recitation of the Roman Breviary in English, the numerous parochial and educational initiatives in Scripture studies, the fostering of Bible vigils, *Living Room Dialogues,* renewal groups, retreats, and houses of prayer.[32] It was not surprising that one of the key measurements for successful renewal was fidelity to the Scripture's understanding of service, authority, and love of neighbor. The phenomenal spread of the Catholic charismatic movement placed the importance of Scripture as constitutive of a common "spiritual ecumenism" at the center of the Christian Catholic experience of thousands.[33]

This turn toward the personal appropriation of the Word of God in meditative listening, group discussion, and application to life in a society and church in change would be thoroughly mainstreamed in RENEW, the most widespread program of parochial revitalization of the postconciliar period.[34] In addition, the most universal pathway for the "biblical turn" toward similarity expressed itself in the adoption by all the major churches of a common cycle of liturgical readings. The Roman Catholic Church published its revision of the readings to be done at Eucharistic services in 1969. A three-year cycle of Sunday Scripture selections, now in the vernacular, was developed, which then became the model for use in the *Worshipbook* of the three Presbyterian churches in the United States, the Episcopal *Book of Common Prayer*, the Lutheran *The Church Year*, and the services of the Methodists, Disciples of Christ, and others.[35] What developed was a common biblical-liturgical exposure shaped according to a shared calendar and paschal emphasis. The lectionary pushed the faith traditions toward similarity in origins, responsiveness to the Word, and journey into Christ.

One of the most significant dimensions of this new ecumenical consensus was the involvement of the various churches in the social issues of the day. Within Roman Catholicism, solidarity with others as a key component of church life was encoded into communal identity through the restoration of the general intercessions or "prayers of the faithful" in the course of the Sunday liturgy. Mandated by the Council and almost immediately instituted, the prayers enabled the community in its own voice to "intercede for all humanity." The petitions were to be "offered for the church, for civil authorities, for those oppressed by various needs, for all people, and for the salvation of the world."[36] A survey of diocesan liturgical practice taken in the spring of 1966 indicated that ninety out of the ninety-five dioceses reporting used the new form at Sunday Eucharist; fifty-eight used the prayers at weekday celebrations.[37] Guidelines for the prayers were issued in 1969 and again in 1979. They remain the staple of Catholic Eucharistic praying to the present. Some of the Eucharistic prayers themselves contained an explicitly social dimension in both Catholic and Protestant reforms.[38] This basic orientation, shaped not only by the Council's *Constitution on the Sacred Liturgy* but also by the social teaching of the *Pastoral Constitution on the Church in the Modern World*, received substantial strengthening in the teachings of Paul VI (*Populorum Progressio*, 1967;

Octogesima adveniens, 1971) and the synods on *Justice in the World* (1971) and *Evangelization* (1974). *Justice in the World* emphasized ecumenical cooperation:

> . . . we highly commend cooperation with our separated Christian brethren for the promotion of justice in the world, for bringing about development of peoples and for establishing peace. This cooperation concerns first and foremost activities for securing human dignity and man's fundamental rights, especially the right to religious liberty. This is a source of our common efforts against discrimination on the grounds of differences of religion, race and colour, culture and the like. . . . In the same spirit we likewise commend collaboration with all believers in God in the fostering of social justice, peace, and freedom.[39]

A good percentage of the ecumenical endeavors in the constitutive phase of conciliar renewal attempted to relate the churches to the "social systems" of the time, engaging the people together in community action, work with minorities, housing, help for the aged, criminal justice, and prison reform. Notably enough, in a trend that reflected both the ecumenical consensus and its future difficulties, a study released in 1975 observed, "It seems worth noting that many Roman Catholics feel that their ecumenical participation has included a tacit agreement to ignore issues where consensus within the ecumenical agency does not exist." The divisive issues that were tacitly ignored were abortion and public aid to parochial schools.[40]

This ecumenism took place, of course, in the midst of four of the most influential social movements of the 1960s: civil rights, the war on poverty, women's liberation, and the anti–Vietnam War protests. Their crossover influence on the ecumenical consensus cannot be ignored, and numerous studies have indicated the interpenetration of these movements with Roman Catholics open to ecumenically oriented social change. For some Catholics, the experience of the Freedom Riders revealed the social possibilities inherent in new religious alliances and direct action for justice.[41] Shared commitments to racial justice cut through all the denominations during the height of the movement.[42] The National Conference on Religion and Race (1963) networked Protestant, Catholics, and Jews, branched out in numerous directions, and pushed a cross-denominational alliance for the Civil Rights Act of 1964.[43] The march on Selma involved priests and ministers, nuns and women of all denominations.

It was a consciousness-changing experience leading to new alliances among women religious.[44] The war on poverty in its multiple dimensions and numerous networks of social-justice activities engaged people in the shared public space of social change.[45] The newly formed National Organization for Women established an Ecumenical Task Force on Women and Religion, "which until 1972 was run primarily by Catholic feminists and focused predominantly on Catholic women's concerns."[46] The desire of women for ordained ministry was a concern that cut across all church bodies, and the practice of Protestants in this area was an example for the movement among Catholics. Was this an ecumenical issue meaning that it was "widely felt," or was it an ecumenical issue that should develop into a common practice?[47] Finally, Catholic participation in the antiwar effort, both moderate and radical, placed members of different faith traditions in the same acts of protest, united them in a methodology of direct action, and helped in some cases to create a common missionary understanding of social reform, a "sacramental resistance" to all forms of oppression.[48]

While the impact of all of these trajectories of the new ecumenical consensus is difficult to measure, the overall impression is that a definite shift had occurred in the public construction of Catholic identity. In a community that had historically privileged its association with the American way of life in the 1950s, the new ecumenical consensus dissolved the ritual, legal, and social boundaries between peoples, critiqued the basic racial, political, and economic structures of society, and placed a whole host of new questions about creedal cooperation and the limits of the consensus before the Catholic community.[49] The church was now struggling to find coherence between its internal reforms and its external mission in society. To be sure, there were immediate signs of polarization and the beginnings of a counterreaction, but during the constitutive phase of conciliar reform this ecumenical consensus held fast. For those riding the high wave of social change, disagreements were muted; authenticity, freedom, dialogue, and cooperation became the watchwords of the day. The language of personal rights and religious liberty, helped considerably by the Council's own *Declaration on Religious Liberty*, entered into the Catholic handbook of life in the modern world. Now their own religious convictions merged easily with the "politics of human rights" and liberation that swept the entire world.[50] In a detailed study of the Archdiocese of Washington that may be taken as indicative of the dominant trend, one historian has noted the centrality of this new ecumenism. The experience exposed Catholics to different forms of religious truth, forced a new awareness of cooperation with others, and argued for participative structures in the formation of common policy. It raised the possibility of a public morality shaped by conscience, a discriminating application of doctrine to life, a methodology of concession to the views of others, and tactical compromise so as to achieve a common goal.[51]

The "ecumenical consensus" was ritually, legally, educationally, and pastorally in place by the mid-1970s. Buttressed by a concomitant intellectual period of intense theological dialogue, this common social and spiritual ecumenism had dramatically shifted the fulcrum of Catholic identity toward the pole of similarity with others.[52] Its mainstreaming into the Catholic body politic would be analogous to the amalgamation of many of the social movements of the 1960s into the cultural mores, laws, organizations, and networks of American society.[53] The "constitutive moment," again to use the framework developed by Paul Starr—that moment of decision when "ideas and culture come into play, as do constellations of power, preexisting institutional legacies, and models from other countries"—had become "institutionally entrenched."[54] The post–Vietnam War era would build on its foundations. An ecumenical emphasis on the relationship between official liturgical order and questions of social ethics would continue in the subsequent decades.[55] Studies completed in 1975, 1983–1984, 1990, and 2004 would indicate how this type of common religious culture had taken root, branched out into all sectors of church life, and shifted the locus of self-understanding and practice toward a focus on the affinities between Catholicism and other religious traditions.[56] A re-centering of Catholic identity on similarity with others had occurred. It was a truly epochal change from the public identity of a church that until the 1960s had been primarily shaped by the dynamics of the Counter-Reformation and, in the United States, by the enclave world of the immigrant communities.

However, given the many different currents involved and its close affinities with the social changes of the period, the ecumenical consensus was inherently unstable. After the end of the Vietnam War, new configurations would emerge, and the many currents that had joined in a common riverbed would now begin to claim their differences. Ironically, however, even in the differences, a consensus would be presupposed. The very diverse currents that would form new rivers all shared a commitment to social change, a comingling of internal church policies with external political orientations, and a conviction that institutional change could be accomplished by a strategic use of social networking, media exposure, direct action, focused publications, alliances with the powerful, and the mobilization of like-minded people in a participative process.[57] They would also share an ecumenical openness to others, not the pan-ecumenism of the sixties to be sure, but now an ecumenism directed to people of any faith profession who shared a similar socioreligious conviction. In the *longue durée*, it would be these new ecumenical alignments as well as the older ones that would shape the contemporary terrain on which a now fragmented and pluriform Catholic community does public battle. It is to that transformation that we now turn.

STRUGGLING TO CONTROL PUBLIC SPACE, 1976–1988

Just as the initial thrust toward religious dialogue and unity among the mainline churches had been influenced by the participative, egalitarian, and reformist movements of the 1960s, so a new ecumenical approach paralleled the more conservative post–Vietnam War movements in American society and the public ascendancy of the new right.[58] In a socioreligious world no longer preoccupied with the Vietnam War, reactive to the second and more radical phase of the rights movements, critical of the entitlements of the Great Society and its welfare liberalism, and suddenly conscious of the cultural extremes of the 1960s, three key questions began to mobilize opinion: How much had these interfaith ecumenical initiatives reflected a more pervasive and leveling secularism? How much had they aided and abetted a doctrinal relativism? Were the churches losing their congregational cohesion through a capitulation to modernity?[59] After 1974, a "cultural opening" thus occurred, and those who had always been uncomfortable with the institutional disarray that had marked the previous decade could publicly mobilize into a more vocal if heterogeneous choir.[60] The simultaneous public ascendancy of a new and more radical brand of feminism and the extension of social rights to sexual minorities served as a potent and shaping counterinfluence.[61] While the varieties of these religious voices cannot be examined here—they ranged from the ultraconservatives through the traditionalists to the neoconservatives[62]—an overview of the emergence of the most prominent and new ecumenical alliance over the past forty years, that of Roman Catholics with Evangelical Protestants, will indicate once again how, for the most part, the definition of Catholic identity had shifted toward that end of the spectrum closer to similarity than to difference.

In the spring of 1974, two Lutherans, the sociologist Peter Berger and the theologian Richard John Neuhaus, drew up twelve themes that they perceived to be weakening the work of the churches. What emerged from their initial efforts and a consultation among six Lutherans, five Roman Catholics, two Orthodox, two Christian Reformed, a Methodist, a Presbyterian, and a member of the United Church of Christ, in January 1975, was the "Hartford Appeal." Coming as it did just as the unifying forces for social reform that had dominated the 1960s were dissolving and a more radical phase was developing, the Appeal was not a congregationally based ecumenical statement. Nevertheless, it united major theological voices across denominational lines and pointed in the direction of a loosely connected public movement critical of the perceived alliances between the churches and modernity.[63] In general terms, the document emphasized the transcendence of the church's mission with respect to society. Touching the theologically leveling forces associated with ecumenical extremism, theme five severely critiqued what the authors perceived as a growing tendency to argue that "all religions are equally valid." While recognizing the importance of "learning from the riches of other religions," the signers of the Appeal opined: "But we repudiate this theme because it flattens diversities and ignores contradictions. In doing so, it not only obscures the meaning of Christian faith, but also fails to respect the integrity of other faiths. Truth matters; therefore differences among religions are deeply significant."[64]

The following year a Roman Catholic theologian and a Protestant ecumenist, both of whom had signed the Hartford Appeal, argued in one of the most prestigious ecumenical journals that unity among Christians as reflected in the practice of intercommunion should not degenerate into a "mere expression of courtesy, civil friendship, or solidarity in some secular cause."[65] Ritual activities needed to be more directly related to Christian tradition and to the church. Ecumenical practices should become more discriminating so as to reinforce boundaries and project institutional consolidation. Such an emphasis would combat the secularism that now characterized modern American society, Western developed nations, and the churches themselves.[66] The Appeal occurred at the same time that many others in the Catholic Church were beginning to note the development among some of a new-style Catholicism, one marked by institutional tenuousness and much closer but not exactly similar core beliefs to mainline Protestant churches. "Communal Catholics," the sociologist Andrew Greeley argued, were caught in the midst of two transitions, "from Counter-Reformation to Ecumenical Age, and from the immigrant old neighborhood to the professional class suburb." A new pluralism had entered into the church's identity: "Communal Catholics will no longer accept what the church says on social and moral issues merely because the church has said it."[67] Apparently, the forces of religious freedom and personal rights embedded in the ecumenical consensus had begun to differentiate themselves and become institutionally visible.

At the time, the Hartford Appeal represented a relatively moderate, intellectually thoughtful, cross-denominational presentation of the church's identity and role in the public square.[68] Theme ten captured this attempt both to engage society and to critique it from a specifically Christian viewpoint: "The Church must denounce oppressors, help liberate the oppressed, and seek to heal human misery. Sometimes the Church's mission coincides with the world's programs. But the norms for the Church's activity derive from its own perception of God's will for the world." This search for the boundaries separating the church from the world, focus on the transcendent elements in Christian teaching, and opposition to the many forms of subjectivism in the modern world was pitched at a very high level. It emerged from within the mainstream of America's religious bodies and carefully tried to avoid the polarized thinking that had been developing for over a decade. As Lutheran theologian George Lindbeck described it, "Unfaithful Christians divide into a right and a left (for example, into papists and enthusiasts). But true faith opposes both. Both capitulate to culture, to the wisdom of this world, but in different ways."[69]

Yet the Appeal clearly had its sights focused on the "progressives" and the growth in all the churches of "rampant immanentism, humanism, secularism, psychologism, sociologism of our age—a convergent movement that leaves no room for the transcendent except as a kind of psychological 'peak experience.' "[70] Catholic theologian Avery Dulles noted the affinities between the proposals of the Appeal and the recent writings of the historian James Hitchcock in his attacks on "liberal Catholicism." As future events would have it, this type of defense of a middle ground defined in relation to the socially dissolving forces of the "progressives" would soon find its popular religious corollary in the mounting institutional and personal opposition to the moral and social challenge of women's reproductive rights.

The Supreme Court's recognition of a woman's right to obtain an abortion in 1973 galvanized religious bodies across the ecumenical spectrum, eventually splitting them into liberal and conservative extremes.[71] For purposes of this essay, this approval of legalized abortion, as the decision was popularly understood, rearranged the ecumenical consensus from that of the reforms of the 1960s and forced the creation of new theological and social alliances—ecumenical to be sure, but now battling in the fractious territory where morality and social policy collided. Within the Roman Catholic community, clearly opposed to abortion in its received teaching, various groups argued almost immediately over political tactics and public positioning. A few of them may be mentioned, as their ferocious arguments in the 1980s demonstrate the wide spectrum of views in the community and would shape the course of the church well into the twenty-first century.[72]

As early as November 1973, the bishops announced their commitment to the passage of a constitutional amendment forbidding abortion.[73] Analysis of their statements from 1973 through the early 1990s indicates their consistent opposition to abortion but disagreement over a "single issue" approach, and some flexibility as to the tactics to be used. These differences would become more marked in the following decade, when Cardinal Joseph Bernardin would argue for a "consistent-ethic approach" and archbishops Bernard Law of Boston and John O'Connor of New York would push for a single-issue agenda.[74] It is important to note that the disagreements at the episcopal level were not over rejection of abortion, but over the centrality of particular moral issues in the formation of public policy in a pluralistic democracy. They were over how to apply the meaning of religious freedom within a democratic and religiously pluralistic polity.[75]

Among the middle leadership in the church, the 1976 Leadership Conference of Women Religious, some of whom had been strongly influenced by the justice and rights movements of the 1960s, formed a task force on how women religious at local and regional levels could support the pro-life stand of the bishops. When *Choose Life* was published in 1977, the ad hoc committee of the bishops severely critiqued it for not being strong enough. The Leadership Conference issued a stance in support of a pro-life position, but this tussle over how to support women and still achieve clarity of teaching in a public pro-life stance would percolate for many years among men and women at the grassroots level. Mixed up in the imbroglio would be the different strands of the women's movement.[76] More strident in tone and even more deeply rooted in the justice and rights movements of the 1960s, the National Coalition of American Nuns argued that it was "firmly opposed to abortion, as such," but it publicly rejected the various forms of the Human Life Amendment that the bishops supported.[77] Among the laity, more than 115,000 responses dealt with concerns related to the human person during the bicentennial consultation before the Detroit Conference on Liberty and Justice for All (October 21–23, 1976). The summary statements noted the defense of a "rich pluralism" in the church and that "many also defended the individual's right to choose how to apply gospel values to the conditions of her or his own life." With respect to abortion, eight thousand responses connected abortion with other social problems in the community (housing, the elderly, unemployment). They wanted "the Church to support the right to life in every phase of life."[78]

Particular advocacy groups of the laity also multiplied in the wake of the Supreme Court decision. Catholics for a Free Choice, founded in 1970 but joining ranks after 1973 with the Religious Coalition for Abortion Rights, supported the decision of the Court. Ten years later, they would sponsor a *New York Times* ad (October 7, 1984) that spoke of a "diversity of opinions regarding abortion" among "committed Catholics." The ad was supported by the Catholic Committee on Pluralism and Abortion. At the same time, the National Coalition of American Nuns released a statement accusing the American bishops of sexism on abortion.[79] The signing of the ad by some religious women became a national *cause célèbre*.[80] In the minds of many, the support for abortion would be of one piece with the work of Catholics for a free choice, the feminist focus on the experience of women, the acceptance of abortion in mainline Protestant churches, theories of moral probabilism, and the misinterpretation of the *Declaration on Religious Freedom* of Vatican II; this whole complex would need to be rejected in the struggle for a clearer definition of a public Catholic identity.[81] Lastly, as early as 1975, at a meeting of groups supportive of a pro-life amendment to the Constitution, one of the groups, the Committee for the Pro-Life Amendment, felt it had to oppose "any [congressional] candidate who is a pro-abortionist, and also any of those who are sympathetic." Confrontational in tone and approach, the committee severely disagreed with one of the archbishops, who had hired a layman who had publicly backed abortion rights. A group designed to educate clergy and laity, in 1974–1975 the committee visited nineteen cities and gave twenty-one workshops trying to encourage people to pressure Congress.[82] Its approach would be paralleled in the decades to come in that brand of the pro-life Catholic movement involved in direct action campaigns and in groups such as Catholics United for the Faith, which used the classification "dissenter" for almost anyone advocating different views.[83]

In short, in the wake of the 1973 decision, the Catholic community faced a host of questions that touched the complex relationships between church teaching, the ecumenical consensus, the respective authority of lay and clerical members, the role of experience in the definition of faith, women's rights, the interpretation of the Council's decrees, political advocacy, and the formation of public policy. Should the movement for an amendment cross denominational boundaries? How active should the bishops be in shaping public policy? Should the laity have an independent role? What was the relationship between support for the Equal Rights Amendment and support for abortion? How was the struggle against abortion related to "doing away with wars and fighting poverty," or rejecting the death penalty? Should the church use the pro-life amendment as a litmus test for the rejection or support of any particular candidate? Would a "consistent ethic" approach open the doors to moral relativism? Would a confrontational approach push the church in the direction of sectarianism? Where did one draw the line between Roman Catholic similarity with others as citizens and as believers, and how much or with what intensity did the Catholic difference in the area of abortion and other areas of sexuality need to shape the public moral consensus?[84] In a survey of ecumenical activities in the fall of 1979, the respondents considered the two greatest obstacles to ecumenism to be theological differences on abortion and the issue of women's ordination.[85] The connection of both issues with the radicalization of the rights and gender movements of the 1960s was unmistakable. Published in early 1975, the moderately centered Hartford Appeal would fast lose its appeal in an increasingly polarized society.

The impact of abortion and other issues on the fifty-year realignment within the ecumenical consensus illustrates very clearly how an institutionalized pluriformity would enter deeply into the church's structures and policies. In November 1975, the National Conference of Catholic Bishops released its *Pastoral Plan for Pro-Life Activities*. The document called for the organization of pro-life groups in parishes and congressional districts and asked the community to mobilize "through all institutions, agencies, and organizations." While specifically focusing on abortion as the denial of a basic human right to life, the plan also linked this most basic right with other social rights and called on all sectors of the community to promote dialogue "among churches and religious groups."[86] Immediately, many in the mainline churches reacted. On January 26, 1976, the Religious Coalition for Abortion Rights, to which Catholics for a Free Choice became affiliated, released a statement. Bishop James Armstrong, president of the Board of Church and Society of the United Methodist Church, noted the stresses and strains the activist approach of the bishops placed on the inherited ecumenical consensus: "Strenuous efforts by the Catholic Bishops to legislate their particular religious view on abortion is a blow to the integrity with which we have engaged in other ecumenical pursuits. . . . Efforts to deny the rights of others to follow the dictates of their consciences on this matter could also detract from the ecumenical accords which have been achieved after many years." Armstrong was joined in this appeal by the chairperson of the executive council of the United Church of Christ, the associate general secretary of American Baptist Churches, the national president of the National Council of Jewish Women, the president of United Presbyterian Women, the director of the Commission on Social Action of Reform Judaism, and the president of the Unitarian Universalist Association.[87]

This initial parting of the ways was only the beginning. On October 3, 1977, 209 Protestant and Jewish subscribers published an abortion rights statement, "A Call to Concern." If the Roman Catholic Church was successful, the broadside argued, "it would violate the deeply held religious convictions of individual members and official bodies of many other religious groups about when human personhood begins, the relative rights of a woman and a fetus, and responsible family life."[88] On October 14, in response, another Protestant group, the Christian Action Council based in Washington D.C., supported the Catholic initiative and labeled "A Call to

Concern" an "irresponsible" attack on the Church."[89] Thirty-two Evangelical Protestants signed this counterstatement, among them Dr. C. Everett Koop, Richard John Neuhaus, Albert Outler, and several prominent Catholic leaders. Joining the fray to defend the Court's decision, the National Abortion Rights League lumped together the National Conference of Catholic Bishops, the John Birch Society, the Ku Klux Klan, the Christian Crusade, and the National States Rights Party. Included in its mailing was a list of the Catholic dioceses that sent monetary support to the National Committee for the Human Life Amendment.[90] The National Organization for Women described the Roman Catholic initiative as "a major attack on your human rights."[91] John C. Bennett, a leading Protestant ethicist and ecumenist, supporter of civil rights, and former president of Union Theological Seminary, noted that in contrast to the Roman Catholic Church, "the highest judicatories" of numerous "Protestant denominations have declared themselves in favor of laws that permit abortion in a variety of situations."[92] Two weeks later, Alfred Moran, executive director of New York Planned Parenthood, spoke on *CBS Evening News* of the work of "the National Conference of Catholic Bishops and some other extreme religious groups to impose their theological views on American women, but only certain American women. Only poor American women who can not afford medical care."[93] The next month, the *New York Times*, noting the disagreements between President Carter (opposed to federal funding for abortion) and his female staff and HEW Secretary Joseph Califano (a Catholic) and his staff, wryly cited one congressman: "It would take the wisdom of Augustine or Thomas Aquinas to settle the question."[94]

In January 1978, the secretary of public affairs for the United States Catholic Conference argued that a pattern was emerging that attempted to identify the abortion issue "not merely as a 'Catholic issue' but as a 'Catholic bishops' issue—the intent being, it seems, to isolate Catholic leadership not only from the non-Catholic community but from the Catholic community as well."[95] That same month, a columnist in the *New York Times* noted that in the past year some antiabortion activists had raided a Planned Parenthood clinic; others had chained themselves to furniture in a Washington office of the organization; still others had begun to make common cause for family values with the constituency of George Wallace's American Independent Party. In November, Phyllis Schlafly, a Roman Catholic opponent of abortion and the Equal Rights

Amendment and a founder of the anticommunist Cardinal Mindzenty Foundation and the Eagle Forum, had protested the National Women's Conference in Houston by calling a counter meeting at the same time. All of this appeared to be similar to the attack on gay rights in Florida. The reporter for the *Times* warned that a grassroots cross coalition was beginning to form and it would provide the bishops with extraordinary political clout.[96] The bishops' Office of Public Affairs pondered a public response to what it considered a new anti-Catholicism now growing exponentially within society. Among the alternatives considered was an " 'interreligious statement.' "[97] The war over the public moral space had begun in earnest, creating an atmosphere in which new ecumenical alliances were called for.

In the 1980s, the various approaches to abortion and to numerous other areas of life, both internal and external to the church, used mechanisms of public advocacy and marketing to shape the moral contours of society. These mechanisms had first come to the fore in the 1960s: the mobilization of institutions, petition writing, direct mail contact, advocacy networking, media spin control, direct protest actions, etc. The key questions, the answers that accompanied them, and their delivery systems would shape the external public discourse and the internal definition of Catholic identity for several decades. They all came together in the abortion debate and grew more pronounced as the society itself engaged in arguments over family values, homosexuality, and reproductive ethics.[98] In the wars of the 1980s, the ideological lines would be drawn and the broad middle place of public discourse eventually hollowed out. Indicative of the problem would be the fact that the pastoral letters on *The Challenge of Peace* (1983) and *Economic Justice for All* (1986) searched for a broad middle ground through the use of listening sessions, dialogue with others, and the articulation of consensus public policy. Both pastorals contained arguments from natural law, scripture, and papal social teaching. The methodology had emerged from the ecumenical consensus of the constitutive period; the positions taken had much in common with the reformist currents of the same era.[99] The first pastoral took two years; the second, five years. The pastorals received sharp critiques from those on the right and left, both in the church and in society, but they still passed. In contrast, the pastoral on women, product of an even longer and more complex listening process (1982–1993), withered completely under pressure from all sides.[100] Eventually, in the minds of many, all the issues would be conflated with the issue of authority:

the challenges of gender, personal rights, ecclesial participation, and the importance of a Catholic "difference" from modern society.

With respect to ecumenism, the Roman Catholic–Evangelical Protestant alliance that would be formed in the 1990s and have a great impact on the internal policies of the church and its external public voice was deeply rooted in the two developments described above: (1) the initial intellectual search, as exemplified in the Hartford Appeal, for a transcendent moral pole to counteract the dissolving effect of social change—in some instances named "natural law," in others the "Bible," in still others "the teaching authority"; and (2) the early struggles against abortion and its support by the more radicalized proponents in the rights movements. One of the earliest people to point out the possibility of a new ecumenical alliance to struggle against a dissolving secular humanism was St. Louis University historian James Hitchcock, who wrote in the midst of the debates of the late 1970s: "The effort must, ultimately, become ecumenical. . . . most of the major Protestant churches will have little sympathy for it. . . . More importantly, those Protestants broadly designated evangelicals (sometimes derogatorily called fundamentalists) are the only Christians in the country who at present seem to have retained their sense of purpose, identity, and self-confidence."[101] Hitchcock's call was a little too early. During the 1980s, while there was increasing differentiation within Protestantism on the social issues related to family values and sexuality, the Moral Majority with its anti-Catholic tone controlled the religious debate in society.[102] At the same time, the ferocity of the open arguments over war and peace, the economy, abortion rights, women's ordination, moral theology, and dissent and authority in a Catholic Church torn between extremes and just beginning to grapple with the sexual abuse of minors made any partial institutional mobilization almost impossible.[103] In these circumstances any public and influential Catholic-Evangelical alliance seemed remote.[104] But a more self-conscious and new ecumenical alliance lay just beyond the horizon.

THE ADVENT OF PLURIFORMITY: 1989–2010

On the side of Evangelicals, the Christian Coalition and Focus on the Family emerged in the early 1990s in the wake of the collapse of the Moral Majority. Both organizations, more astute in their political insight, manifested an opening to Catholics, and internally many members of the

Catholic community found the new socioreligious movements attractive.[105] In such a context and armed with the perceived support of the Roman curia and new coalitions at the base, many Roman Catholics now joined forces politically and religiously with Evangelical Protestants. A new popular ecumenical consensus, paralleling but not supplanting that of the 1960s, emerged to actively influence the church's role in society. It found its popular base in an ecumenical realignment that had been happening for two decades within the American Catholic community. It found its episcopal supporters in a new cadre of church leadership. It found its articulate spokespersons within the Catholic community in one of the authors of the Hartford Appeal, Lutheran pastor Richard John Neuhaus (1936–2009) and in numerous lay intellectuals.[106]

Neuhaus, who had been involved in the civil rights movement and had been an early opponent of the Vietnam War, converted to Roman Catholicism in 1990. His 1984 *Naked Public Square*, numerous other books, and the periodical *First Things* (1990–) would articulate one form of church presence in a secularized society, a presence that was ecclesiastically consolidating, publicly engaged, and generally committed to neoconservative causes.[107] He would be linked with another lay intellectual in the church, George Weigel, whose 1987 *Tranquillitas Ordinis* was a sharply worded argument over just-war theory against those he identified as inheritors of the 1960s and members of the "consensus" wing of American public Catholicism: Dorothy Day, Thomas Merton, James Douglass, Daniel Berrigan, J. Bryan Hehir, John Coleman, and David Hollenbach.[108] In the 1990s, Weigel and Neuhaus would consider themselves moderate compared to the Catholics on the far right. They themselves did not agree on all issues. Still, their neoconservative critique, both within the church and outside of it, would be identified by many with similar themes that emerged from some of the teachings of John Paul II (1978–2005).[109] The vision, as with that of the Hartford Appeal, was shaped by the struggle against a militant secularism; it was helped theologically by the astute Catholic theologian Avery Dulles and presented a united front against the radicalized forces surfacing in the debates of the 1980s on internal church issues. It found a ready audience in many leaders among the hierarchy.

The new ecumenical trend that developed was captured very well on March 29, 1994, in a document authored by Richard John Neuhaus, Charles Colson, George Weigel, and Kent Hill: *Evangelicals and Catholics*

Together: The Christian Mission in the Third Millennium.[110] Among the Catholic signatories were James Hitchcock, Peter Kreeft, Matthew Lamb, Ralph Martin, and Michael Novak. Among the episcopal signers was Cardinal John O'Connor of New York. The document made significant references to the differences between the two traditions, among which were the sacraments of the Catholic Church. But it argued that these extensive doctrinal differences should not prevent cooperation in other areas of life. The statement called particular attention to the joint responsibility of "the right ordering of society." The two communities, Catholics and Evangelicals, joined hands in their contention "for the truth that politics, law, and culture must be secured by moral truth." They supported religious freedom, which also involved the "renewal of the constituting vision of the place of religion in the American experiment." They wished publicly to "secure the legal protection of the unborn" and, in the educational system, to ensure that the cultural heritage of Judaism and Christianity was transmitted to the next generation: "the morality of honesty, law observance, work, caring, chastity, mutual respect between the sexes, and readiness for marriage, parenthood, and family." "We reject the claim that, in any or all of these areas, 'tolerance' requires the promotion of moral equivalence between the normative and the deviant." The agreement went on to argue for a "renewed spirit of acceptance, understanding, and cooperation across lines of religion, race, ethnicity, sex, and class." It supported a "vibrant market economy," a "realistic and responsible understanding of America's part in world affairs," and a "renewed appreciation of Western culture." It contended against pornography and sexual depravity. *Evangelicals and Catholics Together* saw all of these issues as "a set of directions oriented to the common good and discussable on the basis of public reason."

This Catholic-Evangelical alliance broke from the pattern of liturgical, doctrinal, and social consensus that marked the earlier period and still received institutional recognition in national, diocesan, parochial, and educational ventures throughout the country. Although the document was contested among the various wings of Evangelical Protestantism and diverse networks in Roman Catholicism, its publication and general circulation captured the heart of a great change, from the ecumenical consensus of the 1960s to a newer parallel consensus emerging both intellectually and popularly from the mid-1970s to the early 1990s. It served as the intellectual and popular progenitor of the later "Manhattan

Declaration: A Call of Christian Conscience," issued November 20, 2009, by Orthodox, Catholic, and Evangelical Christians, and authored by Robert George, Timothy George, and Chuck Colson.[111] The Manhattan Declaration, like its predecessors, has received the support of Catholic bishops, priests, people, specific periodicals, and various congregations, churches, and petitioners throughout the United States. This new alliance, like the ecumenical consensus before it—because of its popular base, its episcopal support, its intellectual arguments, and its support in national, diocesan, parochial, and educational ventures throughout the country—has shaped our contemporary church. The result is that American Catholics, in a fashion analogous to the society around them, have sorted themselves into enclaves of like-minded reformers.[112] The residual effects of the battles of the 1980s are still being felt, and a broad middle where the two ecumenisms meet within the boundaries of the Catholic tradition has disappeared from view.

With the public articulation and consolidation of the Evangelical-Catholic alliance, alongside an already entrenched ecumenical consensus that had emerged in the immediate postconcilar period, the Catholic Church in the United States entered into a new era—the era of pluriformity. Initially, as the impact of the Second Vatican Council took hold, the arguments over basic creedal statements and Protestant-Catholic Counter-Reformation self-definitions had seen their day. The new thrust toward unity expressed itself in a common language, a turn toward Scripture, a similar structure in liturgical celebrations, and shared struggles against the social problems of race, poverty, and war. It is a testament to the institutionalized movement in the fulcrum of Catholic identity toward similarity that as the points of tension began to intensify in the community after 1975, countermovements within Roman Catholicism did not define themselves as separate from their Christian and Jewish neighbors so much as split themselves into warring subgroups, forming religious and political cross-denominational alliances on the left and on the right. Presupposing the initial ecumenical consensus and the linkage established between theological convictions and social vision, Catholic identity assertion migrated to dichotomous positions on social order, gender, human rights, family life, and particularized ethical markers of identity, such as opposition to abortion. A new ecumenism, parallel to but not supplanting an earlier one, arose among many members of the community as they began to make common cause not with traditionally mainline Protestant churches but with the inheritance of American Evangelicalism. Taking the *longue durée*, the past fifty years in American Catholicism have seen a struggle for the control of public space in church and society precisely because an awareness of a common public political and social space has begun to dominate the religious horizon of the imagination. At the end of the process, what has been created has been an American Roman Catholicism with a pluriform public identity. American Roman Catholicism has entered into the politics of history.

To some extent, this history of Christian ecumenical relationships serves only as a dense case study of what has happened in numerous other areas of church life. Studies of the priesthood, sexuality, institutional authority, and sociological trackings of religious practice have all pointed to a fragmented, polarized, and publicly weakened Catholic identity.[113] R. Scott Appleby, one of the most astute of contemporary Catholic historians, describes one major trend in these words: "a fractious pluralism threatens to undermine the possibility of a genuinely diverse but unified moral and religious community."[114] Numerous examples of this polarized "battle for Catholic identity" have recently been described by John Gehring.[115] As the Obama presidency gave way to the Trump presidency, a debate took place within the community between a future structured around the more sectarian "Benedict option" and the more publicly engaged *Commonweal* option.[116] In all of this, the Catholic Church has followed a path parallel to dominant trends both in Protestant Christianity and in a fractured society.[117]

Yet, in terms of Roman Catholicism, the argument here is that in the future this pluriformity within the church will not go away, tied as it is to the Second Vatican Council's own teaching, the changing geopolitical emphases of the papacy, and the reception of both Council and papacy among the Catholic people in the largest and most religiously pluralistic democratic country in the world. Entrenched within networks of personal exchange, supported by different approaches in the leadership, propagated in divergent publications and media outlets, advocated by pressure groups from within and without the church, argued at the highest academic levels, sometimes sorted into enclaves of like-minded people, and taking expression in liturgical rituals and social visions, the pluralism inherent in Catholic identity and traditionally identified with divergent theological traditions or distinct religious charisms has become both laicized and democratized. Different "constitutive events" have created divergent institutional pathways of pluriformity. What is called for in this situation will be a new conceptualization of American Catholic identity within the context of an increasingly globalized church. In conclusion, leaving historical method behind and presupposing the established pattern of pluriformity, I would like to conclude with a few general but tentative comments as to the future.

2013 AND BEYOND

When Pope Francis appeared on the balcony of St. Peter's Basilica with the crowds gathered before him on the night of March 13, 2013, the world sensed something new was occurring in the Roman Catholic Church. The pope knelt and asked for the people's blessings. Since that time, after numerous visits to various parts of the world, innumerable speeches, two major apostolic exhortations, one encyclical, and a picture book full of symbolic encounters, and without changing any of the teachings of his immediate predecessors or the inherited Catholic tradition, Pope Francis has attempted to set a new style of leadership for the Roman Catholic Church.[118] Francis brought to his own ministry several distinct traits that differentiated him from his predecessors: a non-European, he saw the world church from a different vantage point; pastor of a local church, he knew firsthand the vitality of popular religiosity and the religious and social struggles of the urban poor; a member of the Society of Jesus, he was the first vowed religious trained in a distinctive spirituality and elected to the papacy since Gregory XVI (1831–1846); an Argentinian, he inherited and helped shaped some of the most creative documents of the regional churches of the postconciliar world. The impact of all of these dimensions of the pope's life on the face of a global Catholicism would soon become evident.

Pope Francis's approach occurs within the context of a universal church that had become, in practice and structure, pluriform. The Second Vatican Council inaugurated the advent of a world church, one in which for the first time the church in the United States was to play a significant shaping role.[119] In liturgy, governance, cultural adaptation, and social engagement, the Council argued for a new equilibrium between the center and the periphery, between the local and the universal poles of catholicity, between the national conferences of bishops and the Roman curia, between the bishops and the pope, between the enculturated churches of distinct regions and the unifying principle of shared faith expressed in a now globalized Roman Catholic Church. These tensive relationships that necessarily accompanied the broader processes of globalization impacted the pontificates and shaped the policies of Paul VI, John Paul II, and Benedict XVI, each reacting in slightly different ways.[120] The newness of this church and this world that they faced should not be discounted. Yet Pope Francis is now trying something new. Structurally, he wants to revive the atrophied conciliar teaching on collegiality and the implementation of synodality.[121] Pastorally, he calls for a pedagogy of discernment and an application of John XXIII's "medicine of mercy."[122] Spiritually, he asks for a deeper conversion to the following of Christ as the starting point for action.[123] He wants all three areas to percolate within the global church.

In an age of pluriform but antagonistic relationships, one of the pope's favorite images is that of a polyhedron. He writes in *Evangelii Gaudium* (no. 236): Our model "is not the sphere, which is no greater than its parts, where every point is equidistant from the center, and there are no differences between them. Instead, it is the polyhedron, which reflects the convergence of all its parts, each of which preserves its distinctiveness." The image of the polyhedron responds creatively to the reality of multipolarity, as the pope points out in his address to the Council of Europe, November 25, 2015: "Creatively globalizing multipolarity, and I wish to stress this creativity, calls for striving to create a constructive harmony, one free of those pretensions to power which, while appearing from a pragmatic standpoint to make things easier, end up destroying the cultural and religious distinctiveness of people."[124] The image is similar to that of a prism:

We are in the epoch of globalization, and we think about what globalization is and what unity would be in the church: perhaps a sphere, where all points are equidistant from the center, all equal? No. This is uniformity. And the Holy Spirit doesn't create uniformity! What shape can we find? Let us consider a prism: the prism is unity, but all its parts are different; each has its own peculiarity, its charisma. This is unity in diversity. It is on this path that we Christians do what we call by the theological name of ecumenism: we seek to ensure that this diversity may be more harmonized by the Holy Spirit and become unity; we try to walk before God and be blameless; we try to go and find the nourishment we need to find our brother. This is our path, this is our Christian beauty![125]

This image of the polyhedron is accompanied in the apostolic exhortation *Evangelii Gaudium* by four principles, all of which are related to core Catholic beliefs and a specific Catholic Gospel identity: "Time is greater than space" is related to the Gospel acceptance of coexistence between the wheat and the weeds and the necessity of addressing challenges and differences patiently, over time, under God's grace; the prevailing of "unity over conflict" is related to the Gospel's message of peace; the rejection of "angelic forms of purity, dictatorships of relativism, empty rhetoric, objectives more ideal than real," and the primacy of reality over ideas are united to the principle of the Incarnation; the necessary tension between the whole and the part, the individual and the community, with the whole being greater than the part, is related to the totality embraced by the Gospel. The polyhedron's methodology of realization is encounter, dialogue, accompaniment, listening, mutual communal participation, mercy, and patience.[126]

Pope Francis's approach to global multipolarity, what I have referred to in this chapter as American "pluriformity," has begun to shape the church in the United States. Many interpret the pope's appointment of Bishop Blaise Cupich of Spokane as Archbishop of Chicago on September 20, 2014, as the beginning of the "Francis era" in the American church.[127] Two years later, on November 19, 2016, the pope raised Cupich and two other Americans—Joseph W. Tobin, the Archbishop of Indianapolis and then Archbishop of Newark, and Kevin Farrell, in charge of the Vatican Dicastery for Laity, Family and Life—to the rank of cardinal. Following Francis's call for the development of synodality in the church, the Archdiocese of Washington, D.C., and the Diocese of San Diego, in June 2014 and October 2016 respectively, conducted broad listening sessions among the people of God and held local diocesan synods. Although no detailed general report has been published, many of the dioceses in the United States participated in the pope's call for wide consultation amongst the laity in preparation for the two-year Synod on the Family (2014–2015). It is indicative of the pluriformity described in this essay that the United States Conference of Catholic Bishops' "Report on Reception and Implementation of *Amoris Laetitia* in the United States" and the examples now given from the Archdioceses of Washington, Los Angeles, and Philadelphia take very rich and extensive, but in some places cautious, approaches to implementing the pope's Apostolic Exhortation on the family.[128] This is in contrast to particular episcopal statements and more detailed guidelines for irregular situations offered by the bishops of Malta and Argentina. In complete opposition to the pope, another American, Cardinal Raymond Burke, has publicly disagreed with parts of *Amoris Laetitia*.[129] Given the history in the United States, the area of common ground among the laity or among the clergy is still hard to find. Yet something that breaks from the established pattern is beginning.

The stylistic and methodological change characteristic of Pope Francis comes into focus in the pope's apostolic visit to Cuba and the United States, September 19–28, 2015. One major commentator argues that during that visit, the pope wanted to reorient the American church in three different ways: (1) toward the political center; (2) to the geographical and existential margins; (3) to the heart of the Christian Gospel. Neither conservative nor liberal, the pope seems to be coming from a different place.[130] His style of leadership from 2013 onward, and then his apostolic visit, appears to open up a small but growing public space for dialogue and bridge building in an American church whose middle path of discourse and practice had been hollowed out.[131]

The pope's approach can be easily seen in three major speeches: to the bishops of the United States, September 23, 2015; to the United States Congress, September 24, 2015; and to a gathering of Hispanics, immigrants, and others at Independence Hall, Philadelphia, September 26, 2015. In all three speeches, in one form or another, Pope Francis raises issues of "ideological delusion," whether religious or economic, conservative or liberal. While not avoiding pressing issues such as the evil of abortion, care for the poor, abolition of the death penalty, and religious freedom, Francis argues for a personalistic methodology based on the "spirit of cooperation, solidarity, common good, bridge building, and dialogue.[132] Significantly, when speaking to Congress, he held up for cultural emulation the political leader Abraham Lincoln, the civil rights leader Martin Luther King, the social advocate for the poor Dorothy Day, and the religious leader Thomas Merton. To the bishops, Francis spoke words of pastoral care, prayer, and the "culture of encounter": "Dialogue is our method, not as a shrewd strategy but out of fidelity to the One who never wearies of visiting the marketplace, even at the eleventh hour, to propose his offer of love (Mt. 20.1–16). The path ahead, then, is dialogue among yourselves, dialogue in your presbyterates, dialogue with lay persons, dialogue with families, dialogue with society." Employing the same image he uses for the global church, the pope noted in Independence Hall: "If globalization is a sphere, where every point is equidistant from the center, it cancels everything out; it is not good. But if globalization is like a polyhedron, where everything is united but each element keeps its own identity, then it is good; it causes a people to grow, it bestows dignity and it grants rights to all."

In the context of this essay, Pope Francis is pressing for a "new ecumenism," both within and without the church. It is an ecumenism that has global implications, and it carries both a new vision of the church touching how pluriform parts fit together into a whole and a new methodology for bridging divides. This globalized perspective indicates that how the church in the United States handles its own pluriformity has implications for the world church. In this country, as we have seen, the two broad orientations of ecumenical alliances have within them a wide spectrum of opinions and stances; neither the ecumenical consensus of the constitutive period of reception nor the Catholic-Evangelical alliance of the past twenty years is monolithic. Our history shows us that once entering into the politics of history, the church must always both search for the outward limits of its unity and negotiate the inward tensions of its pluriformity. It must engage at the same time both similarity and difference. Sometimes within history there is more public coherence; at other times, the pluriformity that is intrinsic to Catholicism stretches toward breaking point; at still other times, one group or another appears to have the institutional ascendancy. But now entrenched in the ecclesial body politic on both the national and global scenes, the pluriformity will not disappear.

Seen from the historian's point of view, the trick is elasticity—similarity and difference together. Both authoritative hierarchical teaching and continuing communal growth are important, and they must be kept within the same spectrum of belief and communion in order to remain church. Internally, it is the push of pluriformity within communion that creates vitality and enables freedom; externally, it is this push of communion and pluriformity that enables a Catholic mission in a complex and pluralistic democratic society. In such a situation, in the church of the future, a large burden will be placed on leadership and authoritative teachers, and an equally large burden will be placed on the people to believe and to practice communion with each other. In the final analysis, the Catholic Church, with its hierarchical and communal dimensions, is comprised of a pilgrim people making their journey in faith through the politics of history to a plentitude of life that lies beyond. That historical vision is the legacy of the Council; it will be the distinguishing mark of the church of the future. Constructing an identity within the politics of history will be an ongoing task. And building this new public identity in its self-conscious theological explanations, pastoral applications, institutional expressions, catechetical formations, and spiritual discernments will be some of the challenges facing the American church in a global world.

NOTES

1. See Daniel O'Hanlon to Dan Carson, December 31, 1966, and "Dialogue on Post-Council Themes," October 30–November 1, 1965, O'Hanlon Papers, Box 8, file 15, and Box 8, file 6, Graduate Theological Union Library, Berkeley, California.

2. Joseph Bernardin, "Called to Be Catholic: Church in a Time of Peril" and Bernard Law, "Response to 'Called to Be Catholic,'" in *Origins* 26 (August 29, 1996): 166–171, at 168, 170. For further comment, see "Reaction to the Catholic Common Ground Project," *Origins* 26 (September 12, 1996); Philip J. Murnion, "Introduction," Cardinal Joseph Bernardin and Archbishop Oscar H. Lipscomb, *Catholic Common Ground Initiative: Foundational Documents* (New York: Crossroad, 1997).

3. For recent examples of public disagreement, see Paul J. Dieltz, "Catholicism and the Road to the American Presidency" (master's thesis, Graduate Theological Union, Berkeley, California, 2007); Donald W. Trautman, "How Accessible Are the New Mass Translations?," *America*, March 21, 2007, 9–11; Anthony J. Cernera and Eugene Korn, "The Latin Liturgy and the Jews," *America*, October 8, 2007, 10–13; Laurie Goodstein, "U.S. Bishops Urged to Challenge Obama," *New York Times*, November 11, 2008, A19; Matthai Durvila, "Prop. 8 Backlash Grows," *San Francisco Chronicle*, November 10, 2008, A1, 16; Ian Urbina, "New Turn in Debate Over Law on Marriage," *San Francisco Chronicle*, November 13, 2009; Amy Sullivan, "A Tale of Two Priests," *Time*, November 16, 2009; Joseph Bottom, "And the War Came," *First Things*, June/July 2009, 63–68; Ian Urbina, "Patrick Kennedy Says His Politics Led to Communion Ban," *New York Times*, November 23, 2009, A20; Ian Urbina, "New Turn in Debate Over Law on Marriage," *New York Times*, November 13, 2009; Robert Mickens, "Unlocking the Door of the Vernacular," *Tablet*, June 18, 2010, 11–12; Joshua J. McElwee, "Bishop to Congress: Religious Freedom Subject to 'Rapid Erosion,'" *National Catholic Reporter*, November 11–14, 2011, 5; Laurie Goodstein, "Illinois Bishops Drop Program Over Bias Rule," *New York Times*, December 29, 2011, A 1, 18; Roebert Mickens, "Rome's Three-Line Whip," *Tablet*, May 5, 2012, 9–10; LCWR, "Leadership Conference of Women Religious Decides Next Steps in Responding to CDF Report," press release, August 10, 2012.

4. "A New Pope from the Americas," *New York Times*, March 14, 2013, A1, 10–11; Edward Pentin, "Full Text and Explanatory Notes of Cardinals' Questions on 'Amoris Laetitia,' " *National Catholic Register*, January 26, 2017, 1–8; Tom Kington, "Backlash Grows Over Pope's 'Love,' " *Los Angeles Times*, April 14, 2017, A3; "Conservative Opposition to Pope Francis Spurs Talk of Schism in the Catholic Church," *Los Angeles Times*, April 20, 2017," World/Europe section.

5. Paul Starr, *The Creation of the Media: Political Origins of Modern Communications* (New York: Basic Books, 2004), 1–12, is a helpful analysis of how events become institutionalized in new pathways.

6. The "public" sphere, essential to the emergence of modern participative government, was first defined by Jurgen Habermas as a free zone between the individual and the state where "individuals participate in discussions about matters of common concern." See Mark E. Warren, "The Self in Discursive Democracy," in *The Cambridge Companion to Habermas*, ed. Stephen K. White (New York: Cambridge University Press, 1995), 167–200, at 171. An historiographical overview of the much debated meaning of "public" as religious interpreters see it is given in E. Harold Breitenberg, Jr., "To Tell the Truth: Will the Real Public Theology Please Stand Up," *Journal of the Society of Christian Ethics* 23 (Fall/Winter 2003): 55–96. In this essay, I take "public" in the widest sense to refer to society's broader religious, institutional, social, economic, political, intellectual, and cultural values and means of organization.

7. The identification of different time frames has been informed by Fernand Braudel, "History and the Social Sciences: The *Longue Durée*" (1958), reprinted in *Histories: French Constructions of the Past*, ed. Jacques Revel and Lynn Hunt (New York: New Press, 1995), 115–145.

8. For a parallel timeline in an entirely different field, see Stephen Schloesser, "'Dancing on the Edge of the Volcano': Biopolitics and What Happened After Vatican II," in *From Vatican II to Pope Francis: Charting a Catholic Future*, ed. Paul Crowley (Maryknoll, NY: Orbis Books, 2014), 3–26.

9. Christine Dubois, "Intercommunion: Guess Who's Been Coming to Dinner?," *U.S. Catholic*, April 1984, 31–37, at 36. The information in this paragraph is taken from public documents in the form of pastoral circulars, newspapers, and the documentary organ of the National Conference of Catholic Bishops, *Origins*: "When Other Christians May Be Admitted to Eucharistic Communion in the Catholic Church," April 12, 1976; Hunthausen to Dear People of God, March 27, 1984; Hunthausen to Dear Father, March 27, 1984. For general background, see Timothy P. Schilling, *Conflict in the Catholic Hierarchy: Coping Strategies in the Hunthausen Affair* (Utrecht, Netherlands: Labor Grafimedia BV, 2002).

10. Taken from *The Priorities and Goals of the Roman Catholic Church in Western Washington 1986–1990* and "Ecumenical Report for Pontifical Commission," Archives of the Archdiocese of San Francisco (hereafter AASF).

11. See "Apostolic Visitation Results Review," copy in author's possession. For an example of this conflation of issues, see Joseph Sobran, "Catholic Feminists

Gather in Washington," *Wanderer* 119, October 23, 1986, 1, 6; Gary Bullert, "Is Archbishop Hunthausen a Dissenter?," *Wanderer* 119, December 4, 1986, 3; Frank Morriss, "Is 'Hunthausen Panel' Only Looking at One Side?," *Wanderer*, April 9, 1987), 4, 6; Gary Bullert, *The Hunthausen File*, privately printed, St. Thomas League, Bellevue, Washington, 1992.

12. It is significant that one of the most perceptive of modern historical and theological commentators, Yves Congar, reflects extensively on Vatican II's departure from "Tridentinism." See Yves Congar, *Fifty Years of Catholic Theology: Conversations with Yves Congar*, ed. Bernard Lauret (Philadelphia: Fortress Press, 1988), 3–21. See more recently the collection of articles in Raymond F. Bulman and Frederick J. Parrella, eds., *From Trent to Vatican II: Historical and Theological Investigations* (New York: Oxford University Press, 2006). As an example of the recent explorations of the more latent elements of sameness during this same time frame, see Wietse de Boer, "Calvin and Borromeo: A Comparative Approach to Social Discipline," in *Early Modern Catholicism: Essays in Honour of John W. O'Malley, S.J.*, ed. Kathleen M. Comerford and Hilmar M. Pabel, eds. (Toronto: University of Toronto Press, 2001), 84–96.

13. See Will Herbert, *Protestant—Catholic—Jew* (Garden City, NY: Doubleday, 1955, 1960). For more recent evaluation, see the entire issue of *U.S. Catholic Historian* 23 (Winter 2005).

14. See the important document "The Use of English in the Liturgy," in *Prayer and Practice in the American Catholic Community*, ed. Joseph P. Chinnici and Angelyn Dries (Maryknoll, NY: Orbis, 2000), document 71, 218–222.

15. For some specific social background to the emergence of this shared public culture, see Robert Wuthnow, *The Restructuring of American Religion* (Princeton, NJ: Princeton University Press, 1988); Lizabeth Cohen, *A Consumer's Republic: The Politics of Mass Consumption in Postwar America* (New York: Knopf, 2003); William W. Bassett, ed., *The Bond of Marriage: An Ecumenical and Interdisciplinary Study* (Notre Dame, IN: University of Notre Dame Press, 1968); Timothy D. Lincoln, "Mobile Sheep and Stable Shepherds: The Ecumenical Challenge of Porous North American Denominational Boundaries," *Journal of Ecumenical Studies* 36 (1998): 425–436; James R. Kelly, "Sources of Support for Ecumenism: A Sociological Study," *Journal of Ecumenical Studies* 8 (1971), 1–9; and John E. Lynch, "Mixed Marriages in the Aftermath of 'Matrimonia Mixta,'" *Journal of Ecumenical Studies* 11 (1974): 637–659.

16. All citations and references taken from Austin Flannery, ed., *Vatican Council II: The Conciliar and Post Conciliar Documents* (Collegeville, MN: Liturgical Press, 1992).

17. I have decided here to concentrate on relationships between Christian bodies, but a parallel analysis could be developed for Catholic-Jewish relationships and Catholic-Muslim relationships. See Egal Feldman, *Catholics and Jews in Twentieth-Century America* (Urbana, IL: University of Illinois

Press, 2001); Charlotte Kelin, "Catholics and Jews—Ten Years After Vatican II," *Journal of Ecumenical Studies* 12 (1975): 471–483; Pim Valkenberg, Anthony Cirelli, eds., *Nostra Aetate: Celebrating Fifty Years of the Catholic Church's Dialogue with Jews and Muslims* (Washington, DC: Catholic University of America Press, 2016).

18. For more general studies, see the entire issue on "Ecumenism," *U.S. Catholic Historian* 28, no. 2 (Spring 2010).

19. Kevin Lynch, "Living Room Dialogues: Grass-Roots Ecumenism," *Ecumenist* 4, no. 1 (November/December 1965): 14–15; William B. Greenspun and Cynthia C. Wedel, eds., *Second Living Room Dialogues* (Glen Rock, NJ: Paulist Press, 1967), ix–xiv.

20. "Educating for Ecumenism," *Ecumenist* 4, no. 4 (May/June 1966): 69–70.

21. Chinnici and Dries, *Prayer and Practice*, document 83.

22. "Directory Concerning Ecumenical Matters: Part One," May 14, 1967, in *Vatican Council II: The Conciliar and Post-Conciliar Documents*, ed. Austin Flannery (Collegeville, MN: Liturgical Press, 1975), 483–501.

23. *Guidelines for Ecumenism, Diocese of Superior, Wisconsin* (Superior, WI: Chancery Press, 1967), "addenda." For a later example, see Archdiocese of Detroit, *Ecumenical Guidelines* (Detroit, MI: Division of Ecumenical and Interreligious Affairs, June 1977). For some more concrete examples, see Jeremy Bonner, *The Road to Renewal: Victor Joseph Reed & Oklahoma Catholicism, 1905–1971* (Washington, DC: Catholic University of America Press, 2008), 225–235; and Mary Christine Athans, "Jewish-Catholic Relations Since Vatican II: An Historical Overview," in *In Service of the Church*, ed. Victor J. Klimoski and Mary Christine Athans (St. Paul, MN: Saint Paul Seminary School of Divinity, University of St. Thomas, 1993), 79–98.

24. Complete results of the questionnaire are given in "*America's* Survey of Diocesan Post-Conciliar Programs," Part I, *America*, June 11, 1966, 825–831; Part II, *America*, July 9, 1966, 28–30; Part III, *America*, August 6, 1966, 136–138; Part IV, *America*, September 24, 1966, 343–344.

25. The step-by-step process can be followed in Frederick R. McManus, ed., *Thirty Years of Liturgical Renewal* (Washington, DC: Bishops' Committee on the Liturgy, National Conference of Catholic Bishops, 1987), documents 1, 2, 3, 5, 13.

26. For a full exposition, see Frederick R. McManus, "ICEL: The First Years," in *Shaping English Liturgy: Studies in Honor of Archbishop Denis Hurley*, ed. Peter C. Finnan and James M. Schellman (Washington, DC: Pastoral Press, 1990), 433–439, and supplementary material from other commentators, 461–489.

27. See David R. Holeton, "Anglican Liturgical Renewal, Eschatological Hope, and Christian Unity," in *Liturgical Renewal as a Way to Christian Unity*, ed. James F. Puglisi (Collegeville, MN: Liturgical Press, 2005), 1–19.

28. Donald Gray, "Common Words and *Common Worship*: Praying Together and Apart," in Puglisi, *Liturgical Renewal*, 21–33, at 31.

29. For full description, see Annibale Bugnini, *The Reform of the Liturgy 1948–1975* (Collegeville, MN: Liturgical Press, 1990); Frederick R. McManus, "The Roman Order of Mass from 1964–1969: The Preparation of the Gifts," in Finn and Schellman, *Shaping English Liturgy*, 107–138; McManus, *Thirty Years of Liturgical Renewal*, documents 22, 23.

30. Gordon Lathrop, "Knowing Something a Little: On the Role of the *Lex Orandi* in the Search for Christian Unity," in *So We Believe, So We Pray, Towards Koinonia in Worship*, ed. Thomas F. Best and Dagmar Heller (Geneva: WCC Publications, 1995), 39–48, at 40. For studies of the revision in all the churches, see Frank C. Senn, ed., *New Eucharistic Prayers: An Ecumenical Study of their Development and Structure* (New York: Paulist Press, 1987).

31. See Mary Alice O'Connor, *The NPM Reference for Prayers We Have in Common: A Catalog, Collection, and Evaluation of the ICET Texts* (Washington, DC: Pastoral Press, 1990).

32. I have tried to cover the initial development of some of these movements and their roots in the biblical renewal in "The Catholic Community at Prayer, 1926–1976," in *Habits of Devotion: Catholic Religious Practice in Twentieth-Century America*, ed. James M. O'Toole (Ithaca, NY: Cornell University Press, 2004), 9–87.

33. See Edward D. O'Connor, *The Pentecostal Movement in the Catholic Church* (Notre Dame, IN: Ave Maria Press, 1971), 141–175, for one of the first descriptions of the ecumenical convergence in the charismatic movement; Jim Scully, "Spirit-Baptism," *Catholic Charismatic* 2, no. 2 (June/July 1977), 26–29 (CROG, 2/9, Archives of the University of Notre Dame), for a description of the prayer groups and the centrality of scripture.

34. For initial descriptions, see James R. Kelly, "Does the RENEW Program Renew?," *America*, March 7, 1987, 197–199; Margaret Gallagher, "Participation in RENEW: Why and Why Not?," *Living Light* 21 (June 1985), 320–327.

35. See Normand Bonneau, *The Sunday Lectionary: Ritual Word, Paschal Shape* (Collegeville, MN: Liturgical Press, 1998); Henry C. Winter, "Presbyterians Pioneer the Vatican II Sunday Lectionary: Three Worship Models Converge," *Journal of Ecumenical Studies* 38 (2001), 127–150; Horace T. Allen Jr., "Common Lectionary: Origins, Assumptions, and Issues," *Studia Liturgica* 21, no. 1 (1991), 14–30.

36. For history of the development, see McManus, *Thirty Years of Liturgical Renewal*, 129–133; Bugnini, *The Reform of the Liturgy*, 402–404.

37. Bishops' Commission on the Liturgical Apostolate, "Survey of Diocesan Liturgical Practice," *Newsletter* 2 (October 1966).

38. See Arlo D. Duba, "Presbyterian Eucharistic Prayers," in Senn, *New Eucharistic Prayers*, 117–118.

39. Synod of Bishops, *The Ministerial Priesthood: Justice in the World* (Washington, DC: National Conference of Catholic Bishops, 1972), 48.

40. David J. Bowman, ed., *U.S. Catholic Ecumenism—Ten Years Later* (Washington, DC: United States Catholic Conference, 1975). This fine overview studies reports from state, metropolitan, county, city, parish, and personal works throughout the country.

41. See Raymond Arsenault, *Freedom Riders: 1961 and the Struggle for Racial Justice* (New York: Oxford University Press, 2006), particularly the tables on 533–587; for Catholic participation, see *A Report by the Members of the Chicago Interreligious Delegation to Albany, Georgia*, September 1962, in Catholic Interracial Council, AASF.

42. See "Racial and Cultural Relations: Denominational Statements, 1961–1963," *Interracial News Service* 325 (January/February 1964).

43. Mathew Ahmann, ed., *Race: A Challenge to Religion* (Chicago: Henry Regnery, 1963); John T. McGreevy, *Parish Boundaries: The Catholic Encounter with Race in the Twentieth-Century Urban North* (Chicago: University of Chicago Press, 1996); James F. Findlay, "Religion and Politics in the Sixties: The Churches and the Civil Rights Act of 1964," *Journal of American History* 77 (June 1990), 66–92; Joseph P. Chinnici, "Ecumenism, Civil Rights, and the Second Vatican Council: The American Experience," *U.S. Catholic Historian* 30, no. 3 (Summer 2012): 21–49.

44. See Amy L. Koehlinger, *The New Nuns: Racial Justice and Religious Reform in the 1960s* (Cambridge, MA: Harvard University Press, 2007); National Catholic Conference for Interracial Justice, *Selma*, pamphlet in Eugene Boyle Collection, Box A, AASF.

45. For examples, see the numerous articles in Sister M. Charles Borromeo Muckenhirn, ed., *The Changing Sister* (Notre Dame, IN: Fides, 1965); Beryl Satter, *Family Properties, Race, Real Estate, and the Exploitation of Black Urban America* (New York: Metropolitan, 2009); National Catholic Conference for Interracial Justice, "Report of the Director of Urban Services," NCCIJ, Correspondence, 1967, AASF; James F. Donnelly, "America: Metaphor and Method for Social Commitment," *America*, October 12, 1974.

46. Mary J. Henold, *Catholic and Feminist: The Surprising History of the American Catholic Feminist Movement* (Chapel Hill: University of North Carolina Press, 2008), 65 and passim.

47. "Ordination of Women in Other Christian Churches," Memorandum, July 25, 1972, Committee on Pastoral Research and Practices, AASF; "Women Priests," a report of the Committee on Pastoral Research and Practices, *Origins* 2 (December 29, 1972): 437–443.

48. Insightful on the crossover between Catholics and Protestants in this area is Amanda Porterfield, *The Transformation of American Religion: The Story of a Late Twentieth-Century Awakening* (New York: Oxford University Press, 2001), chap. 2 and 3.

49. For a complex analysis of the "consensus" around the American way of life, see Wendy Wall, *Inventing the "American Way": The Politics of Consensus from the New Deal to the Civil Rights Movement* (New York: Oxford University Press, 2008).

50. See Joseph P. Chinnici, "*Dignitatis Humanae Personae*: Surveying the Landscape for Its Reception in the United States," *U.S. Catholic Historian* 24 (Winter 2006): 63–82; Kenneth Cmiel, "The Emergence of Human Rights Politics in the United States," *Journal of American History* 86 (December 1999): 1231–1250; J. Bryan Hehir, "Religious Activism for Human Rights: A Christian Case Study," in *Religious Human Rights in Global Perspective: Religious Perspectives*, ed. John F. Witte and Johan David Van der Vyver (The Hague: Martinus Nijhoff, 1991), 97–119.

51. See Kristine LaLonde, " 'What We Believe Must Be Put Into Action': The Church and Social Activism 1960–1967," paper delivered at the Catholicism in Twentieth-Century America Project of the Cushwa Center for the Study of American Catholicism, University of Notre Dame.

52. The numerous theological dialogues during this period and beyond cannot be overlooked, but they are one manifestation of a common ecumenical turn. See Joseph A. Burgess and Brother Jeffrey Gros, eds., *Building Unity: Ecumenical Dialogues with Roman Catholic Participation in the United States* (New York: Paulist Press, 1989); Lydia Veliko and Jeffrey Gros, eds., *Growing Consensus II: Church Dialogues in the United States, 1992–2004* (Washington, DC: Bishop's Committee for Ecumenical and Interreligious Affairs, United States Conference of Catholic Bishops, 2005).

53. My own framing of the overall developments in the postconciliar era and its periodization has been influenced by the series of essays in Van Gosse and Richard Moser, eds., *The World the Sixties Made: Politics and Culture in Recent America* (Philadelphia: Temple University Press, 2003); and Beth Bailey and David Farber, *America in the Seventies* (Lawrence: University Press of Kansas, 2004).

54. Starr, *The Creation of the Media*, 1.

55. For various examples, see Mark Searle, "Liturgy and Social Ethics: An Annotated Bibliography," *Studia Liturgica* 21 (1991): 220–235.

56. See Bowman, *U.S. Catholic Ecumenism*; Charlotte Klein, "Catholics and Jews— Ten Years After Vatican II," *Journal of Ecumenical Studies* 12 (1975): 471–483; Gregory Baum, "After Twenty Years," *Ecumenist* 21 (January/February 1983): 17–19; James R. Kelly, "Roman Catholic Catechists and Their Ecumenical Attitudes," *Review of Religious Research* 25 (June 1984): 379–386; Eugene J. Fisher, "Research on Christian Teaching Concerning Jews and Judaism: Past Research and Present Needs," *Journal of Ecumenical Studies* 21 (1984): 421–436; Thaddeus D. Horgan, ed., *Walking Together: Roman Catholics and Ecumenism Twenty-Five Years After Vatican II* (Grand Rapids, MI: Eerdmans, 1990); Philip A. Cunningham, *Education for Shalom: Religious Textbooks and the Enhancement of the Catholic and Jewish Relationships* (Collegeville, MN: Liturgical Press, 1995); Mark R. Francis and Keith F. Pecklers, eds., *Liturgy for the New Millennium: A Commentary on the Revised*

Sacramentary (Collegeville, MN: The Liturgical Press, 2000); Arleon L. Kelley, ed., *A Tapestry of Justice, Service, and Unity: Local Ecumenism in the United States, 1950–2000* (Tacoma, WA: National Association of Ecumenical and Interreligious Staff Press, 2004).

57. The shared convictions of participative democracy are well articulated in Jon A. Shields, *The Democratic Virtues of the Christian Right* (Princeton, NJ: Princeton University Press, 2009), esp. 153–155.

58. For background, see David Farber and Jeff Roche, eds., *The Conservative Sixties* (New York: Peter Lang, 2003); Bruce J. Schulman, *The Seventies: The Great Shift in American Culture, Society, and Politics* (New York: Free Press, 2001); Bruce J. Schulman and Julian E. Zelizer, eds., *Rightward Bound: Making America Conservative in the 1970s* (Cambridge, MA: Harvard University Press, 2008); Donald T. Critchlow, *The Conservative Ascendancy: How the GOP Right Made Political History* (Cambridge, MA: Harvard University Press, 2007); William Martin, *With God on Our Side: The Rise of the Religious Right in America* (New York: Broadway, 1996, 2005); Thomas M. Gannon, "The New Christian Right in America as a Social and Political Force," *Archives de sciences sociales des religions* 52 (Juillet–Septembre, 1981): 69–83.

59. See "Neo-Conservatives in the Church," *Ecumenist* 21 (November/December 1982): 1–5.

60. I have tried to deal with the origins of this split in the community in "An Historian's Creed and the Emergence of Postconciliar Culture Wars," *Catholic Historical Review* 94 (April 2008): 219–244. For the notion of "cultural opening," this time applied to the new left, see Daniel Geary, " 'Becoming International Again': C. Wright Mills and the Emergence of a Global New Left, 1956–1962," *Journal of American History* 95 (December 2008): 710–736.

61. See Sara M. Evans, "Beyond Declension: Feminist Radicalism in the 1970s and 1980s," in *The World the Sixties Made: Culture in Recent America*, ed. Van Gosse and Richard Moser (Philadelphia: Temple University Press, 2003), 52–66; Jeffrey Escoffier, "Fabulous Politics: Gay and Lesbian, and Queer Movements, 1969–1999," in Gosse and Moser, *The World the Sixties Made*, 191–218; David Eisenbach, *Gay Power: An American Revolution* (New York: Carroll & Graf, 2006).

62. For a beginning overview, see William D. Dinges, "Roman Catholic Traditionalism," in *Fundamentalisms Observed*, ed. Martin E. Marty and R. Scott Appleby (Chicago: University of Chicago Press, 1991), 66–101; James Hitchcock, "Catholic Activist Conservatism in the United States," in Marty and Appleby, *Fundamentalisms Observed*, 101–135; Michael W. Cuneo, *The Smoke of Satan: Conservatives and Traditionalist Dissent in Contemporary American Catholicism* (New York: Oxford University Press, 1997); Patrick Allitt, *The Conservatives: Ideas and Personalities Throughout American History* (New Haven, CT: Yale University Press, 2009), 224–276.

63. See Peter L. Berger and Richard John Neuhaus, eds., *Against the World for the World: The Hartford Appeal and the Future of American Religion* (New York: Seabury

Press, 1976), particularly the article by Avery Dulles, "Unmasking Secret Infidelities: Hartford and the Future of Ecumenism," 44–62. For its importance, see Patrick W. Carey, *Avery Cardinal Dulles, SJ: A Model Theologian, 1919*–2008 (Mahwah, NJ: Paulist Press, 2010), 281–288.

64. "Hartford Appeal," reprinted in appendix I of Avery Dulles, *The Resilient Church: The Necessity and Limits of Adaptation* (Garden City, NY: Doubleday, 1977), 191–195, at 192, with commentary 62–91.

65. Dulles, *The Resilient Church*, 160–161, and 153–171 on Eucharistic sharing. See Avery Dulles, "Intercommunion Between Lutherans and Roman Catholics," and "Lutheran Response by George A. Lindbeck," *Journal of Ecumenical Studies* 13 (1976), 60–67.

66. For a consistent effort to frame the interpretation of modern Catholicism against a backdrop of secularism, see James Hitchcock, *On the Present Position of Catholics in America* (New York: National Committee of Catholic Laymen, 1978); *Catholicism and Modernity: Confrontation or Capitulation?* (New York: Seabury Press, 1979); *What Is Secular Humanism? Why Humanism Became Secular and How It Is Changing Our World* (Ann Arbor, MI: Servant Books, 1982). The charter for the forces opposed to "liberalization" was considered to be Msgr. George A. Kelly, *The Battle for the American Church* (Garden City, NY: Doubleday, 1979).

67. Andrew M. Greeley, *The Communal Catholic: A Personal Manifesto* (New York: Seabury Press, 1976). For another indication somewhat later, see George Gallup and Jim Castellli, *The American Catholic People: Their Beliefs, Practices, and Values* (Garden City, NY: Doubleday, 1987), chap. 2.

68. See, for example, Richard John Neuhaus, "Calling a Halt to Retreat," in Berger and Neuhaus, *Against the World for the World*, 138–164.

69. George A. Lindbeck, "A Battle for Theology," in Berger and Neuhaus, *Against the World for the World*, 20–43, at 22.

70. Dulles, *The Resilient Church*, 36–44, and "Unmasking Secret Infidelities," 59. In the latter article, Dulles notes the affinities between the Hartford Appeal and the work of James Hitchcock, *The Decline and Fall of Radical Catholicism* (Garden City, NY: Image Books, 1972).

71. Scott Flipse, "Below-the Belt Politics: Protestant Evangelicals, Abortion, and the Foundations of the New Religious Right, 1960–1975," in Farber and Roche, *The Conservative Sixties*, 127–141; Kristin Luker, *Abortion and the Politics of Motherhood* (Berkeley: University of California Press, 1984); Part III, "The Politics of Sexuality and Reproduction," in *Church Polity and American Politics: Issues in Contemporary American Catholicism*, ed. Mary C. Segers (New York: Garland, 1990); Rosalind Pollack Petchesky, "Antiabortion, Antifeminism, and the Rise of the New Right," *Feminist Studies* 7 (Summer 1981): 206–246.

72. For presentation of various views on an intellectual level, see Patricia Beattie Jung and Thomas A. Shannon, eds., *Abortion and Catholicism: The American Debate* (New York: Crossroad, 1988).

73. Complete background on the activities of the bishops throughout this period may be found in Timothy A. Byrnes, *Catholic Bishops in American Politics* (Princeton, NJ: Princeton University Press, 1991).

74. Michele Dillon, "Institutional Legitimation and Abortion: Monitoring the Catholic Church's Discourse," *Journal for the Scientific Study of Religion* 34, no. 2 (June 1995): 141–151; Timothy A. Byrnes, "The Politics of the American Catholic Hierarchy," *Political Science Quarterly* 108, no. 3 (Fall 1993): 497–514.

75. The conflicting interpretations of the legacy of John Courtney Murray and the interpretation of religious freedom are too complex to cover here. As starting points, see the different views expressed in David Hollenbach, "Theology and Philosophy in Public: A Symposium on John Courtney Murray's Unfinished Agenda," *Theological Studies* 40, no. 4 (December 1979), 700–715; Dennis P. McCann, "Natural Law, Public Theology and the Legacy of John Courtney Murray," *Christian Century*, September 5–12, 1990, 801–803; Todd David Whitmore, "What Would John Courtney Murray Say?," *Commonweal*, October 7, 1994, 16–22; and most recently, J. Leon Hooper, "Locked Together in (Religious) Argument: Justifying Vatican II's Declaration on Religious Liberty," in Crowley, *From Vatican II to Pope Francis*, 101–111.

76. See Leadership Conference of Women Religious Task Force, *Choose Life: A Statement Affirming the Value of Human Life and Promoting the Quality of Life*, 1977; and Msgr. James T. McHugh, "Analysis and Critique of *Choose Life*," Rose Eileen Masterman Papers, 2/21, Archives of the University of Notre Dame. For a sampling of biographies, see Ann Patrick Ware, ed., *Midwives of the Future: American Sisters Tell Their Story* (Kansas City, MO: Leaven Press, 1985).

77. National Coalition of American Nuns, "Statement on Its Opposition to the Hatch Act," April 14, 1982, AASF. For background in the 1960s, see Koehlinger, *The New Nuns*, 234.

78. A Call to Action, preparation for the Detroit Conference, "Personhood," in USCC Publications, collection 226, box 10, folder 32, 4–11, U.S. Bishops Conference on Liberty and Justice for All, Archives of the Catholic University of America.

79. "Nuns' Group Accuses Bishops of 'Sexism' on Abortion," *Florida Catholic*, October 19, 1984; and "Statement of the National Coalition of American Nuns on the Current Abortion Debate," 10/8/84, AASF.

80. As examples of this extended controversy, see Bernard J. Cooke, "The Church Turns to Power, Not Truth," *Los Angeles Times*, January 1, 1985; and William J. Levada, "Abortion: Catholic Faith Is Not Selective," *Los Angeles Times*, January 24, 1985.

81. See Richard Doerflinger, "Who Are Catholics for a Free Choice?," *America*, November 16, 1985, 312–317; Michele Dillon, *Catholic Identity: Balancing Reason, Faith, and Power* (New York: Cambridge University Press, 1999); "A Diversity of Opinions Regarding Abortion Exists Among Committed Catholics," *New York Times*, October 7, 1984; Kenneth A. Briggs, "Threat By Vatican Reported By Nuns," *New York Times*, December 15, 1984, A1.

82. See Report of a meeting held in Kansas City, Missouri, February 11, 1975, where the representatives of the National Committee for the Human Life Amendment, the Family Life Association, and the Right-to-Life Association argued over the tactics the bishops should employ in supporting the pro-life amendment. The document is in AASF.

83. See Michael W. Cuneo, "Life Battles: The Rise of Catholic Militancy Within the American Pro-Life Movement," in *Being Right: Conservative Catholics in America*, ed. Mary Jo Weaver and R. Scott Appleby (Bloomington: Indiana University Press, 1995), 271–299; James A. Sullivan, "Catholics United for the Faith: Dissent and the Laity," in Weaver and Appleby, *Being Right*, 107–137; Keith Cassidy, "Pro-Life Direct Action Campaigns: A Survey of Scholarly and Media Interpretations," in *Life and Learning VI*, ed. Joseph W. Koterski (Washington, DC: University Faculty for Life, 1997), 235–244. For general background, see Carol Mason, *Killing for Life: The Apocalyptic Narrative of Pro-Live Politics* (Ithaca, NY: Cornell University Press, 2002). For an illuminating contemporary reflection on the history of the pro-life movement and its need to return to its "consistent ethic" and nonviolent roots, see James R. Kelly, "Finding Renewal," *America*, February 16, 2009, 11–14.

84. For an overview, see John T. McGreevy, *Catholicism and American Freedom: A History* (New York: Norton, 2003), chap. 8–10; more particularly, Timothy A. Byrnes, "The Politics of the American Catholic Hierarchy," *Political Science Quarterly* 108, no. 3 (Fall 1993): 497–514; Michael Warner, *Changing Witness: Catholic Bishops and Public Policy, 1917–1994* (Grand Rapids, MI: Eerdmans, 1995).

85. James R. Kelly, "Managing Ecumenism: An Empirical Study of National, Arch/Diocesan Ecumenical Officers," *Journal of Ecumenical Studies* 17 (1980): 589–605.

86. "Pastoral Plan for Pro-Life Activities," November 20, 1975, in *Pastoral Letters of the United States Catholic Bishops, Vol. IV 1975–1983*, ed. Hugh J. Nolan (Washington, DC: National Conference of Catholic Bishops, 1984), 81–91, at 82, 87. For background and analysis, see Margaret Ross Sammon, "The Politics of U.S. Catholic Bishops: The Centrality of Abortion," in *Catholics and Politics: The Dynamic Tension Between Faith and Power*, ed. Kristin E. Heyer, Mark J. Rozell, and Michael A. Genovese (Washington, DC: Georgetown University Press, 2008), 11–26.

87. Statement released by "Religious Coalition for Abortion Rights," January 21, 1976, AASF.

88. "A Call to Concern," *Christianity and Crisis*, October 3, 1977, 222–224.

89. "Scholars Call Pro-Abortion Statement Irresponsible," *Our Sunday Visitor*, November 13, 1977.

90. See National Abortion Rights Action League, in Abortion file, 1977, AASF.

91. See letter of Eleanor Smeal, NOW President, in Abortion file, 1977, AASF.

92. John Bennett, "How to Argue About Abortion," *Christianity and Crisis*, November 14, 1977, 264–266, at 264. Bennett listed United Methodist, United Presbyterian, Presbyterian US, Episcopal, Lutheran (LCA), Reformed (RCA), American Baptist, and United Church of Christ.

93. Burrelle's T.V. Clips, November 29, 1977, in Abortion file, 1977, AASF.

94. Martin Tolchin, "Opponents on Abortion Issue Gear for a New Battle," *New York Times*, December 9, 1977.

95. January 4, 1978, Abortion file, 1977, AASF.

96. Lawrence Lader, "Abortion Opponents' Tactics," *New York Times*, January 1, 1978; Donald T. Critchlow, *Phyllis Schlafly and Grassroots Conservatism: A Woman's Crusade* (Princeton, NJ: Princeton University Press, 2005).

97. Russell Shaw to Bishop Kelly, "Anti-Catholicism in abortion controversy—NCCB/USCC response," January 13, 1978, Abortion file, 1977, AASF.

98. For the 1980s culture wars, see Andrew Hartman, *A War for the Soul of America: A History of the Culture Wars* (Chicago: University of Chicago Press, 2015); Anthony M. Petro, *After the Wrath of God: AIDS, Sexuality, and American Religion* (New York: Oxford University Press, 2015); James Davison Hunter, *Culture Wars: The Struggle to Define America* (New York: Basic Books, 1991).

99. For general background, see Jim Castelli, *The Bishops and the Bomb: Waging Peace in a Nuclear Age* (Garden City, NY: Doubleday, 1983); Bradford E. Hinze, "Developing a New Way of Teaching with Authority," in *Unfailing Patience and Sound Teaching: Reflections on Episcopal Ministry in Honor of Rembert G. Weakland, O.S.B.*, ed. David A. Stosur (Collegeville, MN: Liturgical Press, 2003), 165–196; and Kenneth R. Himes, "*The Challenge of Peace* and *Economic Justice for All*: Reflections Twenty Years Later," in Stosur, *Unfailing Patience and Sound Teaching*, 213–235.

100. See, for examples, LCWR Executive Committee, "Critiquing the Women's Pastoral Draft," *Origins*, August 30, 1990, 186–187; Archbishop Pilarczyk, "Vote on Women's Pastoral Delayed," *Origins*, September 27, 1990, 250–251.

101. Hitchcock, *On the Present Position of Catholics in America*, 44.

102. John H. Evans, "Polarization in Abortion Attitudes in U.S. Religious Traditions, 1972–1998," *Sociological Forum* 17 (2002): 397–422.

103. I address some of these issue and their impact on the church in *When Values Collide: The Catholic Church, Sexual Abuse, and the Challenges of Leadership* (Maryknoll, NY: Orbis, 2010).

104. See Gallup and Castelli, *The American Catholic People*; Mark J. Rozell, "Political Marriage of Convenience? The Evolution of the Conservative Catholic-Evangelical Alliance in the Republican Party," in *Catholics and Politics: The Dynamic Tension Between Faith and Power*, ed. Kristin E. Heyer, Mark J. Rozell, and Michael A. Genovese (Washington, DC: Georgetown University Press, 2008), 27–42. Very illuminating is the article by Seth Dowland, " 'Family Values' and the Formation of the Christian Right Agenda," *Church History* 78 (2009): 606–631.

105. Mary Bendyna, John C. Green, Mark J. Rozell, and Clyde Wilcox, "Catholics and the Christian Right: A View from Four States," *Journal for the Scientific Study of Religion* 39 (2000): 321–332.

106. For Neuhaus, see the entire issue of *First Things*, no. 192 (April 2009).

107. See in particular Neuhaus, *The Naked Public Square: Religion and Democracy in America* (Grand Rapids, MI: Eerdmans, 1984); *The Catholic Moment: The Paradox of the Church in the Postmodern World* (San Francisco: Harper & Row, 1990).

108. George Weigel, *Tranquillitas Ordinis: The Present Failure and Future Promise of American Catholic Thought on War and Peace* (New York: Oxford University Press, 1987). See in particular chap. 4 and pp. 314–324.

109. This movement in American Catholicism needs to be correlated with the insights in Herminio Rico, *John Paul II and the Legacy of Dignitatis Humanae* (Washington, DC: Georgetown University Press, 2002).

110. Printed with several significant commentaries in Charles Colson and Richard John Neuhaus, eds., *Evangelicals and Catholics: Towards a Common Mission Together* (Dallas: Word, 1995), xv–xxxiii. For history and reaction, see Norman L. Geisler and Ralph E. MacKenzie, *Roman Catholics and Evangelicals: Agreements and Differences* (Grand Rapids, MI: Baker, 1995), 491–502. For background, see Patrick Allitt, "The Transformation of Catholic-Evangelical Relations in the United States," in *The Sixties and Beyond: Dechristianization in North America and Western Europe, 1945–2000*, ed. Nancy Christie and Mchael Gaubreau (Toronto: University of Toronto Press, 2013), 144–156.

111. "Manhattan Declaration: A Call of Christian Conscience," http://www.manhattandeclaration.org/. For background, see David D. Kirkpatrick, "The Right Hand of the Fathers," *New York Times Magazine*, December 20, 2009, 24–29.

112. See Bill Bishop, *The Big Sort: Why the Clustering of Like-Minded America Is Tearing Us Apart* (Boston: Houghton Mifflin, 2008); for parallels in the Catholic community, see Charles R. Morris, *American Catholic: The Saints and Sinners Who Built America's Most Powerful Church* (New York: Random House, 1997), chap. 15.

113. See Dean R. Hoge and Jcqueline E. Wenger, *Evolving Visions of the Priesthood: Changes from Vatican II to the Turn of the New Century* (Collegeville, MN: Liturgical Press, 2003); Leslie Wookcock Tentler, "Sex and Subculture: American Catholicism Since 1945," in Christie and Gauvreau, *The Sixties and Beyond*, 156–185; James D. Davidson, "The Catholic Church in the United States: 1950 to the Present," in *The Church Confronts Modernity: Catholicism Since 1950 in the United States, Ireland, and Quebec*, ed. Leslie Woodcock Tentler (Washington, DC: Catholic University of America Press, 2007), 177–207. But also see, as a caution from the local experience, the vibrant description of the styles of parish life in Jerome P. Baggett, *Sense of the Faithful* (New York: Oxford University Press, 2009).

114. R. Scott Appleby, "Decline or Relocation? The Catholic Presence in Church and Society, 1950–2000," in Tentler, *The Church Confronts Modernity*, 208–235, at 230.

115. John Gehring, *The Francis Effect: A Radical Pope's Challenge to the American Catholic Church* (Lanham, MD: Rowman & Littlefield, 2015).

116. See Patrick Gilger, "Navigating the Benedict Option," *America*, April 17, 2017, 19–23; Bill McCormick, "An Interview with Rod Dreher," *America*, April 17, 2017, 24–25; Paul Baumann, "Detachment Plan: A Review of Rod Dreher's 'The Benedict Option'," *Commonweal*, March 16, 2017.

117. James Davison Hunter, *To Change the World: The Irony, Tragedy, and Possibility of Christianity in the Late Modern World* (New York: Oxford University Press, 2010); Daniel T. Rodgers, *Age of Fracture* (Cambridge, MA: Harvard University Press, 2011).

118. For biography, see Austen Ivereigh, *The Great Reformer: Francis and the Making of a Radical Pope* (New York: Holt, 2014). For vision, see Pope Francis, *Evangelii Gaudium: The Joy of the Gospel* (Boston: Pauline, 2013).

119. Joseph P. Chinnici, "The Cold War, the Council, and American Catholicism in a Global World," *U.S. Catholic Historian* 30, no. 2 (Spring 2012): 1–24.

120. For the general tensions, see Niall Ferguson, Charles S. Maier, Erez Manela, and Daniel J. Sargent, eds., *The Shock of the Global: The 1970s in Perspective* (Cambridge, MA: Belknap Press, 2010); Samuel Moyn, *The Last Utopia: Human Rights in History* (Cambridge, MA: Belknap Press, 2010); Mark A. Noll, *The New Shape of World Christianity: How American Experience Reflects Global Faith* (Downers Grove, IL: InterVarsity Press, 2009).

121. See "Address of His Holiness Pope Francis" commemorating the fiftieth anniversary of the institution of the Synod of Bishops, October 17, 2015, http://w2.vatican.va/content/francesco/en/speeches/2015/october/documents /papa-francesco_20151017_50-anniversario-sinodo.html.

122. See Pope Francis, *The Church of Mercy* (Chicago: Loyola Press, 2014); Pope Francis, *The Name of God Is Mercy: A Conversation with Andrea Tornielli*, trans. Oonagh Stransky (New York: Random House, 2016).

123. See Ivereigh, *The Great Reformer*, 300, with its application in *Evangelii Gaudium*, no. 1–19. The same methodology is applied in his exhortations and encyclical.

124. "Address of Pope Francis to the Council of Europe," November 25, 2014, https://w2.vatican.va/content/francesco/en/speeches/2014/november /documents/papa-francesco_20141125_strasburgo-consiglio-europa.html.

125. Meeting with the Pentecostal community in Caserta, July 18, 2004, as cited in Walter Kasper, *Pope Francis' Revolution of Tenderness and Love* (Mahwah, NJ: Paulist Press, 2015), 244–266.

126. Pope Francis, *Evangelii Gaudium*, 222–237.

127. See Gehring, *The Francis Effect*, 131–169.

128. The *Report* and the various diocesan implementing documents are available at http://www.usccb.org/.

129. For Burke, see Marco Politi, *Pope Francis Among the Wolves: The Inside Story of a Revolution* (New York: Columbia University Press, 2014), 180–181.

130. John L. Allen, Jr., *Francis: The Pope's Bold Message Comes to America* (New York: Time, 2015), 7.

131. The middle path or search for common ground is well covered, with several examples, in Gehring, *The Francis Effect*, 193–206.

132. The speeches can be accessed on the Vatican website, https://w2.vatican.va /content/vatican/en.html.

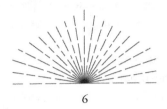

6

Catholic Worship in a Contentious Age

Andrew H. Walsh

It is two o'clock on a November Sunday, and St. Patrick's Catholic Church on Mission Street in San Francisco—a sturdy, red brick, Victorian Gothic structure rebuilt after the great earthquake and fire of 1906—is packed with worshippers deeply engaged in the Mass. The singing is energetic, and almost everyone present receives the Eucharist.

Surrounded by towering office blocks and hotels, the church faces the Yerba Buena Gardens. It was established in 1851 to serve Irish immigrants drawn to California's gold rush. As its choice of patron saint suggests, this parish was one of the first manifestations of English-speaking Catholic presence on the west coast of the United States. Like many other churches named for St. Patrick, it served as a focal point of Irish Catholic community for generations. Its large stained-glass windows still depict the patron saints of each of Ireland's thirty-two counties. St. Patrick's Irish days, however, are far behind it. The Mass this afternoon is celebrated in Tagalog, the chief language of the Philippines. The parish's current mission is to meet the religious needs of conventioneers, tourists, downtown workers, and Filipino immigrants.

The Catholic Church in the United States has been a multiethnic enterprise for most of its long history. But the scope of ethnic and racial diversity among the Catholic population of the country has multiplied dramatically since the 1960s, and the impact of that change can be most readily assessed by considering contemporary worship. At the moment, the Archdiocese of San Francisco, which is not atypical in this respect, provides formal pastoral services to twenty-three immigrant groups, with worship conducted not only in English and Spanish (in thirty-four of ninety-eight parishes), but in Tagalog, Vietnamese, Chinese, Korean, Tongan, Samoan, Polish, Burmese, Aramaic, Croatian, Portuguese, Arabic, and many other tongues.

Fifty years ago, the racial and ethnic diversity of the Catholic population did not have much impact on worship, which in America, and around the world, was a fairly uniform commodity. The language of the Mass, and of almost all forms of Catholic worship, was Latin, as it had been for centuries. Routine "low Mass" in American parishes looked and sounded very much the same, no matter what the native language of the congregation. All used a uniform Latin text, the *Roman Missal*, first published in 1570 in the wake of the Council of Trent. There might be some variations in the musical forms, if any, that accompanied services and in the popular devotions observed in different parishes. But the only major variable among parishes on Sunday morning was the language used in preaching the sermon.

The new and profound variety of contemporary Catholic worship in the United States, however, runs deeper than the languages in use. In the Archdiocese of San Francisco, worshippers can pick a Mass accompanied by "contemporary music," Gospel music, Gregorian chant, or many different ethnic styles of religious music. A third layer of diversity might be described as theological.[1] In recent years, a small group of American Catholics who wish to worship with the text and norms of the Mass used from 1570 to 1965 have gained permission to do so. In the Archdiocese of San Francisco, four parishes celebrate what Pope Benedict XVI denominated the "Extraordinary Form" of the Mass, some once a week and others once a month. A few others use the Latin text of the "Novus Ordo" Mass, the post–Vatican II liturgy authorized in 1970.

And so, in the second decade of the twenty-first century, individual Catholics can find, in most parts of America, a range of worship options to meet their religious needs and tastes. This diverse "new normal" developed in the wake of the Second Vatican Council, which met in four sessions from 1962 to 1965. On December 4, 1963, the world's Catholic bishops voted 2,147 to 4 to approve the *Constitution on the Sacred Liturgy*, the first major document produced at the Council. It was then approved by Pope Paul VI, paving the way for dramatic revision in Catholic worship.

The *Constitution* outlined a strong case for liturgical restoration and revitalization. It directed that

> the rite of the Mass is to be revised in such a way that the intrinsic nature and purpose of its several parts, as also the connection between them, may be made more clearly manifested and that devout and active participation of the faithful may be more easily achieved. For this purpose the rites are to be simplified, due care being taken to preserve their substance; elements which, with the passage of time, came to be duplicated, or were added with but little advantage, are now to be discarded; other elements which have suffered injury through accidents of history are now to be restored to the vigor which they had in the days of the Holy Fathers, as may seem useful or necessary.[2]

In the United States, the first wave of liturgical change driven by Vatican II took effect in December 1964. American Catholics were not elaborately prepared for change; indeed, they received only a few weeks' notice. So when the liturgical changes introduced after Vatican II are discussed, words like avalanche, revolution, and upheaval shower down upon the reader. While there is no doubt Catholics experienced an unprecedented degree of liturgical change from the mid-1960s to the mid-1970s,[3] it is also true that this burst of change has receded into the past. Those with adult memories of pre–Vatican II worship are now in their seventies—a rapidly diminishing cohort in the vast sea of American Catholics. In the United States, the texts and rubrics for Catholic worship have been largely stable for the past forty years, which permits an assessment.

In 1960, few American Catholics entertained even the possibility that any significant change in the patterns and practices of worship could or should take place. The reception given to the surprising and major liturgical changes that followed was stunningly positive and pervasive. By 1976, survey research indicated that about 85 percent of American Catholics preferred the new, English-language Mass to the old one, with an even higher percentage of priests agreeing.[4] Since then, scores of surveys have reported that American Catholics overwhelmingly value the Mass and other sacraments of the church in their current form, feel profoundly shaped by them, and treasure the communion with God and each other that Catholic worship produces. For example, 89 percent of Catholics surveyed in 2011 by the *American Catholics in Transition* project said they valued the Mass and other sacraments, and 75 percent agreed with the statement "the sacraments of the Church are essential to my relationship with God."[5]

Despite these very high levels of approval, criticisms of the changes, and remorse in some quarters over the loss or diminution of many traditional devotional practices, have produced some resistance, which began to get better organized in the late 1980s. Although these increasingly loud critiques have not produced notable rollbacks, they have weight because of the passion of the critics, their access to impressive resources, and the sympathy they have generated among the church's leaders. Both Pope John Paul II and Benedict XVI harbored reservations about post–Vatican II liturgical change and the messages that it communicated to believers. Both popes leaned in traditionalist directions and supported accommodation with Catholics who sought to resurrect the old pre–Vatican II, Tridentine Mass, which Pope VI had discouraged from being celebrated anywhere when the "New Order" Mass was approved in 1969. Most notably, in 2007, Benedict made it much easier for priests everywhere to choose to celebrate the Tridentine form of the Mass, on their own initiative. In doing so, he raised the hopes of "restorationists" that more significant reversals could be expected.

While celebrations of the Tridentine rite have not attracted a broad base of support, there have been efforts in recent years to revive flagging pre–Vatican II devotional practices, and a lively "neo-traditional" movement in church architecture has emerged. Catholic "traditionalism" also finds much support among the younger clergy and many of the nation's bishops. Anyone reading journalistic accounts of Catholic life in recent years is aware that there have been many skirmishes around the nation as priests and bishops have advocated the return of older religious norms; forbidding female altar servers and instructing priests not to administer the Eucharist "in two kinds" to the laity (communing laity with only the consecrated host and not from the communion chalice as well) are two widespread examples.

But even here, some limiting factors appear to reduce the prospect of rollback. Pope Benedict, in particular, grounded his willingness to authorize the celebration of the Tridentine rite, as a valid "extraordinary" form of the Eucharist, on the grounds that the Catholic Church does not and cannot change its core teachings. It is hard to see how, under that kind of rationale, liturgical changes with strong records of papal approval could be wholly reversed. It can thus be argued that Pope Benedict's actions largely added to the diversity of legitimate practice, rather than restricting it. Further, the recently elected Pope Francis, to the disappointment of liturgical restorationists, does not harbor the sympathy to older forms of Catholic worship that his two predecessors shared. He seems to be a man shaped by the forms and values of the 1969 Mass, most notably by its spirit of simplicity—a man who wants the church to focus on the poor, and to look forward.

Whether one supports or opposes the liturgical reformation of the late twentieth century, at least one further general conclusion must be put forward in any estimate of the state of Catholic worship. Since the 1960s, the participation of American Catholics in worship and other activities has declined sharply, probably by more than half. American Catholics say they like Catholic worship, but they participate in it much less often than they used to. This is a sharp disappointment to supporters of the Catholic liturgical movement, who believed and taught that worship in English would strengthen the faith and practice of ordinary believers—indeed that, because of the inherent power of the liturgy, it would do a better job of forming Catholics than formal religious education programs. That position is hard to sustain when the Gallup Poll reports that the percentage of Catholics who say they have attended Mass in the past seven days has dropped from levels above 70 percent in the mid-1950s to 45 percent in 2008.[6] Other surveys indicate even lower attendance, with the Center for Applied Research in the Apostolate (CARA) at Georgetown University reporting that only 23 percent of Catholic adults say they attend Mass at least once a week.[7] In the 2013 report *American Catholics in Transition*, 32 percent of those surveyed said they attended Mass at least once a week.[8]

Until the mid-1960s, Catholics were the most observant religious group in American society. Since then, they have dropped into the middle of the pack. In 2009, Gallup reported that, for the first time, Catholics attended worship less frequently than American Protestants, and they are certainly far less observant than Evangelical Protestants. Catholics, who were once taught that failing to attend Mass at least once a week is a mortal sin, now are more likely to decide for themselves how often to go and how to value that decision. A survey of American Catholics that was part of the American Religious Identification Survey (ARIS) of 2008 found that 17.3 percent of Catholics thought that someone "considered to be a good Catholic" should attend Mass at least "a few times a year"; 12 percent said they didn't know how often that might be.

Like some other bishops, Cardinal Timothy Dolan of New York acknowledged that challenge in 2010, when he declared a "Year of the Mass" in his archdiocese. He told Laurie Goodstein of the *New York Times* that "he was chagrined when he saw a long line of people last Sunday on Fifth Avenue. 'I'm talking two blocks, a line of people waiting to get into,' he said, pausing for suspense, 'Abercrombie and Fitch. And I thought, wow, there's no line of people waiting to get into St. Patrick's Cathedral, and the treasure in there is of eternal value. What can I do to help our great people appreciate that tradition?' "9

THE CATHOLIC TRADITION OF WORSHIP

Catholic worship—the most widespread and widely practiced form of Christianity, both in the United States and the world—has its roots in the earliest days of the Christian community. Rome was an early center of Christian life in the Roman Empire. Roman Rite traditions of worship—in Latin and in Greek—form one of a cluster of ancient regional traditions of Christian worship (the others are Alexandrian, Antiochian, Armenian, and Chaldean), out of which Catholic, Orthodox, and Oriental Orthodox worship have developed. These traditions share important elements; perhaps most significantly, they are all both liturgical (traditions of public worship by a body of Christians acting together) and sacramental. (According the *Catechism of the Catholic Church*, a sacrament is an "efficacious sign of grace, instituted by Christ and entrusted to the Church, by which divine life is dispensed to us.") Sacraments, in other words, put believers into direct contact with God's grace and with the reality of God's life. They are agents of initiation, transformation, sustenance, healing, and above all, salvation. They come from God, through the church, to believers, making and sustaining them as members of the Body of Christ.

All of these ancient regional rites embody the gradual transformation of Jewish worship into Christian worship. They are all complex, incorporating and signifying many elements of belief and teaching. In all, the two foundational sacraments are baptism and the Eucharist, with the Eucharist in particular evolving as an amalgam. It contains elements inherited from both synagogue worship (reading and explaining Scripture) and temple worship (repentance and ritual sacrifice), as well as distinctly Christian ideas about Christ's incarnation, sacrifice at the crucifixion, salvific role, and the practice of believers gathering for a common meal. From its earliest days, the Eucharistic texts have incorporated references to a host of themes—creation, the fall of humanity, the incarnation of Christ, the Last Supper, Passover, the Crucifixion, and Resurrection. The first section of the Eucharistic service (called the "Liturgy of the Word" in contemporary terminology) involves the reading of selections from Scripture and commentary by the celebrant. It presents few interpretive complexities. The second major part, "the Liturgy of the Eucharist," is and was harder to summarize. One of its two major clusters of themes is the celebration of a common meal, the blessing and sharing of bread and wine, understood as the consecrated body and blood of Christ, and as a continuation of the Last Supper. The other cluster of themes and references are to Christ's sacrifice, as the innocent Lamb of God sacrificed for others in a cosmic Passover of universal significance. As celebrated in the early centuries of the Christian church, the Eucharistic service in all of the early regional rites and piety presumed that the baptized believers present would receive the Eucharist. No attempts were made to prioritize the mysteries.

By the sixth century, the Roman Eucharistic rite had begun to stabilize in a form recognizable today, and the authority of the papacy was broadly acknowledged, especially in the West. In a world where all texts were copied by hand, uniformity was impossible, and under the umbrella of the Roman rite, several regional sub-rites flourished among Latin-speaking Christians in various parts of the empire. As late as the Middle Ages, across Europe, many regional rites were recognized as valid by the leaders of the church, as parts of a "family" of Roman rites: two non-Roman ones in Italy, three in little England, several on the Iberian Peninsula, and many "Gallican" rites in what is now France. In addition, at least nine Catholic religious orders had their own liturgical traditions and practices.

Interpretation of the liturgy evolved, particularly after the development of the sacrament of individual penance, which placed questions about individual sin and repentance into clearer focus and gave them higher priority. How and when are Christians worthy to receive the sacraments? In the Western church, worship in this period was also shaped in the monastic setting, and scholastic philosophy and theology began to press for clarification of the church's complex, mystical teachings about the liturgy. Clear-reasoning scholastics wanted to know what the hierarchy of teachings was: was the Mass chiefly about sacrifice or about the common meal?

A major interpretive change became clear in the eleventh century: the common meal dimension of the Eucharist was subordinated to the sacrificial dimension. That was followed in the twelfth century by changes in piety that made it very uncommon for laypeople to receive the Eucharist when they attended Mass. The architectural evolution of medieval churches illustrates this change. Laypeople attending Mass stood in a nave, separated from the altar by a carved wooden screen and by the chancel, an area of the church reserved for clergy. The ritual actions of the celebrant were, in the words of James White, a sacred action glimpsed from afar. The consecrated host was treated as a relic, a holy thing that needed to be protected in a fallen world. Ordinary, sinful mortals approached the Eucharist in trembling and on rare occasions. The sixteenth-century Council of Trent, which aimed to *increase* the frequency of communion, mandated that lay Catholics should receive communion at least once a year. Medieval Catholics—and their successors for hundreds of years thereafter—attended Mass chiefly to observe the consecration of the body and blood of Christ, to "commune visually" in the "sacrifice of the mass."[10]

The Catholic liturgical reforms of the sixteenth century, framed at Trent, were all aimed to counter the attacks of Protestant reformers on Catholic institutional practices, teaching, and worship. The liturgical decisions of the Counter-Reformation were enshrined in a new set of uniform and printed liturgical books issued in Rome, notably the *Roman Breviary* (a prayer book for priests) and the *Roman Missal*, a standard text of the Roman Rite Mass in 1568 and 1570. Over the next several centuries, these Roman texts were gradually imposed across Europe, with a big push occurring in the nineteenth century. This produced a much more uniform world of Catholic worship than had ever existed, and one far more clearly keyed to Rome.

A new, Counter-Reformation style of church emerged to provide a more coherent setting for revised Catholic worship. The Jesu Church in Rome, completed in 1575, set a pattern soon followed worldwide. It dispensed with the chancel and altar screen and structured sacred space in an explicitly theatrical way. The altar and pulpit were designed for maximum visibility—the central ritual act for most worshipers was *observing* the consecration of the Eucharist, so they needed to see it clearly. The priest celebrated the sacrament on behalf of the people, but without their direct involvement and, most often, without offering them the chance to receive it during the service itself. For the next several hundred years, those receiving communion often did so before or after the Mass, or at various points in the Mass when a noncelebrant priest might distribute communion from a side altar, and not after the celebrant himself received it.

A Baroque pattern of church design evolved to heighten the new interpretation yet further. In the medieval era, consecrated elements were stored close to the altar in a separate cabinet or even in a hanging storage vessel. After Trent, the tabernacle where the consecrated host—understood as Christ himself present in the church—was stored was moved onto the main altar. Baroque and Rococo architects then imagined the altar as a heavenly throne room for God, which produced immense and magnificent high altars, often separated from the nave of the church by a low railing where communicants might kneel to receive the Eucharist.

If Catholics attending Mass and other services mostly did not understand Latin, could not hear the priest clearly since his back was turned to them, and rarely received the Eucharist, what were they doing? Most of them came to church to be in the presence of God, to follow the rules the church made for them, and, increasingly, to pray privately during church services. Catholic devotional practices—prayers like the Rosary, practices like adoration of the consecrated Eucharist, prayers directed to Mary the Mother of God and to particular saints—all developed rapidly after the seventeenth century. For most of this period, Catholics were forbidden to use translations of the Latin texts of the Mass or other sacraments. In fact, they rarely followed the prayers and actions of the priest celebrating the sacrament before them. Instead, Catholics used the sacred setting of the church—filled with sacred symbols and icons—and the occasion of the Mass for private prayer, repentance, and communion with their own chosen patrons among the saints. Catholics "visited" the Blessed Sacrament—going to church to pray before the tabernacle containing the consecrated host. At other times, the consecrated host was "exposed," or displayed as in the Forty Hours Devotion, elevated in the Benediction of the Blessed Sacrament, or carried in procession. Individual religious orders often promoted particular devotions, as with the Jesuits and the cult of the Sacred Heart of Jesus, the Claretian Fathers and the cult of St. Jude the Obscure in Chicago, or the Franciscans who sponsor a weekly novena at the Shrine of St. Anthony of Padua in Cincinnati.

This kind of disjuncture—private worship in a public setting—could crop up even among proponents of "liturgical reform," as with the "dialogue mass," an experimental twentieth-century precursor of the post–Vatican II reforms that was permitted by some bishops in some places during the 1940s and 1950s. In it, a priest and his altar servers celebrated the Mass at the altar, in Latin and in a low voice. Simultaneously, another priest stood in the nave before the congregation, reading the prayers of the Mass aloud in the local language, and the congregation then responded to him. But the "real" Mass, the canonically valid celebration, was considered to be the quiet Mass at the high altar.

Liturgical Reform

To many laypeople, it still seems that the liturgical changes of the 1960s erupted from nowhere. But there is a substantial prehistory to the reforms. Even at Trent, there was considerable awareness that the church's worship traditions had evolved, although this was emphasized less in subsequent Catholic apologetics than claims about the church's unwavering fidelity to early church teachings and practice. As early as the late seventeenth century, liturgical scholars, many of them Benedictines and Jesuits, began to document the history of Catholic worship and to grasp the degree of change that took place in the medieval and early modern period. A "liturgical movement" sprang up in the nineteenth century and spread in the twentieth, aimed at restoration and revitalization of a fuller set of Catholic worship practices. More directly, in the twentieth century, two popes began to teach about the need to revitalize Catholic worship in order to respond to challenges to Catholic identity that accompanied modernization. Pope Pius X, a conservative, antimodern figure in most respects, wanted to strengthen Catholic identity, which was eroding rapidly as Catholic countries like France and Italy underwent modernization and urbanization. In 1903, he issued a *motu proprio* on sacred music (supporting the revival of Gregorian chant), which argued that key to increasingly the intensity of Catholic identity was "active participation in public prayer."[11] He followed that in 1905 with a decree, *Sancta Tridentia Synodus*, calling attention to the Council of

Trent's teaching that Catholics should commune at every liturgy they attend, a practice not actually followed since before 1000. That encouraged a frequent-communion movement that gathered strength over the course of the century. And as Catholic scholars considered the challenge of increasing participation in worship, they inevitably turned to the question of how and to what degree the language of the Mass, Latin, a language few Catholics understood, impeded participation.

Pope Pius XII moved this agenda forward in the 1950s. He authorized the use of vernacular languages in the celebration of sacraments and services like baptism, matrimony, and the funeral, so that participants could grasp the religious teachings conveyed by these rites. In 1951, he authorized a new text for the Easter vigil based on ancient sources. In 1955 followed the revision of all the services of Holy Week, restoring early Christian prayers and practices recovered by modern scholars. Throughout the 1950s, a pontifical Commission for the Restoration of the Liturgy worked within the Congregation on Sacred Rites. One of the pivotal recoveries influencing discussion was a text called the *Apostolic Tradition*, rediscovered in the nineteenth century and widely republished in the early twentieth, which offered an account of worship in early-third-century Rome attributed to the theologian Hippolytus. It enormously increased knowledge about early Christian practices, including the Eucharist, initiation, ordination, and daily prayer.[12] Among other things, it stressed centrality of the common-meal tradition in the Eucharist.[13]

WORSHIP AFTER VATICAN II

Liturgical change came rapidly after the First Sunday of Advent in 1964. The initial wave included the limited use of the vernacular in the Mass, although for several years the text itself remained that of the old *Roman Missal*. One of the most striking early changes was the shift of the location of the celebrant so that he faced the congregation—a move that restored early Christian practice and emphasized the assembly of baptized believers for collective worship. In most Catholic churches, this change required the use of a new and temporary altar located much closer to the people, since almost all churches had an altar affixed to the back wall of the sanctuary. Congregants could now see what the priest was doing at the altar, which had not been possible when he stood with his back to the congregation.

Priests were also instructed that preaching was a vital part of the new liturgy and directed to base their homilies on the day's Scripture readings, emphasizing the proclamation of the Gospel rather than moral exhortation. Another dramatic change was the instruction to receive the Eucharist in a standing posture, rather than kneeling at an altar rail. "Most of the physical changes surrounding the reception of the sacrament were implemented to reflect the fact that those receiving the Eucharist were eating a meal," the historian Margaret McGuiness wrote. "Kneeling, liturgists explained, was a posture associated with penance, contrition, begging, beseeching, apologizing, asking for forgiveness, not a normal posture for eating."[14] This was one of a series of shifts in what McGuiness calls "liturgical etiquette"—the gestures, postures, and rituals though which Catholics approached the communion chalice. She notes that even before Vatican II, religious educators and liturgical scholars were expressing concern that the very elaborate codes of behavior—standing, kneeling, genuflection, making the sign of the cross repeatedly—had the effect of discouraging many, especially children, from participating in the Eucharist. Before the Council, this discussion was part of a growing effort to encourage the frequent reception of the Eucharist that Pope Pius X had initiated at the beginning of the twentieth century. McGuiness estimated that by the mid-1960s, about 30 percent of those attending a typical American Mass received the Eucharist. By the mid-1970s, in the new climate of liturgical reform, the percentage had doubled. The most dramatic change in liturgical piety involved receiving communion "in two kinds"—both the consecrated host and a sip of consecrated wine from a chalice—instead of just the host, as had been the practice of the laity for centuries. Perhaps an even greater symbolic departure was the shift in the manner in which communicants received the host. Rather than kneeling and having it placed directly on their tongues, communicants were encouraged to stand and receive it in their hands. Liturgical scholars tended to argue that those attending a shared meal did not wait for their hosts to place food in their mouths; they took it with their own hands and fed themselves. This was more appropriate for baptized believers who shared fully in the Body of Christ. Reception of communion in the hand was more controversial than reception standing, and it took until 1976 for the nation's Catholic bishops to formally approve the practice—although the practice had become widespread by the late 1960s. Some Catholics never felt comfortable receiving in the hand and continued to receive the Eucharist on their tongues.

One of the challenges of changing Eucharistic etiquette involved the problem of how to rebalance popular understanding of the Eucharist—to renew emphasis on the shared sacred meal aspect of the sacrament, which had been drastically deemphasized for almost one thousand years. While most Catholics welcomed the new and joyful emphasis on the resurrected Christ and the less formal celebration of the rite, some who had been brought up to respect and fear Christ's sacrifice of himself and the miracle of the transformation of bread and wine into the body and blood of Christ felt a sense of loss. "A significant part of the older Mass celebrated since Trent had taken the form of a ritual focused on a thing untouchable in both a metaphorical and a physical sense," the historian Mark Massa wrote. "All of that now seemed banished with the sound of guitars, the sudden appearance of banners, and an easy familiarity with the 'bread of celebration' that left a number of Catholics reeling between confusion and feelings of betrayal."[15]

Key explanations of the changes and reassurances of their Catholicity came from a rising generation of liturgical scholars produced in the earlier stages of liturgical reform. One of the most important for the United States, Massa argued, was Frederick McManus of the Catholic University of America, a distinguished canon lawyer, a columnist for *Worship* magazine in the 1950s and 1960s, and editor of the newsletter of the Committee on Worship of the National Conference of Catholic Bishops. His "historical consciousness allowed the readers of McManus's columns to understand how and why history makes different demands on Church worship in different cultural periods."[16]

The revision of Catholic worship led, in the late 1960s and 1970s, to an enormous wave of church renovations and new church construction to create sacred spaces suitable to the new liturgy. "It is as if," James F. White wrote,

the church building shifted from being a theater with a stage and a house clearly distinguished to a structure in which everyone is on stage. . . . The result was that thousands of churches were found unsatisfactory for reformed worship and underwent drastic renovation. New churches were built on an entirely difference principle. God was now imagined as not somewhere out beyond the east window but present in the midst of God's people. This produced buildings whose focus said more about immanence than transcendence. Attention shifted from the church building as the house of God to the church as the house of God's people.[17]

Two themes from the *Constitution* reverberated: first that the Mass was "the summit and source of the Church" and that the goal was "full, conscious, and active" participation by the laity. The church's liturgical books—and its chapels, churches, and cathedrals were reshaped to reveal the "noble simplicity" native to the Roman rite. These dictates "triggered an avalanche of change. It is likely that the 1960s saw as much iconoclasm in Roman Catholic churches as the Reformation had in some Protestant lands. Thousands of plaster images bit the dust or ended up in flea markets. Communion rails and confessional booths disappeared. Secondary altars were discarded. Stations of the cross and all kinds of devotional images disappeared."[18]

The result was a new and aesthetically severe "Catholic plain style" that often embraced architectural modernism. Good examples of the new aesthetic include the chapel at Our Lady of Gethsemane Monastery in Kentucky (although austerity was not a new style for Cistercian monks). A much more modest example is the Church of the Blessed Sacrament in East Hartford, Connecticut. Built for a working-class congregation in 1971, the church, located a few blocks from the giant Pratt & Whitney aircraft engine factory, is a simple, boxy structure often mistaken from the adjacent highway for a warehouse. From the highway, it is marked only with a simple black cross on the side of the church. Many new churches of the 1970s and 1980s favored a fan-shaped layout, with the altar at the base of the fan, surrounded on several sides by pews. The goal was to place as many people as possible close to the altar. St. John the Evangelist Church in West Chester, Ohio, is a good example, as is Mother Elizabeth Ann Seton Church in Carmel, Indiana, a widely honored church of the 1980s.

Thousands of other churches were extensively renovated in the decades after 1965; in almost all of them, the key alterations were to pull the altar away from the wall of the church, so that priests could celebrate facing the people, and to reduce emphasis on church elements that supported devotional practices. The tabernacle containing the consecrated hosts was usually moved off the main altar, the number of side altars was diminished, and much religious iconography, especially statues of the saints, were removed.

Space in the sanctuary was often expanded, at least partly because of the changing sense of ministry in the church. While the priesthood remains restricted to celebrate males (with the exception of the growing number of married Episcopalian and Lutheran priests who become Catholic), in many Catholic churches worship is conducted by relatively large groups of ministers working together, many of them laypeople. Surrounding the altar during a given sacrament might be married male deacons (who might also preach and themselves conduct liturgical rituals like marriages and funerals) and also lectors charged to read Scripture; "extraordinary ministers of the Eucharist," who might be needed to help distribute it to those communing; and acolytes, or altar servers, to assist the priest and deacon. The lectors, Eucharistic ministers, and altar servers might be male or female, some might be children and others adults, and some might well be vested in simple liturgical garments. Laypeople also lead congregational singing, participate in the responses to communal prayers, and offer one another a sign of peace before the Eucharist.

Another major influence on church design was the increased symbolic weight given to the sacrament of baptism. A postconciliar Rite of Christian Initiation for Adults (RCIA) that began to develop in the late 1960s and reached its current form in 1986, is a good example. The Sacred Constitution had called for the restoration of the ancient Christian practice of preparing "catechumens" for reception into the church. Now, as in the early church period, much of a parish's attention during Lent is given to instructing catechumens in the context of parish worship Sunday by Sunday. The RCIA now culminates with the ceremonial admission of candidates to communion at the Easter Vigil Mass. As part of this general thrust, baptismal fonts have become increasingly prominent features of church design. Many churches now have fonts large enough to enable adult baptism by full immersion, rather than a small basin of water from which water was sprinkled on the heads of converts. In some African American parishes, like St. Benedict the Moor in Chicago, the baptismal pools are enormous features of the church. Some newer churches, like St. Philip in Falls Church, Virginia, which was renovated in 2008, are designed on an axial plan, with the altar at one end of a rectangular church structure and a large baptismal pool at the other. At St. Philip, the chairs in which the congregation sits can be turned to face in either direction.

As noted above, in 1969, the Vatican approved the text of a new Missal, the authorized text for the Mass, which incorporated the liturgical changes developed since the end of the council. It was briefer than the Tridentine rite and gave the celebrating priest some choice in the form of prayers; three Eucharistic prayers were authorized, for example, rather than the one in the previous Missal. A third Scripture reading (from the Old Testament) was restored to the Mass. The new Latin text was then distributed for translation into the vernacular, a responsibility given to the bishops of the places where each language was spoken. The International Commission for English in the Liturgy, then already at work on the translation of other services, produced an English translation that was approved by the various national groups of bishops and the Vatican and put into place in 1976, toward the end of the decade of rapid change that followed the Second Vatican Council. The ICEL translation of the Mass aimed for a plain and direct style of spoken English, intended to convey the meaning of the Latin text, not to reproduce the style or syntax of the Latin master text.

The flood of change began to slow in the late 1970s, and the texts for worship had largely stabilized by the early 1980s. During that decade, it also became clear that not everyone was pleased with the changes.

Some felt that change had not gone far enough. During the 1970s, a large number of unofficial liturgical texts had been published, and there were many places where clergy and others experimented with liturgy to suit their own priorities. Some demanded more change, including the restoration of old practices. Theologian Chester Gillis reported in 1999 that many American groups of lay Catholics, often women religious and other women working in church jobs, were regularly conducting their own liturgical celebrations without male clerical leadership.[19] There are small groups of Catholics who have split with Rome and ordained women clergy to lead them.

Far more numerous among the discontented were conservatives unhappy with the changes. "The post-conciliar period saw a cataclysmic breakdown in traditional Catholic beliefs, practices, and discipline," the Catholic journalist Philip Lawler wrote in 2008.

Of all the changes that emerged in the 1960s and 1970s, the most striking and significant were the changes in liturgy. The Mass—the central act of Catholic worship—was altered almost beyond recognition. The Latin that had been used in the Roman rite throughout the world was replaced by vernacular languages. . . . New prayers were added, new translations of the Scriptures introduced, new theories continually tested on unsuspecting congregations. . . . From week to week, year after year, bewildered parishioners did not know what to expect at Sunday Mass, and the experiments would continue whether or not they approved.[20]

Like many conservatives, Lawler protested louder and louder during the 1980s and 1990s, using his position as editor of the *Boston Pilot* and as a key staffer for Cardinal Bernard Law, who became the most influential conservative voice in the American hierarchy during the 1980s and 1990s. But Lawler eventually grew frustrated with Law, who rarely actually punished Boston priests whose liturgical practices dismayed conservatives. The conservatives supported the positions of Popes John Paul II and Benedict XVI. They complained to Rome, they publicized, and they began to organize and fund new "conservative" or restorationist organizations, including a network of colleges like Thomas Aquinas College in California and Ave Maria University in Florida. Conservatives like Lawler also insisted that liturgical change was at the root of falling rates of Catholic attendance at worship.

Others less than pleased by the trends of change included some church musicians, who complained that new patterns of worship had displaced older ones without creating a beautiful new culture of worship music. Thomas Day, the best-known writer on this topic, blamed a deep-rooted culture of inhibition in the Irish-dominated American Catholic Church, but thought that the results had only gotten worse after Vatican II. In fact, before Vatican II, despite a long effort to revive Gregorian chant, there was no singing in most celebrations of the Mass, and not much of a repertoire.[21] During the revision of the liturgy, many congregations adapted Protestant hymns, the contemporary popularity of folk music shaped a new genre of popular worship embodied in the "guitar Mass," and Pentecostal-inflected styles of religious music made considerable impact on all sorts of American worship in the 1990s and 2000s. New hymnals, issued by all sorts of organizations, reflect the full gamut of Catholic viewpoints, from restorationist to womanist.

Another critique of the post–Vatican II turn away from devotional practice also arrived in the mid-1980s, from an entirely different direction: a group of historians interested in the history of popular or "lived" religion.

While these scholars often came from Catholic backgrounds, they viewed themselves as cultural historians, tended to teach in secular institutions, and did not position themselves as Catholic insiders, as liturgical scholars trained in doctoral programs at Notre Dame, the Graduate Theological Union, and the Catholic University of America largely tend to do.

Robert Orsi's *Madonna of 115th Street: Faith and Community in Italian Harlem, 1880–1950* was published in 1985. The following year saw the publication of both Ann Taves's *The Household of Faith: Roman Catholic Devotions in Mid-Nineteenth-Century America* and Colleen McDannell's *The Christian Home in Victorian America, 1840–1900*. All three shared a keen interest in the meanings of Catholic devotional practices to the people who practiced them. What they documented was the depth and passion of Catholic devotional practice in the years before Vatican II. They did not begin, as liturgical scholars tended to do, with the sense that Catholics had been excluded for centuries from participation in Eucharistic worship, a participation that was restored through the changes that followed Vatican II. Nevertheless, by the 1990s, these historians' distinctive focus on devotional Catholicism dominated the emerging field of Catholic studies.

Orsi, Taves, and McDannell agreed that much of Catholic devotional practice and many of the publications used in devotional practice came originally from clerical sources. But they, and especially Orsi, emphasized the appropriation of these practices by the faithful themselves, and especially by women. Examined in this way, devotional practices were not deviations from the central themes and traditions of Christian worship, but rather profoundly legitimate expressions of lay piety, the building blocks of Catholic lives.

Orsi's initial work focused on the cult of the festival of Our Lady of Mt. Carmel, a ritual transferred from Southern Italy to an Italian immigrant neighborhood in New York at the end of the nineteenth century. "The sacred theater of the *festa*," Orsi wrote, took place in the streets as well as in the Church of Our Lady of Mt. Carmel. In the processions and complex devotional rituals of the *festa*, "men and women of Italian Harlem revealed their deepest values and perceptions, their cosmology, the way they understood the world to work." Orsi stressed that laypeople functioned as "as both audience and as actors."[22] For him, clerical leadership was a marginal matter, and clergy often struggled with mixed success to steer, redirect, and constrain the passionate devotional practices of the believers.

In the 1990s, Orsi shifted his attention to the devotional practices of the cult of St. Jude the Obscure, focused on a shrine at the Church of Our Lady of Guadalupe in Chicago. The cult, which had followers nation-wide, was established in the 1920s and was promoted vigorously during the mid-twentieth century by the Claretian Fathers, an order of priests rooted in Spain, who used the contributions of devotees of St. Jude to fund their own work. Orsi was drawn to study the devotion to St. Jude in large measure because of the enormous appeal of St. Jude, the patron saint of hopeless causes, to young Catholic women from immigrant backgrounds who were becoming middle class. In the study, he focused explicitly on the changes to the devotion that followed Vatican II.

In Orsi's reading, the reform of the liturgy undertaken at and after the Council, strengthened rather than diminished the hold of the clergy on Catholic worship. While others stressed the communal focus of the new Mass, Orsi noted that in the reformed worship, believers were asked to focus their thoughts and prayers on those of the priest, to respond to the promptings of the priest, rather than following their own agendas and their own relationships with the Mother of God or with favorite saints during the course of a Mass. "The saints," Orsi noted drily, "did not go quietly from their niches in America's neo-Gothic cathedrals. . . . The effort to change the inner lives of American Catholics, to reconfigure the way they engaged the sacred, practiced their faith, and indeed, the way they faced the everyday challenges of their lives, unfolded as a tense and complex practice that met with resistance, ambivalence and uncertainty."[23] What followed was a "bitter internecine struggle [that] erupted over the continued appropriateness of some of the most beloved practices associ-ated with American Catholic popular piety and the cult of the saints."[24]

This reversal of interpretation—Vatican II as retrogressive and clericalizing—was not universally accepted, but it made a consider-able impression. The most vigorous response came from scholars, often liturgical scholars, who drew different conclusions about the history of devotional practice in the twentieth century. Joseph Chinnici, in a wide-ranging essay on prayer, countered that the driving force in mid-twentieth-century devotional Catholicism was not the life problems and experiences of individual Catholics, but rather a distinct set of responses to the social position of Catholics in mid-century America, the cold war, and the threat of communism. He noted that many of the era's most popular devotional practices were projects promoted by new national movements and organizations.

> Certainly, the prayer forms of the immigrant church—devotion to the saints, especially Mary, sodalities and confraternities; novenas, stations of the cross; the rosary and indulgenced prayers and holy cards, and the paraliturgical practices of holy hour, adoration of the Blessed Sacrament and benediction grew in popularity in the first half of the twentieth century. . . . However, from the World War I era to the early 1940s the old immigrant prayer forms associated with the Eucharist and Mary began to change their social base. So strongly rooted in the nineteenth century in local neighborhoods, ethnic identity, and a sacrificial ethic, they now became . . . much more aligned with institutional structures, organizational hierarchies, diocesan and national secretariats.[25]

Chinnici then noted that many of these devotional practices were already in decline in the 1950s because they had less resonance with a new, better-educated, and more assimilated generation of Catholics. In his reading, these sorts of devotional practices fell away abruptly in the late 1960s when new spiritual practices—Cursillo, Marriage Encounter, Renew (a parish revitalization movement), and most notably, the Charismatic movement—that were better attuned to that cultural moment arrived on the scene. These featured increased emphasis on Scripture, were keyed to the reformed liturgy, and emphasized "personal participation in the Spirit, group sharing, and communal interchange."[26]

While the dramatic decline of traditional devotional Catholicism in the late 1960s and 1970s is universally acknowledged, even by those who lament it, these practices have not disappeared. Eucharistic adoration and the related service of Benediction—where those in attendance pray together before the exhibited consecrated host, which is then elevated to bless the assembly—are still widely available, if not that widely attended. They are promoted by both advocacy organizations of the faithful and by clerical authorities. Thousands of parishes around the nation sponsor fixed periods in which consecrated host is "exposed" for adoration in a special vessel called a monstrance, often for a few hours a week or a month. In a far smaller group of parishes, the practice of "perpetual adoration" has made a comeback. In it, volunteers take turns praying in the presence of the consecrated host around the clock, often in a special chapel set aside for the purpose. Perpetual adoration requires a robust organization to staff, usually at least two hundred or so volunteers willing to spend a shift of an hour or so in prayer before God. In Connecticut, for example, scores of parishes schedule Eucharistic adoration at least occasionally, while about ten are hosts to perpetual adoration and have often maintained the practice for decades on end.

The Catholic cable television network EWTN often airs programs based on devotional practices, and many websites actively promote a wide range of devotional practices, showing instructional and inspiration films and distributing devotional items—icons, scapulars, rosaries, religious statues, service books, and texts of all sorts. There are websites where devotees can participate in perpetual adoration online. Devotional practices are also encouraged at many of the scores of Catholic pilgrimage sites scattered around the nation, especially at sites that serve growing immigrant populations. For example, devotional activities honoring Our Lady of Guadalupe have expanded from the Southwest, where they have long histories, into many parts of the nation, especially in places where Mexican immigrants have located. Since 1978, up to seventy thousand Vietnamese Americans have gathered for a weekend each August in Carthage, Missouri, at the headquarters of the Congregation of Mary Co-Redemptrix (an order of Vietnamese priests) for Marian Days. The gathering is held in honor of the Immaculate Heart of Mary, and its devotional practices are linked to the pilgrimage of Our Lady of Fatima. The National Shrine of Our Lady of Czestochowa outside Philadelphia has been a center for Polish American pilgrimages since the 1950s, but "walking pilgrimages" to the shrine, modeled on Polish custom, began in 1987 and now attract more than three thousand pilgrims each year on August 15.

Large pilgrimage processions following a statue of Our Lady of Consolation began in May 1875 in Carey, Ohio, in the state's northwest corner, but now the crowds at the Basilica of Our Lady of Consolation near Toledo that gather for the Feast of the Assumption on August 15 are far larger—reaching toward ten thousand. The current group of pilgrims is dominated by recent Arab American immigrants from nearby Detroit, who come for a candlelit procession and an outdoor vigil Mass in Aramaic held on the evening of August 14. A series of novenas preparing pilgrims for the feast begins at the basilica on August 6, and each evening's schedule offers a full roster of devotional practices, including "a rosary procession around the basilica, exposition of the Blessed Sacrament, a scripture reading, homily, benediction of the Blessed Sacrament, and the hymn to Our Lady of Consolation."[27]

None of these major pilgrimages has a particularly conservative or restorationist flavor, although it isn't hard to find vocal restorationists focused on the revival of traditional devotions, especially on the internet. Instead, they seem to reflect a return to devotional practice on the part of some, but not most, American Catholics, perhaps especially recent immigrants, of whom there are millions. In a work focused on the reception of Vatican II in the United States, the historian Colleen McDannell has argued that some traditional devotional practices and religious art began to filter back into many Catholic parishes in the 1980s. "Many American parishes that emptied their churches during the sixties and seventies have undertaken renovations that reintroduce crucifixes, statues, ranks of candles, Stations of the Cross, small chapels, and pipe organs."[28] One example is Blessed Trinity Church in Ocala, Florida, to which McDannell's parents belong. Built in 1974, the church's fan-shaped sanctuary placed worshippers close to the altar and reflected the austere architectural preference of the post–Vatican II years. It was, she wrote, "a poster child for modernist Catholicism: abstraction, simplicity, emptiness and informality encouraged all to focus on the Mass and the assembled congregation."[29]

But in the following years, pastors and people began to fill up the worship space with more traditional iconography and church furniture. "Obviously, no one at Trinity particularly liked the Vatican II aesthetic of simplicity," McDannell wrote, "but still it was the very cluttering of the altar area over 30 years that began to cause problems for the something that everybody did like about the Vatican II era: the active participation of parishioners in church rituals."[30] The result was an ambitious renovation that created space for both devotional practices and the comfortable participation of the congregation in the church's rituals.

The pastors and members of Holy Trinity interviewed by McDannell weren't unhappy about the changes to worship that followed the Council, but they valued many aspects of the devotional tradition and are pleased to see some of them reintroduced. They were not, however, lining up for an internecine struggle between "modernists" and "restorationists." In 1993, spurred by requests from the congregation, the church set aside an office for chapel space and launched perpetual adoration of the Blessed Sacrament, a ritual practice that involves 168 parishioners regularly, with 200 providing backup. In recent years, the parish has reintroduced "the blessings of homes, animals on St. Francis's feast day, and Easter foods" and practices like "a Divine Mercy novena, St. Peregrine's Mass for a cure for cancer, or Easter Processional devotions."[31] Further, the practices take place alongside a vast array of parish ministries with a strong post–Vatican II flavor of lay participation, including a parish elementary school and a diocesan high school paid for with the tithing of members, and many social justice ministries, including global ones.

> Almost everything at Blessed Trinity is run by volunteers. With the exception of school teachers and a paid church staff of sixteen, parishioners do everything from plumbing to serving lunches at funerals to working at Habitat for Humanity. They help with a prison ministry and drive trucks to pick up used furniture for their thrift shop. A year-round soup kitchen provides daily meals to the hungry. . . . They make rosary beads, run marriage preparation classes and distribute ashes on Ash Wednesday. There is an equally long list of ministries available for Spanish speakers.[32]

The devotions practiced at Blessed Trinity "have been streamlined and given a modern theological spin," and lay participation and management extend to conducting many of the devotional rituals that do take place, such as house blessings.[33]

Despite the revival of some devotional practices and their integration with Vatican II–style Catholicism, devotional practice is powerfully attractive to only some American Catholics. In the *American Catholics in Transition* survey, 37 percent of respondents thought that "participating in devotions such as Eucharistic Adoration or praying the rosary" is very important. In contrast, 63 percent said participating in the sacraments was very important, 68 percent believed that the church's teachings on Mary the Mother of God were very important; 68 percent thought that helping the poor was very important; and 73 percent said belief in the resurrection of Jesus was very important. An additional 41 percent did say they thought participating in devotions was "somewhat important," which suggests that most contemporary Catholics are not deeply engaged by the devotional tradition. My own students, for example, are curious about devotional practice, but few of them report participating in public devotions, or even do so in the setting of their families. In a recent class of twenty-four students, all Catholic and mostly from New England and the Middle Atlantic region, about one-third reported that they attend Mass weekly. All of them could recite the rosary prayers, but none had ever done so either with their families or in public worship.

ROME AND THE "REFORM OF REFORM"

From 1978, when Pope John Paul II was elected, until March 2013, when Pope Francis was elected, the church was led by bishops who were not entirely satisfied with the ways in which the decisions of the Second Vatican Council were implemented, including in worship. John Paul II, and especially Pope Benedict XVI, who was John Paul's chief assistant for almost all of John Paul's long papacy, believed that many of the decisions of the late 1960s and 1970s broke too abruptly with preconciliar Catholicism. While neither advocated a simple return to the old Tridentine rite, both looked for ways to emphasize continuity rather than change. Their position emerged gradually as John Paul transformed the American and worldwide episcopate, appointing men who supported him and his sense of the church's mission. In the 1980s, a few examples of pushback emerged; more arrived in the 1990s, as Rome exerted more control over Catholic worship. And in the 2000s, under Benedict, more significant change occurred—most notably, a decision to allow priests to celebrate the old Tridentine rite, if they chose to do so, and the imposition of a new and controversial English translation of the 1970 Novus Ordo Mass. In America, some of the new generation of bishops also stirred controversy by either reviving older devotional practices or attempting to ban post–Vatican II practices such as the use of female altar servers, restricting laity to communing only with the consecrated host and not with consecrated wine from the chalice, and turning priests celebrating the Mass back around to face the altar rather than the congregation.

This generation of change began quietly in October of 1984, when John Paul, who was trying to bring Catholic traditionalists, including a group of schismatic Catholics who condemned Vatican II, back into the fold, authorized limited celebration of the Tridentine rite, which Pope Paul VI had sharply restricted in 1969. John Paul ruled that it was acceptable for occasional celebrations of the Tridentine rite to take place for the benefit of those who wanted it, provided the local bishop had approved and that both priest and people made it clear that they did not oppose the Novus Ordo Mass. In 1985, a small number of Tridentine celebrations began in the United States. One took place in Hartford, Connecticut, where about 165 people gathered in a large, neo-Gothic church to hear a thirty-seven-year-old priest celebrate the rite for the first time in his career. "I've always loved the Tridentine rite," one woman told the *Hartford Courant*. "In this Mass, you don't have to give canned responses to the prayers. You can say the rosary during mass or meditate or say your own prayers."[34] In 1988, John Paul went further, authorizing more widespread use of the Tridentine rite, with the permission of local bishops. This encouraged the development of some religious orders, like the Priestly Fraternity of St. Peter, devoted to the Tridentine rite. Its founders had reentered the Catholic Church from the schismatic Society of St. Pius X.

As late as 1994, the Vatican was still willing to ratify practices associated with the post–Vatican II period. It granted a request by American bishops to permit girls to serve as acolytes during services. This largely ended a kind of rearguard action in the United States, but the Vatican stipulated that no bishop or priest had to use girls. At the moment, only one diocese in the United States (Lincoln, Nebraska) flatly forbids the use of female altar servers, but there continue to be parish-level disputes over the practice.

During the 1990s, John Paul set the stage for what has come to be called "the reform of the reform." In May 1989, he released an apostolic letter, *Vicesimus Quintus Annus* (On the twenty-fifth anniversary of the liturgical constitution), marking the twenty-fifth anniversary of the *Sacred Constitution.* He opened by offering strong support for the translations and new texts prepared after the council. They were, he wrote, prepared "in accordance with the conciliar principles of fidelity to tradition and openness to legitimate development, and so it is possible to say that the reform of the Liturgy is strictly traditional and in accordance with the ancient usage of the holy Fathers." But, the pope continued, there were problems, both with abuses in the celebration of Catholic rites (most notably, failure to follow the prescribed texts exactly) and in the texts themselves. It was time to reevaluate—in Rome—the processes by which translations of the official Roman texts were made. In the late 1960s, Rome had given authority to supervise translations to a series of international commissions that represented the bishops of the countries where a given language was spoken. For English, that meant the International Commission on English in the Liturgy (ICEL), which had begun work in 1967. "The time has come to evaluate this commission, its past activity, both the positive and negative aspects, and the guidelines and the help which it has received from the episcopal conference regarding its composition and activity."[35]

Over the course of the next decade, this evaluation process turned so strongly negative that ICEL was, in 2003, taken over by the Vatican.[36] In the mid- and late 1990s, proposed translations submitted by ICEL—first of the Psalter, then a comprehensive revision of the 1973 *Missal* (the Mass text), and finally of ordination rites—were shelved in Rome, despite the approval of all of the national bishops' conferences involved. This was a stunning blow to the staff of ICEL, and to liturgical scholars. Over the course of this process, several things were happening in the United States as well. The first was the rise of a new generation of bishops, some of whom were sharply critical of the ICEL texts, usually because they saw them as insufficiently literal translations of the original Latin. The second was the rise of active advocacy groups like Adoremus, founded in 1995, which pressed for revisions of liturgy in a traditional direction. Adoremus stressed its acceptance of Vatican II but, in the mode of Pope John Paul II and Cardinal Joseph Ratzinger, affirmed the conciliar documents but criticized the implementation of Council decisions. The organization's mission statement called on the church "to rediscover and restore the beauty, the holiness, and the power of the Church's rich liturgical tradition while remaining faithful to an organic, living process of renewal."[37] The organization explicitly endorsed Ratzinger's views expressed in his 1985 book *Feast of Faith*.

In 2001, the Vatican issued what the writer John Wilkins called "its knockout blow," an instruction on the use of vernacular languages in Catholic worship called *Authentic Liturgy*, "which overturned the entire basis on which ICEL's worked had rested for forty years"—the proposition that vernacular translations should convey the meaning of the Latin master texts, but not necessarily by reproducing Latin vocabulary and syntax. Instead, the new edict said the proper goal was to reproduce the sense of individual Latin words in the text as closely as possible. "*Liturgam authenticam* did not recommend," Wilkins wrote, "it commanded. It insisted that translations follow an extreme literalism, extending even to syntax and rhythm, punctuation and capital letters."[38]

The instruction was followed the next year by a new *General Instruction on the Missal*, replacing a document of 1975. The *General Instruction* directed how the Mass and sacraments should be celebrated, prescribing in more detail how celebrants should express reverence (by more and deeper bows), pushing to curtail informality, and mandating the use in the liturgy not simply of a processional cross but of a crucifix—a cross with an image of the body of the crucified Christ. All were designed to push Catholic worship back in a more traditional direction. Over the next few years, further messages came from the Vatican discouraging highly visible forms of lay participation in the conduct of the Mass—restricting the use of Eucharistic ministers when priests and deacons are present, and forbidding them from assisting in the purification of sacred vessels after communion.

In 2004, another Vatican instruction was issued "on certain matters to be observed or avoided regarding the Most Holy Eucharist. It "singled out as abuses . . . homilies delivered by lay people, too much commotion and moving around during the sign of the peace, alteration of texts set down for use in the liturgy, the use of leavened bread in the Eucharist, and the administration of communion by lay people when a priest or deacon is present."[39]

That same year, drafts of a new English translation of the Novus Ordo Mass, composed at the Vatican, began to circulate. It brought joy to *Adoremus* and Latin literalists, but misery to liturgical scholars and many pastoral leaders. Over the next few years, the new, word-for-word translation worked its way through the Vatican process. It was mandated for use in Advent at the end of 2012, an echo of the 1964 changes to the Mass. Few outside the "reform of the reform" community had anything positive to say about it. As a group, liturgical scholars were apoplectic.[40]

The old ICEL translation was "simple and direct," Rita Ferrone wrote on the blog Pray Tell. "It follows the speech patterns and rhythms of contemporary spoken English." The new translation was "mannered and complex," she complained. Spurning clarity and intelligibility, *Liturgiam authenticam* placed top priority on "the exact rendering of each word and expression in Latin, the use of sacral vocabulary remote from ordinary speech, and reproduction of the syntax of the Latin original whenever possible. The result," she wrote, is "a translation that is filled with expression not easily understood by English speakers. It has resulted in prayers that are long-winded, pointlessly complex, hard to proclaim and difficult to understand."[41]

The new translation was also challenged on theological grounds. Biblical scholars, in particular the Jesuit John R. Donahue, complained in *Commonweal* "of a significant translation error"—the use of the word "chalice" rather than "cup" in the Eucharistic prayer (the prayer of consecration). To call the vessel a chalice, a technical Christian term, rather than a cup, "disguises the relation of the Christian Eucharist to an anamnesis [enacted memorial] of the Pascal Meal celebrated by the Jewish Jesus as he approached his suffering and death."[42]

A larger debate focused on the translation of the Latin phrase *pro multis* in the Mass text, a phrase describing the meaning of Christ's sacrifice of himself for the salvation of fallen humanity. In the ICEL version, it was translated "for all"; in the new version, it is "for many." While "for many" conforms more exactly to the Gospel texts, "for all" conveys the church's formal doctrine more accurately.

Finally, there has been widespread dismay about a change to the lay part of an exchange of greetings between priest and people. In the ICEL version, the priest said, "The Lord be with you," and the people responded, "And also with you." Left not translated in ICEL was the Latin phrase *et cum spiritu tuo.* The new translation of the lay response is "And with your spirit." Translators and biblical scholars disagree about which is better, but much of the concern expressed arises from the fact that the ICEL translation has been widely adopted by Protestants since 1973 precisely because Catholics used it. Critics see the language change as an insult to Protestants and a conscious attempt to build a new barrier to ecumenical relations. It also seems to be a matter of conscious policy, John Wilkins noted. *Liturgian authenticam* advises that "great caution is to be taken to avoid a wording or style that the Catholic faithful would confuse with a manner of speech of non-Catholic ecclesial communities."[43]

The measure of grief associated with these changes among Catholic liturgical scholars can be sensed in the words of a recent eulogy preached by the abbot of St. John's Abbey in Collegeville, Minnesota, the center of American liturgical scholarship. In it, Abbot John Klassen reviewed the life and work of the Rev. Kevin Seasoltz, a scholar at the center of the movement, who taught liturgy at the Catholic University of America for twenty-five years and then served as editor of *Worship*, the most important American journal on liturgy.

> With the publication of *Liturgiam authenticum* and its revised principles for translation of liturgical texts, Father Kevin and many other liturgical scholars felt that the vision of liturgy and life that inspired the creation of *Sacrosanctum conciliam* at the Second Vatican Council was being abandoned. Though intellectually Father Kevin knew that history moves, that the pendulum must swing, on an emotional level these changes were heartrending. For Kevin and many others in liturgical studies, it was like their life's work was being ravaged.[44]

Yet many "restorationist" conservatives have been frustrated that Pope Benedict did not go further with his reconstruction. They were delighted with his 2005 speech, soon after taking the papal throne, which called for the "desecularization" of the church and denounced "the hermeneutics of discontinuity and rupture" (the argument that Vatican II brought fundamental change to church teaching and worship). And they cheered in 2007, when he issued a *motu proprio, Summorum pontificum,* which dramatically loosened the conditions that Pope John Paul II had attached to the celebration of the Tridentine rite. Benedict argued that the Tridentine rite was valid and that priests could celebrate it on their own initiative, without seeking the approval of their bishop. Nevertheless, Benedict insisted on the entire validity of the 1970 Mass, calling it the "ordinary form" of Mass and the Tridentine rite the "extraordinary form" (OF and EF to disputants in the blogosphere). In his own liturgical style, Benedict did a great deal to revive traditional forms of piety. He loved and revived abandoned forms of papal vestments and garments, and he greatly expanded the use of Latin in the services he personally presided over. His personal aesthetic was clearly more Baroque than modern. But Benedict never used the Tridentine rite in public or, as far as is known, in private either, to the disappointment of many traditionalist bloggers who constantly begged him to do so. Instead, Benedict seemed to anticipate the eventual adoption of a new Mass text that wove together OF and EF.

What liturgical conservatives seem to prefer, at the moment, is something quite novel—the acceptance of a certain pluralism in Catholic worship. Others can keep the *Novus Ordo* mass, if they can keep the Tridentine one. "Conservative liturgical discussion is increasingly characterized by advocacy of a necessary pluralism," noted Eamon Duffy, the English church historian. This sort of reluctant pluralism might even be ascribed to Pope Benedict, who, after all, established a distinction between "ordinary" and "extraordinary" rites of the Mass. Writing in 2002, Archbishop Rembert Weakland of Milwaukee, who had been deeply involved in ICEL earlier in his career, agreed that an uncomfortable pluralism might be the only way forward, even for those suspicious of modernity. "It is the only way in which they can attempt to return to pre-Vatican II and Vatican II sources without at the same time repudiating totally the council and the papally-controlled implementation that followed it or declaring both to be aberrations."[45]

In recent years, the efforts of liturgically conservative American bishops to restore traditional practices have attracted headlines but have usually ended without producing much, if any, change beyond their diocese. In October 2011, for example, Bishop Thomas Olmsted of Phoenix and Bishop Robert Morlino of Madison, Wisconsin, citing instructions in the newly approved third edition of the 1969 Missal, both announced plans to restrict the number of occasions at which laypeople in their diocese might receive the Eucharist "in both kinds"—that is, receive both the consecrated host and consecrated wine from the chalice at communion. In their judgment, neither the new Missal nor the documents of Vatican II called for laity to receive from the chalice regularly, even though that had become almost universal practice in the United States. They foresaw risks of spilling and even profanation in crowded situations, doubted whether laity were adequately instructed, and were worried that universal use of the chalice called for undue use of lay Eucharistic ministers. Olmsted and Morlino said the appropriate standard was for laity to receive from the chalice only at events like first communion and confirmation and at annual events like the feast of Corpus Christi, which honors the body of Christ.

The result was an explosion of negative commentary, from the media and from many Catholics. "It's true that the bread alone is sufficient for the full theological reality of Christ's Eucharistic presence, but why we should settle for sufficient when we can have the entire Eucharistic symbol, which better communicates the fullness of the mystery we celebrate?" thundered Bryan Cones in *U.S. Catholic.* "Should we restrict the amount of water used in baptism or the amount of oil when we anoint the sick? Neither should we settle for a merely vicarious drinking from the cup."[46]

Morlino defended his instruction in a letter to his priests on October 11, 2011, arguing that his reservations about distributing communion in two kinds were rooted in his concern that contemporary Catholics didn't understand the sacrament and took it too casually.

> I have been told of, and have personally experienced, the reality that the provision both that the faithful be well instructed and that there be no danger of profanation of the Sacrament, is not being met. . . . So many do not understand the Eucharist as the memorial of Christ's Sacrifice, his death and resurrection; nor the real presence of Christ, body, blood, soul, and divinity, under both species of bread and wine; nor the role of the ordinary and, if necessary, extraordinary ministers of the Eucharist. Most of all (and this has been my point from the start) so many of our people do not understand the kinds of reverence due at all times to the sacrament, whether within the Eucharistic Liturgy or outside the celebration.[47]

But other American bishops weighed in saying they disagreed that the faithful were poorly instructed, and it became clear that Olmsted had misinterpreted the canonical language in Roman norms. Both Morlino and Olmsted backed down.

SORTING OUT CHANGE

One way to understand this complex situation is that despite all of the institutional activity and advocacy since the mid-1980s, not that much has changed in the worship of American Catholics in the parishes that the vast majority of them attend. "Most of the people in the pews . . . don't read Pray Tell or *Worship* magazine," Pray Tell blogger Benedictine Anthony Ruff wrote on April 6, 2013. "They go to Mass on Sunday and Father does it in their language."[48] The overwhelming majority of them still receive the Eucharist standing rather than kneeling and in their hand, rather than on their tongues. Those who worship in Spanish in the United States have seen no changes whatsoever in their texts for worship in recent decades. While most priests prefer the language of the 1973 ICEL translation of the

Missal, they are using the new one, and its English is intelligible to most people. This is not to deny that the pendulum did swing away from the norms of the 1970s and 1980s, but rather that the effects of that have been mostly felt by the most engaged—the defenders of the post–Vatican II changes and those who yearn for "reform of the reform."

The election of Pope Francis in March 2013 promised to change the situation yet again. It is evident that his personal liturgical sensibilities reflect the imprint of the post–Vatican II style of worship. His liturgical tastes are much different from those of his immediate predecessor. Both liturgical progressives and restorationists have been examining minutely the choices Pope Francis makes when presiding over worship, both in public and in his private Masses. "It is astonishing how, from the first minute of his election, Pope Francis chose a new style: unlike his predecessor, no miter with gold and jewels, no ermine-trimmed cape, no made to measure shoes and headwear, no magnificent throne," Hans Kung wrote in the *National Catholic Reporter* on May 31, 2013.

Compared to Benedict, Francis moved immediately toward simplicity— in his choice of residence (a Vatican City guest house and not the papal apartment or the Castel San Gadolfo), his vestments, the forms of transportation he chooses, his liturgical style, and much more. In his first few months in office, he set a pattern of informal and gregarious contact with others, and he made repeated gestures of inclusion—visiting a prison on Holy Thursday to wash the feet of prisoners, including women and Muslims, picking for his first trip outside Rome the Sicilian island of Lampedusa, the landfall of thousands of undocumented immigrants from Africa. At Lampedusa, he prayed at an altar built from the wreckage of ships in which desperate immigrant had drowned. Where John Paul and Benedict usually wore brand new vestments at each public occasion of worship, Francis has repeatedly worn vestments brought with him from Argentina, which have been often described as "seventies style" in their simplicity.

At his daily Mass in the Vatican guest house, he concelebrates with visiting priests and bishops and celebrates with young altar servers dressed in street clothes. Where Benedict had drastically increased the amount of Latin used in papal ceremonies, Francis immediately reverted to the vernacular, especially when acting specifically as bishop of Rome. When he made his first international trip to Brazil in July 2013, he chose an ordinary Fiat with the windows rolled down instead of the Popemobile, and he shifted the language of his Masses from largely Latin to overwhelmingly Portuguese. For traditionalists, who valued Benedict's taste and traditionalism, this was not encouraging. "The Latin in Latin America is becoming harder and harder to find," the traditionalist website *Rorate Caeli* reported mournfully on July 24. "Latin has been almost entirely removed from the *novus ordo* celebrations by Pope Francis."[49]

Liturgical progressive, on the other hand, found much to celebrate in Francis's tone and style. "Benedict's 'hermeneutic of continuity' was never about continuity with the past fifty years of Catholic liturgical renewal," Anthony Ruff wrote in the Pray Tell blog on April 6, 2013. "It wasn't about the sensitivities of *current-day* worshipers or continuity with *current* liturgical practices. It was about establishing continuity with practices lost fifty years ago."

"For those of us who track what's going on behind the scenes and what it means for the future of Catholic liturgical renewal, Pope Francis' Mass this Sunday at the Cathedral of John Lateran is one more indication of the direction of his papacy," Ruff exclaimed. "It is part of Francis' 'hermeneutic of continuity'—with Vatican II, with Pope Paul's reform of the rites, and with the rest of the Catholic Church."

The mood among liturgical conservatives has been increasingly anxious since the election of Pope Francis. "Liturgical traditionalists (myself included) can only be depressed by this election—it is almost the worst result possible for those of us who think the new liturgy lost the theological profundity and ritual beauty of the Tridentine Mass," Michael Brendan Dougherty wrote in *Slate* just after Francis's election.[50]

Speaking in the middle of Pope Francis's visit to Brazil in July 2013, the plainspoken Archbishop Charles Chaput of Philadelphia told the *National Catholic Reporter*'s John Allen that many on the right wing of the church—his wing—"generally have not been really happy about his election, from what I've been able to read and to understand. He'll have to care for them, too."[51]

However, Francis did not move briskly to address liturgy early in his papacy. In November 2014, he even appointed a prelate associated with Benedict's position on worship, Cardinal Robert Sarah, as prefect of the Congregation for Divine Worship and the Discipline of the Sacraments, the Vatican dicastery in charge of worship. What followed was an escalating series of disagreements as Sarah tried to extend the policies that prevailed during Benedict's years and Pope Francis overruled him with increasing vigor.

The first round of disputation began in December 2014, when Francis asked the Congregation on Divine Worship to revise its rubrics for the foot-washing ceremony that takes place on Holy Thursday to explicitly endorse the participation of women in the service. Francis, who values the ritual because it emphasizes the servanthood of Catholic clergy, had made global headlines for his foot-washing ceremonies in a juvenile detention center, a home for the elderly, a refugee center, and a maximum security prison. Contrary to recent precedent, Francis included women and even non-Christians in the groups whose feet he washed. The Congregation on Divine Worship did not act promptly on the request, and about a year later, in January 2016, the pope issued a decree making the changes. "I have decided to make a change to the *Roman Missal*. I therefore decree that the section according to which those persons chosen for the Washing of the feet must be men or boys, so that from now on the Pastors of the Church may choose the participants in the rite from among all the members of the People of God," Francis wrote in a letter to Sarah, which was released along with the decree.[52] Cardinal Sarah revealed his own position in a speech in March 2016, in which he said that the changes introduced by Pope Francis were not mandatory—that Catholic priests and bishops were not obliged to include women among those whose feet are washed.

Sarah then took the initiative. In July 2016, in a speech given to a liturgical conference in London, he called on priests to return to the pre–Vatican II practice of facing east (with their back to the congregation) for much of the Mass. "It is very important that we return as soon as possible to a common orientation, of priests and the faithful turned together in the same direction—eastwards or at least towards the apse—to the Lord who comes."[53] On that occasion, Sarah also recommended kneeling to receive communion and suggested the eventual reconciliation of the ordinary and extraordinary forms of the Mass into a new version of the Mass, a change also sought by Pope Benedict but unpopular with conservatives who revered the unadulterated Tridentine rite.

The Vatican's response was rapid. Pope Francis called Sarah in for a private meeting, and on July 11 the Vatican issued a statement saying Sarah had been misinterpreted. "There are not, therefore, any new liturgical directives beginning next Advent as some have wrongly inferred from the words of Cardinal Sarah, and it is best to avoid using the expression 'reform of the reform,' referring to the liturgy, as sometimes it has been a source of misunderstanding. This was the agreed view expressed during a recent audience granted by the Pope to the Cardinal Prefect of the Congregation of Divine Worship."[54] This kind of pointed criticism of a high-ranking Vatican official startled many.

The pope then acted even more dramatically in October 2016, when he made sweeping reassignments of the hierarchs appointed to serve on the Congregation of Divine Worship (CDW). Among the liturgical conservatives turned out of the Congregation were Cardinals Raymond Burke, Angelo Scola, Marc Ouellet, and George Pell. Initial reports circulating on conservative blogs depicted a massacre. "Pope Francis, in one fell swoop has today carried out a stunning mass removal of all conservative cardinals and bishops from the Vatican's Congregation for Divine Worship," Father Brian Harrison wrote in his blog.[55] It turned out that Francis had not replaced the entire Congregation—only seventeen of the twenty-nine members—and had appointed some conservatives in the new group, but panic among conservative bloggers was palpable.

In January 2017, Pope Francis set up a special commission to study changes to the rubrics for worship made by his predecessors, a move that sidestepped Cardinal Sarah. At the end of August, Francis gave a talk to Italian bishops that defended the liturgical changes that followed Vatican II and declared "the reform of the liturgy irreversible." He specifically knocked down any return to priests celebrating the Mass while "looking to the east," saying that having the priest face the congregation across the altar made the altar "the center to which attention converges in all our churches."[56]

The pope moved further in September 2017, releasing a *motu proprio* called *Magnum Principium* (The Great Principle), which rolled back many of the rules for approving liturgical translation imposed by Pope John Paul's *Liturgiam Authenticam* of 2001. The pope simultaneously decreed changes in canon law to ensure that result. In the decree, Francis returned chief responsibility for translation to the various national bishops' conferences and overturned the translation rules promulgated by John Paul and Benedict that insisted on highly literal translations of official Latin texts. Instead of insisting on strict conformity to Latin vocabulary and syntax, even at the expense of turgid or unidiomatic usages, Francis said liturgical translations should show "triple fidelity": to the Latin texts, to the local language in question, and to the comprehensibility of the text for those who would use it. This last stipulation was aimed at the CDW's reinsertion of Latin technical vocabulary, most famously the use of "consubstantial" in the Nicaean Creed recited by the congregation at every Mass. The Congregation of Divine Worship would still have the power to "confirm" translations, but would not be able to impose its own translations of bishops' conferences, as had happened with English after the repudiation of ICEL.[57]

Sarah rallied gamely, writing in October 2017 in a French theological magazine that the rules imposed in *Liturgiam Authenticam* remained in effect and that the CDW would continue to play an active role in reviewing and evaluating translations up to the point of producing its own translations. He wrote that the distinction made in *Maximum Pontificum* between the authority of the bishops' conferences to translate and "recognize" liturgical texts and the CDW's continuing responsibility to "confirm" texts didn't amount to meaningful change because "recognatio" and "confirmatio" were synonyms. Pope Francis didn't sit still, sending Sarah a remarkably forceful public letter saying he had misinterpreted *Maximum Pontificum*.[58] "The process of translating relevant liturgical texts into a language . . . must not bring a spirit of 'imposition' over the episcopal conferences with a translation handed down from the Dicastery, as that would betray the right of the bishops as set forth in canon law."[59]

Despite the series of slap-downs, Sarah remained in office in late 2017, but it seemed clear that Pope Francis would go to considerable lengths to correct Vatican officials who don't support his program of decentralizing authority away from Rome and toward bishops' conferences. Outside Rome, the reaction of hierarchs to *Maximum Pontificum* and the rebuke of Sarah was nearly ecstatic, with the bishops' conferences of Germany, France, New Zealand, and Switzerland publicly stating their satisfaction with the return of responsibility for translations to local bishops. In the United States, where there are many liturgical conservatives in positions of authority, the reaction of bishops was more muted, although Cardinal Donald Wuerl of Washington told the *National Catholic Reporter* that Francis's action restored a practice explicitly endorsed by Vatican II.[60]

So, while it was clear that the pendulum had swung away from the "reform of the reform" staked out by Pope Benedict, it was not necessarily true that the "liturgy wars" had ended, despite Pope Francis's desire to make his policies irreversible. While disputes over translations didn't have much discernible impact on ordinary American Catholics, the tenacity of the ideologically committed remained impressive, with partisans on both sides leaping into dispute in scholarship, Catholic journalism, and the blogosphere. In the next few years, the movement of the debate will probably depend on how long Pope Francis is in office and whether he has the time to appoint a decisive cohort of bishops who support his approach. Time will tell about that.

On the ground in the United States, worship is likely to remain one of the defining factors in the complex linguistic, theological, and cultural "pluriformity" of American Catholicism. While those holding a wide range of commitments have generally come to see this plurality as at least tactically desirable to preserve their own preferences, internal Catholic pluralism does not necessarily defuse all conflict. A good example of deep and persistent tensions over worship at the grassroots level came in November 2017 in the Archdiocese of Hartford, Connecticut, which had just completed a sweeping reorganization and merger of parishes to deal with its declining cohort of priests. Archbishop Leonard J. Blair suddenly reversed the merger of three parishes in Enfield that had taken place the previous June, stating blandly that after "the merger was effected, some issues developed regarding these extinct entities, requiring further changes in the merger of the three parishes."[61] The *Hartford Courant* in a follow-up reported that St. Martha Parish had been separated from the merger and reestablished because of conflicts that focused on worship style. "A clash of cultures—more traditional worship vs. more contemporary worship—was the driving force behind the failure of a merger involving three Roman Catholic parishes in Enfield, making St. Martha Church the only parish to be separated from an established merger under the in the Archdiocese of Hartford's pastoral plan."[62] Given the general unpopularity of the archdiocesan merger plan, which merged 140 parishes into fifty-nine new parishes, Archbishop Blair's decision to undo one of these mergers so quickly must have been made reluctantly. The *Courant* quoted lay leaders saying the merger had created such a "toxic atmosphere" that the archdiocese had to act.

It did not start out "as some sort of, 'it's them and us and we don't agree with what they're doing,'" Walter Wojciehowski, former parish council president at St. Adalbert's parish said. "Certainly we have some differences, but we felt we could work with them. We never had that opportunity. From what I could see, there was very little interest in seeing our side of the story. They had their view of the world and they were going to stick with it." The sticking point for St. Martha's parishioners was apparently the focus on social justice and contemporary worship at St. Adalbert's and St. Patrick's. They were particularly unhappy to see their parish's Latin celebration of the Tridentine rite moved to St. Adalbert's old building.

That sort of conflict suggests the functional segmentation of Catholicism that has arrived with the reality of internal pluralism. How widespread the division is remains to be seen, but this sort of tension over how to worship faithfully may emerge as a major challenge to Catholic life in coming decades.

NOTES

1. The diversity of Catholic worship has yet another level—about one million American Catholics belong to eight Eastern Catholic Churches that have diocesan structures in the United States. They are all fully "Catholic," just as Catholic as the Roman rite and just as "united with Rome," but use their own liturgical traditions, usually rooted in eastern Mediterranean, Eastern European, or Syriac Christian traditions. Probably about 70 percent of them (in Ukrainian and Ruthenian jurisdictions) follow the worship of the Byzantine tradition. Next in size are the Maronite and Melkite traditions, rooted in Syria and Lebanon, which have about 150 parishes in the United States. In recent years, immigrants from Syriac traditions, Chaldean Catholics from Iraq, and Syro-Malabar and Syro-Malankara Catholics from India have established a vital new presence in this country. These rites have undergone their own reforms and restorations since Vatican II, but this chapter will focus on Roman rite worship in the United States.

2. *Sacrosanctum Concilium*, December 4, 1963, http://www.vatican.va/archive/hist _councils/ii_vatican_council/documents/vat-ii_const_19631204_sacrosanctum -concilium_en.html, no. 50.

3. Latin revisions of the texts for all of the sacraments—Eucharist, baptism, ordination, marriage, confirmation, penance, and anointing of the sick— were completed by 1973. English translations, approved by the American bishops and by the Vatican, were all authorized for use in the United States by September 1977. See the useful table in Joseph Chinicci, "The Catholic Community at Prayer, 1926–1976," in *Habits of Devotion: Catholic Religious Practice in Twentieth-Century America*, ed. James M. O'Toole (Ithaca, NY: Cornell University Press, 2004), 18.

4. See Andrew Greeley, William McCready, and Kathleen McCourt, *Catholic Schools in a Declining Church* (Kansas City, MO: Sheed and Ward, 1976), 130. Greeley also discusses the survey findings in chapter 7 of *The American Catholic: A Social Portrait*, (New York: Basic Books, 1977).

5. William V. D'Antonio, Michele Dillon, and Mary L. Gautier, *American Catholics in Transition* (Lanham, MD: Rowman & Littlefield, 2013), 167, 168. In the survey, 63 percent described the sacraments as "very important" and 26 percent as "somewhat important"; 41 percent strongly agreed with the statement "the sacraments of the Church are essential to my relationship with God," and an additional 34 percent said they somewhat agreed.

6. Lydia Saad, "Churchgoing Among U.S. Catholics Slides to Tie Protestants," Gallup, April 9, 2009, http://www.gallup.com/poll/117382/church-going-among-catholics-slides-tie-protestants.aspx.

7. CARA reports that 32 percent of Catholic adults say they rarely or never attend Mass. Only 17 percent of adults under thirty say they attend Mass at least once a week. http://cara.georgetown.edu/CARAServices/FRStats/mattend.jpg.

8. D'Antonio, Dillon, and Gautier, *American Catholics in Transition*, 24.

9. Laurie Goldstein, "A New Leader Confronts Disaffection in Catholics," *New York Times*, November 23, 2010, 18.

10. James F. White, *Roman Catholic Worship: Trent to Today* (Mahwah, NJ: Paulist Press, 1995), 79.

11. White, *Roman Catholic Worship*, 79.

12. White, *Roman Catholic Worship*, 98

13. The recovery of the *Apostolic Tradition* had a great impact on liturgical reform in Protestant circles as well as Catholic ones and on the developing academic field of liturgical studies in the twentieth century. The early-twentieth-century attribution of the Apostolic Tradition to third-century Rome is now disputed. Some believe it reflects somewhat later practices in Alexandria, Egypt, or in Syria, rather than in Rome.

14. Margaret M. McGuiness, "Let Us Go to the Altar," in O'Toole, *Habits of Devotion*, 223.

15. Mark S. Massa, *The American Catholic Revolution: How the Sixties Changed the Catholic Church Forever* (Oxford: Oxford University Press, 2010), 3.

16. Massa, *The American Catholic Revolution*, 16.

17. White, *Roman Catholic Worship*, 117.

18. White, *Roman Catholic Worship*, 118.

19. Chester Gillis, *Roman Catholicism in America* (New York: Columbia University Press, 1999), 15–16.

20. Philip F. Lawler, *The Faithful Departed: The Collapse of Boston's Catholic Culture* (New York: Encounter Press, 1999), 72.

21. Thomas Day, *Why Catholics Can't Sing* (New York: Crossroad, 1990). He intensifies the criticism in *Where Have You Gone, Michelangelo: The Loss of Soul in Catholic Culture* (New York: Crossroad, 1993), where he complains about highly amplified priests and cantors blasting through worship.

22. Robert A. Orsi, *The Madonna of 115th Street: Faith and Community in Italian Harlem, 1880–1950* (New Haven, CT: Yale University Press, 1985), xliii.

23. Robert A. Orsi, *Thank You, St. Jude: Women's Devotions to the Patron Saint of Hopeless Causes* (New Haven, CT: Yale University Press, 1996), 32.

24. Orsi, *Thank You, St. Jude*, 32.

25. Joseph Chinnici, "The Catholic Community at Prayer, 1926–1976," in O'Toole, *Habits of Devotion*, 52. In a footnote, Chinnici notes that Orsi's *Thank You, St. Jude* did a good job of describing the transformation of the cult of St. Jude into a national movement and described well the efforts of its Claretian sponsors to reform and redirect the devotional movement in the 1960s.

26. O'Toole, *Habits of Devotion*, 87.

27. Our Lady of Consolation, accessed July 20, 2013, http://www.olcshrine.com.

28. Colleen McDannell, *The Spirit of Vatican II: A History of Catholic Reform in America* (New York: Basic Books, 2011), 211.

29. McDannell, *The Spirit of Vatican II*, 209.

30. McDannell, *The Spirit of Vatican II*, 210.

31. McDannell, *The Spirit of Vatican II*, 220, 219.

32. McDannell, *The Spirit of Vatican II*, 225.

33. McDannell, *The Spirit of Vatican II*, 219.

34. Andrew Walsh, "For Catholic Worshipers, Latin Mass Like Heaven," *Hartford Courant*, October 28, 1985, A1.

35. Pope John Paul II, "Apostolic Letter on the 25th Anniversary of *Sacrosanctum Concilium*," December 31, 2007, http://www.adoremus.org/JPII25SC .html#sthash.EKFurmHL.dpuf.

36. For an account of the rise and fall of ICEL, see John Wilkins, "Lost in Translation: The Bishops, the Vatican and the English Liturgy," *Commonweal*, November 28, 2005.

37. http://www.adoremus.org/faq.htm. Accessed on June 23, 2013.

38. Wilkins, "Lost in Translation."

39. Bob Harvey, "Vatican Lays Down Law to Curb 'Abuses' of Mass: New Rules Target Role of Lay People, but Not Women," *Ottawa Citizen*, April 24, 2004, A13.

40. See, for example, Rita Ferrone, "It Doesn't Sing," pray-tell.org, June 30, 2011; Rupert Shortt, "Tactical Missal," *Times Literary Supplement*, December 12 2012. For a defense of Pope Benedict's liturgical reforms, see Trent Beattie, "Benedict XVI Put Liturgy Front and Center," *National Catholic Register*, March 20, 2013; and Tom Esolen, "Restoring the Words: The New Translation of the Mass Restores Its Beauty and Splendor," *First Things*, November 2012.

41. Ferrone, "It Doesn't Sing."

42. John R. Donahue, "Cup or Chalice? The Large Implications of a Small Change," *Commonweal*, June 1, 2012, 12.

43. Wilkins, "Lost in Translation." For a defense of the change, see Austin J. Miller, "Why 'And with Your Spirit' Is Right," *Catholic Herald*, January 27, 2011.

44. John Klassen, "RIP Kevin Seasotz: "These Changes Were Heartrending . . ." pray-tell.org, May 3, 2013.

45. Rembert Weakland, "The Liturgy as Battlefield: What Do Restorationists Want?" *Commonweal*, January 11, 2002, 10.

46. Brian Cones, "You're Cut Off: No More Cup for the People," *U.S. Catholic* 76, no. 12 (December 2011): 8.

47. Robert Morlino, "Letter to Priests," October 10, 2011 https://madisondiocse.org/documents/2016/12Species_Bishop%20Memo.pdf.

48. Anthony Ruff, "Vernacular Liturgy and Pope Francis' Hermeneutic of Continuity," pray-tell.org, April 6, 2013.

49. Rorate Caeli, accessed July 24, 2013, http://rorate-caeli.blogspot.com/.

50. Michael Brendan Dougherty, "Why Pope Francis May Be a Catholic Nightmare," *Slate*, March 13, 2013, http://www.slate.com/articles/news_and_politics/foreigners/2013/03/pope_francis_to_lead_the_catholic_church_cardinal_bergoglio_s_election_as.html.

51. John Allen, "Right Wing Generally Not Happy with Pope Francis, Chaput Says," *National Catholic Reporter*, June 23, 2013.

52. Vatican Information Service, January 21, 2016.

53. Dan Hitchens, "Cardinal Sarah Asks Priests to Start Celebrating Mass Facing East This Advent," *Catholic Herald*, July 5, 2016.

54. Communication of the Holy See Press Office, "Some Clarifications on the Celebration of Mass," July 11, 2016.

55. Brian Harrison, "Francis Purges Conservatives from Divine Worship Congregation," *Catholic Family News*, accessed November 20, 2017, http://www.cfnews.org/page88/files/22a89f85bceeed07846bd8db23a92171-647.html.

56. Gerald O'Connell, "Pope Francis says with magisterial authority: The Vatican II liturgical reform is 'irreversible,'" *America*, August 24, 2017.

57. Jason Horowitz, "Pope Gives Nod to Liberals in 'Liturgy Wars,'" *New York Times*, September 10, 2017.

58. The force of the pope's very unusual public rejection is conveyed in headlines on stories reporting on his letter to Sarah: "Pope Disavows Cardinal Sarah on Liturgical Translation," in the French Catholic wire service, La Croix; "Pope Francis Rebukes Cardinal Sarah on Liturgy," in *America*; "Francis Corrects Sarah: Liturgical Translations Not to Be 'Imposed' from Vatican," in the *National Catholic Reporter*.

59. Joshua J. McAlwee, "Francis Corrects Sarah," *National Catholic Reporter*, October 22, 2017.

60. Joshua J. McAlwee, "Cardinal Wuerl: Francis' Liturgical Reform Is 'What the Council Said,'" *National Catholic Reporter*, October 30, 2017.

61. Jordan Otero Sisson, "St. Martha Parish Reestablished in Enfield," *Hartford Courant*, November 11, 2017.

62. Jordan Otero Sisson, "Clash of Culture Leads to Failed Parish Merger in Enfield," *Hartford Courant*, November 20, 2017.

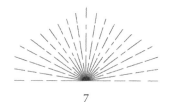

7

Public Catholicism

CONTEMPORARY PRESENCE AND FUTURE PROMISE

Richard L. Wood

This chapter presents a bird's-eye view of the public profile of contemporary Roman Catholicism in the United States. It pays attention both to the high-level national picture within church and society, and to more diffuse dynamics within broad segments of the Catholic community and American society as a whole. I argue that, although an institutional analysis leads to an impressive picture of public Catholicism's presence at all levels of church and society, specific dynamics within the church continue to undermine the wider impact of public Catholicism. Thus, this chapter offers a reflective essay on the condition of American public Catholicism, synthesizing information and insight from a variety of sources. Such a wide-angle look into public Catholicism cannot delve into a fully detailed analysis; what is lost through generality I hope to gain through a broad assessment that can offer insight, if not into the future itself, at least into the key dynamics that will partly give birth to that future.

Any thoughtful citizen of the United States—Catholic or otherwise—might well be troubled by the state of American public Catholicism today. Catholicism has not lost its public voice, but the credibility of that voice has been undermined by the sectarian tone of some Catholic leaders and by clericalist misuse of authority to shelter sexual abusers. Catholicism's historically fruitful dialogue with American culture—carried on in diverse ways by leaders both lay and clerical, from Bishop John Carroll and Orestes Brownson in the eighteenth and nineteenth centuries to John Ryan, Dorothy Day, Jack Egan, and Cardinal Joseph Bernardin in the twentieth century—in some ways continues today. But amid the sexual abuse scandal in the church and acute political polarization in the wider society, leaders in both church and society seem increasingly tone-deaf to the appropriate give-and-take of public dialogue in a democratic society. This chapter argues that if the Catholic Church can reestablish its public credibility and vigorously relaunch that historic dialogue, its social teaching and institutional presence hold vast potential to play a leavening role in American public life. Alternatively, if recent patterns continue, the church risks sacrificing both its public efficacy and its historical role in society, in the name of what I will argue below is a more sectarian self-understanding.

The chapter begins by outlining an analytic framework through which to examine the relationship between public Catholicism and American society. The second section then extends José Casanova's influential analysis of "public religion in the modern world" to document Catholicism's public presence in three sectors of American life:[1] *ecclesial institutions*, from the national bishops' conference and state-level bishops' conferences to dioceses/archdioceses, Catholic universities, and local parishes and schools; *other public institutions*, ranging from Congress and the Supreme Court to state and local elected officials and nongovernmental institutions; and *lay-centered social movements*. The third section portrays public Catholicism in action through a brief case study of the Catholic involvement in the 2009–2010 health-care reform debate. The fourth section deepens the earlier analysis by considering cultural and institutional factors in three areas: institutional leadership; authority dynamics within the church; and the culture of prayer, spirituality, and worship in parishes. Finally, the concluding section discusses the key dynamics likely to shape the future of public Catholicism in America.

Throughout the chapter, I frame the argument within an analysis of the relationship between three dynamics of social life: the dynamics of democratic politics in society, the dynamics of authority within the Catholic tradition and in the wider society, and the dynamics of individual identity formation.

THINKING ABOUT "PUBLIC CATHOLICISM": AN ANALYTIC FRAMEWORK[2]

Catholics and non-Catholics alike may be tempted to identify "public Catholicism" with the public voice of the bishops in addressing social policy. Certainly the bishops represent one crucial dimension of the church's public witness, but it is a mistake to reduce public Catholicism only to this dimension. Far better to start with an adequate understanding of the notion of "the public" in order to properly consider what we mean by public Catholicism. This section thus begins by summarizing current understandings of the public sphere and why it is crucial to democratic society, then identifies the institutional settings and cultural dynamics that are key to public Catholicism. Doing so will also clarify why everyone, not just Catholics, has a stake in the status and efficacy of public Catholicism in American society.

Note that evidence of significant direct Catholic impact on American public life appears thin. A plausible case might be made for a Catholic role in changing American policy with regard to Central America in the 1980s and fighting domestic-partnership legislation at the state level more recently. But even in these limited areas, it would be hard to argue for a dominant Catholic role, and it would be indefensible to argue for Catholic efficacy with regard to a wide variety of other issues, even those on which the church has expended considerable resources: against abortion and sexual promiscuity, or in favor of humane immigration reform or vouchers for private education. On balance, the record of public Catholicism's *direct impact* appears markedly thin, especially for an organization claiming as its own more than a fifth of all Americans, and with the institutional resources documented below. To offer insight into why this may be so, and into the strengths and weaknesses of public Catholicism, I turn first to current democratic theory.

The Public Sphere

The notion of the "public sphere" has profoundly shaped the thinking of democratic theorists in recent years.[3] In briefest summary, the core notion holds that democracy is not simply the product of elections and representative institutions, but rather is built upon a foundation of societal-wide dialogue through which citizens reflect upon their experience and current situation and establish priorities and commitments that flow into and shape the political process through those elections and representative institutions. Democratic deliberation thus occurs at multiple levels: among citizens, between leaders of all kinds of institutions, and among political leaders. All such sites constitute what democratic theorists call the "public sphere." Note that the concept of the public sphere does not posit only a bottom-up flow of influence; political decisions also flow down to shape the deliberative dynamics in society. To the extent that these political processes approximate reflective dialogue about the direction of society, they also constitute part of the public sphere. Thus, the public sphere is made up of all those settings in which people come together to discuss, debate, deliberate, and make decisions regarding the life of society and its future direction. It includes venues from the most grassroots dinner table and watercooler settings to the most elite institutions—anywhere that public issues or political orientations are discussed and shaped.

Two caveats are immediately important. First, by emphasizing "dialogue" and "deliberation," the above description risks presenting too cordial a view of the public sphere. The public sphere also includes the much more conflictive processes of partisan politics and its whole infrastructure of contesting parties, electoral battles, talk radio, and blogs. Conflict-based and dialogue-based dynamics are equally central in shaping the public sphere.[4] Second, though the democratic ideal posits that all members of a society participate in the public arena on an equal footing, in reality differing levels of power mean some people shape public dynamics more than others—and some people may be excluded nearly completely (for lack of cultural or economic resources, as noncitizens, for reasons of gender or sexual orientation, etc.). Egalitarian themes within Catholic social teaching become especially relevant here because of that tradition's emphasis on judging societal arrangements partly through the lens of their impact on those who were previously marginal in society.[5]

Note that this analytic understanding of "the public" does not parallel either of the popular usages of the word: the public in this sense is neither to be identified narrowly with debate and voting in political bodies such as legislatures, nor broadly with "public opinion" understood as the sum total of everyone's private opinions. Importantly, although the notion of the public was originally developed by looking historically at the face-to-face settings of premodern Europe, that conception is no longer adequate. Instead, the public must include the ways that mass media and specialized media now constitute crucial sites of public discussion. Democratic deliberation thus occurs in settings as various as in-person or online conversations in which people draw on their experience and cultural understandings to reflect on societal-level concerns, to congressional and presidential debates, to television programming that provokes political discussion, to the give-and-take of legal precedent setting by the Supreme Court—and even to Twitter exchanges (albeit here only in a constricted sense of "deliberation").

In this way of understanding the public sphere, "public Catholicism" cannot be narrowed to the role of the Catholic bishops. Doing so would collapse to a few voices what is objectively a far more diverse set of individual voices and institutional channels through which the Catholic tradition shapes American consciousness. Thus, we are dealing with public Catholicism everywhere that the Catholic worldview is brought to bear in deliberations within the public sphere undergirding American democracy. In a sense, then, it is the whole Catholic tradition that sustains a dialogue with American culture, with that dialogue carried on at many levels simultaneously—by theologians and Catholic scholars in their intellectual work; by deacons, religious sisters and brothers, and priests in preaching and teaching; by lay Catholic leaders within secular institutions; by Catholic businessmen and politicians within corporations and government. Ultimately, the Catholic understanding of the authoritative office of the bishops means that they are arbiters of the Catholic tradition's stance in this societal-wide dialogue, but as we shall see, without these other voices that dialogue would be much impoverished. The voice of the bishops thus constitutes the central flow among many that make up the overall current of American public Catholicism, with other important channels, crosscurrents, and subterranean flows also important to the overall picture. This portrayal emphasizes the actual ways that Catholicism relates to American culture; it is also consistent with democratic political norms, in which social policy is driven by effective argumentation and political discernment, not via a privileged church voice directly shaping political life.

In utilizing this model of church-society relations within the public sphere, we must remember that there are two different modes of authority at work in the two settings: Within the church, authority is ultimately hierarchical in structure. It is "top-down" although not absolutist, in that when internal church dynamics are healthy, multiple currents of Catholic teaching are in play within that hierarchically structured authority; but it is inherently hierarchical. In contrast, within the wider society, authority is democratically structured through participative and representative institutions, often colloquially described as "from the bottom up." In fact, democratic authority is a good deal more complex than that phrase implies, with multiple hierarchical authority structures in play, including scientific authority, authority rooted in corporate and labor union hierarchies, and the authority attached to icons of popular culture and religious belief. But the top-down versus bottom-up imagery captures a key distinction between authority within Catholicism, structured by complex hierarchy, and authority within the democratic public sphere, structured by democratic relations.[6]

Used poorly, such a broad understanding of the public sphere might risk becoming analytically useless by requiring us to pay attention to everything at once. But we can avoid this risk: As a relatively coherent spiritual and intellectual tradition that revolves around specific institutional nodes, Catholicism lends itself to a focused analysis limited to a relative handful of such institutions.

Institutions of Public Life: Ecclesial and Secular

Here I sketch the analytic tools for conceiving of how public Catholicism exerts influence in society. As an initial approximation, we can think of Catholic public influence being exerted through the two broad channels sketched above—one in a top-down direction, the other in a bottom-up direction. On one hand, Catholic teaching might flow down and out to the wider society through ecclesial institutions explicitly committed to Catholic worldview and practice. On the other hand, Catholic worldview and social commitments might flow upward through the institutions of society, as a result of cultural influence of individual Catholics in civil institutions and electoral politics. Figure 7.1 sketches these complementary potential channels of Catholic influence, as well as an important "middle" route of influence.

As depicted in figure 7.1, analyzing public Catholicism requires paying attention to a diverse array of institutional settings, from parishes and diocesan organizations to national-level episcopal structures and from local civil society to the Supreme Court. This chapter offers an initial assessment of the Catholic institutional presence, but for now note how public Catholicism both shapes and is shaped by American society through high-level contact between national leaders of church and

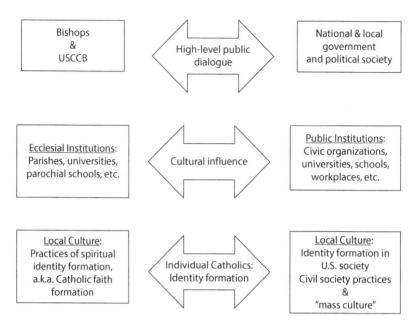

Fig. 7.1 Public Catholicism: Channels of influence between church and society

society *and* by the bottom-up diffusion of identities and practices that subsequently shape public life. We will later consider concrete examples of each process; here, the crucial point lies in recognizing the multiple levels of potential cross-influence between church and society.

Note that the bottom of figure 7.1 assumes a relatively free flow of culture between the ecclesial sector and the wider social world. This is in keeping with the contemporary reality that American Catholics no longer exist in a separate, sectarian subculture within American society, as arguably was the case up through the 1950s. Rather, Catholics have fully joined the broad American cultural and social milieu, with most individual Catholics operating competently within both Catholic settings and the wider culture.[7]

Public Catholicism as Identity and Culture

Fundamental to analyzing public Catholicism is understanding the cultural position of individual Catholics. How central a "Catholic" identity is to individual Catholics surely varies greatly, but to the extent such an identity is significant, it has presumably been shaped by parish-level cultural dynamics. This is so because worship services, rituals marking life transitions of birth, adulthood, marriage or religious life, and death mostly occur through parishes. More importantly, the central constitutive ritual of Catholic spiritual community, the Eucharist (or communion), occurs primarily in parish settings. Even highly individualized spiritual practices such as the rosary often occur in communal settings, and in any case make reference to and are understood within scriptural and theological commitments that prioritize the communal dimensions of the Christian message.

Yet almost no American Catholics today live their lives closed off within these communal Catholic settings. Rather—except for the tiny minority who have chosen monastic or quasi-monastic lifestyles—American Catholics also share in the hum and blare of contemporary American culture in all its variegated complexity: hyperconsumption and the marketing of the stylized "self," but also the wide availability of diverse techniques of spiritual self-discipline; endless and continual electronic entertainment, but also a wealthy society's ability to create islands of serenity via public parks or private meditation centers. Thus, though parishes are key to my analysis and do sustain internal cultural lives based upon Catholic practices and worldviews, parish members swim partly within that parish-based Catholic culture and partly within the wider culture.

Although (as depicted in figure 7.1), public Catholicism exerts social influence through both elite dialogue and more dispersed cultural flows above the level of the individual, in the long term it will only have significant influence to the extent that the complex and crosscutting identity-forming pressures produce individuals with discernibly "Catholic" identities. For if there is no distinction between being Catholic and being American, then American Catholicism simply dissolves into the wider mainstream culture. This makes understanding what Catholics call "faith formation" crucial to assessing public Catholicism. This is the "identity formation" level shown in figure 7.1; it includes the practices of spirituality and worship centered in parishes, as well as the intellectual commitments shaped by theologians and disseminated through Catholic teaching and preaching.

Though some regret the fact that lay Catholics now live fully within both church and society, lamenting it as the death of a distinctively traditional Catholicism, sociologically it reflects American Catholics' successful upward mobility over several generations and American society's successful dismantling of anti-Catholic nativism. It also represents the opportunity for American Catholicism to effectively shape the wider society. As long as Catholics resided in a subculture of their own, their ability to reshape the wider culture was quite limited. By bridging between broad American cultural patterns and the Catholic worldview carried within parish life, contemporary American Catholics bring Catholicism to bear within the ongoing evolution of American culture, both at the grassroots and at higher institutional levels. This brings us to the "cultural influence" level shown in figure 7.1.

Beyond Identity: Thinking About Cultural Flow Between Church and Society

Beyond individual identity formation, equally or more important is the way that public Catholicism shapes and is shaped by broader American culture. To think about this, it is helpful to imagine American society not only as a collection of individual Americans, but also as the product of interweaving cultural strands that shape American life.[8] American life is a stream made up of a variety of cultural currents, intermingling in complex ways yet preserving themselves as evolving cultural traditions (including traditions based upon democratic commitments, religion, ethnic and racial identities, mass consumerism, "new age" and artistic humanism, utilitarianism, nationalism, etc.). In this metaphor, public Catholicism is one such cultural current, shaping and being shaped by American culture in ways not reducible to individual identity formation. Rather, public Catholicism also bridges between authoritative teaching internal to the church and the flow of democratic authority in American society.

From the standpoint of advocates of public Catholicism, this bridging represents an advance, rather than a retreat, only if Catholic culture preserves sufficient coherence to play that role. Theologically, such an understanding harmonizes well with Gerhard Lohfink's analysis of the early church as a "contrast society" to the wider culture.[9] Two points are crucial here, which can be best appreciated by extending the "bridging" metaphor: A bridge must be securely anchored at both ends, or it cannot function as a bridge. Thus, at one end, the church as contrast society must coherently articulate and clearly live out its own identity and self-understanding. At the other end, the church must not only affirm democratic life and freedom of conscience in principle, but also accept *in practice* the dynamics of democratic authority in political decision making. From the standpoint of Catholics, "bridging" must be faithful to the church's self-understanding; simultaneously, from the standpoint of the non-Catholic public, this bridging represents a legitimate voice for public Catholicism only if the key actors in public Catholicism accept the rules of the democratic public sphere—namely, that religious leaders (1) enter the public arena to try to convince others that their views will best serve the common good; (2) recognize that pursuit of the common good is a complex political art and a skilled craft, in which specialists (called politicians) pursue partial victories that pave the way for deeper future victories; and (3) enter the public arena open to the possibility of others' providing convincing counterarguments that might cause them to revise their views.[10] Refusal to accept these terms of democratic life, in the name of a purer absolute good, potentially leads to the situation of the Catholic Church behaving as a sect—an oxymoron in traditional Catholic self-understanding, but nevertheless a contemporary alternative, as we shall see.

Catholics (whether conservative or progressive) who prefer a more prophetic/critical stance toward American culture will surely respond that no prophetic social role is possible if American Catholicism simply embraces the wider culture. I do not argue for a blind embrace of the wider culture: If the church understands itself as "leaven" for the "dough" of the wider society, it must to a significant degree serve as a contrast to that society— "leavening" presumes a distinction between the leaven and the dough. Thus, the notion of the church as contrast society returns us to the theme of identity formation: If church institutions can effectively shape an American Catholic identity that holds its own amid the pressures of popular culture, then American Catholics are, as demonstrated below, impressively positioned to shape the wider culture in ways not previously possible. However, the point here is that prophetic Catholicism cannot reject all normal political compromise if it wants to play this leavening role.

Thus, American public Catholicism in the early twenty-first century stands institutionally and culturally on complex terrain. The next two sections begin a concrete analysis of that terrain by considering the American Catholic institutional profile and role in an important current debate.

CATHOLICISM'S INSTITUTIONAL PRESENCE IN AMERICAN LIFE

Catholicism is brought to bear in public life both through explicitly church-sponsored institutions and through the presence of Catholic individuals within nonchurch institutions and broad social movements.

In briefly outlining Catholicism's presence in American life, I pay attention both to the raw numerical weight of Catholic institutional and individual presence in these settings and to the subtler dynamics of Catholic influence within these institutions. I divide the discussion into ecclesial institutions, other public institutions, and lay-centered social movements—recognizing that the level of institutional control by Catholic bishops varies substantially across these levels. Such episcopal control is strongest in official ecclesial institutions directly affiliated with dioceses, weaker in those affiliated with religious orders, and weaker still vis-à-vis public institutions and lay-centered social movements (although episcopal influence in the latter varies greatly). This creates a significant pluralism of Catholic perspectives and directions of influence, despite outside perceptions of a monolithic Catholic voice.

Ecclesial Institutions

In terms of sheer institutional presence, Catholicism maintains an impressive and growing weight in American society. In 2007, there were 19,044 parishes in the United States, spread broadly across the geographic regions, social settings, and—importantly—the districts that elect presidents, congressional representatives, state officials, city council members, and school boards.[11] This represents an increase of 1,102 parishes since 1967 (a 6 percent increase), though a decrease of 583 parishes since 2000 (a 3 percent decline), as dioceses strapped for financial resources and ordained clergy have closed some churches.

Far outpacing this slow, four-decade rise in the number of American parishes, the number of Catholics per parish has increased significantly, from 2,614 to 3,544 members in the average parish (a 36 percent increase). This has been driven by a dramatic increase in the total Catholic population, from 46.9 million to 67.5 million (a 44 percent increase), primarily due to immigration. Simultaneously, the number of ordained men who lead most of these parishes has declined 40 percent, and the number of religious sisters and brothers who once provided crucial additional staffing in parishes, schools, and other settings has fallen most precipitously of all (63 percent). As a result, the number of Catholics per priest or religious has risen by 220 percent during this four-decade period.

From the point of view of cultural sociology, we can assume that where institutional Catholic influence wanes (as reflected roughly in declining numbers of priests and religious sisters/brothers, or thinner institutional life generally), the identity-formation dynamics among lay Catholics will be increasingly influenced by mass American culture.[12] That is, individual identity formation is shaped by both internal Catholic and wider cultural dynamics; where the former is weaker, the latter may hold greater sway.

But a wide Catholic institutional presence remains within American culture. Beyond parishes, the church's presence includes 557 hospitals assisting some 83 million patients per year, often at times of personal crisis, and often with explicitly Catholic pastoral care offered alongside medical expertise. In addition, approximately 1,004 day-care centers and 2,856 specialized social service centers serve a broad constituency of low- and middle-income non-Catholic and Catholic clients. Some 769 parish-affiliated high schools and 583 other Catholic high schools serve approximately 608,000 students during the key identity-shaping teen years; and more than 6,500 Catholic schools serve more than 1.6 million elementary school students. Finally, more than 3.8 million elementary- and high-school-age children are reported to partake in religious education through parishes nationwide. All this adds up to an impressive Catholic institutional presence in American life, albeit one whose cultural influence has likely waned significantly in the face of societal changes of recent decades.[13]

Meanwhile, the state of American ecclesial finances has deteriorated markedly: As Francis Butler noted in 2006, U.S. dioceses "face an era of rising costs, diminishing reserves and insufficient income. . . . Dioceses appear to be running through their reserves at an alarming rate. . . . The reason for this is simple: It's due to the outflow of grants to sustain parishes operating at a loss."[14] Butler went on to note that these deficits are primarily associated with parishes housing parochial schools.

These structural deficit problems have been exacerbated by the costs of settlements with victims of clergy sexual abuse.[15] From 2004 to 2008,

American dioceses and their equivalents faced costs related to sexual misconduct allegations that varied between $139 million and $498 million *annually*. With a total of almost $1.7 billion paid out over that period and approximately 60 percent paid directly by dioceses (40 percent paid by insurance), this has been an enormous drain on church finances. In addition, the finances of men's religious communities deteriorated dramatically, with $281 million paid out to settle sexual abuse cases from 2004 to 2008. Whether these financial liabilities have peaked or will continue unabated remains unclear, as the financial sums and the numbers of new allegations show no consistent pattern.

Incalculable but serious damage to the church's public credibility has also been done by the supervisory negligence of some bishops, which exacerbated the sexual abuse scandal. The resulting authority scandal is beyond my purposes here, but has surely undermined the credibility and legitimacy of the bishops' authoritative voice.

More complex has been the financial situation of women's religious communities. Some have prospered financially by selling off medical and other institutions to endow their communities or to promote social justice and charitable endeavors; many others confront profound financial crises as members age and face high medical costs while recruitment of new members declines.

The resulting ecclesial financial difficulties, combined with the rising influence of some bishops resistant to national episcopal influence in their dioceses, led to an important downsizing of the United States Conference of Catholic Bishops (USCCB) during 2005–2006. The retrenchment instituted a leaner organizational structure and sharp reductions in staffing. While some of this reorganization may have been overdue, it is hard to avoid the conclusion that it also represented a significant scaling back of organizational aspiration and capacity, and a lower priority to some areas of historic episcopal priority: Whereas the bishops' most prominent interventions in public discourse in the 1980s involved criticism of nuclear weapons policy, economic inequality, and American intervention in Central America, in recent years they have involved criticism of abortion rights, embryonic stem cell research, and domestic-partnership legislation. This represents an important shift of public profile, albeit one that should not be exaggerated—after all, throughout these decades the bishops have also continued to speak out on a wide spectrum of social issues, including opposition to the death penalty, concern about poverty in America, and support of immigrants' rights. Nonetheless, a greater emphasis on "conservative" issues and a more partisan tenor of political messages has been widely perceived, along with a deemphasis of the integrated "seamless garment" approach advocated by the late Cardinal Joseph Bernardin (see chapters 3, 5, and Killen's conclusion to this volume).

Throughout these shifts, the USCCB has remained the Catholic bishops' primary voice in national public affairs, through such activities as educating and lobbying congressional representatives regarding the bishops' issue priorities; the periodic promulgation of statements such as *Faithful Citizenship*, intended to inform Catholic political choices during the 2008 elections; and the antipoverty program Catholic Campaign for Human Development, which each year distributes some ten million dollars in funding to empower poor communities.

Other ecclesial institutions have fared far better in recent years. A less-known story involves the continuing work and influence of Catholic lobbying efforts through the "Catholic conferences" sponsored by groups of bishops in some thirty-two states.[16] David Yamane argues that the bishops' lobbying efforts at this level have been largely unaffected by the recent sex and authority scandals and remain quite strong (at least as of 2004). Much less certain is the effect of the recent church financial implosion and the broader economic downturn, and whether the state conferences have been able to sustain their funding and activity.

Catholic universities and colleges represent another key facet of the public profile of American Catholicism. It is a diverse profile, from small colleges that are quite insular to large liberal arts colleges and research universities that are very much engaged with the wider culture. Furthermore, their political and theological profiles vary enormously. Some have embraced traditionalist efforts to reinstate a tightly defined Catholic orthodoxy; others have largely fused with the mainstream culture of American higher education; and still others have embraced Catholic teaching on social justice as defining their central mission.

These complex internal dynamics too often obscure what is in any case an impressive profile in higher education: 236 Catholic colleges and universities, spread out across all fifty states, enroll more than 900,000 students and represent a rich pluralism of emphases and identities within an at least potentially unifying Catholic vision of contemporary life.[17]

Enrollment grew by almost 61 percent between 1980 and 2005. This strong institutional presence does not necessarily translate into effective identity-formation processes; we simply do not know a great deal about whether these colleges and universities are effectively passing on a Catholic ethos, spirituality, vision, and social commitment (in whatever terms a given observer defines those things). The best data come from Christian Smith's *National Study of Youth and Religion*; these data do raise important doubts about the efficacy of current church practice in this regard.[18]

Finally, church-sponsored communications media remain an important aspect of the Catholic public profile, although the focus and technological basis of the media used continue to shift. A Catholic media profile that once emphasized magazines, newspapers, and radio today increasingly emphasizes different media.[19] Catholic television stations and websites now abound, and the Vatican now sponsors a sophisticated internet projection. Thus, though such publications as *America*, *First Things*, the *National Catholic Reporter*, the *National Catholic Review*, and the *Wanderer* continue to be read and to exercise significant influence in their particular markets, the broader Catholic market appears increasingly to belong to television and the internet.

Good studies of this shifting religious media terrain are rare, but a few generalizations seem warranted. First, and perhaps most important, all these media outlets combined appear to have lost market share to the dynamic growth of two other sectors of religious media. More evangelically inclined media and magazines reach out to a broad mass market across nearly all regions and social sectors. At the same time, a smaller set of media outlets promote "contemporary spirituality" of Buddhist, Hindu, Sufi, Sikh, "new age," and other varieties, especially among the future societal leaders being educated in elite universities and socialized in urban centers.[20] Second, Catholic television appears to be dominated by traditionalist Catholicism, with programming devoted to some of the least intellectually reflective pietistic practices of contemporary Catholicism and to the most sectarian Catholic intellectuals. This programming both reflects and promotes an authentic part of the current spectrum of Catholic practice; its dominance nonetheless reflects a dearth of televised presence for others points on that spectrum. Third, the Catholic internet presence is far more diversified, better reflecting the broad "catholic" spectrum of views and emphases; here, conservative and liberal positions, official and alternative Catholic voices, and clergy and lay perspectives all find a voice.

Two final notes regarding ecclesial institutions: First, the Vatican's extension into a sophisticated multilingual presence via an official website and YouTube channel should make official teaching more directly available in forms accessible to lay Catholics. But this will only serve to advance ecclesial insight if it is accompanied by a parallel effort to foster dialogue within the church and critical engagement across perspectives and cultures.[21] Second, political historians have shown that the most successful civil associations in American history have been built on "federated" organizational forms, combining intensive local participation with state- and national-level structures.[22] The Catholic structure of parishes, (arch)dioceses, state conferences, and the national bishops' conference constitutes precisely such a federated structure—suggesting that the Catholic tradition might still be capable of articulating a strong external voice vis-à-vis American public life. For such a voice to be effective, legitimate, and authentically Catholic, it must emerge from long-term symbiosis between authoritative central teaching and decentralized lay initiative, both appropriately affirming the pluralistic principles of a democratic public arena.

Other Public Institutions

Beyond the official and semiofficial ecclesial institutions discussed above, individual Catholic leaders in prominent positions in other public institutions also project public Catholicism into the wider society. Three such settings appear especially important at present.

First, notable Catholic intellectuals teach and write from within high-profile universities, including public, religiously affiliated, and elite secular private universities. No exhaustive list of such figures exists, but a few luminaries will serve to flag the significance of this sector. Charles Taylor, Alisdair MacIntyre, Mary Ann Glendon, the legal scholars John T. Noonan and Robert P. George, and theologian Bryan Hehir all write and speak extensively as Catholic commentators. Though not emanating from universities, important intellectual work is also done via the news media, exemplified in the "Beliefs" column in the *New York Times* written for twenty years by Peter Steinfels, the liberal opinion column of E. J. Dionne, and the conservative commentary of Michael Gerson (the last two published in the *Washington Post* and further syndicated).[23] Although not Catholics, Robert Bellah and Jean Bethke Elshtain might be considered part of this group, given their linkages and influence in the Catholic world.

In addition, a series of endowed chairs of Catholic Studies (or similar positions) have been created in recent years. Richard Gaillardetz, previously as the Murray/Bacik Endowed Chair in Catholic Studies at the University of Toledo and now at Boston College, has played the most prominent public intellectual role, but such endowed chairs also exist at the University of Kansas, University of Illinois at Chicago, Iowa State University, Northwestern University, Washington University in St. Louis, Case Western Reserve, University of Pittsburgh, University of California at Santa Barbara, University of Kentucky, University of Rochester, Virginia Commonwealth University, Nassau Community Colleges New York (Center), Yale University, University of New Mexico, Hofstra University, Tulsa University, and Harvard Divinity School.

Second, Catholics have come to play a remarkably prominent position in the court system of the United States, particularly at the level of the U.S. Supreme Court. There, Republican and Democratic presidents have appointed a series of Catholic judges: Antonin Scalia, Clarence Thomas, Samuel Alito, John Roberts, and Sonia Sotomayor. The first four helped shift the Supreme Court in a markedly more conservative direction: Scalia (until his death), Thomas, Roberts, and usually Alito have been among the most reliably conservative voices on the Court. Sotomayor brings a liberal Catholic orientation rooted in a different reading of Catholic social teaching and a more liberal tradition of jurisprudence, or perhaps simply reflecting a vaguely "New Deal" Catholic upbringing. The current transition in justices may shift things further: the recently retired Anthony Kennedy was Catholic and the crucial centrist on a range of 5–4 decisions; Neil Gorsuch is a strong conservative and currently attends an Episcopalian church, but some sources identify him as still Catholic; and Brett Kavanaugh (in confirmation hearings as this goes to press) would constitute another presumably conservative voice. In any case, the nation now faces the extraordinary situation of two-thirds of the Supreme Court justices being broadly Catholic (counting Gorsuch and assuming Kavanaugh is confirmed).[24]

Third, Catholic elected officials continue to exert influence at all levels of American government, from school boards, city councils, and mayors' offices to the halls of Congress. No systematic data on this phenomenon exist—though studies on this terrain would be enormously valuable, both in assessing the current picture and in understanding shifts in Catholic representation over recent decades. It would be most interesting, for example, to know whether the shift in public Catholicism—from being a core part of the "New Deal Democrat" coalition from the 1930s to the 1980s to being a key swing constituency in the 1980s, 1990s, and 2000s, when Catholics supported Reagan, Clinton, Bush, and Obama in successive presidential elections—has been reflected in the profile of elected local and state-level Catholic officials nationwide. Likewise, the outspoken intervention of some American bishops in opposition to Catholic candidates deemed insufficiently committed to Catholic teaching on "life issues" has been widely viewed as undermining the candidacies of top-of-the-ticket Democratic candidates, from Mario Cuomo to Geraldine Ferraro to John Kerry, while failing to produce strong Catholic candidates on the Republican ticket. Has it also negatively influenced Democratic Catholic candidates for local or statewide office? Has it fostered Catholic Republican candidacies at these levels? We simply do not know much, although anecdotal accounts abound.

Finally, only future elections will show whether the widespread Catholic swing toward Barrack Obama in 2008, despite episcopal criticism of his stance on life issues, simply reflected widespread disenchantment with the Republican Party following the Iraq occupation, Hurricane Katrina, and the "Great Recession," or instead signaled a long-term increase in autonomous political judgment by lay Catholics. If the latter is the long-term pattern, research will be needed to assess whether it results from a widespread turning away from episcopal authority, or from heightened lay political discernment kept in dialogue with episcopal authority. The 2016 election showed how closely split the Catholic electorate remains.

Lay-Centered Movements

At a more grassroots level, a wide variety of lay-centered movements are shaping the cultural terrain of American Catholicism. Some of these are familiar, such as the pro-life/antiabortion movement, which is partly episcopally funded and draws on Catholic parish life in significant ways. A variety of Catholic social-justice movements, although only weakly present in most parishes, engage students at public and Catholic universities via campus ministry efforts, worship at "Newman Centers," and issue-specific outreach efforts. The Catholic charismatic movement and other apostolic movements continue to exert an important influence, both through local parishes and in less institutionally organized venues.[25] Meanwhile *Opus Dei*, Catholics United for the Faith, and other conservative movements seek to bolster more traditionalist interpretations of Catholicism, lobby for "restorationist" interpretations of Vatican II, and pressure bishops and priests to clamp down on liberal trends within American Catholicism. On the more liberal side, movements such as Call to Action and Catholics United seek to heighten the profile of Catholic social teaching on a variety of issues and to press for changes in Catholic teaching and authority structures. All these are important and understudied facets of public Catholicism.

Less-known lay-centered Catholic movements also play significant roles in American Catholic life. Many Catholic parishes in low-income urban areas, and some suburban and rural parishes, participate actively in "faith-based community organizing" efforts (FBCO), also known as broad-based or congregation-based community organizing (not to be confused with the presidential "faith-based initiative" for social service funding). Community organizing has received recent attention because of Barrack Obama's early experience in Chicago, but such efforts have for more than six decades involved Roman Catholic, historic black Protestant, liberal and moderate Protestant, Jewish, Unitarian, and (more recently) Pentecostal congregations in work to influence local and state-level public policy. They have built a track record of influencing public policy to benefit low- and middle-income communities on such issues as public education, economic development, housing, health care, and policing. Sponsoring most of this work are several national FBCO networks, including the PICO National Network, the Industrial Areas Foundation, the Gamaliel Foundation, and Direction Action and Research Training; the regional Inter-Valley Project and Regional Congregations and Neighborhood Organizations; plus a few independent efforts. These networks link more than 160 local organizations, present in essentially all major metropolitan areas and many other primary cities of the country.[26] As of 1999, for which systematic national data exist, those organizations incorporated four thousand member institutions (87 percent of which were religious congregations, the rest mostly unions, public schools, and neighborhood associations) in thirty-eight states, which together included approximately two million institutional members. Since then, the field has grown significantly and now has a presence in all but a handful of states.[27] About a third of the sponsoring congregations are Catholic parishes. When well implemented, this organizing model empowers lay leadership reflective of Vatican II's emphasis on the laity's mission "in the world."

FBCO work on issues has often reflected the public policy priorities embodied in Catholic social teaching as articulated in papal and American episcopal statements. That is no coincidence. For thirty-five years, the bishops' Catholic Campaign for Human Development has been the most consistent source of funding for faith-based community organizing efforts throughout the country; many religious orders also fund this work. That support has been crucial to strengthening the field's organizational infrastructure, in that it often provides the start-up funding that has helped the field grow from a scattering of struggling organizations in the early 1980s to its current wide geographic profile. In the current debate over health-care reform in the United States, the PICO National Network has provided the primary voice of the faith community in articulating the moral basis for health-care reform, via congressional testimony in favor of expansion of the State Children's Health Insurance Program, grassroots organizing in local congressional districts nationwide, and high-profile participation in the White House Forum on Health Reform in March 2009. Rare indeed is the FBCO organization that has not benefited from CCHD funding or sponsorship from the local Catholic diocese.[28]

Two other important lay movements are also not widely recognized: the many small "faith sharing" groups functioning within or alongside Catholic parishes and the grassroots movement Voice of the Faithful. The faith-sharing groups are decentralized and reflect many different strands of Catholicism, typically meeting weekly or monthly to read scripture, reflect on their faith lives, pray together, and (more rarely) engage in service or advocacy work together.[29] Voice of the Faithful argues for increased accountability of episcopal structures and a greater lay share in church leadership, partly in response to the sexual abuse crisis. Though sometimes perceived as hostile to church leaders, the organization appears to combine strong Catholic religious identity, a desire for a thriving institutional profile for public Catholicism, and insistence on greater transparency and accountability.

As carried in ecclesially linked institutions, other public institutions, and lay movements, public Catholicism thus constitutes an impressive Catholic profile in American public life. Yet whether it all adds up to significant Catholic influence on American society today is less clear. Indeed, in its direct impact, public Catholicism appears to add up to less than the sum of its parts.

In order to understand the complex place of the Catholic tradition within the American democratic arena, the next section analyzes the role of public Catholicism in one crucial national debate of recent years.

CASE STUDY OF PUBLIC CATHOLICISM: THE HEALTH-CARE REFORM DEBATE

The 2009–2010 national health-care debate, along with the health reform efforts preceding it, offer a glimpse into public Catholicism in action. As has been widely noted, the recent debate follows decades of efforts to broaden health-care coverage in American society. The U.S. bishops had long supported egalitarian access to health care, and already in 1981 had issued a major pastoral letter strongly endorsing some form of universal coverage, giving as the first principle to guide national health policy that "every person has a basic right to adequate health care."[30] Despite that advocacy, the desire (of the bishops and others) for broad health reform had remained largely frustrated by the difficulties inherent in reshaping a sector that, by the end of the century, made up nearly a sixth of the national economy. The bishops weighed in on the national debate again with a major public resolution in 1993, and with official press releases and voter education efforts in 2002, 2004, and 2006.[31] Over the years, other Catholic public actors also weighed in on the issue, including the Catholic Health Association, various Catholic politicians and intellectuals, and a variety of religious orders.

But all this had gained little traction. That began to change as the nation's health crisis worsened, as children's health became a wedge issue for broader calls for health reform, and when one of the faith-based community-organizing networks described above set expansion of health-care access as one of its primary goals. I focus attention here on the third factor because of its links to public Catholicism and because the first two factors have been widely reported.

As it first sought to influence national policy, the PICO National Network could draw on the experience of its sophisticated statewide effort in California.[32] PICO California had been active in organizing for broad health-care access for several years, and its affiliate in San Jose had been central in winning passage of the nation's first legislation to cover all children in a county (the Santa Clara County Health Initiative). Out of these initiatives, in May 2005 some 315 PICO leaders met in Washington, DC, to begin building PICO's national strategic capacity. After meeting with about one hundred congressional representatives, staffers, and DC-based policy think tanks, they recommended to local affiliates that health care become the initial focus of national organizing.[33]

Eventually, PICO became a key part of an alliance of groups working for major national expansion of coverage for uninsured children and their parents, focused on the reauthorization of the State Children's Health Insurance Program (SCHIP) scheduled for 2007. In alliance with other organizations, PICO mobilized the primary religious voices that brought faith-based moral framing into the congressional debate.[34]

In retrospect, this framing of the policy debate within faith-based language appears to have been important, but in one sense secondary; the Catholic bishops and other religious voices had, after all, been providing such moral framing for years. The PICO National Network's distinctive role emerged as it amplified, diversified, and gave urgency to that faith-based moral framing, but also gave it "political legs." With the ability to organize people to articulate the case for children's health-care coverage in the nation's capital and, crucially, in congressional home districts, PICO's organizing federations in fifteen states and some hundred congressional districts (roughly split 55 percent Democratic and 45 percent Republican) made the case for bipartisan support for SCHIP expansion. Several times in 2005–2007, PICO brought two to five hundred leaders from low- and moderate-income communities to Washington, DC. In March 2007 alone, these constituents reportedly held sixty-eight meetings with their U.S. senators and representatives and another eighty-five meetings with congressional staff. PICO also worked to move the policy conversation out of the Beltway: Local affiliates held forty-seven town hall meetings and press conferences in congressional representatives' home districts, and claim to have generated more than ten thousand phone calls and 6,700 emails to those representatives regarding SCHIP.

Public letters arguing for health-care coverage for children were delivered to Congress and the White House in December 2006 (with two hundred clergy signees) and September 2007 (with 1,900 clergy signees). The media provided public exposure to wider audiences, both locally and nationally, via 112 separate stories in local, regional, and national newspapers plus in-depth stories featuring PICO leaders on National Public Radio and the *PBS NewsHour*.[35]

Ultimately, the SCHIP debate was advanced by the combination of (1) authoritative religious framing of the health-care issue in moral terms provided by the Catholic bishops and other national leaders of faith communities; (2) the PICO National Network's ability to provide convincing political "legs" and a prophetic edge to that moral voice; (3) the wider alliance of secular and faith-based policy think tanks, advocacy groups, and organizing projects that spearheaded the drive to shift the debate from simple reauthorization of the program to significant expansion of children's health coverage; and (4) the congressional leadership's decision to make SCHIP reauthorization a legislative priority. The efficacy of this alliance is signaled most clearly by hard dollars: in 2006, the discussion revolved around whether $12 billion could be provided for reauthorization; by early 2007, the debate had shifted to bipartisan congressional support for $35 billion to underwrite SCHIP expansion. Twice (October 2007 and March 2008) the alliance worked with SCHIP champions in Congress to pass major SCHIP expansion with bipartisan support, but twice the law was vetoed. Neither PICO nor the wider alliance could overcome opposition to expanding government's role in health care.

The inability to overcome these presidential vetoes was a significant setback that could have demobilized the effort, but in retrospect it is clear that it laid the moral and political groundwork for a significant victory: In early 2009, having made comprehensive health-care reform a centerpiece of the presidential campaign, the new Obama administration made SCHIP expansion one of its first legislative priorities; legislation was passed by Congress almost immediately and signed into law on February 4, 2009. At the signing ceremony in the White House, PICO leaders sat in the front row, flanking both sides of Michelle Obama, as President Obama signed the legislation. PICO's announcement of the signing thanked its "key child health allies who helped make this victory happen," and listed the U.S. Conference of Catholic Bishops among those allies.[36]

The passage of SCHIP represented partial implementation of the moral vision of health care carried in Catholic social teaching and for which the American bishops had argued for decades. But, despite the difficulty of this struggle, children's health care would turn out to have been the easy issue. The bigger issue of comprehensive reform remained on the horizon, but it had become imaginable with the change of presidential administrations. The Obama administration followed up the SCHIP signing with an effort to move legislation forward that would fundamentally reshape health-care delivery and provide near-universal coverage.

As Congress struggled through much of 2009 to forge some kind of bipartisan health-care agreement, the United States Conference of Catholic Bishops once again weighed in on the public debate, favoring reform but insisting that it be guided by specific principles. In place of the broad overarching principles of some of the earlier documents (solidarity, subsidiarity, etc.), the bishops specified three principles that they wanted to shape health-care reform.[37] First, they noted that "reform should make quality health care affordable and accessible to everyone"; that is, it should include effective coverage for the poor and working class. Second, it was "essential" that health-care reform "clearly include longstanding and widely supported restrictions on federal funding of abortion and protections for rights of conscience." Third, the bishops strongly urged that immigrants receive access to adequate health care regardless of their immigration status. The bishops' position—strong support for deep reform of health care, but with affordability, immigrant access, and protection of the legal status quo on abortion as guiding principles—would be reiterated repeatedly throughout the health-care debate.

As debate raged in mid-2009, fueled by the early "Tea Party" protests, policy stagnation seemed to set in. The entire reform effort was stuck between liberal insistence on a full "public option" and libertarian protests that had effectively killed the public option. Meanwhile, the PICO National Network and its affiliates were already engaged in extensive educational efforts, and PICO had launched a website devoted to its health-care work, providing comprehensive information regarding various denominations' stances in support of reform and resources for congregational study groups and religious leaders' sermons related to the topic. PICO and its allied organizations, Faith in Public Life (interfaith), Sojourners (Evangelical Christian), and Catholics in Alliance for the Common Good (Roman Catholic), had already become the primary religious voices in a broad health-reform coalition.[38] To break the policy impasse, in August 2009 PICO held a "National Faith-Based Day of Action" involving fifty prayer vigils and reform rallies in eighteen states, specifically intended to counter what organizers viewed as the uncivil and antireform character of public debate.[39] PICO and the three organizations listed above also launched a high-profile organizing campaign and an advertisement on religious television. In the "40 Days for Health Reform" campaign, PICO mediated into the national public arena the human stories of doing without health care, told in local leaders' own voices through testimony before Congress and in national press conferences.

These efforts helped counter the policy stagnation and put health legislation back on track, but congressional support for health-care reform remained razor thin. In two cliffhanger votes, the fate of health-care legislation ultimately hung on the votes of a handful of pro-life members of the House of Representatives—many of whom were Catholic. This group of about a dozen lawmakers was led by Representative Bart Stupak, a Catholic who explicitly tied the group's votes on health legislation to their opposition to federal funding of abortion services. Another central player in the debate was Speaker of the House Nancy Pelosi, also a Roman Catholic but strongly in favor of women's access to abortion services. The first vote (November 7, 2009) led to the extraordinary situation described by the *New York Times* as follows:

> On Friday (November 6), Ms. Pelosi met twice with Democratic lawmakers from the Pro-Choice Caucus. In between, she huddled with staff members from the bishops conference (USCCB), Mr. Stupak and two other leading Roman Catholic lawmakers, Representative Mike Doyle, Democrat of Pennsylvania, and Representative Brad Ellsworth, Democrat of Indiana. The representatives of the nation's bishops made clear they would fight the bill if there were not restrictions on abortion. In an extraordinary effort over the last 10 days, the bishops conference told priests across the country to talk about the legislation in church, mobilizing parishioners to contact Congress and to pray for the success of anti-abortion amendments. The bishops sent out information to be "announced at all Masses" and included in parish bulletins, and urged priests and parishioners to tell House members: "Please support the

Stupak Amendment that addresses essential pro-life concerns." They added: "If these serious concerns are not addressed, the final bill should be opposed." In the end the abortion opponents had the votes, and Ms. Pelosi yielded, allowing Mr. Stupak to offer his amendment.

The Stupak amendment passed relatively comfortably (240–194), with support from pro-life Democrats and most Republicans—despite some consideration among Republicans of voting against the amendment as a way to defeat the overall health legislation.[40] With this settled, the overall health-care reform legislation passed 220–215.

As the legislation moved to the Senate, the potential impact of the Stupak amendment was a matter of sharp debate. Supporters argued that it preserved the long-standing status quo represented by the "Hyde Amendment" of 1974, whereby no federal funds appropriated through Health and Human Services can be used to pay for abortion services. They also argued that this coincided with the policy preferences of most Americans, who continue to oppose government funding of abortion even as they support women's access to it under some circumstances. Opponents argued that, by prohibiting the provision of abortion services via any insurance that is paid or subsidized by federal funds—and given the broad impact of the health-care reform bill on existing health insurance programs—the Stupak amendment would take away abortion coverage already in effect, and thus change the status quo. The complex nuances of the amendment's impact allowed both sets of advocates to frame the issue as a mortal threat to their supporters. Abortion thus reemerged as the potential third rail of health reform, lethal no matter how it was handled.

In December 2009, the Senate passed the overall health-care reform bill, but without the Stupak language. In its place, the Senate version of the bill included language for which Senator Ben Nelson—a Methodist and longtime pro-life ally of the Catholic bishops—negotiated, neither requiring nor prohibiting funding for abortion services, but (1) requiring insurance companies to segregate premium monies that would cover such services, thus keeping federal money separate and (in some sense) not "paying for" abortion; and (2) allowing individual states to exclude abortion coverage in the state-based insurance "exchanges" created in the health reform legislation. Thus, as of the start of 2010, two versions of health reform were on the table; that both included language restricting federal funding for abortion provides evidence of the significant weight of public Catholicism in political deliberation. But which would prevail?

The contrasting House and Senate versions—and particularly their divergent language on abortion coverage—led directly to the second cliff-hanger vote. By early 2010, larger political dynamics dictated that health reform would only move forward by a two-step process: the House would approve the Senate bill without changes, then immediately pass further legislation "fixing" specific problems (including one central to the Catholic bishops' position: providing funding to make health insurance more affordable to low-income Americans). In this situation, the precise Stupak language was dead and Republican opposition to the health-care reform package was unanimous, so the entire health-care vote hung on whether an accommodation on abortion language could be found that kept pro-life Democrats (many of them Catholic) on board. In the balance: the fate of health legislation sought by every Democratic president since Harry Truman (1944–1952), projected to expand coverage to some 32 million uninsured Americans, subsidize care for the poor and the working class, improve prescription drug benefits for the elderly, eliminate insurance industry practices widely seen as abusive, and do so while lowering federal deficits over the next ten years.[41]

Also in the balance was a key goal of the American Catholic bishops for several decades: a health bill that would dramatically expand access to health care while respecting other elements of Catholic teaching. Recall that in addition to abortion and the "conscience clause," the bishops had focused attention particularly on affordability and the rights of immigrants. Affordability was largely addressed in the final bill, which was also essentially neutral on immigrant health care (neither expanding nor curtailing existing immigrant rights). As the final vote approached in mid-March 2010, the politics of it were clear: Passage would dramatically expand affordability and empower those in Congress likely to support subsequent immigration reform, while defeat would empower those in Congress most opposed to the bishops on matters of immigration. But what the health reform bill would do on abortion—that third rail of health-care reform—was still open to interpretation and negotiation even in the days leading up to the final vote. Here, public Catholicism spoke with several voices. The USCCB remained opposed to anything short of the Stupak language and thus refused to endorse the final bill. If Catholic legislators and their allies adopted this position, it would effectively kill the reform effort, because there appeared to be no other way for the legislation to pass in the current Congress.

However, other Catholic institutions weighed in as well. Three emerged most prominently in public discussions. First, the Catholic Health Association, which had argued throughout the debate for health reform meeting the three USCCB criteria, issued a statement implicitly endorsing the bill up for a vote.[42] Second, an organization named NETWORK: A Catholic Social Justice Lobby issued a strongly worded endorsement signed by the Leadership Conference of Women Religious and the heads of more than fifty women's religious orders that together include more than 95 percent of American nuns.[43] Third, Catholic public intellectuals also endorsed the final bill in explicitly Catholic terms, most prominently the *Washington Post* columnist E. J. Dionne Jr.[44] As noted previously, these voices of public Catholicism carry differing degrees of authority within the church, with the bishops holding official authoritative power. But in the public arena, this distinction is not so clear. Public Catholicism spoke in a complex voice representing various views, all appealing to democratically elected congressional representatives on the basis of Catholic worldviews and commitments.

Ultimately, it was those representatives who had to vote for or against the final legislation. That vote came on the evening of March 21, 2010. At the insistence of the pro-life members of Congress led by Representative Stupak, President Obama agreed that afternoon to issue an executive order clarifying that the bill authorized no use of federal funds to pay for abortion. With this step, Stupak and several others agreed to support the final bill. That night the bill passed on a 219–212 vote, and it was signed into law later that week.[45]

Thus health reform came to the United States after decades of failed efforts and intense debate over what precisely would constitute "reform." That debate will continue, over implementation questions (such as the new law's impact on abortion and how immigrants are to receive medical care in the new health marketplace) and over ethical questions (including the debate on the law's impact on abortion).[46] My purpose here is not to engage in those debates, but rather to analyze the dynamics of public Catholicism both within and beyond the great health reform debate of 2009–2010. Before doing so in depth, I note several features that seem clear from the foregoing analysis.

First, the "Catholic contribution" to the debate was both enormous and complex. The overall weight of public Catholicism clearly pushed in favor of substantial reform within strong ethical guidelines. The USCCB strongly and consistently spoke to Catholics and policy makers about the dimensions of health reform that the church would support. The final issues in the debate were partly focused around key areas of Catholic concern, with Catholic voices very much "in the room," itself a significant achievement. And the diversity of Catholic voices in the legislative endgame reflected with reasonable accuracy the complexity of the moral, fiscal, societal, and human implications of tinkering with the massive health sector—and the political complications that inevitably came into play when restructuring a huge sector of the American economy during an election year. Some Catholic leaders will praise the final result while others will criticize it as either too weak on abortion protections or too weak on universal coverage. But it seems incontestable that Catholic voices rooted in authentically Catholic concerns and commitments significantly influenced the health reform debate.

Second, various Catholic actors skillfully used their institutional resources to shape the debate. Through USCCB press releases, conversations with policy makers, and requests that local parishes make announcements and distribute information at key moments of the debate, the bishops made their position clear and mobilized constituents in support of it. Significantly, they did so repeatedly over the course of nearly a year of focused debate. Similarly, the CHA and the women's religious congregations utilized their networks to support reform and intervened at strategic moments to publicly buttress their allies in Congress—and, in the legislative endgame, arguably created the crucial political space for Catholic legislators to support the final bill.

Third, together with its secular and religious allies, the PICO National Network brought into the public arena an effective set of faith-based voices from poor, working-class, and middle-class communities. Furthermore, those voices contributed powerfully to a successful pilot run at health-care reform (the SCHIP reauthorization) and to moving comprehensive health-care reform through the congressional process. PICO's role reflects the Catholic connections of faith-based community organizing noted above, but also transcends them: the organization brought people into the public arena as citizens rooted in poor to middle-class communities and as people of a variety of faith traditions, not as sectarian Catholics. Yet PICO's overall thrust (in favor of reform that significantly expanded health coverage and made it affordable for poor folks) clearly reflected the emphases of its core religious constituencies: Catholic as well as Jewish congregations, and liberal to moderate Protestant, Unitarian, and African American and Latino Pentecostal churches. In that sense, PICO's work during much of the debate bridged between public Catholicism, the public voices of other religious traditions, and the democratic public arena.

Fourth, where the teachings of those core constituencies differed, PICO remained silent; the organization never endorsed or opposed a specific bill. Embracing the Catholic bishops' final position would have alienated the organization's Pentecostal, liberal Protestant, Jewish, and Unitarian constituents. Rejecting that position would have alienated some of the organization's Catholic constituents. Instead, in the final legislative push, PICO encouraged its members to seek guidance in their own religious tradition's statements on the topic. In this sense, although PICO represented a salient voice of public Catholicism through much of the debate, in the political endgame that role fell to other figures and organizations.

Fifth, the various voices of public Catholicism, though largely united during most of the debate, differed acutely in their assessments of the final legislation. Although that diversity of public views contributed to final passage of health reform, it also reflects a certain incoherence in American Catholicism today. I suggest below that this incoherence is rooted in divergent understandings of authority and the nature of the church—though not in the ways one might expect.

Finally, one must wonder how the health debate has reshaped the overall impact of public Catholicism. Presumably, the experience deepened the reservoir of democratic skills, policy expertise, and public orientation at many of the levels of public Catholicism summarized in figure 7.1 earlier in the chapter. High-profile involvement in this debate may have strengthened public Catholicism's political capital for future policy debates. Alternatively, the Catholic bishops may have lost considerable political capital by staking their final position on health-care reform on what some—including some figures within public Catholicism who appear to have been acting in good faith—regarded as a tendentious and perhaps partisan interpretation of the final health-care bill. Only ongoing political events will make clear which has actually occurred, but one fairly immediate way to gauge this lies in these events' impact on figures of "public Catholicism" within Congress. Initial signs include Bart Stupak's decision not to seek reelection, the result of his demonization by pro-life political forces, despite his having gone to bat repeatedly for pro-life provisions in the health-care bill. One interpretation: the bishops' ultimate position on health-care reform—portrayed by some as intransigent and by others as prophetic—made it impossible for their own allies to navigate the complex crosscurrents of public life and remain viable candidates for public office. The bishops' stance simply offered no cover for their own allies to make the prudential judgments and political compromises that are inevitable in a democratic public arena. Thus, while the overall Catholic influence in the health-care debate (from the USCCB and other voices) certainly appears to have strengthened the strategic position of public Catholicism, the bishops' failure to provide their allies with public room to maneuver appears to have weakened that strategic position.

But the health-care debate can only show us so much. To gain greater perspective, I step back from that specific debate to examine broadly the dynamics of public Catholicism in America today.

ANALYZING INSTITUTIONAL AND CULTURAL DYNAMICS

Analyzing three additional institutional and cultural arenas will offer further insight into the nature of Catholicism within American public life. These arenas are leadership in mediating institutions; authority dynamics; and the culture of worship, prayer, and spirituality.

Institutional Leadership

Catholicism has a rich intellectual tradition of thinking broadly about how laypeople contribute to public life through leadership in the diverse institutions of civil and political society. Separately, whole subfields of social science and organizational management analyze the roles of institutions and organizations in shaping society, especially through what sociologists have long called "mediating institutions" or "voluntary associations." Here, I note only a few insights important for thinking about public Catholicism.

In the future, public Catholicism will be influential to the extent that it (a) advocates for those Catholic ideals for which a democratic consensus can be built and (b) mediates into American culture a more intense encounter between mainstream culture and those Catholic ideals that now stand outside it. In the latter encounter, Catholicism will have to challenge contemporary consumer culture's idolization of individual autonomy. That task is made more complex by the fact that Catholicism itself has been affected by this same idolization of individual autonomy—and made more complex still by the fact that the vestiges of premodern Catholicism itself are challenged by modern affirmation of personal rights, egalitarian ideals, and democratic norms.[47]

Crucial for shaping public Catholicism's future will be the presence of engaged Catholics as leaders of mediating institutions at all levels of society, from local nonprofits to national civil associations, from neighborhood associations to state political parties to Congress, from school teachers to international scholarly associations, and from family businesses to major corporations (the middle level of figure 7.1). Such leadership roles in differentiated institutional sectors are too myriad to discuss coherently as a group here, much less to coordinate nationally through some national Catholic structure. Nor would such central coordination be desirable. But Catholics already occupy many such leadership roles, and more will do so in the future as Latino Catholics in particular move into higher-level leadership in American society. Catholics in positions of institutional leadership can serve as bridges between the Catholic tradition and American institutional life, to the extent that they are deeply immersed in the former and capable of bringing their resulting worldview insightfully to bear within secular institutions.

The efficacy of lay Catholic leaders in this bridging role will be shaped crucially by higher education. In one sense, there is nothing new in this: for generations, Catholic leaders have sought to use universities to train laypeople for leadership in the secular world, and the Second Vatican Council reaffirmed the centrality of this dimension of lay vocations in *Gaudium et Spes*. But two recent shifts make this yet more central. First, as educational levels have risen throughout American society, a university degree followed by postgraduate studies or professional credentialing has become the gateway to institutional leadership in most sectors of society. Second, as Catholic lay leaders have attained higher levels of education and embraced a culture of democratic and professional sources of authority, they expect a more consultative relationship with the church hierarchy. As illustrated by the health reform debate, educated laypeople who exert autonomous authority in mediating institutions simply will not respond to the assertion of a central command-and-control model of clerical or episcopal authority.

What mediating institutions will be most crucial for shaping public Catholic leaders of the future? As argued above, universities will be central, and the Catholic universities briefly catalogued earlier will surely be one important location. But at least as crucial—and perhaps more so—will be *public* universities. Three factors make this so. First, in purely demographic terms, public universities simply touch the lives of huge numbers of young Catholics, especially from the less privileged sectors that Catholic social teaching seeks to make central agents of social transformation.

Second, widespread questions have been raised about how successful Catholic colleges and universities are at adult faith formation of their students. Without prejudging that debate, I would simply note that the psychodynamics of young adult stages of development may necessarily make this difficult. As young adults go about defining themselves, healthy identity formation often includes at least a measure of self-definition in *opposition* to whatever institutional forces predominate in one's life. A strongly "Catholic" institutional setting may thus produce a certain resistance to appropriating an adult faith, or at least lead to complex psychological relationships to the tradition. In contrast, the same oppositional identity-formation processes may play out quite differently in public university settings, in which the Catholic institutional presence is far from dominant but rather represents an identity *alternative* to the dominant one promoted in dorms, social networking venues, fraternities, and sororities. Catholicism brought to bear at public universities through Newman Centers and other campus ministry efforts can thus become the locus of choice for young adults, precisely because it offers a source of resistance to the dominant, often anomic, and sometimes hedonistic or alienating dynamics of mass university student culture.

Third, public university settings incorporate important parallels to the situation that will be faced later in life by Catholic lay leaders of secular institutions. In both settings, Catholics link the values and social commitments learned from their tradition and bring them to bear within more pluralistic and secular settings. Bridging successfully across that institutional divide is a learned skill, and public universities with strong Catholic campus ministries offer students experience in precisely that kind of cross-institutional engagement.

The future of public Catholicism will thus depend greatly on the quality of (mostly lay) Catholic leadership at the level of mediating institutions (the middle level of figure 7.1), which will in turn depend greatly on the quality of faith formation occurring in higher education—at both Catholic and public universities, colleges, and graduate/professional schools.

Authority Dynamics: Church and Sect in American Catholicism

Authority is central to understanding Catholicism's relationship to American public life because, within any society, the various forms of authority represent "alternative processes by which values are allocated, styles by which decisions are made, and objects to which deference and obedience are rendered."[48] More broadly, authority represents one of the core "social forms" or constitutive building blocks upon which communities and societies are built.[49]

American culture rests uneasily on a tension between two relationships to authority. On one hand, it rests on the knee-jerk rejection of all authority in pursuit of the "unencumbered self," free of all restraints on its liberty.[50] But the self unencumbered of all restraints and all authority is markedly unstable and subject to subtle manipulation by external agents. So, paradoxically, American culture rests also on unquestioning acceptance of external authority—in the form of populist demagoguery, media "experts," and cultural icons. In the early twenty-first century, American culture sails precariously between the Scylla that rejects all authority beyond the self and the Charybdis that unreflectively accepts manipulative authority.[51] Thus, if Catholicism offers a different understanding and practice of authority than other American cultural strands, then—in addition to shaping views on specific issues—public Catholicism may become crucial for the wider American culture by promoting more constructive ways of relating to authoritative figures (among Catholics and non-Catholics alike).

The key here rests in the last phrase, "authoritative figures," for it allows an alternative to American culture's uneasy shifting between endless flight from authority in pursuit of the unencumbered self and vesting blind authority in external agents. Rather, authority can reside in the complex flow between the personal judgment of individuals with relative autonomy in their own lives, and authoritative figures to whom deference is given in recognition of greater insight or experience or knowledge.[52] Such deference might be limited to specific areas, such as that given to medical personnel or scientists; or it might be more general, such as that given to the Dalai Lama, Mother Theresa, or Rick Warren by those who see each as an authoritative figure. In either case, between authoritarianism and radical autonomy lies a realm in which authoritative relations can be combined with personal judgment and control of one's life.

To look for positive dynamics of authority within the Catholic Church will strike some as outrageous, amidst ongoing revelations of Catholic abuse of authority, both through sexual abuse by clergy and through related episcopal malfeasance. Yet I suggest that American Catholicism, inchoately and partially, has indeed begun to generate a set of practices and self-understandings that treat authority as substantive, authoritative, and self-transcending—without violating individual responsibility for decision making, moral discernment, and political judgment. We saw glimpses of this in the health-care debate, but it is a far more widespread phenomenon in contemporary Catholicism.

With this suggestion, I certainly do not imply that Catholicism has fully overcome the legacy of obeisance to religious authority that it inherited from the premodern past. Religious authoritarianism remains a significant strand within Catholicism, in sectors of both the hierarchical structure and a laity that yearns for simple definitions of truth from above. Any fair assessment must recognize that American Catholicism retains strands that would deny any moral autonomy to the individual. Nor do I imply that Catholicism has remained unaffected by the powerful cultural force of hyperindividualism in American life. Any fair assessment must also recognize that (like all religious traditions) Catholicism on American shores has internalized elements of radical individualism that in practice reject all moral authority beyond the self.[53]

Alongside these patterns, however, American Catholicism is germinating a different and important set of authority dynamics. This should not surprise us. Given its communion with the long sweep of Catholic history, its institutional structure, and its practice of at least weekly Eucharist,

American Catholicism carries at least the potential for a strong communitarian counterweight to cultural individualism.[54] Likewise, given American Catholics' embeddedness in the American cultural commitment to individualism, we should not be surprised that American Catholics have developed resources for autonomous moral discernment. More generally, the Catholic intellectual tradition's understanding of authority (considerably more complex than the tradition's too frequent recourse in practice to simple obeisance to authority) stands in significant tension with the culture of American individualism.

Space precludes me from fully redeeming this suggestion, beyond noting that recent analyses do so for me. Exemplars from a liberal perspective include works by Michele Dillon and Jerome Baggett showing moral decision making grounded in Catholic principle and sacraments, yet with the locus of authority linked also to individual autonomy.[55] From a conservative direction, the interrogation of episcopal authority by self-described traditionalists such as Richard John Neuhaus, George Weigel, and Michael Novak has the same effect: insistence on moral and theological discernment by active individual intellects that are both in communion and in tension with hierarchically defined truth.

That current cultural and ecclesial pressures drive progressive, liberal, conservative, *and* traditionalist church members in the direction of lay-clerical dialogue reflects a powerful cultural logic underlying global Catholicism today: the strong claims of authoritative teaching embedded within long-standing institutions and spiritual practices, combined with modernity's strong current of individual empowerment. That these cross-pressures so frequently produce incoherent spiritual chaos does not necessarily mean that they cannot ultimately resolve in a coherent authoritative culture.[56] The recent scandals, as well as the internal church tensions revealed in the health reform debate, may move public Catholicism in such a direction.

None of this analysis should suggest that American Catholics have gotten authority dynamics "right." Catholics struggle mightily to balance the roles of authoritative teaching and personal judgment in Catholic lives and structures. But to the extent that American Catholics can "get it right" in balancing healthy individualism and communitarianism, authority and autonomy, Catholic culture can contribute to reconstructing the wider society's tenuous relationship to accountable authority. To the extent that

Catholics do so both in their personal faith lives and in the public arena, they can contribute to reconstructing a coherent and critical authoritative culture both within the church and in the wider society. The dynamics of authority are thus crucial at all levels of figure 7.1

We saw this struggle played out very publicly in the debate over health-care reform.[57] Some analysts no doubt will emphasize the diversity of Catholic viewpoints in the final debate, while others will emphasize the fundamental unity of principles underlying those viewpoints. Among the former, some will celebrate this diversity of viewpoints as one of the great strengths of public Catholicism, allowing complex discernment of policy in a complex social world, while others will decry the diversity of viewpoints as reflecting incoherence and bad faith among some Catholic public actors. At risk of being lost in that debate lies an insight about the current situation among one set of key actors within public Catholicism: the American Catholic bishops themselves. For this observer, viewing that debate from outside, it is hard to deny a certain episcopal incoherence—not among the bishops themselves, since any disagreements there were well shielded from public view. I note, rather, a certain incoherence between the historic tone and content of public Catholicism in America, discussed earlier, and the tone and content of some bishops' interventions in the public arena.

The point may be made most clearly by invoking the sociological distinction between "church" and "sect."[58] Religious leaders operating within a self-understanding as "church" operate with an eye toward pragmatism, maximizing possible gains in public policy, as judged through the lens of their own religion but always in dialogue with other views; and recognizing the trade-offs with competing social goods that cannot be built into policy now but may be attained later. In contrast, religious leaders operating within a self-understanding as "sect" operate with an eye toward absolute definitions of the good, with public policy judged as an all-or-nothing affair, as a matter of purity rather than pragmatism. During the course of much of the health-care debate, the USCCB's role struck this observer as a remarkably savvy and principled "church"-based intervention in the public arena, operating appropriately within Catholic understandings of authoritative teaching *and* the norms of a democratic public sphere. But during the endgame, as the policy process moved toward a final vote, what had seemed a symphony of episcopal intervention in public life suddenly seemed off key: the insistence on the specific Stupak language that would have doomed the overall health reform effort simply clanged. At least for this observer, it seemed out of tune with the historic Catholic understanding of politics in a fallen world, where progress requires accepting partial victories in order to lay the groundwork for future gains. Such a stand might have qualified as prophetic if the alternative were clear violation of Catholic norms, but alternative language on abortion and conscience protection was available (and had been negotiated by the bishops' allies in the Senate).

In these circumstances, the final decision to oppose health-care reform appeared either partisan or sectarian. Though some individual bishops may have wandered into blind partisan identification, overall I discount the partisan explanation. Little in Catholic self-understanding lends itself to unproblematic partisan identification with either major political party in America today. Rather, these events suggest a deeper and more troubling dynamic that may be at work within the American Catholic episcopacy: In the desire to be prophetic and principled, some bishops may be unconsciously willing to shed long-standing Catholic self-understanding as truly a *church*, both theologically and sociologically. If true and if it continues, this would mark an extraordinary shift away from ecclesiological orthodoxy.

However, any episcopal shift toward Catholic sectarianism is unlikely to go unchallenged. Presumably, significant sectors of the Catholic leadership recognize the dangers of such a shift—the danger of squandering potential influence on public policy, the danger of discrediting public Catholicism more generally, the danger of positioning the Catholic Church as just another sect within a crowded landscape, and the danger of being unfaithful to historic Catholic self-understanding as church. If such a sectarian tendency exists within the American episcopacy, much of the future of public Catholicism will depend on whether it is fostered or countered by Catholic leaders—papal, episcopal, clerical, religious, and lay.

If public Catholicism is to thrive, it must be built upon an authoritative culture that can engage educated Catholics. So perhaps the single most fundamental challenge facing American Catholicism in the twenty-first century lies in learning how to effectively confront the hyperindividualism of American culture while simultaneously shedding the church's own clerical authoritarianism inherited from the past and countering any implicit shift toward Catholic sectarianism. This leads us to the next analytic level, for getting authority right involves the cultural practices of worship, prayer, and spirituality.

Culture of Worship, Prayer, and Spirituality

How might constructive dynamics of authority play out in contemporary Catholicism? The days are clearly gone when Catholic leaders could issue authoritative pronouncements and expect American Catholics to simply follow them. If such a time in fact ever existed, its death knell was sounded sometime between *Humanae Vitae* in 1968 and the recent sex-and-authority scandals. Yet Catholic teaching continues to shape members' worldviews and values. As Jerome Baggett shows, even in the hotbed of liberalism called the San Francisco Bay Area, Catholics in the pews come to their moral and ethical views in a dialogical relationship with the magisterium. That is, American Catholics are not simply "cafeteria Catholics" picking and choosing teachings that they like. Rather, at least the more reflective among them arrive at their moral and ethical views by listening to a variety of "voices" in the surrounding culture, from politicians to church leaders, from peers to popular music, and from Bible study groups to talk radio. Some even read official church teaching about the issues. They evaluate these sources in relationship to their intuitions about the moral life and their own lived experience, and gradually build their moral lives in light of that emergent process. Michele Dillon likewise demonstrates this process of moral decision making, framing it explicitly within democratic theory, as the reflexive process through which Catholic teaching develops over time to meet new challenges.

Thus, to the extent that Catholic leaders can draw Catholics into dialogue with the church's teaching via preaching, adult formation classes, and the Catholic media, precisely to that extent will the authority of Catholic teaching actually shape the lives of mature adult Catholics. Such individuals will not and cannot simply adhere unthinkingly to Catholic tradition handed down from above; this would violate the very nature of being a mature adult in the contemporary world.

Though this may risk a fair degree of moral messiness as people find their way—and surely infuriates those who advocate a more deductive, rule-following approach to the moral life—at its best it brings a reflective quality to moral formation that respects the maturity of adult Catholics and affirms their responsibility for their own spiritual lives. In a world of individual empowerment, the church might well aspire to make its teaching more clearly the primary voice within this discernment, but it will have to do so not by fiat but by building its own moral credibility and the plausibility of its authoritative teaching. In any case, whether or not church leaders like this style of moral discernment, it appears to be the dominant mode among a broad swath of American Catholics serious about their faith commitment, especially among those positioned (by education and by leadership skills) to actively engage the secular world. To spite this approach would be to reject out of hand some of the most dedicated and mature American Catholics from whom the church draws financial support and leadership (both elite and grassroots).

On this view, the wrong way forward would be the sectarian one, trying to compel intellectual assent to magisterially prescribed public policy, or to directly induce more rigorous adherence to moral rules flowing from that teaching. On such a path, public Catholicism in American life will likely be destined to wither: Powerful demographic, educational, and cultural trends will dilute the effectiveness of any such approach. Those advocating such a path for public Catholicism do so in hope of transforming American culture, but risk disconnecting Catholic teaching from the actual personal and societal lives of most Catholics, and thus becoming irrelevant to all but a few.

An alternative path lies in affirming the present capacity and future promise of mature Catholic adults—lay, religious, and clergy—to responsibly internalize their faith tradition and carry it into the world not as subservient followers but as thoughtful adherents (which implies sometimes being critical adherents). In shaping lay Catholics fully capable of this role, center stage must be taken by the identity-shaping role of Catholic ministry. In its core pastoral work, the church shapes identities via faith-formation classes, small faith-sharing groups, adult discussion groups, and especially worship with its shared prayers, music, preaching, and Eucharist. Education can train better-informed Catholics, and to a certain degree shape their identities and worldviews. But recent cognitive science confirms a key insight of the social sciences: the core processes of identity formation occur via repetitive ritual processes that tap into brain regions reflecting our deep evolutionary development.[59] In Catholic terms, those ritual processes involve worship and liturgy in community, and their internalization at the individual level in prayer and spirituality.

A fundamental challenge for Catholic leaders will be to foster the cultural dynamics and authoritative relationships that form such strong, engaged, and thoughtful "public Catholics." Parishes—where most Catholics receive the Eucharist, hear the Word, baptize their children, marry their spouses, bury their dead, and pray their way through good times and bad—are the crucial institutional spaces for this. At the bottom of figure 7.1, the identity-formation processes that occur through practices of worship, prayer, and spirituality are thus foundational. Unless Catholicism can be made meaningful there by dynamically engaging everyday Catholics on terms relevant for their daily lives, public Catholicism will be built on hollow foundations.

Public Catholicism is thus partly founded upon the culture of worship, prayer, and spirituality that are the heart of thriving parishes. If these parish-based religious dynamics richly engage Catholics, the overall tradition can advance as a source of authoritative insight in modern adherents' lives. Such a role need not undermine the authority of the episcopacy in ecclesial leadership, but it does call into question the rigid boundary definition whereby strong lay leadership is perceived as a threat to clerical authority. This model reflects the central role of "the sense of the faithful" long recognized as a key partner of episcopal authority.[60] Such an internal dynamic might produce a church focused less on internal power struggles over authority and more on external engagement with the world, with such engagement facilitated by a constructive internal model of collaborative authority.

In sum, whether public Catholicism thrives or withers in American society will be shaped by complex dynamics occurring at multiple levels and differing time horizons. At the highest level, and with the most obvious and immediate impact, are the public actions of bishops and Catholic leaders of elite institutions, how these actions are covered by the media, and how these leaders exert direct influence on the rest of American society. At the lowest level and with the longest timeline are the dynamics of authority and processes of identity formation rooted in mass culture and the worship lives of local parishes. In between lies the role of universities, university-linked ministries, and parish-based faith-formation programs in shaping future leaders of mediating institutions, thus bringing Catholic values, ethos, and worldview into the democratic public arena.

WHITHER THE "CATHOLIC MOMENT"?
AMERICAN PUBLIC CATHOLICISM'S BRIGHT
AND FOREBODING FUTURE

This bird's-eye view can hardly do justice to the complexity of public Catholicism. But it provides enough empirical and analytic framing to say a little about the contemporary moment in American Catholicism and its place in public life.

Most obviously, it seems clear that the Catholic Church remains enormously well positioned to influence public debate across a variety of issues: With a strong institutional presence in neighborhoods, the educational field, the legal and political systems, and public communications media, the potential Catholic voice in the societal conversation underlying American democracy is impressive. This is all the more true given the status of American Catholics as an important swing constituency in national elections, as well as the Catholic Church's presence (though by no means hegemony) among Latinos, the largest emerging ethnic vote now and in coming decades.

The importance of this potential Catholic voice is multiplied again by the fact that current Catholic teaching cuts against the grain of American popular culture in a number of salient areas, from the death penalty to international diplomacy, from prenatal and end-of-life issues to the nature of a just economy, and from sexual morality to the rights of undocumented immigrants. This author, the reader, Catholic institutional leaders, and the mass of American Catholics surely do not agree on all these issues. That is not the point. Rather, the point is that democratic deliberation needs diverse viewpoints to be represented in both politics and civil society. Democratic deliberation within American politics and the wider culture will better face these issues if they draw on thoughtful and divergent voices. The Catholic tradition represents one strong, thoughtful voice on these issues, and one in significant tension with contemporary culture on some of them. This tension makes it all the more important.

Much more problematic for making the Catholic voice effective within that societal conversation is a very different tension between Catholicism and contemporary culture: the tension between divergent understandings of authority outlined previously. At its worst, that tension becomes a dialogue of the deaf, across an unbridgeable gulf that separates those bishops, priests, and lay leaders firmly ensconced in a traditionalist subculture from their peers (in the church and in the wider society) who simply will not abide command-and-control authority within the democratic arena. Transcending this gulf will only be possible if divergent players recognize differing authoritative claims and if the public voices of American Catholicism speak consistently in authoritative rather than authoritarian tones.

On the model of democratic deliberation outlined here, accepting the democratic public arena need not marginalize Catholic truth claims. Rather, the Catholic voice becomes one set of claims about what is true, what is meaningful, and what is the best way forward in social policy. The Catholic public voice is well positioned to be influential if it is articulated in authoritative tones in keeping with ecclesial self-understanding as "church," rather than in more authoritarian and sectarian tones. When spoken with confidence born of faith, intelligence born of deep Catholic intellectual resources, a humane tone born of Catholic pastoral experience, and appropriate humility born of acceptance of the democratic rules of the game, such a voice could be profoundly influential in democratic deliberation. This assertion is premised on the idea that reflective adults and mature communities can actually *value* authoritative voices that respect their maturity of discernment and appropriate autonomy of decision making—and that those unschooled in reflective decision making can learn those skills and orientations. In contrast, public claims made in a more sectarian tenor may gain an immediate following, but within a healthy democratic public arena they ultimately prevail only in the rarest of cases. Nothing indicates that recent Catholic strategy is one of those cases.

Thus, a stark choice faces the leaders of public Catholicism in the United States in the years ahead. Such leaders obviously include individual bishops, but they also include Catholic intellectuals, lay institutional leaders within church structures and in the wider society, the heads of religious orders, local priests, and religious women and men. On what model of Catholic authority are we going to proceed in the future? Public Catholicism has extensive institutional resources to offer as the United States and the Catholic Church confront their respective challenges. But the cultural resources within public Catholicism can lead it to play a healthily critical and constructive role, premised on the complex authority dynamics within a church that fully engages the wider society; or to play a narrowly sectarian role, premised on an understanding of authority exported from the church's internal life to the wider society, but which is not viable within a modern democratic polity.

An appropriate understanding of the parallel structures of authority operative within church and society—mutually recognizing the other's legitimacy in its own context—can help leaders of public Catholicism effectively operate in the public arena. In doing so, they can offer the wisdom of the Catholic tradition to American society as it seeks to define its future. Doing so can also help leaders of public Catholicism to gradually revise Catholic self-understanding in light of the tradition's ongoing experience in history. Something akin to this is clearly the inspiring vision that animated the Second Vatican Council. Liberals tend to affirm the "revise the tradition" side of this vision, and conservatives to affirm the "wisdom of the tradition"—but either stance by itself is surely inadequate. If public Catholicism is not to squander the remarkable institutional resources on which it can draw to influence American culture and society, its leaders will have to forego the effort to produce change by fiat and instead engage in societal dialogue on the terms of the democratic public arena. This, in turn, will require a new interface between the cultural models of authority operative within church and society.

A deep irony thus lies in the American Catholic situation: In its most thoughtful and constructive mode, the Catholic understanding of authority may represent the tradition's crucial potential contribution to American and global culture in the twenty-first century. Yet, when pulled in more sectarian directions, the Catholic understanding of authority undermines the church's very credibility as a contributor to modern democratic dialogue, and thus undermines public Catholicism itself.

In 1987, Richard John Neuhaus famously diagnosed a distinctive "Catholic moment," in which the Catholic Church was uniquely and fortuitously positioned to influence American culture in profound ways.[61] In the quarter-century since then, that moment has taken a severe beating: The clerical sex scandal harmed basic trust in the clergy, the primary face of the church in most Catholics' lives. The associated authority scandal at least temporarily undermined many Catholics' assumption that the church would protect its members and its core spiritual vocation in the world when these things were in tension with immediate institutional self-protection. And the willingness of some members of the episcopacy and clergy to narrow Catholic teaching in a way that appears to serve the narrowest of partisan interests—most commonly Republican interests, but in other settings Democratic interests—have diminished the integrity and transcendence of one of the tradition's richest intellectual resources. This pattern risks transforming Catholicism from church to sect, and giving up entirely on wide Catholic cultural influence.

Yet an important Catholic moment may endure. The institutional and cultural presence of the Catholic tradition in American life makes its public role significant. The tradition's continuing intellectual depth, (usually) nonsectarian ethos, constructive engagement with competing religious traditions, and voice on key questions facing contemporary societies make its public role important. And America's contemporary situation makes the church's public role vital. Our democracy faces vast challenges in the twenty-first century, and America will only succeed in addressing those challenges via active engagement with diverse ethical traditions. Roman Catholicism clearly represents one such ethical tradition.

So the state of public Catholicism is a crucial matter both for the internal life of the church and for the external health of the societal conversation that constitutes democratic deliberation. Internally, if American Catholicism fails to integrate lay and clerical leadership within dynamics of authority mutually recognized as legitimate by mature Catholics, ongoing conflicts over authority will continue to undermine the coherence and plausibility of any public Catholic voice. On the other hand, if such integration can be achieved, the coherence and impact of public Catholicism in the future may be impressive. Externally, given the model of democratic deliberation outlined here, such an articulate and effective public Catholicism may contribute to American society in important ways: by adding significant depth and insight to moral-political discussions; by providing moral resources for new kinds of democratic political action in favor of marginalized members of society; and by contributing to a new synthesis of personal autonomy and communitarian authority in American culture. A Catholic moment may endure—but if so, it must simultaneously be humbler and more confident, less triumphal and yet fully engaged in public life. In short, it must be more "catholic" in both its ecclesiology and its politics.

EPILOGUE: THE CHURCH UNDER FRANCIS I

This chapter was originally drafted well before the election of the Argentine cardinal Jorge Bergoglio as Pope Francis I. In my view, that important new direction changes essentially none of the foregoing analysis, except in one very important way: Early signs suggest that his papacy increases the likelihood of something like the constructive integration called for above, assuming it survives the 2018 recrudescence of the sexual abuse and clerical authority scandals. Such an outcome remains only a hope, for a great deal of intellectual, theological, and ecclesiastical work would be necessary before the full promise of American public Catholicism could flower.

NOTES

1. See José Casanova, *Public Religions in the Modern World* (Chicago: University of Chicago Press, 1994).
2. For important analyses of "public Catholicism," though understood somewhat differently than that term is used here, see David J. O'Brien, *Public Catholicism*, 2nd ed. (Maryknoll, NY: Orbis, 1996); George Weigel, *Soul of the World: Notes on the Future of Public Catholicism* (Washington, DC: Ethics and Public Policy Center, 1996).
3. Key sources in contemporary democratic theory regarding the public sphere include Jeffrey C. Alexander, *The Civil Sphere* (Oxford: Oxford University Press, 2006); Seyla Benhabib, "Models of Public Space: Hannah Arendt, the Liberal Tradition and Jurgen Habermas," in *Habermas and the Public Sphere*, ed. Craig Calhoun (Cambridge, MA: MIT Press, 1992); Casanova, *Public Religions in the Modern World*; Jean L. Cohen and Andrew Arato, *Civil Society and Political Theory* (Cambridge, MA: MIT Press, 1992); Nancy Fraser, "Rethinking the Public Sphere: A Contribution to the Critique of Actually Existing Democracy," in Calhoun, *Habermas and the Public Sphere*; Jürgen Habermas, *The Structural Transformation of the Public Sphere: An Inquiry Into a Category of Bourgeois Society* (Cambridge, MA: MIT Press, 1989); Jürgen Habermas, *The Theory of Communicative Action* (Boston: Beacon Press, 1984); Jürgen Habermas, "A 'Post-Secular' Society—What Does That Mean?," *Reset Dialogues on Civilizations*, September 16, 2008; Margaret R. Somers, "Narrating and Naturalizing Civil Society and Citizenship Theory: The Place of Political Culture and the Public Sphere," *Sociological Theory* 13, no. 3 (November 1995), 229–274; Margaret R. Somers, "What's Political or Cultural About Political Culture and the Public Sphere? Toward an Historical Sociology of Concept Formation," *Sociological Theory* 13, no. 2 (July 1995), 113–144; Alfred Stepan, "Religion, Democracy, and the 'Twin Tolerations,' " *Journal of Democracy* 11, no. 4 (October 2000), 37–57.

Note that the discussion of the public sphere here concerns the relationship of the Catholic Church to its wider societal context within the United States, in which a democratic public sphere is the consensual ideal. Of course, in its internal life the church itself is not a democracy, neither in ideal nor in practice, but rather an authoritative institution in which the vertical definition of truth holds a prominent position. See discussion below of the interface between internal church life and the external relationship with democratic society.

4. On conflict and dialogue in the public arena, see Hannah Arendt, *Between Past and Future: Eight Exercises in Political Thought* (New York: Viking Press, 1968); Hannah Arendt, *The Human Condition* (Chicago: University of Chicago Press, 1958).

5. For introductions to the vast literature on Catholic social teaching, including the "option for the poor," see Charles E. Curran, *Catholic Social Teaching, 1891– Present: A Historical, Theological, and Ethical Analysis* (Washington, DC: Georgetown University Press, 2002); Kenneth R. Himes and Lisa Sowle Cahill, *Modern Catholic Social Teaching: Commentaries and Interpretations* (Washington, DC: Georgetown University Press, 2005); Thomas Massaro and Thomas A. Shannon, eds., *American Catholic Social Teaching* (Collegeville, MN: Liturgical Press, 2002); David Matzko McCarthy, *The Heart of Catholic Social Teaching: Its Origins and Contemporary Significance* (Grand Rapids, MI: Brazos Press, 2009).

6. This brief description suffices here because we are concentrating on authority relations. A full analysis would have to further account for the ways that authority dynamics, in both church and society, are further bisected by the influence of economic power.

7. For the classic portrayal of the earlier Catholic subculture and its emergence into being part of "mainstream" American society, see Will Herberg, *Protestant—Catholic—Jew: An Essay in American Religious Sociology* (Garden City, NY: Doubleday, 1960); also see this volume's introduction. On the contemporary situation of American Catholics vis-à-vis American culture, see Jerome P. Baggett, *Sense of the Faithful: How American Catholics Live Their Faith* (New York: Oxford University Press, 2009); and Michele Dillon, *Catholic Identity: Balancing Reason, Faith, and Power* (Cambridge: Cambridge University Press, 1999).

8. For the iconic analysis of the cultural strands of American life, see Robert N. Bellah, Richard Madsen, William M. Sullivan, Ann Swidler, and Steven M. Tipton, *Habits of the Heart: Individualism and Commitment in American Life* (Berkeley: University of California Press, 1985).

9. See Gerhard Lohfink, *Jesus and Community: The Social Dimension of Christian Faith* (Philadelphia: Fortress Press, 1984).

10. The notion of the church as a contrast society is thus different from the notion of a Catholic subculture. In the former, the Catholic community exists in relationship to, but in some tension with, the wider society and accepts the terms of the "bridging" metaphor discussed here. In the latter, the Catholic

community understands itself, and to some degree actually exists, in isolation from the wider society—and often as simply resistant to it. Accepting the democratic norms of contemporary public life has been historically difficult for the Catholic tradition to embrace, coming only via the Second Vatican Council and subsequent papal statements—both influenced by the American Catholic experience via the theologian John Courtney Murray. For the touchstone statement of the theological argument that ultimately shaped new church thinking on democracy, see John Courtney Murray, *We Hold These Truths: Catholic Reflections on the American Proposition* (Kansas City, MO: Sheed and Ward, 1960). The key Vatican statement is *Gaudium et Spes: The Pastoral Constitution of the Church in the Modern World*, December 7, 1965, http://www.vatican.va/archive/hist_councils/ii_vatican_council/documents/vat-ii_cons_19651207_gaudium-et-spes_en.html.

11. All data in this and the following paragraph come from *The Official Catholic Directory, 1967–2007*.

12. This discussion assumes that the preponderance of Catholic institutional presence is carried by priests and religious. This may be changing as lay leadership gradually emerges at ever-higher levels of ecclesial institutions. But at present, control still lies largely in the hands of clergy. Note, too, that a dynamic countervailing the one discussed in the text is also possible, whereby laypeople actively appropriate Catholic identity-formation resources (perhaps via books, other media, spiritual formation opportunities, and the like) independent of a strong Catholic institutional presence. This surely represents an important process—and can be intensive in the lives of some individual Catholics—but is more idiosyncratic and less systematic than more institutionally centered mechanisms of identity formation.

13. All data in this paragraph come from *The Official Catholic Directory, Anno Domini 2008* (New Providence, NJ: P. J. Kenedy & Sons, 2008), p. 2069 ff.

14. See Francis Butler's address to the National Leadership Roundtable on Church Management at the Wharton School of the University of Pennsylvania on July 29, 2006, available via *Origins* 36, no. 9 (July 20, 2006): 132–134.

15. Data here come from "2008 Survey of Allegations and Costs: A Summary Report for the Secretariat of Child and Youth Protection," chapter 4 of the *2008 Annual Report of the Office of Youth and Child Protection, USCCB* (Washington, DC: United States Conference of Catholic Bishops and the Center for Applied Research in the Apostolate at Georgetown University, February 2009), accessed March 15, 2010, http://www.usccb.org/ocyp/annualreport2008.shtml. Estimates of payouts from sexual abuse settlements vary. The *New York Times* reports "over $2 billion"; Rachel Donadio and Alan Cowell, "Pope Offers Apology, Not Penalty, for Sex Abuse Scandal," *New York Times*, March 20, 2010, 6.

16. See David Yamane, *The Catholic Church in State Politics: Negotiating Prophetic Demands and Political Realities* (Lanham, MD: Rowman and Littlefield, 2005).

17. Data in this paragraph are from *The Official Catholic Directory, 1967–2007*, which also lists 110 seminaries run by religious orders and seventy-one seminaries run by (arch)dioceses. The student enrollment count is for the 2006–2007 academic year, as reported by the U.S. Department of Education's IPEDS system. The Association of Catholic Colleges and Universities notes only thirty-seven seminaries, but their lower number presumably reflects the ACCU restriction that counts only those that accept lay students (see http:// www.accunet.org; enrollment growth data are also from this site). In any case, the diversity of Catholic institutions of higher education means that they provide university- and graduate-level educations of varying academic quality.

18. See Christian Smith and Patricia Snell, *Souls in Transition: The Religious and Spiritual Lives of Emerging Adults* (New York: Oxford University Press, 2009), esp. chap. 4.

19. The Catholic Radio Association coordinates a loose network of Catholic radio stations nationally, as a kind of trade association. The Catholic Academy for Communication Arts Professionals links Catholic radio professionals. CRA data suggest that approximately 150 self-identified Catholic radio stations existed at the end of 2007, and noted that CRA was involved in helping submit applications for 220 others. Fewer data exist regarding Catholic television. The author could identify only fourteen clearly Catholic stations in the United States, most affiliated with (arch)dioceses, but this appears to severely undercount both the number of stations and their influence: The Catholic Television Network, for example, is seen via cable service in seven states, including the most populous states in the nation, as well as on the internet. The best-known Catholic TV is Mother Angelica's EWTN, which broadcasts internationally. Most Catholic TV represents the strongly conservative and traditionalist end of the contemporary spectrum of American Catholicism, not always in concert with the American bishops. In addition, more than a dozen Catholic-affiliated "production centers" are engaged in producing television content; these represent a much broader spectrum of American Catholicism, though how broadly telecast the resulting content may be remains unknown.

20. On spirituality on elite college campuses, see Courtney Bender, *The New Metaphysicals: Spirituality and the American Religious Imagination* (Chicago, 2010). Not all the spiritual alternatives necessarily undermine Catholic formative influence, in that some may be combinable with Catholic practice and identity. But they may, by exposing Catholics to diverse traditions, reduce the centrality and efficacy of Catholic identity formation. Or such exposure may actually heighten the centrality of Catholic identity formation for some Catholics while diluting it for others.

21. Catholic leaders recently appear to have become more reflective regarding their presence in the new media. See, for instance, the reflections of Federico

Lombardi in "Perspective on the Problems of New Communications," *Origins* 39, no. 6 (June 18, 2009): 91–95.

22. See Theda Skocpol, Marshall Ganz, and Ziad Munson, "A Nation of Organizers: The Institutional Origins of Civic Voluntarism in the United States," *American Political Science Review* 94 (2000): 527–546.

23. See especially Dionne's regular commentary during the health-care reform debate, and Gerson's commentary on the controversy surrounding President Obama's invitation to speak at Notre Dame University, *Washington Post*, April 1, 2009, A21. Amidst these dynamics, Archbishop Michael Sheehan's later comments on the topic were important for opening space within public Catholicism; see Tom Roberts, "Bishop Decries 'Combative Tactics' of a Minority of U.S. Bishops," *National Catholic Reporter*, August 26, 2009.

24. For more on these patterns, see Barbara A. Perry, "Catholics and the Supreme Court: From the 'Catholic Seat' to the New Majority," in *Catholics and Politics: The Dynamic Tension Between Faith and Power*, ed. Kristin E. Heyer, Mark J. Rozell, and Michael A. Genovese (Washington, DC: Georgetown University Press, 2008).

25. On the Catholic charismatic movement, see Mary Jo Neitz, *Charisma and Community: A Study of Religious Commitment Within the Charismatic Renewal* (New Brunswick, NJ: Transaction, 1987).

26. For an overview of faith-based community organizing nationally, see Mark R. Warren and Richard L. Wood, *Faith-Based Community Organizing: The State of the Field* (Jericho, NY: Interfaith Funders, 2001); and Richard L. Wood and Mark R. Warren, "A Different Face of Faith-Based Politics: Social Capital and Community Organizing in the Public Arena," *International Journal of Sociology and Social Policy* 22, no. 9/10 (Fall 2002): 6–54. For an in-depth analysis of the religious dynamics within this field, see Richard L. Wood, *Faith in Action: Religion, Race, and Democratic Organizing in America* (Chicago: University of Chicago Press, 2002). On organizing in a Catholic context, see Richard L. Wood, "Up from the Parishes: Reclaiming the Public Voice of Catholicism," *American Catholic Studies*, December 2003, 7–10. On the impact of community organizing on parishes and other faith communities, see Wood's forthcoming *Faith and the Fire of Public Life: Congregational Development through Civic Engagement*.

27. For the first time, good data comparable to the systematic 1999 data have begun to emerge, via the Interfaith Funders National Study of Faith-Based Community Organizing (full disclosure: I served as research director for the study). See Richard L. Wood, Brad Fulton, and Kathryn Partridge, "Building Bridges, Building Power: Developments in Institution-Based Community Organizing" (New York: Interfaith Funders, 2012), http://hdl.handle.net /1928/21413. The 1999 survey documented 133 local faith-based community-organizing efforts nationwide. The field has clearly grown since then, with almost 200 organizations in 2011; a greater than 40 percent increase (see Fulton and Wood, "Building Bridges, Building Power").

28. More controversial was the CCHD's long support of community organizing by the Association of Community Organizations for Reform Now (ACORN), which mobilizes in very-low-income neighborhoods but not through congregations. That support ended in 2008, when ACORN was the center of controversy regarding the cover-up of embezzlement by a staff member related to the longtime national director, the target of coordinated attacks from conservative commentators during the election campaign, and—perhaps most significant in the CCHD funding cutoff—when its new national director explicitly endorsed Barack Obama's presidential bid.

29. For rich data and insightful analysis, see Robert Wuthnow, ed., *"I Come Away Stronger": How Small Groups Are Shaping American Religion* (Grand Rapids, MI: Eerdmans, 1994). Although now rather dated, Wuthnow's analysis still captures important dynamics within small faith-sharing groups.

30. See United States Catholic Conference, *Health and Health Care: A Pastoral Letter of the American Catholic Bishops*, November 19, 1981, http://www.usccb.org/issues-and-action/human-life-and-dignity/health-care/upload/health-and-health-care-pastoral-letter-pdf-09-01-43.pdf, 17.

31. See, for example, United States Conference of Catholic Bishops, *A Framework for Comprehensive Health Care Reform: Protecting Human Life, Promoting Human Dignity, Pursuing the Common Good*, June 18, 1993, https://www.chausa.org/docs/default-source/health-progress/healthcare-at-the-crossroads—a-framework-for-comprehensive-healthcare-reform-pdf.pdf?sfvrsn=0; United States Catholic Bishops, Health Care for the Uninsured, (United States Conference of Catholic Bishops, 2002 [cited]; available from http://www.usccb.org/sdwp/national/uninsbc.shtml.

32. For more on PICO's state- and national-level organizing effort and the strategic capacity underlying it, see Richard L. Wood, "Higher Power: Strategic Capacity for State and National Organizing," in *Transforming the City: Community Organizing and the Challenge of Political Change*, ed. Marion Orr (Lawrence: University Press of Kansas, 2007).

33. This author did research as a participant-observer at the May 2005 meetings and interviewed leaders, did fieldwork, and otherwise monitored subsequent developments.

34. The primary organizations in this initial alliance were the Georgetown Center for Children and Families, the Center on Budget Policy and Priorities, and the organizations First Focus and Community Catalyst.

35. The data in this paragraph come from a PICO source; see Gordon Whitman, "Beyond Advocacy: The History and Vision of the PICO Network," *Social Policy* 37, no. 2 (Winter 2007): 50–59. For detailed information, see Gordon Whitman, "Why SCHIP Sank? Lessons for the Coming Battles," 2008. This author followed these developments as they were occurring, and often verified key claims by monitoring coverage in local media as events were covered there. National press coverage of the network's work includes Bernie Becker,

"Obama Casts Health Effort in Moral Terms," *New York Times*, August 19, 2009; Cyrus Sanati, "Protests Planned for Banks' Shareholder Meetings," *New York Times*, April 8, 2010; David Waters, "Immigration Reform Advocates to Pray, Rally and March in Washington," *Washington Post*, March 19, 2010; and Christi Parsons, "Obama Plan Would Curb Health Insurers on Rate Hikes," *Los Angeles Times*, February 22, 2010.

36. The allies in the SCHIP struggle identified in the announcement were the "Georgetown Center for Children and Families, Center on Budget Policy and Priorities, First Focus, Families USA, Community Catalyst, American Academy of Pediatrics, National Council of Churches, Sojourners, U.S. Catholic Conference of Bishops [*sic*], and other religious denominations."

37. Slight variations in the formulation occurred throughout 2009 and early 2010, depending on the emerging state of the policy debate. The formulation quoted here comes from a USCCB letter to Senators dated September 30, 2009, available at http://www.usccb.org/issues-and-action/human-life-and -dignity/health-care/upload/health-care-letter-senate-2009-09-30.pdf.

38. The coalition also included Families USA, SEIU Healthcare, the American Cancer Society Cancer Action Network, the American Diabetes Association, the American Heart Association, the American Nurses Association, Consumers Union, and the National Association of Community Health Centers.

39. Author accessed http://www.Coverallfamilies.org/pages?id=0021 on November 20, 2014 to obtain a state-by-state listing of these events and the national advertisement put out by the coalition; link no longer active.

40. There have been scattered reports, difficult to verify, that the Catholic bishops weighed in to keep Republicans in line in support of the Stupak amendment, rather than using it as a tool to sink overall health-care reform (which the bishops of course supported, as long as it included no funding for abortion).

41. For initial news analysis of the bill, see David M. Herszenhorn and Robert Pear, "Final Votes in Congress Cap Battle on Health Bill" in *New York Times* (March 26, 2010), p. A17. Available at https://www.nytimes.com/2010/03/26 /health/policy/26health.html. The deficit-reduction claims made for the bill are the least verifiable element of the analysis.

42. In fact, the Catholic Health Association had begun to diverge from the USCCB analysis of the emerging health reform bill in December 2009, when it endorsed the Senate's approach. For the initial statement by the CHA, its later reiteration of support for the final legislation, and its endorsement by Network, see David D. Kirkpatrick, "Catholic Group Supports Senate on Abortion Aid," *New York Times*, December 26, 2009, http://www.nytimes .com/2009/12/26/health/policy/26abort.html?r=1&_r. See also Carol Keehan and Grant Gallicho, "The Time Is Now for Health Reform" in *Commonweal* (March 13, 2010), available at https://www.commonwealmagazine.org/catholic -health-association-prez-time-now-health-reform. For the statement by the

women's religious congregations, see Dennis Coday, "Thousands of Catholic sisters support health care reform" in the *National Catholic Reporter* (March 17, 2010), https://www.ncronline.org/blogs/ncr-today/thousands-catholic-sisters -support-health-care-reform. In essence, the CHA and Network argued that the Senate language—crafted by pro-life senators—adequately protected the long-standing Hyde Amendment provisions against using tax dollars to pay for abortion. The USCCB disagreed. For a sampling of the very prominent news coverage and public discussion, see Michelle Boorstein, "Dissent Among Catholics Seen as Nuns' Groups Back Health Bill," *Washington Post*, March 18, 2010, and David M. Herszenhorn and Robert Pear, "Final Votes in Congress Cap Battle on Health Bill," *New York Times*, March 25, 2010.

43. On the Network intervention and the way differing Catholic views were brought to bear in public deliberation, see previous endnote and Helene Cooper, "Nuns Back Bill Amid Broad Rift Over Whether It Limits Abortion Enough," *New York Times*, March 19, 2010.

44. See E. J. Dionne Jr., "On Health Care, Listen to the Nuns," *Washington Post*, March 18, 2010.

45. On final passage of the main bill and accompanying reconciliation measure, see David M. Herszenhorn and Robert Pear, "Obama Hails Vote on Health Care as Answering 'the Call of History,' " *New York Times*, March 22, 2010. On the comparison between the House and final Senate bills, see Timothy Stoltzfus Jost, Memorandum, March 14, 2010, http://law.wlu.edu/faculty /facultydocuments/jost/Jost_Response_to_Bishops_3.14.10.pdf. On the bishops' role in the final legislative endgame, see Jerry Filteau, "Fact Checked: U.S. Bishops on Health Care Reform," *National Catholic Reporter*, April 12, 2010, http://ncronline.org/news/politics/fact-checked-us-bishops-health-care -reform; and Cardinal Francis George, "Universal Health Care Statement," United States Conference of Catholic Bishops, March 23, 2010, http://www .usccb.org/issues-and-action/human-life-and-dignity/health-care/upload /health-care-cardinal-george-statement.pdf.

46. If one needs evidence that the debate will continue, compare for example the following two posts, both from pro-life analysts: "Abortion in the Affordable Care Act: Responses to Administration Claims" by the USCCB Secretariat of Pro-Life Activities (September 15, 2014) and an untitled legal analysis by Timothy Stoltzfus Jost (March 14, 2010). These are available respectively at http://www.usccb.org/issues-and-action/human-life-and-dignity/abortion /upload/Abortion-in-the-Affordable-Care-Act-Responses-to-Administration -Claims-GAO.pdf and http://law.wlu.edu/faculty/facultydocuments/jost/Jost _Response_to_Bishops_3.14.10.pdf.

47. The Christian personalism strand of Catholic theology, mediated most prominently into the tradition through the writings of Karol Wojtyla both before and after becoming Pope John Paul II, provide one important route through which the latter encounter is occurring. See Patrick Grant, *Personalism*

and the Politics of Culture: Readings in Literature and Religion from the New Testament to *the Poetry of Northern Ireland* (Basingstoke, UK: Macmillan, 1996); and Andrew N. Woznicki, *A Christian Humanism: Karol Wojtyla's Existential Personalism* (New Britain, CT: Mariel, 1980).

48. Quote from p. 618 in Gregory Gleason, "Fealty and Loyalty: Informal Authority Structures in Soviet Asia" in *Soviet Studies* 43, no. 4 (1991): 613–28.

49. For the foundational analyses of authority dynamics in society, see Max Weber, *Economy and Society* [1914–15] (Berkeley: University of California Press, 1968), vol. 1, chap. 3, "The Types of Legitimate Domination" (212–254); vol. 2, chap. 9, sec. 6, "The Distribution of Power within the Political Community: Class, Status, and Party" (926–939); and vol. 2, chap. 11, "Bureaucracy" (956–989). See also Georg Simmel, *On Individuality and Social Forms*, ed. Donald N. Levine (Chicago: University of Chicago Press, 1971).

50. On the unencumbered self, see Michael J. Sandel, "The Procedural Republic and the Unencumbered Self," *Political Theory* 12, no. 1 (February 1984): 81–96, and the extensive commentary it has generated.

51. Note that these do *not* correspond in any simple sense to "liberal" and "conservative" political or theological positions. While exploring these complexities lies beyond my purposes here, I would note that while liberal positions tend toward the "Scylla" side of the cultural tension and conservative positions tend toward the "Charybdis" side, liberals have their own authorities accepted rather blindly (Bono and Barack Obama, at least until recently), and conservatives their own authority-rejectionists (the Tea Party and libertarians).

52. On the distinction between authoritarian, authoritative, and permissive styles, see the pioneering work of Diana Baumrind and Maccoby and Martin. Diana Baumrind, "Child Care Practices Anteceding Three Patterns of Preschool Behavior," *Genetic Psychology Monographs* 75 (1967): 43–88; Diana Baumrind, "Current Patterns of Parental Authority," Developmental Psychology 4, no. 1, pt. 2 (1971): 1–103; E. E. Maccoby and J. A. Martin, "Socialization in the Context of the Family: Parent-Child Interaction," in *Handbook of Child Psychology: Vol. 4. Socialization, Personality, and Social Development*, ed. P. H. Mussen and E. M. Hetherington (New York: Wiley, 1983), 1–101. Also see Susie D. Lamborn, Nina S. Mounts, Laurence Steinberg, and Sanford M. Dornbusch, "Patterns of Competence and Adjustment Among Adolescents from Authoritative, Authoritarian, Indulgent, and Neglectful Families," *Child Development* 62, no. 5 (October 1991): 1049–1065.

53. For a highly sympathetic analysis of how the deification of the self has created a powerful dynamism within American culture, see Harold Bloom, *The American Religion: The Emergence of the Post-Christian Nation*, 2nd ed. (New York: Chu Hartley, 2006). Obviously, I view this dynamic with far less enthusiasm than does Bloom.

54. A fine secular analysis of the possibilities and thin enactment of Catholic communitarianism can be found in Paul Lichterman, *Elusive Togetherness:*

Church Groups Trying to Bridge America's Divisions (Princeton, NJ: Princeton University Press, 2005).

55. See Baggett, *Sense of the Faithful*; Michele Dillon, *Catholic Identity*.

56. On the chaos and incoherence of contemporary Catholic culture, along with its potential, see Peter Steinfels, *A People Adrift: The Crisis of the Roman Catholic Church in America* (New York: Simon & Schuster, 2004).

57. A parallel public controversy was seen in the May 2009 debate regarding the University of Notre Dame's invitation to President Obama to speak on campus and receive an honorary degree, with the more sectarian Catholic voices arguing that he should be excluded because of his support for abortion rights and embryonic stem cell research. On the controversy, see Peter Baker and Susan Saulny, "At Notre Dame, Obama Calls for Civil Tone in Abortion Debate," *New York Times*, May 18, 2009, www.nytimes.com/2009/05/18/us/politics/18obama.html. For the text of Obama's speech there, see "Obama's Commencement Address at Notre Dame," *New York Times*, May 17, 2009, www.nytimes.com/2009/05/17/us/politics/17text-obama.html. On the Vatican's commentary regarding Obama, see, for example, E. J. Dionne Jr., "The Stakes at Notre Dame for President Obama and U.S. Catholics," *Washington Post*, May 7, 2009, http://www.washingtonpost.com/wp-dyn/content/article/2009/05/06/AR2009050603319.html?noredirect=on.

58. The original, classic formulation is found in Ernst Troeltsch, *The Social Teaching of the Christian Churches*, trans. Olive Wyon (London: Allen & Unwin, 1950). In America, "denominations" have come to supplant the full-blown church and sect ideal types rooted in European history, but American Catholicism has closely adhered to a version of denominationalism close to the church type, eschewing more sectarian versions of denominationalism pursued by some traditions.

59. See Paul DiMaggio, "Culture and Cognition," *Annual Review of Sociology* 23 (1997): 263–287. For the sociological foundations of this insight, see Emile Durkheim, "The Dualism of Human Nature and Its Social Conditions," in *Emile Durkheim on Morality and Society*, ed. Robert N. Bellah (Chicago: University of Chicago Press, 1973).

60. On the "sense of the faithful," see Baggett, *Sense of the Faithful*; Paul G. Crowley, "The Sensus Fidelium and Catholicity: Newman's Legacy in the Age of Inculturation," in *John Henry Newman: Theology and Reform*, ed. Michael E. Allsopp and Ronald R. Burke (London: Routledge, 1992); Daniel J. Finucane, *Sensus Fidelium: The Use of a Concept in the Post–Vatican II Era* (San Francisco: International Scholars, 1996).

61. Richard John Neuhaus, *The Catholic Moment: The Paradox of the Church in the Postmodern World* (San Francisco: Harper & Row, 1987).

Conclusion

THE SHAPE OF THE AMERICAN CATHOLIC FUTURE

Patricia O'Connell Killen

Within a single lifetime, the Catholic Church in the United States has moved from being a subculture grounded in class and ethnicity to a denomination parallel to and influential with mainline Protestantism, to a fractious, pluriform community whose leadership often partners with Evangelicals in an "alliance of the embattled." This double transformation has come about through engagement with—and adaptation to—a society that has become ever more voluntary, individualistic, and consumerist. But even as American Catholicism has adjusted itself to social and cultural change at home, it has been buffeted by the no less disruptive dynamics of the global church.

The resignation of Pope Benedict XVI in February 2013 and the election of Jorge Mario Bergoglio as his successor opened a new chapter in the American church. As soon as the Italian-Argentine Cardinal Archbishop of Buenos Aires took office as Pope Francis, his words and actions began unsettling those inside and outside his church. They continue to do so. Some view him as the Spirit-inspired rescuer of the promise of Vatican II, others as a mistaken leader unleashing chaos on a rudderless Barque of Peter. His commitment to simplicity, his call for a church of the poor, his emphasis on the pastoral over the dogmatic, his proclamation of "mercy" as a primary mark of the church, and his powerful use of liturgical symbols— for example, his washing the feet of the disabled, prisoners, women, and non-Catholics at the Holy Thursday Mass—have heartened those inside the church who had grown increasingly disaffected under John Paul II, Benedict XVI, and the bishops they appointed. Francis's very same words and actions have deeply disturbed Catholics committed to the "reform of the reform." They find his writings and actions too imprecise and ambiguous to serve as the forceful presentation of Catholic teaching that they believe is necessary to counter the rising tide of secularism and to preserve the integrity of the church. Anyone who wishes to know what the Catholic Church in America stands for today needs to look in more than one direction.

The contributors to this volume have explained how the American church has arrived at its current state of growing disaffiliation, heightened internal tension, developing pluralism in sensibility and practice, and narrowing public influence. In light of their interpretations, what claims can be made about the foreseeable future of the Roman Catholic community in the United States?

SEVEN PREDICTIONS

1. There Will Be No Return to the Subculture

American Catholics today, regardless of religious and political inclination, breathe the post-subcultural, post-denominational air. All but the most recent immigrants are at home in this environment, have absorbed its attitudes and sensibilities, and have embraced its ideas, proclivities, and practices. Most are not aware how much this context has affected them. Like their neighbors, they value their own experience and prioritize their own beliefs, opinions, and choices. They desire to pursue spiritual quests freely, on their own, and without constraint; so, while many are sad to see their children drift away from the church, they are not inclined to condemn them for it. Catholics share the tendency to trust personal experience and the experience of their peers more than professional expertise, inherited teaching, or designated authorities. Those most involved in the church may consult all three when considering religious, moral, and civic issues, but in the end they trust their own judgment, their own consciences. They claim allegiance to the pronouncements of designated authorities when their views align, but do not consider themselves less Catholic when the opposite is the case.[1] They have absorbed a general suspicion of established institutions and leaders, and have seen that suspicion confirmed by the sexual abuse scandal—hence their willingness, on all manner of issues both ecclesial and civic, to engage in public critique of and dissent from the pope, from bishops, and from authoritative teaching.

Catholics also share the general American proclivity for flatter, more fluid, more interest-based forms of association and social interaction, and for greater democratization and local control. They want a voice in how their parishes are run, and in how their contributions to the diocese are spent. And, just as for other Americans, the internet provides Catholics with unprecedented direct access to an array of interpretations of their religious tradition.[2]

Like their Protestant neighbors, Catholics arrange themselves along a continuum. At one pole is intense preoccupation with maintaining strict boundaries of identity and belonging as fundamental to assuring the purity of the church and its effective witness in the world. At the other is an easy situating of Catholic teaching, practice, and community as part of a much wider cornucopia of spiritual guidance available from the world's traditions as a resource for one's spiritual and life journey—a resource that, through engagement, not pronouncement, can inform deliberations on civic and political issues.

In the nation's religiously pluralistic and voluntary context, Catholics across this continuum have adopted long-honed strategies for bringing faith to bear on public issues, primary among them organizing around a single issue or problem that arouses intense, often emotional commitment and so galvanizes people to action. Within a few years of the conclusion of the Second Vatican Council, Catholics unhappy with the direction of its reforms had organized in this way to bring pressure on church leaders. The other side did the same, especially as the reforms began to be constricted. As John Paul II's appointments came to dominate the American hierarchy, the nation's bishops adopted this same single-issue strategy to bring Catholic teaching to bear on public discussions, a choice that continues to reverberate in the church and in American public life, as Richard Wood has described in chapter 7.

The influence of single-issue activism on the church is illustrated by the bishops' repudiation of the consistent life ethic. First put forth by Cardinal Joseph Bernardin of Chicago in 1983, this ethic, sometimes referred as the "seamless garment," conveyed the integral connection of Catholic teaching on all life issues, including capital punishment and end-of-life care alongside abortion. Such an integrated approach,

Bernardin believed, more accurately conveyed Catholic social teaching and had a better chance of opening a serious conversation in the public square than a focus on abortion alone. Almost immediately, however, the major thought organ of the Catholic neotraditionalists, *First Things*, criticized him for being insufficiently clear and firm in promoting Catholic teaching on abortion. For the neotraditionalists, advocates of the then emerging Catholic-Evangelical alliance, forceful presentation of a single point of Catholic moral teaching took precedence over the more integrated presentation of Catholic social thought.[3] And priority was given to Catholic teaching on issues of sexual morality—teaching more congenial to most on the socially conservative side of the culture wars than was Catholic teaching on other social issues.

That preference, as expressed by the American hierarchy, continued well into Francis's pontificate. At its fall 2017 meeting, the U.S. Conference of Catholic Bishops again repudiated the consistent life ethic by electing Archbishop Joseph Naumann of Kansas City, a strong advocate of the single-issue approach, over Cardinal Blase Cupich of Chicago. Cupich, like his predecessor, was deemed insufficiently committed to asserting abortion as the preeminent moral evil.[4] Cupich's loss also was a rebuke to Pope Francis on the part of prelates for whom opposition to legal access to abortion has become the signature mark of Catholic identity in America.[5] By contrast, Pope Francis—in his informal remarks as well as in formal teaching such as his encyclical on climate change and his apostolic exhortation on the family—employs a more integrated presentation of Catholic moral teaching.[6] The question as of this writing is whether Cupich's defeat was a last victory for socially conservative bishops in the face of increasing numbers of Francis appointments to the American episcopacy, or an indication of continuing opposition to the pontiff.

Over the past thirty years, the American church has come to reflect significantly the divisions in U.S. culture in which religious conservatives have focused primarily on issues of sexual morality while religious moderates and progressives have emphasized issues of structural injustice. This polarization has eroded the deep and essential Catholic value of unity, just as the more individualistic sensibilities of the post-subcultural milieu erode the plausibility of Catholic understandings of the authority of designated leaders and of tradition. Yet, despite strong differences in perspective and sometimes intense conflict, the Roman Catholic Church in the

United States has not split. The Catholic impulse toward unity runs deep. Whether and how it will influence the church as post-subcultural Catholicism continues to develop remains to be seen.

2. The Church Will Be Smaller, but Still the Largest American Religious Body

Since 1990, American society has witnessed a rapid uncoupling of spiritual quests from participation in religious institutions, beginning with liturgically centered traditions and, more recently, in the Evangelical churches. This pattern has been part and parcel of a growing disconnection from social institutions generally. This phenomenon, combined with the decades-long sexual abuse scandal, suggests that the disaffiliation from the Catholic Church described by William Dinges in chapter 1—especially among younger Catholics of Euro-American heritage—is unlikely to reverse in the foreseeable future. Nor will immigrant Catholics and converts be sufficient in number to replenish fully the ranks of those who leave.[7]

Fewer Catholics today have a sense that the church's formal teaching on morals is relevant to their lives; in large numbers, they disagree with what it has to say about contraception, divorce, same-sex marriage, and capital punishment (to say nothing of the necessity of a celibate, all-male priesthood), and they have for a long time. The abuse scandal continues to diminish the hierarchy's credibility. The priest shortage continues to erode the availability and quality of the sacraments, liturgy, pastoral care, spiritual guidance, and faith formation for children and adults. This has lasting effects on the imaginations of Catholics. The closing and merging of parishes in response to the shortage disrupts communities. The growing gap that Katarina Schuth describes in chapter 4 between newer, younger, conservative pastors and their parishioners on the theology of church, lay ministry in the parish, and the nature and practice of leadership complicates the church's ability to provide meaningful liturgy and spiritual sustenance as well. Women, sexual minorities, divorced and remarried Catholics, and single persons question whether they are welcome, especially in light of the hierarchy's tendency to emphasize church teaching on sexual morality and the nuclear family over such socioeconomic issues as poverty, racism, immigration, health care, income inequality, and climate change. Whether the Francis papacy will succeed in shifting this emphasis is a crucial question going forward.[8]

Despite the loss of adherents, the church will remain the country's largest religious body. Some are drawn by Catholicism's long history and tradition, and the fact that its structure, teaching, and communal life contrast in significant ways with the ethos of the wider culture. Its social teachings, even when not championed by much of the hierarchy, are an anchor for others. Still others embrace its rich array of spiritual traditions and devotional practices. A portion of the immigrant population continues to find in the church support and resources for negotiating life in a strange land. And many Catholics will remain in parish communities that are important to them, or seek out such communities as they negotiate family life and personal journeys.

3. The American Catholic Church Will Be More Diverse

Latinos already account for the majority of Catholics in the Millennial generation (born after 1982).[9] By 2060, they are expected to make up more than half of the entire American Catholic population. Catholic immigrants from Asia and Africa are also increasing the diversity of the Catholic community, which has long included African Americans and Native Americans.

By the third generation, ethnic immigrant retention patterns reflect those of Euro-American Catholics. The church's ability to retain a greater proportion of its diverse populations depends, minimally, on its ability to provide culturally sensitive liturgy, pastoral care, and communal support to these populations—to demonstrate that Catholic goods are effective in ways that acknowledge the integrity of immigrants' own lived experience of Catholic faith. Andrew Walsh opens chapter 6 with a description of ethnic and linguistic liturgical richness in a San Francisco parish, but not all dioceses are equipped or have the resources to respond in the same way.

The church also needs to develop intercultural competence in parishes with diverse populations, for while some "ethnic" Catholics have clergy from their own cultures and parishes of their own, most do not. As Timothy Matovina notes in chapter 2, a pivotal issue for Latino Catholics is whether they are received as communities of mature faith or as communities in need of assimilation. To be sure, emphasizing diversity in ethnically mixed parishes can and does generate tension and sometimes balkanization. But as Euro-Americans, African Americans, Latinos, Asians, Africans, and Native

Americans increasingly share a single parish, the capacity to communicate, to make collective decisions, and to imagine a common future becomes ever more important—indeed, essential—for a healthy and vibrant church. Finally, the American Catholic community must face and address more energetically its long history of racism. A promising development was the USCCB's appointment of a committee on racism in the fall of 2017, but the promise was tempered by the fact that it was the first such action since 1979. Whether the bishops will exert their authority and deploy resources to address racism in the church and society remains an open question.

The current wave of racially charged, populist nationalism is itself a challenge to the church in welcoming ethnic immigrants and addressing racism. Those Catholics who are part of it dissent from the church's teachings on immigration and are unlikely to view cultural diversity as an enriching source of forms of spirituality, sensibility, and practice for their parishes. While it is unclear how much younger Catholics share these attitudes, to the extent that they do, their behavior will contribute to the shrinking of the church.

4. Catholics Will Be Catholic as a Matter of Choice

Americans are Catholic because they choose to be. This statement is truer now than it was in 1990, when Andrew Greeley stated it baldly in response to those anxious about the effects of Vatican II.[10] Never has it been easier to opt out of the church. Catholics who remain find in their parishes a community that, with its rituals, pastoral services, and social networks, acknowledges them, supports them, and helps them make sense of the pain, joy, wonder, and agony of life. They find resources for living in Catholicism's theological and spiritual traditions—for some, even when they rarely participate in a parish. For others, the parish is the place where they connect most fully with companions on life's journey. For still others, the pull of family tradition and habit is the thread that keeps them bound to the Catholic community. But with between 10 and 13 percent of the adult population in the United States now made up of former Catholics, the American church has work to do, especially in the face of larger cultural trends propelling disaffiliation.[11]

Ritual is at the heart of the Catholic sacramental tradition. It responds to deep human impulses; access to sacramental rituals marking the cycle of life are often the last thing Catholics relinquish on their way to "former Catholic" status. Ritual shapes imagination, sensibility, and dispositions at a level below rational thought, as Joseph Chinnici describes in chapter 5 and Wood discusses in chapter 7. At its best, it provides a way for human beings, individually and corporately, to negotiate the gap between what is and the imagined ideal, between the "is-ness" and "ought-ness" of life.[12]

Pope Francis understands how ritual molds people and teaches at a deep level. That knowledge is integral to his powerful pastoral presence, especially when, in liturgy, he enacts the reality that the life of faith is lived in the space between the actual and the ideal—as when he baptized the children of unmarried Catholics. Pastors and staffs in vital American Catholic parishes also understand this power of ritual. That is why parishes that can provide different types of liturgy—more contemplative, traditional, praise song, etc.—do so. They are responding to people's hunger for spiritual experience through the liturgy and appreciate that too great a gap between liturgical practice and people's lives may block the satisfying of that hunger.

Pope Francis's delegation of decisions about liturgical texts to local episcopal conferences acknowledges the importance of doing liturgy in a way that resonates with people's larger lives. It also suggests that decisions need to be made closer to where people live, in the particularity of their cultural and social environment. That fine-grained appreciation for people's lives is essential for providing liturgy that not only resonates with but also allows people to transcend their lives, to gain purchase on them—a purchase of deepening understanding, even critique, that will inspire growth and change. Whether the American hierarchy and newer pastors will follow Francis's direction on liturgy remains to be seen. The pope is acknowledging the reality of and the need for a pluralism of liturgical styles. Whereas under his predecessor many American bishops grudgingly endured this pluralism, Francis wants it embraced. Which way the American hierarchy and clergy go will affect the American church's future fortunes.

5. Disconnection and Contestation Will Continue

The American Catholic community has always contained greater diversity of opinion and practice among the lay and the ordained than many perceived. Beginning with implementation of the reforms of Vatican II and with *Humanae Vitae*, the papal encyclical reaffirming the church's position against contraception, more active and visible dissent from Catholic teaching and practice became evident. By the late 1980s, with John Paul II's and his episcopal appointments' retrenching on Council reforms and building an alliance with political conservatives, the assimilation of American Catholics into the nation's larger religious culture was fully visible. By that point, despite the efforts of Cardinal Bernardin and others to esablish common ground, it became clear that the American hierarchy spoke for fewer Catholics, that all Catholics had become more reliant on their own consciences, and that the American Catholic population was beginning to reflect the ideological split coded in the term "culture wars." The rapidity of the change was stunning.

Over the ensuing twenty-five years, the disconnections increased as the majority of American bishops, virtually all John Paul II or Benedict XVI appointments by the end, pursued a strict boundaries approach to Catholic identity and belonging—an approach that, at the beginning, most Catholics did not embrace. The bishops merged the United States Catholic Conference into the U.S. Conference of Catholic Bishops, and in the process reclericalized leadership at all levels, as Steven Avella describes in chapter 3. A failed pastoral letter on women; Vatican actions centralizing to Rome prerogatives that had been assumed by national episcopal conferences in the wake of the Second Vatican Council; a narrowing of space for conversation on women's roles in the church, divorced and remarried Catholics, and sexual minorities; and the bishops' embrace of an alliance with socially conservative American Evangelicals signaled a quite different milieu. Some Catholics embraced these changes; others left the church or found ways to remain on their own terms.

By the sixth year of Pope Francis's reign, the disconnection had shifted in two ways. First, Francis found himself contending with bishops appointed by John Paul II and Benedict XVI, some of whom were quite willing to publicly dissent from his teachings and actively work to undermine him. There was little doubt that the disconnection and contestation would continue unless and until Francis had been in office long enough to replace them with bishops whose vision and practice aligned better with his own.

The tension between Pope Francis and the bishops also exists among the laity. Except for recent immigrants, Catholics under the age of forty-five grew up in the church or joined it in the milieu of the culture wars. This has affected how they think about their relationship to Catholic teaching, practices, including liturgical ritual, and church authorities. It is not yet clear what the attitudes of younger Catholics who remain in the church or who have converted to it will be over the long term. Committed young Catholics are themselves products of the more voluntarist, evangelical culture that has set the norm for Christianity in America over the past three decades, a norm that includes heightened preoccupation with boundaries of identity and belonging. Young Catholics' thinking about the church and their attitudes toward clerical leadership may be more aligned with the "reform of the reform" than with Pope Francis. If they become the majority of the church's lay leaders and ministry professionals, American Catholicism will retain a strong gravitational pull toward liturgical traditionalism and theological conservatism. Whether young Catholics more drawn to Catholic social teaching and progressive theology will remain active in the church is open to question.

What of the role of the laity in leadership, ministry, and liturgical life? Vatican II contended that the laity were called to ministry by virtue of their baptism and encouraged them to take that call seriously. In the decades when John Paul II and Benedict XVI led the church, lay pastoral leadership was viewed as necessitated by circumstance, but not desirable. Some bishops argued that lay ministry is properly an extension of the bishop's ministry and so is to be exercised only under his direction. Some systematically acted to constrain lay ministers, limiting their roles in liturgy. Many preferred volunteers to professional, credentialed lay ministers. Even as the growing priest shortage has made the need for trained lay ministers all the more urgent, enrollment in master's degree programs in lay ministry dropped 16 percent from 2016 to 2017.[13]

Pope Francis appears to have a more expansive view of lay ministry and a greater appreciation for what lay pastoral ministers who share the lived experience of the people can bring to the church. As well, his call for more women in leadership roles in the church, including his initiating a study of the ordination of women to the deaconate, and his exhortation for the church to be a church of the poor in the world, reaffirm for many the Second Vatican Council's emphasis on baptism as the fundamental source of ministry. But his statements calling for a more open and hospitable church stand in marked contrast to the conservative, clericalist tendencies of the American hierarchy over the past two decades. There is thus good reason to believe that the atmosphere of contestation and disconnection will persist.

Events in 2018 foregrounded yet again the extent and depth of the division in the leadership of American Catholicism, a division that is theological, ideological, and political. The presenting issue was clergy sexual abuse and its cover-up by the hierarchy. In June, former Washington, D.C. archbishop, Cardinal Theodore McCarrick was removed from ministry for a credible accusation, and news stories reported that his abuse of seminarians occurred over decades. In mid-August the report of a two-year grand jury investigation of the extent of child sexual abuse in six dioceses in Pennsylvania appeared; and, while the vast majority of cases it described were decades old, its detail on the nature, extent and systematic character of the abuse and episcopal hiding of it, sometimes with the complicity of civil authorities, administered another shock to the laity and spurred another round of remedial activity by the bishops. In late August the former Apostolic Nuncio to the United States, Archbishop Carlo Maria Viganò, published a letter claiming that awareness and a cover up of McCarrick's behavior reached the upper levels of the Vatican, up to and including Pope Francis, whom Viganò called on to resign. As of this writing over thirty American bishops had spoken out on behalf of Viganò and his letter; only a handful in support of Pope Francis. And, while the presenting issue was clergy sexual abuse, how individual bishops viewed the situation was heavily colored by their views of the nature of the church, papal and episcopal authority, and church teaching and discipline on sexuality. Hence, communion for the divorced and remarried, and the death penalty, two issues on which many bishops differ from recent papal statements, lay near the surface. Strikingly absent at this early stage was thoughtful episcopal reflection on what the ongoing revelations were doing to the credibility of the Church; to the plausibility of the Catholic theological tradition linking the authority of office to magisterial teaching authority and the sacraments; and, to the fundamental quality of unity within the People of God.[14]

6. The American Church Will Continue to Struggle with Issues of Sexuality and Gender Diversity

In focusing their moral teaching on contraception, abortion, homosexuality, divorce, and women's place in the church, the American hierarchy has alienated many Catholics, especially younger Catholics. Formal Catholic teaching on women's roles is no longer credible to large numbers of

Catholic women, leading some to abandon the church and others to defect in place.[15] The banning of women from serving as acolytes in some parishes and some bishops' vocal reassertion of Catholic teaching on contraception have done little to help women's sense of being welcome in the church.

The investigations of women's religious communities and of the Leadership Conference of Women Religious, which some members of the American hierarchy instigated and promoted, exemplified to many women the lengths to which some in the hierarchy in the United States and at the Vatican would go to gain control over the lives and financial resources of women religious. The outcry of support for "the sisters" showed the extent to which they exemplify for many lay Catholics a positive experience of the church as an institution and were regarded more highly than some of the episcopacy. Under Pope Francis, the investigations were concluded with a largely positive outcome, but the entire experience reinforced a sense that the church is hostile toward women. While fewer younger women are choosing to stay in the church, a significant portion of those who do embrace what observers describe as the new orthodoxy.[16]

Magisterial statements on homosexuality have ceased to be credible to most American Catholics, creating another disconnection. Determined to proclaim and enforce these, some bishops made matters worse by banning Jesuit priest James Martin from speaking in their dioceses about his 2017 book *Building a Bridge: How the Catholic Church and the L.G.B.T. Community Can Enter Into a Relationship of Respect, Compassion and Sensitivity*—which in fact makes no criticism of official church teaching. While sympathetic engagement with gays and lesbians rather than condemnation is the preferred approach of "Pope Francis bishops" like San Diego's Robert McElroy, they remain in the minority.

As has generally been the case when tension exists between the hierarchy and the laity, the parish is the place where lived experience tempers hierarchically prescribed norms of behavior. Today there are Catholic parishes that welcome sexual minorities, where they engage fully in the sacraments and communal life. There are other parishes that are restrictive. One virtue of the pluriform church is that it provides a wide range of spaces for those who wish to lead a Catholic life. It is unclear, however, if this is sufficient for younger Catholics—or if they want only to be part of a community where the alignment between what is said and what is done is entirely consistent.

7. *Catholicism's Public Presence Will Become More Diffuse and Conflicted*

As the contributors to this volume have made clear, Catholics share in the ethos that has pushed Americans to regard the individual as the locus of religious experience, meaning, and authority. Like their neighbors, Catholics engage whatever biblical, theological, and cultural resources they consider authoritative, then act on their own convictions. They participate in activist American religious politics. The plethora of interest groups created to influence not only public life but also church leadership itself reveals how the democratization of American religious life has taken hold in a hierarchically organized church where, in earlier times, the hierarchy largely guided civic engagement.

Even as lay activism has increased the ways Catholic thought is brought to bear on public issues, it has made the fractures within the Catholic community more visible. Consider what occurred when President Barack Obama was invited to deliver the 2009 commencement speech and receive an honorary degree from the University of Notre Dame.[17] As soon as the invitation became public, organizing began to pressure the university both to rescind the invitation and to hold firm. Opponents believed that the president's support of legal access to abortion disqualified him entirely. Proponents considered the invitation legitimate given Obama's office and his positions on many other issues that aligned with the aims of Catholic social teaching.[18] Some of the organizing was grassroots and animated by student; some was national and led by such professional activists as antiabortion crusader Randall Terry and Catholic League president William Donahue.

Participants on the two sides expressed contrasting understandings of the right way to bring Catholic thought to bear on major issues in the public realm: strong proclamation of church teaching on any given issue, with no compromise, versus ongoing engagement through conversation, the exercise of prudential judgment, and a willingness to compromise in service to a higher goal. For more than a quarter of a century, the American hierarchy has opted for strong proclamation—particularly when it comes to issues of sexuality and gender. The result has been alienation in the rank and file and dissent from Catholic progressives. With Pope Francis's emphasis on a socioeconomic agenda, including immigration, economic justice, and climate change, there has been significant pushback from the

Catholic right. It may be that the pope, through direct influence and his episcopal appointments, can succeed in reorienting the church's public witness in the United States in a way that strengthens and extends its moral authority. The project is up against stiff odds.

RESOURCE FOR RENEWAL

For all the challenges confronting the American Catholic community today, Catholicism is an ancient and varied tradition that over centuries has always been able to renew itself. There is no reason to think that this is impossible now.[19] Indeed, in parishes, on campuses, in communities of religious, seeds of renewal are sprouting—in renewed interest in spiritual practices, in experiments in intentional living, in constructive theological writing, and in social engagement. Times of great social change call out the dynamism of religious traditions.[20] The election to the papacy of a man like Francis, unanticipated as it was, has made clear the capacity for change in what sometimes has seemed a hidebound and sclerotic religious institution.

Shortly after the conclusion of the Second Vatican Council, when he wrote confidently that it was perhaps Christianity's last chance to get its engagement with modernity "right," Thomas O'Dea warranted his confidence with an appeal to a long-standing Catholic way of negotiating historical change: the ability to put two contradictory sentences side by side and act as if they were not contradictory. That approach, he argued, made it possible to maintain the authority and continuity of tradition while accounting for the changing realities within which the church existed. O'Dea believed the church to be durable because it could negotiate its teachings, practice, and community life with elasticity of thought and practice and generosity to difference.[21] All the contributors to this volume have called, similarly, for an embrace of the virtues of elasticity in thought and practice and generosity to difference as pivotal to the American Catholic community's future, especially at this particular moment. Absent those virtues, the dynamics of creative renewal that are endemic in a living faith community are stifled, and the community is less able to respond wisely and effectively to the challenges and opportunities it faces. Chinnici describes this way of being as "pluriformity within communion" and "communion within pluriformity," and notes that it demands maturity on the part of the hierarchy and the people. It demands maturity, in no small part, because it is a reclaiming of a historic Catholic way of proceeding in the face of spontaneous reactions shaped for decades by the nation's culture-war context, with its penchant for drawing sharp divisions designed to drive ecclesial and social ideological politics. From a theological perspective, pluriformity within communion creates room for grace. Pastorally, it invites compassion and a penchant for listening before reacting. Intellectually, it invites an approach of curious reception and appreciation of all the dimensions of Catholic life and the wider world. In the capacity for such hospitality to self and world, so central to Catholic liturgy and life, resides the dynamic durability with which the American Catholic future is being forged.

NOTES

1. For descriptions of how contemporary Catholics engage their authoritative heritage, see Jerome P. Baggett, *Sense of the Faithful: How American Catholics Live Their Faith* (New York: Oxford University Press, 2009); and Terry A. Velling, *Living in the Margins: Intentional Communities and the Art of Interpretation* (New York: Crossroad, 1996). For more historical perspectives on the process, see Colleen McDannell, *The Spirit of Vatican II: A History of Catholic Reform in America* (New York: Basic Books, 2011); and Robert A. Orsi, "U.S. Catholics Between Memory and Modernity: How Catholics Are American," in *Catholics in the American Century: Recasting Narratives of U.S. History*, ed. R. Scott Appleby and Kathleen Sprows Cummings (Ithaca, NY: Cornell University Press, 2012).

2. For a description of shifting institutional forms and participation, see Robert D. Putnam, *Bowling Alone: The Collapse and Revival of American Community* (New York: Simon and Schuster, 2001); Nancy Tatom Ammerman, *Congregation and Community* (New Brunswick, NJ: Rutgers University Press, 1996); Nancy Tatom Ammerman, *Sacred Stories, Spiritual Tribes: Findings Religion in Everyday Life* (New York: Oxford University Press, 2013); Robert Wuthnow, *After Heaven: Spirituality in America Since the 1950s* (Berkeley: University of California Press, 1998); and Wade Clark Roof and William McKinney, *American Mainline Religion: Its Changing Shape and Future* (New Brunswick, NJ: Rutgers University Press, 1987), 11–39.

3. Marjorie Hyer, "Bernardin Views Prolife Issues as a Seamless Garment," *Washington Post*, December 10, 1983; Thomas A. Nairn, ed., *The Seamless Garment: Writings on the Consistent Ethic of Life* (Maryknoll, NY: Orbis, 2008). On the attitudes of the majority of American Catholics at this time, see William D'Antonio, Michelle Dillon, and Mary Gautier, *American Catholics in Transition* (Lanham, MD: Rowman and Littlefield, 2013). For the ongoing critique of

the consistent life ethic, see Matthew Bellisario, "The Corrupt Theology of 'The Seamless Garment,' " *Coalition for Thomism*, August 23, 2010, http://coalitionforthomism.blogspot.com/2010/08/corrupt-theology-of-seamless-garment.html; and William Doino Jr., "Sex and the Seamless Garment," *First Things*, May 7, 2012, http://firstthings.com/web-exclusives/2012/05/sex-and-the-seamless-garment.

4. Michael J. O'Loughlin, "Can the 'Seamless Garment' Approach to Pro-life Issues Make a Comeback in the Catholic Church?," *America*, November 17, 2017, https://www.americamagazine.org/faith/2017/11/17/can-seamless-garment-approach-pro-life-issues-make-comeback-catholic-church; Christopher White, "In a Surprise, Naumann Elected Over Cupich as New Head of U.S. Bishops' Pro-life Committee," *Crux*, November 14, 2017, https://cruxnow.com/church-in-the-usa/2017/11/14/surprise-naumann-elected-cupich-new-head-pro-life-u-s-bishops-committee/.

5. While the American bishops have issued formal statements on an array of social issues, including immigration, poverty, and the environment, these have neither garnered media attention nor aroused the will of the majority of bishops in the way that their condemnation of abortion and support for making it illegal have. Their emphasis has helped to create in the minds of many an impression that Catholicism is only "anti"—antiabortion, antidivorce, anti–sexual minorities. See Robert A. Ludwig, *Reconstructing Catholicism for a New Generation* (Eugene, OR: Wipf and Stock, 2000). The Catholic bishops are full participants in the dominant American way of religious activism in the public realm. The majority prefers strong witness on nonnegotiable boundaries of identity and belonging over public engagement conducted in the mode of democratic discourse of the kind Richard Wood described in chapter 7.

6. Pope Francis, *Laudato Si* (On Care for Our Common Home), May 24, 2015; *Amoris Laetitia* (The Joy of Love), March 19, 2016.

7. See chapters 1 and 2 of this volume.

8. Recent research by Michele Dillon that continues the longitudinal study first reported in *American Catholics in Transition* suggests that the Francis papacy is having a positive influence on Catholic women's attitudes and participation. See Michele Dillon, "Survey of US Catholics Shows Refreshed Enthusiasm Among Women," *National Catholic Reporter*, January 11, 2018, https://www.ncronline.org/news/parish/survey-us-catholics-shows-refreshed-enthusiasm-among-women.

9. Timothy Matovina, chapter 2 of this volume; "America's Changing Religious Landscape," Pew Research Center, Religion and Public Life, May 12, 2015, http://www.pewforum.org/2015/05/12/americas-changing-religious-landscape/; Catherine Denise Tucker, "The Future of Latino Catholicism in the United States: A Population Study, 2010–2060" (Ph.D. diss., Pennsylvania State University, 2014), http://etda.libraries.psu.edu; Michael Lipka, "A Closer Look at

Catholic America," Pew Research Center, September 14, 2015, http://www
.pewresearch.org/fact-tank/2015/09/14/a-closer-look-at-catholic-america/.

10. Andrew Greeley, *The Catholic Myth: Behavior and Belief of American Catholics*
(New York: Simon and Schuster, 1990); Andrew Greeley, *The Catholic
Revolution: New Wine, Old Wineskins, and the Second Vatican Council* (Berkeley, CA:
University of California Press, 2004).

11. "America's Changing Religious Landscape."

12. Jonathan Z. Smith, "The Bare Facts of Ritual," in *Imagining Religion: From
Babylon to Jonestown* (Chicago: University of Chicago Press, 1982), 63.

13. Peter Feuerherd, "Participation in Lay Ministry Training Programs Down
16 Percent," *National Catholic Reporter*, October 12, 2017, https://www.ncronline
.org/news/parish/participation-lay-ministry-training-programs-down
-16-percent.

14. See endnote #28 in the "Introduction" to this volume.

15. Mariam Therese Winter, *Defecting in Place: Women Taking Responsibility for Their
Own Spiritual Lives* (New York: Crossroad, 1995).

16. Dillon, "Refreshed Enthusiasm Among Women"; Patricia Wittberg, "A Lost
Generation? Fewer Young Women Are Practicing Their Faith: How the
Church Can Woo Them Back," *America*, February 20, 2012, https://www
.americamagazine.org/issue/5129/article/lost-generation; Colleen Carroll
Campbell, *The New Faithful: Why Young Adults Are Embracing Christian Orthodoxy*
(Chicago: Loyola Press, 2002).

17. Dennis Brown, "President Obama to Deliver Notre Dame's Commencement Address," *Notre Dame News*, March 20, 2009, https://news.nd.edu/news
/president-obama-to-deliver-notre-dames-commencement-address/.

18. Brent Lang, "Inside the Obama Notre Dame Controversy," *CBS News*,
May 14, 2009, https://www.cbsnews.com/news/inside-the-obama-notre-dame
-controversy/. John M. D'Arcy, "The Church and the University: A Pastoral
Reflection on the Controversy at Notre Dame," *America*, August 31, 2009,
https://www.americamagazine.org/issue/706/article/church-and-university,
and John R. Quinn, "The Public Duty of Bishops: Lessons from the Storm
in South Bend," *America*, August 31, 2009, https://www.americamagazine
.org/politics-society/2009/08/31/public-duty-bishops-lessons-storm-south
-bend, present two different viewpoints on Obama's Notre Dame event from
the perspective of the U.S. bishops.

19. The conditions that call forth renewal evolve over time, and renewal often is
prompted by significant change in the faith community's larger context. See
Yves Lambert, "Religion in Modernity as a New Axial Age: Secularization or
New Religious Forms?" *Sociology of Religion* 60 (1999): 303–333.

20. Religious traditions, by their very nature, contain the seeds of their own
critique, subversion, and renewal that generate both retrenchments and
innovations, which Lambert describes.

21. Thomas F. O'Dea, *The Catholic Crisis* (Boston: Beacon Press, 1968).

Contributors

STEVEN M. AVELLA (Ph.D., University of Notre Dame) is professor of history and chair of the history department at Marquette University in Milwaukee and a priest of the Archdiocese of Milwaukee. His most recent book is *Charles K. McClatchy and the Golden Era of American Journalism, 1858–1936*. He has published book-length studies of the history of the Archdiocese of Milwaukee, the Archdiocese of Chicago, the Diocese of Sacramento, the Society of the Divine Savior, and the Society of the Catholic Apostolate and many articles and book chapters focusing of the history of American Catholicism.

JOSEPH P. CHINNICI, O.F.M. (D.Phil., Oxford University) is professor of history and president emeritus at the Franciscan School of Theology in Oceanside, California. A specialist in American Catholic history and the development of Franciscan spirituality, he is a professed member of the Order of Friars Minor. His most recent book is *When Values Collide: The Catholic Church, Sexual Abuse, and the Challenges of Leadership* (2010). He is general editor of the Franciscan Heritage Series and the author of numerous books and articles, many of which focus on Catholic worship and spirituality.

WILLIAM D. DINGES (Ph.D., University of Kansas) is Ordinary Professor of Religion and Culture in the School of Theology and Religious Studies at the Catholic University of America. He is the author of numerous historical and ethnographic studies of American Catholic life and is at work on a book called *Catholics at Prayer: The "Holy Sacrifice": Ritual, Culture and Social Change in the American Catholic Experience*.

PATRICIA O'CONNELL KILLEN (Ph.D., Stanford University), coeditor of *The Future of American Catholicism*, is professor of religious studies and senior fellow at Gonzaga University. A historian of religion in America, she was professor of American religious history at Pacific Lutheran University for two decades. Her most recent scholarly project was as coeditor of the 2013 volume *Selected Letters of A.M.A Blanchet, Bishop of Walla Walla and Nesqualy, 1846–1879*. Her other major works include studies of religion in the Pacific Northwest, women in religion, and theological reflection.

TIMOTHY MATOVINA (Ph.D., Catholic University of America) is a professor of theology at the University of Notre Dame, where he is department chair in the history of Christianity. He is a former director of Notre Dame's Cushwa Center for the Study of American Catholicism and is a specialist in American Catholic and Latino Catholic life. His most recent book is *Latino Catholicism: Transformation in America's Largest Church.*

KATARINA SCHUTH, O.S.F. (Ph.D., Syracuse University) is professor emerita and holder of the Endowed Chair for the Social Scientific Study of Religion at the St. Paul School of Divinity at the St. Thomas University in St. Paul, MN. Trained as a cultural geographer, her most recent book is *Seminary Formation: Recent History—Current Circumstances—New Directions.* A Sister of St. Francis, she has specialized in social scientific study of training for Catholic ministry.

MARK SILK (Ph.D., Harvard University), coeditor of *The Future of American Catholicism*, is director of the Leonard E. Greenberg Center for the Study of Religion in Public Life and coeditor of the Future of American Religion series. His most recent book, coauthored with Andrew Walsh, is *One Nation Divisible: How Regional Religious Differences Shape American Politics.*

ANDREW H. WALSH (Ph.D., Harvard University) is associate director of the Leonard E. Greenberg Center for the Study of Religion in Public Life at Trinity College. A historian of religion in America, he is coeditor of the Future of Religion in America series. With Mark Silk, he is coauthor of *One Nation Divisible: How Religion Religious Differences Shape American Politics.*

RICHARD L. WOOD (Ph.D., University of California, Berkeley) is associate professor of sociology at the University of New Mexico and founding director of its Southwest Institute on Religion and Civil Society. His research focuses on the cultural and institutional underpinnings of democratic life, especially those carried by religious traditions and faith communities. His most recent book is *Faith and the Fire of Public Life.*

Index

Page numbers in *italics* refer to tables.